NON-LEAGUE
FOOTBALL
TABLES
1889-2006

EDITOR
Michael Robinson

British Library Cataloguing in Publication Data
A catalogue record for this book is available from the British Library

ISBN-10: 1-86223-144-3
ISBN-13: 978-1-86223-144-3   (For use after January 2007)

Copyright © 2006,   Soccer Books Limited

Manufactured in the UK by LPPS Ltd, Wellingborough, NN8 3PJ

FOREWORD

In selecting the Leagues to be included in this fourth edition of Non-League Football Tables we have again chosen those forming the pinnacle of the Non-League Football Pyramid, i.e. The Football Conference and it's three direct feeders.

In addition we have once more included the briefly-lived Football Alliance which became, effectively, the 2nd Division of the Football League in 1892 together with four Midland area leagues. In future editions we expect to continue to include leagues for other parts of the country.

Furthermore, as league sponsors change frequently, we have not used sponsored names (eg. Rymans League) other than in an indicative way on the cover.

We are indebted to Mick Blakeman for providing tables for the three South-Western area Leagues included in this edition of the book.

CONTENTS

FOOTBALL ALLIANCE

1889-90

	P	W	D	L	F	A	Pts
Sheffield Wednesday	22	15	2	5	70	39	32
Bootle	22	13	2	7	66	39	28
Sunderland Albion	21	12	2	7	64	39	28
Grimsby Town	22	12	2	8	58	47	26
Crewe Alexandra	22	11	2	9	68	59	24
Darwen	22	10	2	10	70	75	22
Birmingham St George	21	9	3	9	62	49	21
Newton Heath	22	9	2	11	40	44	20
Walsall Town Swifts	22	8	3	11	44	59	19
Small Heath	22	6	5	11	44	67	17
Nottingham Forest	22	6	5	11	31	62	17
Long Eaton Rangers	22	4	2	16	35	73	10

Sunderland Albion record includes 2 points awarded when Birmingham St George refused to fulfil a fixture which the Alliance committee had ordered to be replayed.

1890-91

	P	W	D	L	F	A	Pts
Stoke	22	13	7	2	57	39	33
Sunderland Albion	22	12	6	4	69	28	30
Grimsby Town	22	11	5	6	43	27	27
Birmingham St George	22	12	2	8	64	62	26
Nottingham Forest	22	9	7	6	66	39	25
Darwen	22	10	3	9	64	59	23
Walsall Town Swifts	22	9	3	10	34	61	21
Crewe Alexandra	22	8	4	10	59	67	20
Newton Heath	22	7	3	12	37	55	17
Small Heath	22	7	2	13	58	66	16
Bootle	22	3	7	12	40	61	13
Sheffield Wednesday	22	4	5	13	39	66	13

1891-92

	P	W	D	L	F	A	Pts
Nottingham Forest	22	14	5	3	59	22	33
Newton Heath	22	12	7	3	69	33	31
Small Heath	22	12	5	5	53	36	29
Sheffield Wednesday	22	12	4	6	65	35	28
Burton Swifts	22	12	2	8	54	52	26
Grimsby Town	22	6	6	10	40	39	18
Crewe Alexandra	22	7	4	11	44	49	18
Ardwick	22	6	6	10	39	51	18
Bootle	22	8	2	12	42	64	18
Lincoln City	22	6	5	11	37	65	17
Walsall Town Swifts	22	6	3	13	33	59	15
Birmingham St George	22	5	3	14	34	64	13

SOUTHERN LEAGUE

1894-95

First Division

	P	W	D	L	F	A	Pts
Millwall Athletic	16	12	4	0	68	19	28
Luton Town	16	9	4	3	36	22	22
Southampton St Mary's	16	9	2	5	34	25	20
Ilford	16	6	3	7	26	40	15
Reading	16	6	2	8	33	38	14
Chatham	16	4	5	7	22	25	13
Royal Ordnance Factories	16	3	6	7	20	30	12
Clapton	16	5	1	10	22	38	11
Swindon Town	16	4	1	11	24	48	9

Second Division

	P	W	D	L	F	A	Pts
New Brompton	12	11	0	1	57	10	22
Sheppey United	12	6	1	5	25	23	13
Old St Stephen's	12	6	0	6	26	26	12
Uxbridge	12	4	3	5	14	20	11
Bromley	12	4	1	7	23	30	9
Chesham	12	3	3	6	20	42	9
Maidenhead	12	2	4	6	19	33	8

1895-96

First Division

	P	W	D	L	F	A	Pts
Millwall Athletic	18	16	1	1	75	16	33
Luton Town	18	13	1	4	68	14	27
Southampton St Mary's	18	12	0	6	44	23	24
Reading	18	11	1	6	45	38	23
Chatham	18	9	2	7	43	45	20
New Brompton	18	7	4	7	30	37	18
Swindon Town	18	6	4	8	38	41	16
Clapton	18	4	2	12	30	67	10
Royal Ordnance Factories	18	3	3	12	23	44	9
Ilford	18	0	0	18	10	81	0

Second Division

	P	W	D	L	F	A	Pts
Wolverton L & NW Railway	16	13	1	2	43	10	27
Sheppey United	16	11	3	2	60	19	25
1st Scots Guards	16	8	5	3	37	22	21
Uxbridge	16	9	1	6	28	23	19
Old St Stephen's	16	6	3	7	34	21	15
Guildford	16	7	1	8	29	41	15
Maidenhead	16	4	1	11	20	49	9
Chesham	16	2	3	11	15	48	7
Bromley	16	2	2	12	16	49	6

1896-97

First Division

	P	W	D	L	F	A	Pts
Southampton St Mary's	20	15	5	0	63	18	35
Millwall Athletic	20	13	5	2	63	24	31
Chatham	20	13	1	6	54	29	27
Tottenham Hotspur	20	9	4	7	43	29	22
Gravesend United	20	9	4	7	35	34	22
Swindon Town	20	8	3	9	33	37	19
Reading	20	8	3	9	31	49	19
New Brompton	20	7	2	11	32	42	16
Northfleet	20	5	4	11	24	46	14
Sheppey United	20	5	1	14	34	47	11
Wolverton L & NW Railway	20	2	0	18	17	74	4

Second Division

	P	W	D	L	F	A	Pts
Dartford	24	16	4	4	83	19	36
Royal Engineers Training Battalion	24	11	9	4	49	37	31
Freemantle	24	12	4	8	58	40	28
Uxbridge	24	11	5	8	62	37	27
Wycombe Wanderers	24	10	6	8	37	54	26
Chesham	24	11	3	10	41	55	25
Southall	24	9	6	9	55	52	24
1st Scot Guards	24	9	6	9	49	50	24
West Herts	24	11	1	12	41	49	23
Warmley (Bristol)	24	10	2	12	44	43	22
Old St Stephen's	24	5	7	12	36	52	17
Maidenhead	24	4	8	12	33	64	16
1st Coldstream Guards	24	3	6	15	30	66	12

1897-98

First Division

	P	W	D	L	F	A	Pts
Southampton	22	18	1	3	53	18	37
Bristol City	22	13	7	2	67	33	33
Tottenham Hotspur	22	12	4	6	52	31	28
Chatham	22	12	4	6	50	34	28
Reading	22	8	7	7	39	31	23
New Brompton	22	9	4	9	37	37	22
Sheppey United	22	10	1	11	40	49	21
Gravesend United	22	7	6	9	28	39	20
Millwall Athletic	22	8	2	12	48	45	18
Swindon Town	22	7	2	13	36	48	16
Northfleet	22	4	3	15	29	60	11
Wolverton L & NW Railway	22	3	1	18	28	82	7

Second Division

Royal Artillery (Portsmouth)	22	19	1	2	75	22	39
Warmley (Bristol)	22	19	0	3	108	15	38
West Herts	22	11	6	5	50	48	28
Uxbridge	22	11	2	9	39	57	24
St Albans	22	9	5	8	47	41	23
Dartford	22	11	0	11	68	55	22
Southall	22	8	2	12	49	61	18
Chesham	22	8	2	12	38	48	18
Olsd St Stephen's	22	7	2	13	47	66	16
Wycombe Wanderers	22	7	2	13	37	55	16
Maidenhead	22	4	4	14	27	81	12
Royal Engineers Training Battalion	22	4	2	16	26	62	10

1898-99

First Division

Southampton	24	15	5	4	54	24	35
Bristol City	24	15	3	6	55	12	33
Millwall Athletic	24	12	6	6	59	35	30
Chatham	24	10	8	6	32	23	28
Reading	24	9	8	7	31	24	26
New Brompton	24	10	5	9	38	30	25
Tottenham Hotspur	24	10	4	10	40	36	24
Bedminster	24	10	4	10	35	39	24
Swindon Town	24	9	5	10	43	49	23
Brighton United	24	9	2	13	37	48	20
Gravesend United	24	7	5	12	42	52	19
Sheppey United	24	5	3	16	23	53	13
Royal Artillery (Portsmouth)	24	4	4	16	17	60	12

Second Division (London Section)

Thames Ironworks	22	19	1	2	64	16	39
Wolverton L & NW Railway	22	13	4	5	88	43	30
Watford	22	14	2	6	62	35	30
Brentford	22	11	3	8	59	39	25
Wycombe Wanderers	22	10	2	10	55	57	22
Southall	22	11	0	11	44	55	22
Chesham	22	9	2	11	45	62	20
St Albans	22	8	3	11	45	59	19
Shepherds Bush	22	7	3	12	37	53	17
Fulham	22	6	4	12	36	44	16
Uxbridge	22	7	2	13	29	48	16
Maidenhead	22	3	2	17	33	86	8

Second Division (South West Section)

Cowes	10	10	0	0	58	8	20
Ryde	10	7	0	3	30	11	14
Freemantle	10	4	1	5	18	31	9
Sandown	10	4	0	6	20	29	8
Eastleigh	10	2	1	7	17	37	5
Andover	10	2	0	8	14	41	4

1899-1900

First Division

Tottenham Hotspur	28	20	4	4	67	26	44
Portsmouth	28	20	1	7	58	27	41
Southampton	28	17	1	10	70	33	35
Reading	28	15	2	11	41	28	32
Swindon Town	28	15	2	11	50	42	32
Bedminster	28	13	2	13	44	45	28
Millwall Athletic	28	12	3	13	36	37	27
Queens Park Rangers	28	12	2	14	49	57	26
Bristol City	28	9	7	12	43	47	25
Bristol Rovers	28	11	3	14	46	55	25
New Brompton	28	9	6	13	39	49	24
Gravesend United	28	10	4	14	38	58	24
Chatham	28	10	3	15	38	58	23
Thames Ironworks	28	8	5	15	30	45	21
Sheppey United	28	3	7	18	24	66	13

Second Division

Watford	20	14	2	4	57	25	30
Fulham	20	10	4	6	44	23	24
Chesham Town	20	11	2	7	43	37	24
Wolverton L & NW Railway	20	9	6	5	46	36	24
Grays United	20	8	6	6	63	29	22
Shepherds Bush	20	9	4	7	45	37	22
Dartford	20	8	3	9	36	44	19
Wycombe Wanderers	20	8	3	9	35	50	19
Brentford	20	5	7	8	31	48	17
Southall	20	6	3	11	21	44	15
Maidenhead	20	1	2	17	16	64	4

1900-01

First Division

Southampton	28	18	5	5	58	26	41
Bristol City	28	17	5	6	54	27	39
Portsmouth	28	17	4	7	56	32	38
Millwall Athletic	28	17	2	9	55	32	36
Tottenham Hotspur	28	16	4	8	55	33	36
West Ham United	28	14	5	9	40	28	33
Bristol Rovers	28	14	4	10	46	35	32
Queens Park Rangers	28	11	4	13	43	48	26
Reading	28	8	8	12	24	25	24
Luton Town	28	11	2	15	43	49	24
Kettering	28	7	9	12	33	46	23
New Brompton	28	7	5	16	34	51	19
Gravesend United	28	6	7	15	32	85	19
Watford	28	6	4	18	24	52	16
Swindon Town	28	3	8	17	19	47	14

Second Division

Brentford	16	14	2	0	63	11	30
Grays United	16	12	2	2	62	12	26
Sheppey United	16	8	1	7	44	26	17
Shepherds Bush	16	8	1	7	30	30	17
Fulham	16	8	0	8	38	26	16
Chesham Town	16	5	1	10	26	39	11
Maidenhead	16	4	1	11	21	49	9
Wycombe Wanderers	16	4	1	11	23	68	9
Southall	16	4	1	11	22	68	9

1901-02

First Division

Portsmouth	30	20	7	3	67	24	47
Tottenham Hotspur	30	18	6	6	61	22	42
Southampton	30	18	6	6	71	28	42
West Ham United	30	17	6	7	45	28	40
Reading	30	16	7	7	57	24	39
Millwall Athletic	30	13	6	11	48	31	32
Luton Town	30	11	10	9	31	35	32
Kettering	30	12	5	13	44	39	29
Bristol Rovers	30	12	5	13	43	39	29
New Brompton	30	10	7	13	39	38	27
Northampton	30	11	5	14	53	64	27
Queens Park Rangers	30	8	7	15	34	56	23
Watford	30	9	4	17	36	60	22
Wellingborough	30	9	4	17	34	75	22
Brentford	30	7	6	17	34	61	20
Swindon Town	30	2	3	25	17	93	7

Second Division

Fulham	16	13	0	3	51	19	26
Grays United	16	12	1	3	49	14	25
Brighton & Hove Albion	16	11	0	5	34	17	22
Wycombe Wanderers	16	7	3	6	36	30	17
West Hampstead	16	6	4	6	39	29	16
Shepherds Bush	16	6	1	9	31	31	13
Southall	16	5	2	9	28	52	12
Maidenhead	16	3	1	12	23	59	7
Chesham Town	16	2	2	12	74	64	6

1902-03

First Division

	P	W	D	L	F	A	Pts
Southampton	30	20	8	2	83	20	48
Reading	30	19	7	4	72	30	45
Portsmouth	30	17	7	6	69	32	41
Tottenham Hotspur	30	14	7	9	47	31	35
Bristol Rovers	30	13	8	9	46	34	34
New Brompton	30	11	11	8	37	35	33
Millwall Athletic	30	14	3	13	52	37	31
Northampton Town	30	12	6	12	39	48	30
Queens Park Rangers	30	11	6	13	34	42	28
West Ham United	30	9	10	11	35	49	28
Luton Town	30	10	7	13	43	44	27
Swindon Town	30	10	7	13	38	46	27
Kettering	30	8	11	11	33	40	27
Wellingborough	30	11	3	16	36	56	25
Watford	30	6	4	20	35	87	16
Brentford	30	2	1	27	16	84	5

Second Division

	P	W	D	L	F	A	Pts
Fulham	10	7	1	2	27	7	15
Brighton & Hove Albion	10	7	1	2	34	11	15
Grays United	10	7	0	3	28	12	14
Wycombe Wanderers	10	3	3	4	13	19	9
Chesham Town	10	2	1	7	9	37	5
Southall	10	1	0	9	10	35	2

1903-04

First Division

	P	W	D	L	F	A	Pts
Southampton	34	22	6	6	75	30	50
Tottenham Hotspur	34	16	11	7	54	37	43
Bristol Rovers	34	17	8	9	66	42	42
Portsmouth	34	17	8	9	41	38	42
Queens Park Rangers	34	15	11	8	53	37	41
Reading	34	14	13	7	48	35	41
Millwall	34	16	8	10	64	42	40
Luton Town	34	14	12	8	38	33	40
Plymouth Argyle	34	13	10	11	44	34	36
Swindon Town	34	10	11	13	30	42	31
Fulham	34	9	12	13	33	34	30
West Ham United	34	10	7	17	38	43	27
Brentford	34	9	9	16	34	48	27
Wellingborough	34	11	5	18	44	63	27
Northampton Town	34	10	7	17	36	69	27
New Brompton	34	6	13	15	26	43	25
Brighton & Hove Albion	34	6	12	16	45	79	24
Kettering	34	6	7	21	30	78	19

Second Division

	P	W	D	L	F	A	Pts
Watford	20	18	2	0	70	15	38
Portsmouth Reserves	20	15	2	3	85	25	32
Millwall Reserves	20	9	4	7	35	39	22
Southampton Reserves	20	9	3	8	59	35	21
Grays United	20	9	3	8	25	55	21
Fulham Reserves	20	8	4	8	40	34	20
Swindon Town Reserves	20	8	3	9	50	44	19
Reading Reserves	20	8	2	10	43	42	18
Wycombe Wanderers	20	5	5	10	29	64	15
Southall	20	4	2	14	25	62	10
Chesham Town	20	1	2	17	19	65	4

1904-05

First Division

	P	W	D	L	F	A	Pts
Bristol Rovers	34	20	8	6	74	36	48
Reading	34	18	7	9	57	38	43
Southampton	34	18	7	9	54	40	43
Plymouth Argyle	34	18	5	11	57	39	41
Tottenham Hotspur	34	15	8	11	53	34	38
Fulham	34	14	10	10	46	34	38
Queens Park Rangers	34	14	8	12	51	46	36
Portsmouth	34	16	4	14	61	56	36
New Brompton	34	11	11	12	40	41	33
West Ham United	34	12	8	14	48	42	32
Brighton & Hove Albion	34	13	6	15	44	45	32
Northampton Town	34	12	8	14	43	54	32
Watford	34	14	3	17	41	44	31
Brentford	34	10	9	15	33	38	29
Millwall	34	11	7	16	38	47	29
Swindon Town	34	12	5	17	41	59	29
Luton Town	34	12	3	19	45	54	27
Wellingborough	34	5	3	26	25	104	13

Second Division

	P	W	D	L	F	A	Pts
Fulham Reserves	22	16	4	2	78	25	36
Portsmouth Reserves	22	14	2	6	75	28	30
Swindon Town Reserves	22	12	3	7	54	47	27
Grays United	22	11	3	8	61	40	25
Southampton Reserves	22	10	5	7	52	35	25
Brighton & Hove Albion	22	9	3	10	48	49	21
West Ham United Reserves	22	8	5	9	45	47	21
Clapton Orient	22	7	7	8	47	56	21
Watford Reserves	22	5	6	11	30	62	16
Southall	22	7	2	13	31	66	16
Wycombe Wanderers	22	6	2	14	37	70	14
Reading Reserves	22	4	4	14	24	57	12

1905-06

First Division

	P	W	D	L	F	A	Pts
Fulham	34	19	12	3	44	15	50
Southampton	34	19	7	8	58	39	45
Portsmouth	34	17	9	8	61	35	43
Luton Town	34	17	7	10	64	40	41
Tottenham Hotspur	34	16	7	11	46	29	39
Plymouth Argyle	34	16	7	11	52	33	39
Norwich City	34	13	10	11	46	38	36
Bristol Rovers	34	15	5	14	56	56	35
Brentford	34	14	7	13	43	52	35
Reading	34	12	9	13	53	46	33
West Ham United	34	14	5	15	42	39	33
Millwall	34	11	11	12	38	41	33
Queens Park Rangers	34	12	7	15	58	44	31
Watford	34	8	10	16	38	57	26
Swindon Town	34	8	9	17	31	52	25
Brighton & Hove Albion	34	9	7	18	30	55	25
New Brompton	34	7	8	19	20	62	22
Northampton Town	34	8	5	21	32	79	21

Second Division

	P	W	D	L	F	A	Pts
Crystal Palace	24	19	4	1	66	14	42
Leyton	24	16	6	2	61	18	38
Portsmouth Reserves	24	12	8	4	52	24	32
Fulham Reserves	24	11	6	7	52	39	28
Southampton Reserves	24	7	9	8	39	41	23
Southern United	24	8	7	9	45	49	23
St Leonard's United	24	9	4	11	54	50	22
Watford Reserves	24	8	5	11	43	47	21
West Ham United Reserves	24	7	5	12	46	48	19
Grays United	24	8	3	13	24	77	19
Reading Reserves	24	6	5	13	36	49	15
Swindon Town Reserves	24	5	5	14	36	51	15
Wycombe Wanderers	24	5	3	16	36	83	13

1906-07

First Division

Fulham	38	20	13	5	58	32	53
Portsmouth	38	22	7	9	64	36	51
Brighton & Hove Albion	38	18	9	11	53	43	45
Luton Town	38	18	9	11	52	52	45
West Ham United	38	15	14	9	60	41	44
Tottenham Hotspur	38	17	9	12	63	45	43
Millwall	38	18	6	14	71	50	42
Norwich City	38	15	12	11	57	48	42
Watford	38	13	16	9	46	43	42
Brentford	38	17	8	13	57	56	42
Southampton	38	13	9	16	49	56	35
Reading	38	14	6	18	57	47	34
Leyton	38	11	12	15	38	60	34
Bristol Rovers	38	12	9	17	55	54	33
Plymouth Argyle	38	10	13	15	43	50	33
New Brompton	38	12	9	17	47	59	33
Swindon Town	38	11	11	16	43	54	33
Queens Park Rangers	38	11	10	17	47	55	32
Crystal Palace	38	8	9	21	46	66	25
Northampton Town	38	5	9	24	29	88	19

Second Division

Southend United	22	14	5	3	58	23	33
West Ham United Reserves	22	14	3	5	64	30	31
Portsmouth Reserves	22	11	6	5	53	24	28
Fulham Reserves	22	11	4	7	47	32	26
Hastings & St Leonards	21	10	4	7	46	31	24
Tunbridge Wells Rangers	22	10	1	11	46	36	21
Salisbury City	22	9	2	11	40	42	20
Southampton Reserves	22	8	2	12	37	56	18
Swindon Town Reserves	22	7	3	12	35	43	17
Reading Reserves	22	6	4	12	32	47	16
Royal Engineers (Aldershot)	21	5	4	12	27	58	14
Wycombe Wanderers	22	4	6	12	28	68	14

The match between Tunbridge Wells Rangers and Royal Engineers
(Aldershot) was not completed.

1907-08

First Division

Queens Park Rangers	38	21	9	8	82	57	51
Plymouth Argyle	38	19	11	8	50	31	49
Millwall	38	19	8	11	49	32	46
Crystal Palace	38	17	10	11	54	51	44
Swindon Town	38	16	10	12	55	40	42
Bristol Rovers	38	16	10	12	59	56	42
Tottenham Hotspur	38	17	7	14	59	48	41
Northampton Town	38	15	11	12	50	41	41
Portsmouth	38	17	6	15	63	52	40
West Ham United	38	15	10	13	47	48	40
Southampton	38	16	6	16	51	60	38
Reading	38	15	6	17	55	50	36
Bradford Park Avenue	38	12	12	14	53	54	36
Watford	38	12	10	16	47	49	34
Brentford	38	14	5	19	49	52	33
Norwich City	38	12	9	17	46	49	33
Brighton & Hove Albion	38	12	8	18	46	59	32
Luton Town	38	12	6	20	33	56	30
Leyton	38	8	11	19	51	73	27
New Brompton	38	9	7	22	44	75	25

Second Division

Southend	18	13	3	2	47	16	29
Portsmouth Reserves	18	10	5	3	39	22	25
Croydon Common	18	10	3	5	35	25	23
Hastings & St Leonard's	18	10	2	6	43	29	22
Southampton Reserves	18	7	4	7	54	46	18
Tunbridge Wells Rangers	18	7	3	8	42	38	17
Salisbury City	18	6	4	8	35	46	16
Swindon Town Reserves	18	5	5	8	36	40	15
Brighton & Hove Albion Reserves	18	4	4	10	34	47	12
Wycombe Wanderers	18	1	1	16	16	72	3

1908-09

First Division

Northampton Town	40	25	5	10	90	45	55
Swindon Town	40	22	5	13	96	55	49
Southampton	40	19	10	11	67	58	48
Portsmouth	40	18	10	12	68	60	46
Bristol Rovers	40	17	9	14	60	63	43
Exeter City	40	18	6	16	56	65	42
New Brompton	40	17	7	16	48	59	41
Reading	40	11	18	11	60	57	40
Luton Town	40	17	6	17	59	60	40
Plymouth Argyle	40	15	10	15	46	47	40
Millwall	40	16	6	18	59	61	38
Southend United	40	14	10	16	52	54	38
Leyton	40	15	8	17	52	55	38
Watford	40	14	9	17	51	64	37
Queens Park Rangers	40	12	12	16	52	50	36
Crystal Palace	40	12	12	16	62	62	36
West Ham United	40	16	4	20	56	60	36
Brighton & Hove Albion	40	14	7	19	60	61	35
Norwich City	40	12	11	17	59	75	35
Coventry City	40	15	4	21	64	91	34
Brentford	40	13	7	20	59	74	33

Second Division

Croydon Common	12	10	0	2	67	14	20
Hastings & St Leonard's	12	8	1	3	42	18	17
Depot Battalion Royal Engineers	12	8	1	3	23	22	17
2nd Grenadier Guards	12	5	0	7	21	33	10
South Farnborough Athletic	12	2	4	6	20	39	8
Salisbury City	12	3	1	8	24	36	7
Chesham Town	12	2	1	9	17	52	5

1909-10

First Division

Brighton & Hove Albion	42	23	13	6	69	28	59
Swindon Town	42	22	10	10	92	46	54
Queens Park Rangers	42	19	13	10	56	47	51
Northampton Town	42	22	4	16	90	44	48
Southampton	42	16	16	10	64	55	48
Portsmouth	42	20	7	15	70	63	47
Crystal Palace	42	20	6	16	69	50	46
Coventry City	42	19	8	15	71	60	46
West Ham United	42	15	15	12	69	56	45
Leyton	42	16	11	15	60	46	43
Plymouth Argyle	42	16	11	15	61	54	43
New Brompton	42	19	5	18	76	74	43
Bristol Rovers	42	16	10	16	37	48	42
Brentford	42	16	9	17	50	58	41
Luton Town	42	15	11	16	72	92	41
Millwall	42	15	7	20	45	59	37
Norwich City	42	13	9	20	59	78	35
Exeter City	42	14	6	22	60	69	34
Watford	42	10	13	19	51	76	33
Southend United	42	12	9	21	51	90	33
Croydon Common	42	13	5	24	52	96	31
Reading	42	7	10	25	38	73	24

Second Division - Section A

Stoke	10	10	0	0	48	9	20
Ton Pentre	10	4	2	4	17	21	10
Merthyr Town	9	4	1	4	16	21	9
Salisbury City	8	2	1	5	7	18	5
Burton United	6	2	0	4	8	21	4
Aberdare	7	1	0	6	6	11	2

Second Division - Section B

Hastings & St Leonard's	9	6	3	0	26	11	15
Kettering	10	6	0	4	34	19	12
Chesham Town	10	5	2	3	25	25	12
Peterborough City	10	4	2	4	16	23	10
South Farnborough Athletic	10	4	1	5	23	19	9
Romford	9	0	0	9	7	33	0

1910-11

First Divison

Swindon Town	38	24	5	9	80	31	53
Northampton Town	38	18	12	8	54	27	48
Brighton & Hove Albion	38	20	8	10	58	35	48
Crystal Palace	38	17	13	8	55	48	47
West Ham United	38	17	11	10	63	46	45
Queens Park Rangers	38	13	14	11	52	41	40
Leyton	38	16	8	14	57	52	40
Plymouth Argyle	38	15	9	14	54	55	39
Luton Town	38	15	8	15	67	63	38
Norwich City	38	15	8	15	46	48	38
Coventry City	38	16	6	16	65	68	38
Brentford	38	14	9	15	41	42	37
Exeter City	38	14	9	15	51	53	37
Watford	38	13	9	16	49	65	35
Millwall	38	11	9	18	42	54	31
Bristol Rovers	38	10	10	18	42	55	30
Southampton	38	11	8	19	42	67	30
New Brompton	38	11	8	19	34	65	30
Southend United	38	10	9	19	47	64	29
Portsmouth	38	8	11	19	34	53	27

Second Division

Reading	22	16	3	3	55	11	35
Stoke	22	17	1	4	72	21	35
Merthyr Town	22	15	3	4	52	22	33
Cardiff City	22	12	4	6	48	29	28
Croydon Common	22	11	3	8	61	26	25
Treharris	22	10	3	9	38	31	23
Aberdare	22	9	5	8	38	33	23
Ton Pentre	22	10	3	9	44	40	23
Walsall	22	7	4	11	37	41	18
Kettering	22	6	1	15	34	68	13
Chesham Town	22	1	3	18	16	93	5
Salisbury City	22	0	3	19	16	92	3

1911-12

First Division

Queens Park Rangers	38	21	11	6	59	35	53
Plymouth Argyle	38	23	6	9	63	31	52
Northampton Town	38	22	7	9	82	41	51
Swindon Town	38	21	6	11	82	50	48
Brighton & Hove Albion	38	19	9	10	73	35	47
Coventry City	38	17	8	13	66	54	42
Crystal Palace	38	15	10	13	70	46	40
Millwall	38	15	10	13	60	57	40
Watford	38	13	10	15	56	68	36
Stoke	38	13	10	15	51	63	36
Reading	38	11	14	13	43	69	36
Norwich City	38	10	14	14	40	60	34
West Ham United	38	13	7	18	64	69	33
Brentford	38	12	9	17	60	65	33
Exeter City	38	11	11	16	48	62	33
Southampton	38	10	11	17	46	63	31
Bristol Rovers	38	9	13	16	41	62	31
New Brompton	38	11	9	18	35	72	31
Luton Town	38	9	10	19	49	61	28
Leyton	38	7	11	20	27	62	25

Second Division

Merthyr Town	26	19	3	4	60	14	41
Portsmouth	26	19	3	4	73	20	41
Cardiff City	26	15	4	7	55	26	34
Southend United	26	16	1	9	73	24	33
Pontypridd	26	13	6	7	39	24	32
Ton Pentre	26	12	3	11	56	45	27
Walsall	26	13	1	11	44	41	27
Treharris	26	11	5	10	44	47	27
Aberdare	26	10	3	13	39	44	23
Kettering	26	11	0	15	37	62	22
Croydon Common	26	8	2	15	43	45	18
Mardy	26	6	6	12	37	51	18
Cwm Albion	26	5	1	16	27	70	11
Chesham Town	26	1	0	25	18	131	2

1912-13

First Division

Plymouth Argyle	38	27	6	10	77	36	50
Swindon Town	38	20	8	10	66	41	48
West Ham United	38	18	12	8	66	43	48
Queens Park Rangers	38	18	10	10	46	35	43
Crystal Palace	38	17	11	10	55	36	45
Millwall	38	19	7	12	62	43	45
Exeter City	38	18	8	12	48	44	44
Reading	38	17	8	13	59	55	42
Brighton & Hove Albion	38	13	12	13	48	47	38
Northampton Town	38	12	12	14	61	48	36
Portsmouth	38	14	8	16	41	49	36
Merthyr Town	38	12	12	14	42	60	36
Coventry City	38	13	8	17	53	59	34
Watford	38	12	10	16	43	50	34
Gillingham	38	12	10	16	36	53	34
Bristol Rovers	38	12	9	17	55	64	33
Southampton	38	10	11	17	40	72	31
Norwich City	38	10	9	19	39	50	29
Brentford	38	11	5	22	42	55	27
Stoke	38	10	4	24	39	75	24

Second Division

Cardiff City	24	18	5	1	54	15	41
Southend United	24	14	6	4	43	23	34
Swansea Town	24	12	7	5	29	23	31
Croydon Common	24	13	4	7	51	29	30
Luton Town	24	13	4	7	52	39	30
Llanelly	24	9	6	9	33	39	24
Pontypridd	24	6	11	7	30	28	23
Mid Rhondda	24	9	4	11	33	31	22
Aberdare	24	8	6	10	38	40	22
Newport County	24	7	5	12	29	36	19
Mardy	24	6	3	15	38	38	15
Treharris	24	5	2	17	18	60	12
Ton Pentre	24	3	3	18	22	69	9

1913-14

First Division

Swindon Town	38	21	8	9	81	41	50
Crystal Palace	38	17	16	5	60	32	50
Northampton Town	38	14	19	5	50	37	47
Reading	38	17	10	11	43	36	44
Plymouth Argyle	38	15	13	10	46	42	43
West Ham United	38	15	12	11	61	60	42
Brighton & Hove Albion	38	15	12	11	43	45	42
Queens Park Rangers	38	16	9	13	45	43	41
Portsmouth	38	14	12	12	57	48	40
Cardiff City	38	13	12	13	46	42	38
Southampton	38	15	7	16	55	54	37
Exeter City	38	10	16	12	39	38	36
Gillingham	38	13	9	16	48	49	35
Norwich City	38	9	17	12	49	51	35
Millwall	38	11	12	15	51	56	34
Southend Unied	38	10	12	16	41	66	32
Bristol Rovers	38	10	11	17	46	67	31
Watford	38	10	9	19	50	56	29
Merthyr Town	38	9	10	19	38	61	28
Coventry City	38	6	14	18	43	68	26

Second Division

Croydon Common	30	23	5	2	76	14	51
Luton Town	30	24	3	3	92	22	51
Brentford	30	20	4	6	80	18	44
Swansea Town	30	20	4	6	66	23	44
Stoke	30	19	2	9	71	34	40
Newport County	30	14	8	8	49	38	36
Mid Rhondda	30	13	7	10	55	37	33
Pontypridd	30	14	5	11	43	38	33
Llanelly	30	12	4	14	45	39	28
Barry	30	9	8	13	44	70	26
Abertillery	30	8	4	18	44	57	20
Ton Pentre	30	8	4	18	33	61	20
Mardy	30	6	6	18	30	60	18
Caerphilly	30	4	7	19	21	103	15
Aberdare	30	4	5	21	33	87	13
Treharris	30	2	4	24	19	106	8

1914-15
First Division

	P	W	D	L	F	A	Pts
Watford	38	22	8	8	68	46	52
Reading	38	21	7	10	68	43	49
Cardiff City	38	22	4	12	72	38	48
West Ham United	38	18	9	11	58	47	45
Northampton Town	38	16	11	11	56	51	43
Southampton	38	19	5	14	78	74	43
Portsmouth	38	16	10	12	54	42	42
Millwall	38	16	10	12	50	51	42
Swindon Town	38	15	11	12	77	59	41
Brighton & Hove Albion	38	16	7	15	46	47	39
Exeter City	38	15	8	15	50	41	38
Queens Park Rangers	38	13	12	13	55	56	38
Norwich City	38	11	14	13	53	56	36
Luton Town	38	13	8	17	61	73	34
Crystal Palace	38	13	8	17	47	61	34
Bristol Rovers	38	14	3	21	53	75	31
Plymouth Argyle	38	8	14	16	51	61	30
Southend United	38	10	8	20	44	64	28
Croydon Common	38	9	9	20	47	63	27
Gillingham	38	6	8	24	43	82	20

Second Division

	P	W	D	L	F	A	Pts
Stoke	24	17	4	3	62	15	38
Stalybridge Celtic	24	17	3	4	47	22	37
Merthyr Town	24	15	5	4	46	20	35
Swansea Town	24	16	1	7	48	21	33
Coventry City	24	13	2	9	56	33	28
Ton Pentre	24	11	6	7	42	43	28
Brentford	24	8	7	9	35	45	23
Llanelly	24	10	1	13	39	32	21
Barry	24	6	5	13	30	35	17
Newport County	24	7	3	14	27	42	17
Pontypridd	24	5	6	13	31	58	16
Mid Rhondda	24	3	6	15	17	40	12
Ebbw Vale	24	3	1	20	23	88	7

1919-20
First Division

	P	W	D	L	F	A	Pts
Portsmouth	42	23	12	7	73	27	58
Watford	42	26	6	10	69	42	58
Crystal Palace	42	22	12	8	69	43	56
Cardiff City	42	18	17	7	70	43	53
Plymouth Argyle	42	20	10	12	57	29	50
Queens Park Rangers	42	18	10	14	62	50	46
Reading	42	16	13	13	51	43	45
Southampton	42	18	8	16	72	63	44
Swansea Town	42	16	11	15	53	45	43
Exeter City	42	17	9	16	57	51	43
Southend United	42	13	17	12	46	48	43
Norwich City	42	15	11	16	64	57	41
Swindon Town	42	17	7	18	65	68	41
Millwall	42	14	12	16	52	55	40
Brentford	42	15	10	17	52	59	40
Brighton & Hove Albion	42	14	8	20	60	72	36
Bristol Rovers	42	11	13	18	61	78	35
Newport County	42	13	7	22	45	70	33
Northampton Town	42	12	9	21	64	103	33
Luton Town	42	10	10	22	51	76	30
Merthyr Town	42	9	11	22	47	78	29
Gillingham	42	10	7	25	34	74	27

Second Division

	P	W	D	L	F	A	Pts
Mid Rhondda	20	17	3	0	79	10	37
Ton Pentre	20	12	7	1	50	14	31
Llanelly	20	10	5	5	47	30	25
Pontypridd	20	10	3	7	33	29	23
Ebbw Vale	20	7	7	6	38	40	21
Barry	20	7	5	8	32	27	19
Mardy	20	7	5	8	29	30	19
Abertillery	20	6	5	9	29	40	17
Porth Athletic	20	4	4	12	30	74	12
Aberaman Athletic	20	4	3	13	28	48	11
Caerphilly	20	1	3	16	20	74	5

1920-21
English Section

	P	W	D	L	F	A	Pts
Brighton & Hove Albion Reserves	24	16	3	5	65	29	35
Portsmouth Reserves	24	13	7	4	44	20	33
Millwall Reserves	24	12	4	8	46	24	28
Southampton Reserves	24	10	7	7	53	35	27
Boscombe	24	10	6	8	25	40	26
Reading Reserves	24	11	3	10	41	34	25
Luton Town Reserves	24	8	8	8	38	35	24
Charlton Athletic	24	8	8	8	41	41	24
Watford Reserves	24	9	4	11	43	45	22
Norwich City Reserves	24	7	7	10	31	39	21
Gillingham Reserves	24	6	5	13	32	47	17
Chatham	24	5	6	13	24	47	16
Thornycrofts	24	4	6	14	29	74	14

Welsh Section

	P	W	D	L	F	A	Pts
Barry	20	13	4	3	35	12	30
Aberdare Athletic	20	12	3	5	29	23	27
Ebbw Vale	20	10	5	5	34	23	25
Pontypridd	20	10	3	7	34	23	23
Mid Rhondda	20	10	3	7	26	18	23
Abertillery Town	20	8	5	7	35	24	21
Ton Pentre	20	7	5	8	32	34	19
Aberaman Athletic	20	5	7	8	30	33	17
Llanelly	20	7	2	11	28	46	16
Mardy	20	2	6	12	18	39	10
Porth Athletic	20	3	3	14	28	54	9

1921-22
English Section

	P	W	D	L	F	A	Pts
Plymouth Argyle Reserves	36	22	5	9	91	38	49
Bristol City Reserves	36	18	8	10	73	50	44
Portsmouth Reserves	36	17	10	9	63	41	44
Southampton Reserves	36	19	5	12	70	47	43
Gillingham Reserves	36	17	9	10	65	47	43
Charlton Athletic Reserves	36	18	6	12	69	54	42
Boscombe	36	17	5	14	38	55	39
Luton Town Reserves	36	17	4	15	50	54	38
Watford Reserves	36	15	7	14	65	53	37
Brighton & Hove Albion Reserves	36	12	13	11	60	52	37
Bath City	36	16	5	15	55	53	37
Swindon Town Reserves	36	14	7	15	59	46	35
Bristol Rovers Reserves	36	13	7	16	50	82	33
Millwall Reserves	36	13	4	19	49	53	30
Reading Reserves	36	11	7	18	46	59	29
Exeter City Reserves	36	10	9	17	42	63	29
Guildford United	36	11	6	19	44	56	28
Norwich City Reserves	36	10	6	20	47	86	26
Southend United Reserves	36	9	3	24	47	92	21

Welsh Section

	P	W	D	L	F	A	Pts
Ebbw Vale	16	11	3	2	33	11	25
Ton Pentre	16	9	4	3	35	14	22
Aberaman Athletic	16	7	5	4	25	19	19
Porth Athletic	16	6	6	4	31	20	18
Pontypridd	16	7	4	5	28	19	18
Swansea Town Reserves	16	7	4	5	24	17	18
Barry	16	3	3	10	14	35	9
Abertillery Town	16	3	2	11	21	45	8
Mardy	16	2	3	11	14	43	7

1922-23

English Section

Bristol City Reserves	38	24	5	9	84	39	53
Boscombe	38	22	7	9	67	34	51
Portsmouth Reserves	38	23	3	12	93	51	49
Bristol Rovers Reserves	38	20	8	10	59	41	48
Plymouth Argyle Reserves	38	20	7	11	74	41	47
Torquay United	38	18	8	12	63	38	44
Brighton & Hove Albion Reserves	38	20	3	15	95	60	43
Luton Town Reserves	38	16	11	11	67	56	43
Southend United Reserves	38	18	6	14	69	68	42
Southampton Reserves	38	18	5	15	65	54	41
Millwall Reserves	38	15	10	13	61	55	40
Coventry City Reserves	38	15	8	15	56	61	38
Guildford Town Reserves	38	15	7	16	65	59	37
Swindon Town Reserves	38	13	6	19	54	73	32
Bath City	38	10	8	20	44	71	28
Watford Reserves	38	11	6	21	34	79	28
Yeovil & Petters United	38	10	6	22	56	104	26
Norwich City Reserves	38	9	7	22	42	68	25
Exeter City Reserves	38	10	5	23	43	81	25
Reading Reserves	38	7	6	25	43	95	20

Welsh Section

Ebbw Vale	12	6	5	1	22	15	17
Aberaman Athletic	12	7	2	3	30	19	16
Swansea Town Reserves	12	6	2	4	25	14	14
Pontypridd	12	6	2	4	18	18	14
Barry	12	4	3	5	15	11	11
Bridgend Town	12	4	2	6	15	21	10
Porth Athletic	12	0	2	10	18	24	2

1923-24

Eastern Section

Peterborough & Fletton United	30	20	2	8	54	31	42
Leicester City Reserves	30	19	3	8	72	30	41
Southampton Reserves	30	18	5	7	60	36	41
Millwall Reserves	30	18	3	9	56	38	39
Portsmouth Reserves	30	16	2	12	66	37	34
Brighton & Hove Albion Reserves	30	13	7	10	55	42	33
Norwich City Reserves	30	13	6	11	46	34	32
Folkestone	30	12	5	13	61	51	29
Coventry City Reserves	30	10	8	12	39	4	28
Watford Reserves	30	11	6	13	36	48	28
Reading Reserves	30	11	6	13	32	43	28
Northampton Town Reserves	30	9	10	11	32	47	28
Luton Town Reserves	30	10	7	13	40	49	27
Guildford United	30	7	5	18	38	72	19
Kettering	30	5	8	17	30	67	18
Bournemouth Reserves	30	4	5	21	40	85	13

Western Section

Yeovil & Petters United	34	25	3	6	71	30	53
Plymouth Argyle Reserves	34	21	5	8	74	37	47
Pontypridd	34	19	8	7	81	44	46
Torquay United	34	19	7	8	59	25	45
Bristol City Reserves	34	17	9	8	63	39	43
Swansea Town Reserves	34	19	5	10	62	38	43
Bristol Rovers Reserves	34	17	6	11	69	43	40
Cardiff City Reserves	34	15	4	15	55	31	34
Exeter City Reserves	34	11	11	12	48	47	33
Weymouth	34	15	3	16	48	60	33
Llanelly	34	14	5	15	47	62	33
Swindon Town Reserves	34	11	6	17	36	60	28
Bridgend Town	34	11	5	18	57	72	27
Newport County Reserves	34	10	7	17	57	79	27
Ebbw Vale	34	8	8	18	38	62	24
Bath City	34	6	9	19	32	71	21
Barry	34	6	7	21	36	74	19
Aberaman Athletic	34	6	4	24	41	87	16

1924-25

Eastern Section

Southampton Reserves	32	17	10	5	65	30	44
Kettering Town	32	17	6	9	67	39	40
Brighton & Hove Albion Reserves	32	15	10	7	68	42	40
Millwall Reserves	32	15	10	7	65	48	40
Peterborough & Fletton United	32	15	9	8	56	29	39
Bournemouth Reserves	32	15	9	8	66	48	39
Leicester City Reserves	32	15	7	10	61	45	37
Portsmouth Reserves	32	15	7	10	51	40	37
Folkestone	32	13	11	8	55	46	37
Norwich City Reserves	32	13	8	11	65	58	34
Coventry City Reserves	32	12	9	11	51	41	33
Luton Town Reserves	32	15	2	15	48	63	32
Northampton Town Reserves	32	10	5	17	38	59	25
Watford Reserves	32	7	7	18	44	71	21
Nuneaton Town	32	8	2	22	37	62	18
Reading Reserves	32	8	1	23	38	87	17
Guildford United	32	4	3	25	40	107	11

Western Section

Swansea Town Reserves	38	25	4	9	73	26	54
Plymouth Argyle Reserves	38	22	10	6	97	35	54
Pontypridd	38	24	4	10	81	39	52
Bridgend Town	38	20	11	7	74	52	51
Mid Rhondda United	38	21	6	11	79	48	48
Weymouth	38	21	4	13	77	50	46
Cardiff City Reserves	38	18	6	14	56	44	42
Newport County Reserves	38	17	8	13	71	60	42
Swindon Town Reserves	38	17	8	13	48	46	42
Bristol City Reserves	38	18	5	15	51	43	41
Yeovil & Petters United	38	15	10	13	49	50	40
Exeter City Reserves	38	16	6	16	78	55	38
Taunton Unied	38	15	6	17	55	51	36
Bristol Rovers Reserves	38	13	6	19	45	50	32
Torquay United	38	9	11	18	41	73	29
Llanelly	38	6	12	20	49	94	24
Ebbw Vale	38	9	6	23	40	91	24
Bath City	38	8	8	22	28	85	24
Barry	38	8	6	24	38	82	22
Aberaman Athletic	38	6	7	25	39	95	19

1925-26

Eastern Section

Millwall Reserves	34	24	6	4	106	37	54
Leicester City Reserves	34	23	2	9	105	60	48
Brighton & Hove Albion Reserves	34	21	4	9	105	69	46
Kettering Town	34	19	5	10	98	68	43
Peterborough & Fletton United	34	19	3	12	76	62	41
Portsmouth Reserves	34	17	5	12	76	67	39
Norwich City Reserves	34	17	4	13	85	90	38
Bournemouth Reserves	34	15	5	14	72	67	37
Southampton Reserves	34	14	7	13	65	72	35
Fulham Reserves	34	13	6	15	86	77	32
Grays Thurrock United	34	13	5	16	63	77	31
Guildford United	34	11	8	15	71	87	30
Watford Reserves	34	12	2	20	62	94	26
Luton Town Reserves	34	11	3	20	70	78	25
Folkestone	34	9	6	19	67	93	24
Reading Reserves	34	10	3	21	58	84	23
Coventry City Reserves	34	9	5	20	54	93	23
Nuneaton Town	34	7	3	24	61	113	17

Western Section

Plymouth Argyle Reserves	26	20	1	5	67	31	41
Bristol City Reserves	26	16	4	6	48	28	36
Bristol Rovers Reserves	26	13	4	9	51	35	30
Swindon Town Reserves	26	13	4	9	57	40	30
Ebbw Vale	26	13	3	10	60	46	29
Torquay United	26	12	5	9	59	46	29
Yeovil & Petters United	26	9	8	9	43	48	26
Mid Rhondda	26	12	1	13	47	49	25
Weymouth	26	10	3	13	64	60	23
Exeter City Reserves	26	8	5	13	40	49	21
Barry	26	8	4	14	47	55	20
Taunton United	26	9	2	15	44	60	20
Pontypridd	26	7	5	14	44	77	19
Bath City	26	7	1	18	38	86	15

1926-27

Eastern Section

Brighton & Hove Albion Reserves	32	21	6	5	86	47	48
Peterborough & Fletton United	32	18	9	5	80	39	45
Portsmouth Reserves	32	19	6	7	95	65	44
Kettering Town	32	15	10	7	66	41	40
Millwall Reserves	32	16	5	11	67	56	37
Bournemouth Reserves	32	14	6	12	69	64	34
Norwich City Reserves	32	14	5	13	79	74	33
Dartford	32	13	7	12	60	71	33
Reading Reserves	32	12	8	12	75	79	32
Luton Town Reserves	32	10	11	11	75	70	1
Leicester City Reserves	32	12	5	15	94	72	29
Watford Reserves	32	10	8	14	74	84	28
Southampton Reserves	32	10	6	16	57	77	26
Poole	32	9	6	17	55	86	24
Grays Thurrock United	32	10	3	19	49	66	23
Guildford United	32	6	7	19	57	106	19
Folkestone	32	7	4	21	57	98	18

Western Section

Torquay United	26	17	4	5	63	30	38
Bristol City Reserves	26	14	10	2	77	37	38
Plymouth Argyle Reserves	26	15	4	7	56	38	34
Ebbw Vale	26	14	2	10	67	45	30
Bristol Rovers Reserves	26	12	4	10	51	43	28
Swindon Town Reserves	26	11	5	10	60	57	27
Barry	26	11	4	11	65	50	26
Essex City Reserves	26	10	6	10	62	49	26
Weymouth	26	12	2	12	48	65	26
Newport County Reserves	26	9	6	11	57	53	24
Bath City	26	7	9	10	44	52	23
Yeovil & Petters United	26	9	5	12	49	66	23
Taunton United	26	4	4	18	36	83	12
Mid Rhondda United	26	2	5	19	22	89	9

1927-28

Easter Section

Kettering Town	34	23	6	5	90	39	52
Peterborough & Fletton United	34	21	3	10	73	43	45
Northfleet United	34	17	7	10	83	54	41
Brighton & Hove Albion Reserves	34	20	0	14	90	63	40
Norwich City Reserves	34	17	6	11	69	69	40
Southampton Reserves	34	16	7	11	92	70	39
Aldershot Town	34	17	5	12	85	66	39
Sittingbourne	34	16	5	13	64	70	37
Millwall Reserves	34	15	6	13	66	59	36
Poole	34	15	5	14	69	84	35
Folkestone	34	12	6	16	71	91	30
Guildford City	34	12	5	17	65	89	29
Dartford	34	12	4	18	46	49	28
Gillingham Reserves	34	10	7	17	72	84	27
Sheppey United	34	11	3	20	57	87	25
Chatham	34	10	4	20	49	70	24
Grays Thurrock United	34	10	3	21	48	88	23
Bournemouth Reserves	34	9	4	21	48	62	22

Western Section

Bristol City Reserves	30	20	3	7	95	51	43
Exeter City Reserves	30	18	4	8	104	56	40
Bristol Rovers Reserves	30	16	3	11	80	64	35
Plymouth Argyle Reserves	30	16	2	12	88	53	34
Newport County Reserves	30	13	8	9	99	70	34
Ebbw Vale	30	15	3	12	67	74	33
Swindon Town Reserves	30	13	4	13	80	74	30
Aberdare & Aberaman	30	12	6	12	62	68	30
Yeovil & Petters United	30	11	7	12	64	57	29
Torquay United Reserves	30	11	6	13	51	67	28
Bath City	30	12	3	15	64	68	27
Taunton Town	30	11	5	14	60	65	27
Weymouth	30	10	6	14	50	83	26
Merthyr Town Reserves	30	9	4	17	50	77	22
Barry	30	8	6	16	45	87	22
Mid Rhondda United	30	7	6	17	36	81	20

1928-29

Eastern Section

Kettering Town	36	24	4	8	96	46	52
Peterborough & Fletton United	36	21	5	10	86	44	47
Brighton & Hove Albion Reserves	36	19	9	8	91	56	47
Millwall Reserves	36	21	4	11	90	67	46
Bournemouth Reserves	36	20	5	11	82	58	45
Aldershot Town	36	18	5	13	68	52	41
Sheppey United	36	17	7	12	58	58	41
Folkestone	36	17	6	13	83	80	40
Northfleet United	36	17	4	15	87	65	38
Gillingham Reserves	36	15	8	13	68	70	38
Guildford City	36	13	11	12	85	78	37
Southampton Reserves	36	14	6	16	86	79	34
Poole	36	13	8	15	62	66	34
Thames Association	36	13	5	18	67	74	31
Dartford	36	10	6	20	55	106	26
Chatham	36	8	8	20	47	81	24
Sittingbourne	36	11	1	24	59	98	23
Norwich City Reserves	36	8	6	22	48	96	22
Grays Thurrock United	36	6	6	24	47	91	18

Western Section

Plymouth Argyle Reserves	26	15	6	5	69	27	36
Newport County Reserves	26	15	2	9	64	58	32
Bristol Rovers Reserves	26	14	3	9	54	45	31
Bristol City Reserves	26	14	2	10	70	46	30
Torquay United Reserves	26	13	4	9	52	42	30
Bath City	26	13	4	9	43	59	30
Exeter City Reserves	26	11	6	9	69	53	28
Lovells Athletic	26	11	6	9	54	48	28
Swindon Town Reserves	26	11	5	10	68	74	27
Yeovil & Petters United	26	11	2	13	49	57	24
Taunton Town	26	9	5	12	58	66	23
Ebbw Vale	26	9	5	12	56	66	23
Barry	26	6	3	17	38	66	15
Merthyr Town Reserves	26	3	1	22	37	92	7

1929-30

Eastern Section

Aldershot Town	32	21	6	5	84	39	48
Millwall Reserves	32	21	3	8	75	56	45
Thames Association	32	17	6	9	80	60	40
Peterborough & Fletton United	32	18	3	11	66	39	39
Northampton Town Reserves	32	17	4	11	86	60	38
Southampton Reserves	32	14	7	11	73	62	35
Sheppey United	32	15	5	12	76	69	35
Kettering Town	32	13	7	12	70	69	33
Dartford	32	14	5	13	57	59	33
Norwich City Reserves	32	14	3	15	69	69	31
Guildford City	32	13	2	17	65	97	28
Bournemouth Reserves	32	10	7	15	59	63	27
Brighton & Hove Albion Reserves	32	12	2	18	56	79	26
Folkestone	32	13	0	19	56	82	26
Sittingbourne	32	10	5	17	55	59	25
Northfleet United	32	6	7	19	53	77	19
Grays Thurrock United	32	7	2	23	54	101	16

Western Section

Bath City	28	16	6	6	85	52	38
Bristol Rovers Reserves	28	16	4	8	64	50	36
Taunton Town	28	14	7	7	50	40	35
Barry	28	15	3	10	65	55	33
Yeovil & Petters United	28	12	7	9	63	47	31
Plymouth Argyle Reserves	28	14	3	11	68	52	31
Newport County Reserves	28	13	4	11	68	76	30
Lovells Athletic	28	13	2	13	59	57	28
Exeter City Reserves	28	11	6	11	49	54	28
Bristol City Reserves	28	11	5	12	59	63	27
Swindon Town Reserves	28	10	6	12	69	67	26
Torquay United Reserves	28	10	6	12	76	77	26
Llanelly	28	10	4	14	55	52	24
Ebbw Vale	28	5	6	17	52	97	16
Merthyr Town Reserves	28	5	1	22	48	93	11

1930-31

Eastern Section

Dartford	16	9	5	2	39	18	23
Aldershot Town	16	10	3	3	50	28	23
Norwich City Reserves	16	9	1	6	47	38	19
Peterborough & Fletton United	16	6	5	5	35	29	17
Thames Association Reserves	16	7	2	7	38	31	16
Millwall Reserves	16	7	0	9	47	40	14
Folkestone	16	4	3	9	31	46	11
Guildford City	16	5	1	10	28	53	11
Sheppey United	16	4	2	10	31	63	10

Western Section

Exeter City Reserves	22	15	2	5	59	28	32
Llanelly	22	10	8	4	72	39	28
Merthyr Town	22	12	3	7	62	49	27
Plymouth Argyle Reserves	22	12	2	8	55	34	26
Bath City	22	10	6	6	47	39	26
Torquay United Reserves	22	9	5	8	66	49	23
Swindon Town Reserves	22	7	7	8	48	52	21
Bristol Rovers Reserves	22	7	6	9	58	64	20
Barry	22	7	5	10	29	39	19
Taunton Town	22	5	7	10	36	62	17
Newport County Reserves	22	6	2	14	36	66	14
Ebbw Vale	22	5	1	16	32	79	11

1931-32

Eastern Section

Dartford	18	12	3	3	53	18	27
Folkestone	18	12	2	4	58	27	26
Guildford City	18	11	1	6	33	24	23
Norwich City Reserves	18	9	2	7	46	33	20
Millwall Reserves	18	9	2	7	41	39	20
Tunbridge Wells Rangers	18	7	5	6	23	25	19
Bournemouth Reserves	18	6	4	8	43	61	16
Peterborough & Fletton United	18	4	5	9	28	29	13
Aldershot Town	18	3	5	10	17	30	11
Sheppey United	18	2	1	15	16	72	5

Western Section

Yeovil & Petters United	24	16	4	4	65	31	36
Plymouth Argyle Reserves	24	15	5	4	81	31	35
Bath City	24	12	7	5	50	33	31
Llanelly	24	12	4	8	65	46	28
Taunton Town	24	13	2	9	53	58	28
Newport County Reserves	24	10	6	8	70	51	26
Exeter City Reserves	24	9	7	8	59	43	25
Merthyr Town	24	9	4	11	66	73	22
Bristol Rovers Reserves	24	8	4	12	54	47	20
Swindon Town Reserves	24	8	4	12	54	95	20
Barry	24	7	3	14	58	76	17
Torquay United Reserves	24	5	6	13	43	66	16
Ebbw Vale	24	3	2	19	34	102	8

1932-33

Eastern Section

Norwich City Reserves	14	9	2	3	34	22	20
Dartford	14	8	2	4	26	23	18
Folkestone	14	7	1	6	35	32	15
Bournemouth Reserves	14	5	4	5	36	33	14
Tunbridge Wells Rangers	14	5	2	7	23	24	12
Guildford City	14	5	2	7	22	28	12
Millwall Reserves	14	5	1	8	27	31	11
Aldershot Reserves	14	3	4	7	24	34	10

Western Section

Bath City	20	13	4	3	62	34	30
Exeter City Reserves	20	12	3	5	62	46	27
Torquay United Reserves	20	12	1	7	56	37	25
Plymouth Argyle Reserves	20	11	2	7	68	38	24
Yeovil & Petters United	20	11	2	7	59	44	24
Llanelly	20	10	2	8	53	33	22
Bristol Rovers Reserves	20	7	3	10	53	65	17
Newport County Reserves	20	6	4	10	42	55	16
Merthyr Tydfil	20	7	1	12	39	58	15
Barry	20	3	4	13	30	72	10
Taunton Town	20	4	2	14	21	63	10

1933-34

Eastern Section

Norwich City Reserves	16	9	4	3	41	15	22
Margate	16	8	3	5	23	20	19
Millwall Reserves	16	7	4	5	28	28	18
Clapton Orient Reserves	16	8	1	7	33	34	17
Bournemouth Reserves	16	6	3	7	38	30	15
Tunbridge Wells Rangers	16	6	2	8	25	36	14
Folkestone	16	5	3	8	26	26	13
Guildford City	16	5	3	8	27	33	13
Dartford	16	4	5	7	15	24	13

Western Section

Plymouth Argyle Reserves	20	13	6	1	62	22	32
Bristol Rovers Reserves	20	14	3	3	56	27	31
Bath City	20	11	3	6	43	25	25
Torquay United Reserves	20	9	4	7	54	36	22
Yeovil & Petters United	20	10	1	9	35	39	21
Exeter City Reserves	20	8	3	9	54	47	19
Merthyr Town	20	8	2	10	39	50	18
Llanelly	20	8	1	11	25	39	17
Barry	20	4	5	11	37	64	13
Newport County Reserves	20	4	3	13	36	54	11
Taunton Town	20	5	1	14	27	65	11

Central Section

Plymouth Argyle Reserves	18	16	1	1	47	14	33
Clapton Orient Reserves	18	9	3	6	35	25	21
Norwich City Reserves	18	8	4	6	41	27	20
Yeovil & Petters United	18	7	4	7	34	38	18
Bath City	18	7	3	8	31	36	17
Dartford	18	6	4	8	28	26	16
Tunbridge Wells Rangers	18	7	1	10	26	37	15
Llanelly	18	6	2	10	28	39	14
Folkestone	18	6	1	11	30	41	13
Guildford City	18	6	1	11	28	45	13

1934-35

Eastern Section

Norwich City Reserves	18	12	1	5	52	21	25
Dartford	18	8	6	4	36	22	22
Margate	18	7	6	7	38	30	20
Bournemouth Reserves	18	8	3	8	34	26	19
Guildford City	18	7	5	6	41	34	19
Aldershot Reserves	18	7	3	8	29	43	17
Folkestone	18	5	6	7	30	39	16
Tunbridge Wells Rangers	18	6	4	8	32	56	16
Clapton Orient Reserves	18	5	4	9	33	35	14
Millwall Reserves	18	3	6	9	26	45	12

Western Section

Yeovil & Petters United	16	11	2	3	49	18	24
Newport County Reserves	16	8	5	3	45	29	21
Plymouth Argyle Reserves	16	7	5	4	40	24	19
Exeter City Reserves	16	7	2	7	38	32	16
Bath City	16	6	4	6	35	32	16
Bristol Rovers Reserves	16	5	5	6	33	37	15
Barry	16	6	3	7	30	40	15
Torquay United Reserves	16	5	3	8	24	29	13
Taunton Town	16	1	3	12	13	66	5

Central Section

Folkestone	20	11	4	5	43	31	26
Guildford City	20	11	4	5	43	39	26
Plymouth Argyle Reserves	20	6	9	5	40	28	21
Torquay United Reserves	20	7	6	7	34	35	20
Bristol Rovers Reserves	20	8	4	8	38	46	20
Margate	20	8	3	9	40	34	19
Dartford	20	8	3	9	43	38	19
Aldershot Reserves	20	8	3	9	33	44	19
Tunbridge Wells Rangers	20	8	2	10	33	37	18
Yeovil & Petters United	20	8	1	11	45	51	17
Bath City	20	6	3	11	34	43	15

1935-36

Eastern Section

Margate	18	13	2	3	49	16	28
Folkestone	18	11	3	4	46	23	25
Dartford	18	9	3	6	47	25	21
Tunbridge Wells Rangers	18	9	1	8	26	41	19
Clapton Orient Reserves	18	7	4	7	39	31	18
Millwall Reserves	18	7	3	8	42	39	17
Norwich City Reserves	18	8	0	10	39	38	16
Guildford City	18	6	3	9	32	52	15
Aldershot Reserves	18	6	1	11	24	45	13
Bournemouth Reserves	18	3	2	13	25	59	8

Western Section

Plymouth Argyle Reserves	16	12	3	1	51	18	27
Bristol Rovers Reserves	16	8	3	5	35	30	19
Newport County Reserves	16	8	3	5	29	30	19
Torquay United Reserves	16	7	1	8	25	28	15
Bath City	16	5	5	6	18	26	15
Cheltenham Town	16	6	2	8	32	28	14
Yeovil & Petters United	16	5	3	8	31	35	13
Barry	16	5	2	9	29	41	12
Exeter City Reserves	16	4	2	10	24	38	10

Central Section

Margate	20	14	3	3	57	18	31
Bristol Rovers Reserves	20	13	1	6	51	37	27
Plymouth Argyle Reserves	20	12	2	6	53	32	26
Aldershot Reserves	20	9	4	7	37	37	22
Folkestone	20	9	3	8	51	36	21
Tunbridge Wells Rangers	20	7	4	9	40	41	18
Dartford	20	7	3	10	34	42	17
Guildford City	20	7	3	10	33	47	17
Cheltenham Town	20	5	5	10	32	45	15
Bath City	20	5	5	10	34	52	15
Yeovil & Petters United	20	3	5	12	40	75	11

1936-37

Ipswich Town	30	19	8	3	68	35	46
Norwich City Reserves	30	18	5	7	70	35	41
Folkestone	30	17	4	9	71	62	38
Margate	30	15	4	11	64	49	34
Guildford City	30	15	4	11	54	60	34
Bath City	30	14	5	11	65	55	33
Yeovil & Petters United	30	15	3	12	77	69	33
Plymouth Argyle Reserves	30	11	8	11	64	58	30
Newport County Reserves	30	11	8	11	72	68	30
Barry	30	12	4	14	58	72	28
Cheltenham Town	30	10	4	16	61	70	24
Dartford	30	9	5	16	41	55	23
Exeter City Reserves	30	8	7	15	57	78	23
Tunbridge Wells Rangers	30	8	6	16	62	64	22
Torquay United Reserves	30	8	5	17	46	76	21
Aldershot Reserves	30	7	6	17	47	74	20

Midweek Section

Margate	18	12	1	5	48	24	25
Bath City	18	10	5	3	38	28	25
Norwich City Reserves	18	9	5	4	44	27	23
Folkestone	18	7	6	5	32	36	20
Millwall Reserves	18	8	3	7	44	47	19
Portsmouth Reserves	18	6	5	7	40	27	17
Tunbridge Wells Rangers	18	5	4	9	30	41	14
Aldershot Reserves	18	6	2	10	20	30	14
Guildford City	18	3	6	9	24	36	12
Dartford	18	4	3	11	19	43	11

1937-38

Guildford City	34	22	5	7	94	60	49
Plymouth Argyle Reserves	34	18	9	7	98	58	45
Ipswich Town	34	19	6	9	89	54	44
Yeovil & Petters United	34	14	14	6	72	45	42
Norwich City Reserves	34	15	11	8	77	55	41
Colchester United	34	15	8	11	90	58	38
Bristol Rovers Reserves	34	14	8	12	63	62	36
Swindon Town Reserves	34	14	7	13	70	76	35
Tunbridge Wells Rangers	34	14	6	14	68	74	34
Aldershot Reserves	34	10	12	12	42	55	32
Cheltenham Town	34	13	5	16	72	68	31
Exeter City Reserves	34	13	5	16	71	75	31
Dartford	34	9	11	14	51	70	29
Bath City	34	9	9	16	45	65	27
Folkestone	34	10	6	18	58	82	26
Newport County Reserves	34	10	6	18	56	86	26
Barry	34	8	7	19	50	88	23
Torquay United Reserves	34	8	7	19	46	81	23

Midweek Section

Millwall Reserves	18	13	3	2	59	21	29
Colchester United	18	13	1	4	42	23	27
Aldershot Reserves	18	11	3	4	38	29	25
Norwich City Reserves	18	9	1	8	45	39	19
Portsmouth Reserves	18	5	5	8	31	30	15
Dartford	18	6	3	9	32	35	15
Folkestone	18	6	3	9	34	38	15
Tunbridge Wells Rangers	18	5	4	9	28	36	14
Bath City	18	5	3	10	27	45	13
Guildford City	18	4	0	14	21	61	8

1938-39

Colchester United	44	31	5	8	110	37	67
Guildford City	44	30	6	8	126	52	66
Gillingham	44	29	6	9	104	57	64
Plymouth Argyle Reserves	44	26	5	13	128	63	57
Yeovil & Petters United	44	22	10	12	85	70	54
Arsenal Reserves	44	21	9	14	92	57	51
Cardiff City Reserves	44	24	3	17	105	72	51
Tunbridge Wells Rangers	44	22	6	16	93	76	50
Norwich City Reserves	44	23	4	17	86	76	50
Chelmsford City	44	18	8	18	74	73	44
Bath City	44	16	12	16	58	74	44
Barry	44	18	7	19	76	90	43
Cheltenham Town	44	16	9	19	76	105	41
Ipswich Town Reserves	44	14	12	18	64	76	40
Worcester City	44	13	14	17	72	90	40
Folkestone	44	16	6	22	74	85	38
Newport County Reserves	44	13	10	21	74	108	36
Exeter City Reserves	44	12	9	23	51	107	33
Torquay United Reserves	44	12	8	24	53	89	32
Swindon Town Reserves	44	11	9	24	66	101	31
Aldershot Reserves	44	12	6	26	69	92	30
Bristol Rovers Reserves	44	9	11	24	66	85	29
Dartford	44	8	5	31	53	119	21

Midweek Section

Tunbridge Wells Rangers	16	8	7	1	37	18	23
Colchester United	16	9	2	5	36	21	20
Norwich City Reserves	16	7	4	5	40	26	18
Millwall Reserves	16	7	4	5	33	23	18
Portsmouth Reserves	16	5	4	7	21	29	14
Guildford City	16	4	6	6	24	39	14
Aldershot Reserves	16	4	5	7	22	25	13
Folkestone	16	4	5	7	24	35	13
Dartford	16	4	3	9	24	45	11

1939-40

Eastern Section

Chelmsford City	7	5	0	2	29	9	10
Guildford City	8	4	1	3	26	13	9
Tunbridge Wells Rangers	7	2	3	2	21	16	7
Dartford	7	2	1	4	17	30	5
Norwich City Reserves	7	2	1	4	9	34	5

Western Section

Lovells Athletic	14	11	1	2	53	22	23
Worcester City	14	9	2	3	55	30	20
Hereford United	14	8	0	6	45	31	16
Yeovil & Petters United	14	7	2	5	30	24	16
Gloucester City	14	5	0	9	35	49	10
Barry	14	4	1	9	31	56	9
Cheltenham Town	13	3	2	8	21	38	8
Bath City	13	3	2	8	21	41	8

1945-46

Chelmsford City	18	15	1	2	66	23	34
Hereford United	20	13	3	4	59	31	29
Bath City	20	12	2	6	62	32	26
Cheltenham Town	18	9	1	8	35	54	22
Barry Town	20	8	4	8	42	42	20
Yeovil & Petters United	18	7	1	10	57	52	18
Worcester City	20	8	2	10	60	58	18
Colchester United	20	7	3	10	29	47	17
Bedford Town	16	4	1	11	30	49	15
Swindon Town Reserves	18	4	3	11	36	65	14
Cardiff City Reserves	20	4	5	11	39	60	13

1946-47

Gillingham	31	20	6	5	103	45	47
Guildford City	32	21	4	7	86	39	46
Merthyr Tydfil	31	21	2	8	104	37	45
Yeovil Town	32	19	6	7	100	49	44
Chelmsford City	31	17	3	11	90	60	38
Gravesend & Northfleet	32	17	4	11	82	58	38
Barry Town	30	14	6	10	89	61	36
Colchester United	31	15	4	12	65	60	35
Cheltenham Town	31	14	3	14	68	75	32
Millwall	24	8	5	11	59	57	29
Dartford	32	10	5	17	71	100	25
Bedford Town	32	8	8	16	63	98	24
Hereford United	32	8	7	17	37	85	23
Worcester City	31	8	5	18	55	90	22
Exeter City Reserves	32	10	2	20	69	126	22
Bath City	32	7	7	18	52	93	21
Gloucester City	32	8	1	23	57	120	17

1947-48

Merthyr Tydfil	34	23	7	4	84	38	53
Gillingham	34	21	5	8	81	43	47
Worcester City	34	21	3	10	74	45	45
Colchester United	34	17	10	7	88	41	44
Hereford United	34	16	10	8	77	53	42
Lovells Athletic	34	17	6	11	74	50	40
Exeter City Reserves	34	15	7	12	65	57	37
Yeovil Town	34	12	11	11	56	50	35
Chelmsford City	34	14	7	13	62	58	35
Cheltenham Town	34	13	9	12	71	71	35
Bath City	34	12	8	14	55	62	32
Barry Town	34	10	9	15	60	70	29
Gravesend & Northfleet	34	11	6	17	52	81	28
Guildford City	34	11	4	19	69	74	26
Dartford	34	10	6	18	35	62	26
Gloucester City	34	8	6	20	45	78	22
Torquay United Reserves	34	6	9	19	43	95	21
Bedford Town	34	6	3	25	41	104	15

1948-49

Gillingham	42	26	10	6	104	48	62
Chelmsford City	42	27	7	8	115	64	61
Merthyr Tydfil	42	26	8	8	133	54	60
Colchester United	42	21	10	11	94	61	52
Worcester City	42	22	7	13	87	56	51
Dartford	42	21	9	12	73	53	51
Gravesend & Northfleet	42	20	9	13	60	46	49
Yeovil Town	42	19	9	14	90	53	47
Cheltenham Town	42	19	9	14	71	64	47
Kidderminster Harriers	42	19	6	17	77	96	44
Exeter City Reserves	42	18	7	17	83	73	43
Hereford United	42	17	6	19	83	84	40
Bath City	42	15	8	19	72	87	38
Hastings United	42	14	10	18	69	93	38
Torquay United Reserves	42	15	7	20	73	93	37
Lovells Athletic	42	14	8	20	73	74	36
Guildford City	42	12	12	18	58	85	36
Gloucester City	42	12	10	20	78	100	34
Barry Town	42	12	10	20	55	95	34
Tonbridge	42	9	7	26	54	105	25
Chingford Town	42	6	9	27	43	94	21
Bedford Town	42	5	8	29	32	101	18

1949-50

Merthyr Tydfil	46	34	3	9	143	62	71
Colchester United	46	31	9	6	109	51	71
Yeovil Town	46	29	7	10	104	45	65
Chelmsford City	46	26	9	11	121	64	61
Gillingham	46	23	9	14	92	61	55
Dartford	46	20	9	17	70	65	49
Worcester City	46	21	7	18	85	80	49
Guildford City	46	18	11	17	79	73	47
Weymouth	46	19	9	18	80	81	47
Barry Town	46	18	10	18	78	72	46
Exeter City Reserves	46	16	14	16	73	83	46
Lovells Athletic	46	17	10	19	86	78	44
Tonbridge	46	16	12	18	65	76	44
Hastings United	46	17	8	21	92	450	42
Gravesend & Northfleet	46	16	9	21	88	81	41
Torquay United Reserves	46	14	12	20	80	89	40
Bath City	46	16	7	23	61	78	39
Gloucester City	46	14	11	21	72	101	39
Hereford United	46	15	8	23	74	76	38
Cheltenham Town	46	13	11	22	75	96	37
Headington United	46	15	7	24	72	97	37
Bedford Town	46	12	11	23	63	79	35
Kidderminster Harriers	46	12	11	23	64	108	35
Chingford Town	46	10	6	30	63	151	26

1950-51

Merthyr Tydfil	44	29	8	7	156	66	66
Hereford United	44	27	7	10	110	69	61
Guildford City	44	23	8	13	88	60	54
Chelmsford City	44	21	12	11	84	58	54
Llanelly	44	19	13	12	89	73	51
Cheltenham Town	44	21	8	15	91	61	50
Headington United	44	18	11	15	84	83	47
Torquay United Reserves	44	20	6	18	93	79	46
Exeter City Reserves	44	16	12	16	90	94	44
Weymouth	44	16	12	16	82	88	44
Tonbridge	44	16	12	16	79	87	44
Gloucester City	44	16	11	17	81	76	43
Yeovil Town	44	13	15	16	72	72	41
Worcester City	44	15	11	18	69	78	41
Bath City	44	15	10	19	66	73	40
Dartford	44	14	11	19	61	70	39
Bedford Town	44	15	9	20	64	94	39
Gravesend & Northfleet	44	12	14	18	65	83	38
Kettering Town	44	13	11	20	87	87	37
Lovells Athletic	44	12	13	19	81	93	37
Kidderminster Harriers	44	13	9	22	58	103	35
Barry Town	44	13	7	24	54	104	33
Hastings United	44	11	6	27	91	143	28

1951-52

Merthyr Tydfil	42	27	6	9	128	60	60
Weymouth	42	22	13	7	81	42	57
Kidderminster Harriers	42	22	10	10	70	40	54
Guildford City	42	18	16	8	66	47	52
Hereford United	42	21	9	12	80	59	51
Worcester City	42	23	4	15	86	73	50
Kettering Town	42	18	10	14	83	56	46
Lovells Athletic	42	18	10	14	87	68	46
Gloucester City	42	19	8	15	68	55	46
Bath City	42	19	6	17	75	67	44
Headington United	42	16	11	15	55	53	43
Bedford Town	42	16	10	16	75	64	42
Barry Town	42	18	6	18	84	89	42
Chelmsford City	42	15	10	17	67	80	40
Dartford	42	15	9	18	63	65	39
Tonbridge	42	15	6	21	63	84	36
Yeovil Town	42	12	11	19	56	76	35
Cheltenham Town	42	15	4	23	59	85	34
Exeter City Reserves	42	13	7	22	76	106	33
Llanelly	42	13	6	23	70	111	32
Gravesend & Northfleet	42	12	7	23	68	88	31
Hastings United	42	3	5	34	41	131	11

1952-53

Headington United	42	23	12	7	93	50	58
Merthyr Tydfil	42	25	8	9	117	66	58
Bedford Town	42	24	8	10	91	61	56
Kettering Town	42	23	8	11	88	50	54
Bath City	42	22	10	10	71	46	54
Worcester City	42	20	11	11	100	66	51
Llanelly	42	21	9	12	95	72	51
Barry Town	42	22	3	17	89	69	47
Gravesend & Northfleet	42	19	7	16	83	76	45
Gloucester City	42	17	9	16	50	78	43
Guildford City	42	17	8	17	64	60	42
Hastings United	42	18	5	19	75	66	41
Cheltenham Town	42	15	11	16	70	89	41
Weymouth	42	15	10	17	70	75	40
Hereford United	42	17	5	20	76	73	39
Tonbridge	42	12	9	21	62	88	33
Lovells Athletic	42	12	8	22	68	81	32
Yeovil Town	42	11	10	21	75	99	32
Chelmsford City	42	12	7	23	58	92	31
Exeter City Reserves	42	13	4	25	71	94	30
Kidderminster Harriers	42	12	5	25	54	85	29
Dartford	42	6	5	31	40	121	17

1953-54

Merthyr Tydfil	42	27	8	7	97	55	62
Headington United	42	22	9	11	68	43	53
Yeovil Town	42	20	8	14	87	76	48
Bath City	42	17	12	13	73	67	46
Kidderminster Harriers	42	18	9	15	62	59	45
Weymouth	42	18	8	16	83	72	44
Barry Town	42	17	9	16	108	91	43
Bedford Town	42	19	5	18	80	84	43
Gloucester City	42	16	11	15	69	77	43
Hastings United	42	16	10	16	73	67	42
Kettering Town	42	15	12	15	65	63	42
Hereford United	42	16	9	17	66	62	41
Llanelly	42	16	9	17	80	85	41
Guildford City	42	15	11	16	56	60	41
Gravesend & Northfleet	42	16	8	18	76	77	40
Worcester City	42	17	6	19	66	71	40
Lovells Athletic	42	14	11	17	62	60	39
Tonbridge	42	15	9	18	85	91	39
Chelmsford City	42	14	10	18	67	71	38
Exeter City Reserves	42	11	13	18	61	72	35
Cheltenham Town	42	11	12	19	56	83	34
Dartford	42	6	13	23	42	89	25

1954-55

Yeovil Town	42	23	9	10	105	66	55
Weymouth	42	24	7	11	105	84	55
Hastings United	42	21	9	12	94	60	51
Cheltenham Town	42	21	8	13	85	72	50
Guildford City	42	20	8	14	72	59	48
Worcester City	42	19	10	13	80	73	48
Barry Town	42	16	15	11	82	87	47
Gloucester City	42	16	13	13	66	54	45
Bath City	42	18	9	15	73	80	45
Headington Town	42	18	7	17	82	62	43
Kidderminster Harriers	42	18	7	17	84	86	43
Merthyr Tydfil	42	17	8	17	97	94	42
Exeter City Reserves	42	19	4	19	67	78	42
Lovells Athletic	42	15	11	16	71	68	41
Kettering Town	42	15	11	16	70	69	41
Hereford United	42	17	5	20	91	72	39
Llanelly	42	16	7	19	78	81	39
Bedford Town	42	16	3	23	75	103	35
Tonbridge	42	11	8	23	68	91	30
Dartford	42	9	12	21	55	76	30
Chelmsford City	42	11	6	25	73	111	28
Gravesend & Northfleet	42	9	9	24	62	97	27

1955-56

Guildford City	42	26	8	8	74	34	60
Cheltenham Town	42	25	6	11	82	53	56
Yeovil Town	42	23	9	10	98	55	55
Bedford Town	42	21	9	12	99	69	51
Dartford	42	20	9	13	78	62	49
Weymouth	42	19	10	13	83	63	48
Gloucester City	42	19	9	14	72	60	47
Lovells Athletic	42	19	9	14	91	78	47
Chelmsford City	42	18	10	14	67	55	46
Kettering Town	42	16	11	15	105	86	43
Exeter City Reserves	42	17	9	16	75	76	43
Gravesend & Northfleet	42	17	8	17	79	75	42
Hereford United	42	17	7	18	90	90	41
Hastings United	42	15	10	17	90	76	40
Headington United	42	17	6	19	82	86	40
Kidderminster Harriers	42	14	7	21	86	108	35
Llanelly	42	14	6	22	64	98	34
Barry Town	42	11	11	20	91	108	33
Worcester City	42	12	9	21	66	83	33
Tonbridge	42	11	11	20	53	74	33
Merthyr Tydfil	42	7	10	25	52	127	24
Bath City	42	7	10	25	43	107	24

1956-57

Kettering Town	42	28	10	4	106	47	66
Bedford Town	42	25	8	9	89	52	58
Weymouth	42	22	10	10	92	71	54
Cheltenham Town	42	19	15	8	73	46	53
Gravesend & Northfleet	42	21	11	10	74	58	53
Lovells Athletic	42	21	7	14	99	84	49
Guildford City	42	18	11	13	68	49	47
Hereford United	42	19	8	15	96	60	46
Headington United	42	19	7	16	64	61	45
Gloucester City	42	18	8	16	74	72	44
Hastings United	42	17	9	16	70	58	43
Worcester City	42	16	10	16	81	80	42
Dartford	42	16	10	16	79	88	42
Chelmsford City	42	16	9	17	73	85	41
Tonbridge	42	14	12	16	74	65	40
Yeovil Town	42	14	11	17	83	85	39
Bath City	42	15	8	19	56	78	38
Exeter City Reserves	42	10	10	22	52	89	30
Merthyr Tydfil	42	9	11	22	72	95	29
Barry Town	42	6	11	25	39	84	23
Kidderminster Harriers	42	7	10	25	60	83	20
Llanelly	42	5	8	29	39	123	18

1957-58

Gravesend & Northfleet	42	27	5	10	109	71	59
Bedford Town	42	25	7	10	112	64	57
Chelmsford City	42	24	9	9	93	57	57
Weymouth	42	25	5	12	90	61	55
Worcester City	42	23	7	12	95	59	53
Cheltenham Town	42	21	10	11	115	66	52
Hereford United	42	21	6	15	79	56	48
Kettering Town	42	18	9	15	99	76	45
Headington Town	42	18	7	17	90	83	43
Poole Town	42	17	9	16	82	81	43
Hasting United	42	13	15	14	78	77	41
Gloucester City	42	17	7	18	70	70	41
Yeovil Town	42	16	9	17	70	84	41
Dartford	42	14	9	19	66	92	37
Lovells Athletic	42	15	6	21	60	83	36
Bath City	42	13	9	20	65	64	35
Guildford City	42	12	10	20	58	92	34
Tonbridge	42	16	7	22	77	100	33
Exeter City Reserves	42	12	8	22	60	94	32
Barry Town	42	11	9	22	72	101	31
Kidderminster Harriers	42	10	10	22	60	101	30
Merthyr Tydfil	42	9	3	30	69	137	21

1958-59

North-Western Zone

Hereford United	34	22	5	7	80	37	49
Kettering Town	34	20	7	7	83	63	47
Boston United	34	18	8	8	73	47	44
Cheltenham Town	34	20	4	10	65	47	44
Worcester City	34	19	4	11	74	47	42
Bath City	34	17	5	12	89	62	39
Wellington Town	34	15	9	10	74	58	39
Nuneaton Borough	34	17	5	12	76	66	39
Wisbech Town	34	16	5	13	77	54	37
Headington United	34	16	3	15	76	61	35
Barry Town	34	15	5	14	64	67	35
Merthyr Tydfil	34	16	3	15	54	59	35
Gloucester City	34	12	6	16	50	65	30
Corby Town	34	10	8	16	59	79	28
Lovells Athletic	34	10	3	21	51	70	23
Rugby Town	34	7	6	21	45	93	20
Kidderminster Harriers	34	7	3	24	42	94	17
Burton Albion	34	3	3	28	41	104	9

South-Eastern Zone

Bedford Town	32	21	6	5	90	41	48
Gravesend & Northfleet	32	21	2	9	79	54	44
Dartford	32	20	3	9	77	41	43
Yeovil Town	32	17	8	7	60	41	42
Weymouth	32	13	11	8	61	43	37
Chelmsford City	32	12	12	8	74	53	36
King's Lynn	32	14	5	13	70	63	33
Poole Town	32	12	8	12	60	65	32
Cambridge City	32	12	7	13	61	54	31
Hastings United	32	13	5	14	60	59	31
Tonbridge	32	14	3	15	51	59	31
Cambridge United	32	11	8	13	55	77	30
Trowbridge Town	32	12	4	16	53	75	28
Exeter City Reserves	32	7	12	13	47	71	26
Guildford City	11	7	6	19	45	67	20
Clacton Town	32	6	7	19	44	81	19
Yiewsley	32	3	7	22	36	78	13

1959-60

Premier Division

Bath City	42	32	3	7	116	50	67
Headington United	42	23	8	11	78	61	54
Weymouth	42	22	9	11	93	69	53
Cheltenham Town	42	21	6	15	82	68	48
Cambridge City	42	18	11	13	81	72	47
Chelmsford Town	42	19	7	16	90	70	45
Bedford Town	42	21	3	18	97	85	45
King's Lynn	42	17	11	14	89	78	45
Boston United	42	17	10	15	83	80	44
Wisbech Town	42	17	10	15	81	84	44
Yeovil Town	42	17	8	17	81	73	42
Hereford United	42	15	12	15	70	74	42
Tonbridge	42	16	8	18	79	73	40
Hastings United	42	16	8	18	63	77	40
Wellington Town	42	13	11	18	63	78	37
Dartford	42	15	7	20	64	82	37
Gravesend & Northfleet	42	14	8	20	69	84	36
Worcester City	42	13	10	19	72	89	36
Nuneaton Borough	42	11	11	20	64	78	33
Barry Town	42	14	5	23	78	103	33
Poole Town	42	10	8	24	69	96	28
Kettering Town	42	9	10	23	60	90	28

First Division

Clacton Town	42	27	5	10	106	69	59
Romford	42	21	11	10	65	40	53
Folkestone Town	42	23	5	14	93	71	51
Exeter City Reserves	42	23	3	16	85	62	49
Guildford City	42	19	9	14	79	56	47
Sittingbourne	42	20	7	15	66	55	47
Margate	42	20	6	16	88	77	46
Trowbridge Town	42	18	9	15	90	78	45
Cambridge United	42	18	9	15	71	72	45
Yiewsley	42	17	10	15	83	69	44
Bexleyheath & Welling	42	16	11	15	85	77	43
Merthyr Tydfil	42	16	10	16	63	65	42
Ramsgate Athletic	42	16	8	18	83	84	40
Ashford Town	42	14	12	16	61	70	40
Tunbridge Wells United	42	17	5	20	77	73	39
Hinckley Athletic	42	14	8	20	62	75	36
Gloucester City	42	13	9	20	56	84	35
Dover	42	14	6	22	59	85	34
Kidderminster Harriers	42	14	6	22	59	97	34
Corby Town	42	15	3	24	75	91	33
Burton Albion	42	11	10	21	52	79	32
Rugby Town	42	10	11	21	67	91	31

1960-61

Premier Division

Oxford United	42	27	10	5	104	43	64
Chelmsford City	42	23	11	8	91	55	57
Yeovil Town	42	23	9	10	109	54	55
Hereford United	42	21	10	11	83	67	52
Weymouth	42	21	9	12	78	63	51
Bath City	42	18	14	10	74	52	50
Cambridge City	42	16	12	14	101	71	44
Wellington Town	42	17	9	16	66	68	43
Bedford Town	42	18	7	17	94	97	43
Folkestone Town	42	18	7	17	75	86	43
King's Lynn	42	16	13	13	68	66	42
Worcester City	42	15	11	16	69	69	41
Clacton Town	42	15	11	16	82	83	41
Romford	42	13	15	14	66	69	41
Guildford City	42	14	11	17	65	62	39
Tonbridge	42	16	6	20	79	85	38
Cheltenham Town	42	15	7	20	81	81	37
Gravesend & Northfleet	42	15	7	20	75	101	37
Dartford	42	13	11	18	57	90	37
Hastings United	42	8	9	25	60	100	25
Wisbech Town	42	9	6	27	58	112	24
Boston United	42	6	8	28	62	123	20

Oxford United were previously known as Headington United.

First Division

Kettering Town	40	26	7	7	100	55	59
Cambridge United	40	25	5	10	100	53	55
Bexleyheath & Welling	40	22	8	10	93	46	52
Merthyr Tydfil	40	23	6	11	88	65	52
Sittingbourne	40	21	10	9	77	63	52
Hinckley Athletic	40	17	13	10	74	59	47
Ramsgate Athletic	40	19	7	14	77	56	45
Rugby Town	40	18	9	13	89	71	45
Corby Town	40	16	10	14	82	73	42
Poole Town	40	18	5	17	71	65	41
Barry Town	40	16	9	15	65	74	41
Yiewsley	40	17	7	16	65	76	41
Trowbridge Town	40	14	10	16	71	73	38
Ashford Town	40	14	8	18	61	67	36
Margate	40	11	12	17	62	75	34
Dover	40	12	7	21	67	74	31
Canterbury City	40	10	10	20	52	75	30
Nuneaton Borough	40	11	7	22	60	91	29
Burton Albion	40	12	4	24	63	85	28
Tunbridge Wells United	40	8	5	27	56	115	21
Gloucester City	40	7	7	26	40	102	21

1961-62

Premier Division

Oxford United	42	28	5	9	118	46	61
Bath City	42	25	7	10	102	70	57
Guildford City	42	24	8	10	79	49	56
Yeovil Town	42	23	8	11	97	59	54
Chelmsford City	42	19	12	11	74	60	50
Weymouth	42	20	7	15	80	64	47
Kettering Town	42	21	5	16	90	84	47
Hereford United	42	21	2	19	81	68	44
Cambridge City	42	18	8	16	70	71	44
Bexleyheath & Welling	42	19	5	18	69	75	43
Romford	42	15	9	18	63	70	39
Cambridge United	42	13	12	17	76	78	38
Wellington United	42	14	10	18	75	78	38
Gravesend & Northfleet	42	17	4	21	59	92	38
Bedford Town	42	16	5	21	73	79	37
Worcester City	42	15	7	20	51	64	37
Merthyr Tydfil	42	13	11	18	62	80	37
Clacton Town	42	13	10	19	74	91	36
Tonbridge	42	10	14	18	71	92	34
King's Lynn	42	12	8	22	59	74	32
Folkestone Town	42	12	6	24	64	103	30
Cheltenham	42	9	7	26	48	86	25

First Division

Wisbech Town	38	21	11	6	76	42	53
Poole Town	38	23	6	9	81	47	52
Dartford	38	21	8	9	89	50	50
Rugby Town	38	20	9	9	82	49	49
Margate	38	20	6	12	73	55	46
Corby Town	38	19	6	13	82	60	44
Sittingbourne	38	16	12	10	69	51	44
Dover	38	19	6	13	66	55	44
Yiewsley	38	18	6	14	64	51	42
Barry Town	38	14	11	13	55	51	39
Ashford Town	38	14	11	13	66	70	39
Hinckley Athletic	38	15	8	15	75	65	38
Burton Albion	38	16	5	17	70	79	37
Nuneaton Borough	38	12	12	14	63	69	36
Tunbridge Wells United	38	12	7	19	60	85	31
Canterbury City	38	11	8	19	60	82	30
Ramsgate Athletic	38	10	9	19	48	70	29
Trowbridge Town	38	9	9	20	45	69	27
Gloucester City	38	6	4	28	46	104	16
Hastings United	38	5	4	29	45	115	14

1962-63

Premier Division

Cambridge City	40	25	6	9	99	64	56
Cambridge United	40	23	7	10	74	50	53
Weymouth	40	20	11	9	82	43	51
Guildford City	40	20	11	9	70	50	51
Kettering Town	40	22	7	11	66	49	51
Wellington Town	40	19	9	12	71	49	47
Dartford	40	19	9	12	61	54	47
Chelmsford City	40	18	10	12	63	50	44
Bedford Town	40	18	8	14	61	45	44
Bath City	40	18	6	16	58	56	42
Yeovil Town	40	15	10	15	64	54	40
Romford	40	14	11	15	73	68	39
Bexleyheath & Welling	40	13	11	16	55	63	37
Hereford United	40	14	7	19	56	66	35
Merthyr Tydfil	40	15	4	21	54	71	34
Rugby Town	40	14	5	21	65	76	33
Wisbech Town	40	15	3	22	64	84	33
Worcester City	40	12	9	19	47	65	33
Poole Town	40	10	12	18	54	66	32
Gravesend & Northfleet	40	10	3	27	62	91	23
Clacton Town	40	3	7	30	50	135	13

First Division

Margate	38	21	13	4	86	47	55
Hinckley Athletic	38	22	9	7	66	38	53
Hastings United	38	22	8	8	86	36	52
Nuneaton Borough	38	21	10	7	82	41	52
Tonbridge	38	22	8	8	81	51	52
Dover	38	22	7	9	78	56	51
Corby Town	38	19	8	11	79	50	46
King's Lynn	38	19	7	15	76	66	45
Cheltenham Town	38	18	7	13	83	52	43
Folkestone Town	38	15	10	13	79	57	40
Canterbury City	38	14	8	16	42	56	36
Yiewsley	38	11	10	17	63	71	32
Ramsgate Athletic	38	12	7	19	58	82	31
Trowbridge Town	38	11	9	18	50	81	31
Burton Albion	38	10	10	18	48	76	30
Gloucester City	38	9	11	18	42	78	29
Sittingbourne	38	12	3	23	56	75	27
Ashford Town	38	9	6	23	58	76	24
Barry Town	38	6	5	27	35	75	17
Tunbridge Wells United	38	6	2	30	43	118	14

1963-64

Premier Division

Yeovil Town	42	29	5	8	93	36	63
Chelmsford City	42	26	7	9	99	55	59
Bath City	42	24	9	9	88	51	57
Guildford City	42	21	9	12	90	55	51
Romford	42	20	9	13	71	58	49
Hastings United	42	20	8	14	75	61	48
Weymouth	42	20	7	15	65	53	47
Bedford Town	42	19	9	14	71	68	47
Cambridge United	42	17	9	16	92	77	43
Cambridge City	42	17	9	16	76	70	43
Wisbech Town	42	17	8	17	64	68	42
Bexley United	42	16	10	16	70	77	42
Dartford	42	16	8	18	56	71	40
Worcester City	42	12	15	15	70	74	39
Nuneaton Borough	42	15	8	19	58	61	38
Rugby Town	42	15	8	19	68	86	38
Margate	42	12	13	17	68	81	37
Wellington Town	42	12	9	21	73	85	33
Merthyr Tydfil	42	12	8	22	69	108	32
Hereford United	42	12	7	23	58	86	31
Kettering Town	42	10	5	27	49	89	25
Hinckley Athletic	42	7	6	29	51	104	20

First Division

Folkstone Town	42	28	7	7	82	38	63
King's Lynn	42	28	5	9	94	44	61
Cheltenham Town	47	25	10	7	92	49	60
Tonbridge	42	24	11	7	98	54	59
Corby town	42	24	7	11	114	56	55
Stevenage Town	42	21	6	15	70	59	48
Ashford Town	42	19	9	14	73	57	47
Burton Albion	42	19	8	15	76	70	46
Poole Town	42	17	11	14	75	61	45
Dover	42	18	9	15	86	75	45
Canterbury City	42	16	12	14	66	66	44
Crawley Town	42	20	2	20	81	71	42
Trowbridge Town	42	16	9	17	71	78	41
Clacton Town	42	19	1	22	76	88	39
Gloucester City	42	17	4	21	88	89	38
Yiewsley	42	15	8	19	63	77	38
Sittingbourne	42	15	8	19	52	70	38
Ramsgate Athletic	42	13	9	20	57	55	35
Tunbridge Wells Rangers	42	10	8	24	47	89	28
Gravesend & Northfleet	42	7	9	26	43	96	23
Deal Town	42	5	7	30	48	106	17
Barry Town	42	3	6	33	33	137	12

1964-65

Premier Division

Weymouth	42	24	8	10	99	50	56
Guildford City	42	21	12	9	73	49	54
Worcester City	42	22	6	14	100	62	50
Yeovil Town	42	18	14	10	76	55	50
Chelmsford City	42	21	8	13	86	77	50
Margate	42	20	9	13	88	79	49
Dartford	42	17	11	14	74	64	45
Nuneaton Borough	42	19	7	16	57	55	45
Cambridge United	42	16	11	15	78	66	43
Bedford Town	42	17	9	16	66	70	43
Cambridge City	42	16	9	17	72	69	41
Cheltenham Town	42	15	11	16	72	78	41
Folkstone Town	42	17	7	18	72	79	41
Romford	42	17	7	18	61	70	41
King's Lynn	42	13	13	16	56	79	39
Tonbridge	42	10	16	16	66	75	36
Wellington Town	42	13	10	19	63	78	36
Rugby Town	42	15	6	21	71	98	36
Wisbech Town	42	14	6	22	75	91	34
Bexley United	42	14	5	23	67	74	33
Hastings United	42	9	14	19	58	86	32
Bath City	42	13	3	26	60	86	29

First Division

Hereford United	42	34	4	4	124	39	72
Wimbledon	42	24	13	5	108	52	61
Poole Town	42	26	6	10	92	56	58
Corby Town	42	24	7	11	88	55	55
Stevenage Town	42	19	13	10	83	43	51
Hillingdon Borough	42	21	7	14	105	63	49
Crawley Town	42	22	5	15	83	52	49
Merthyr Tydfil	42	20	9	13	75	59	49
Gloucester City	42	19	10	13	68	65	48
Burton Albion	42	20	7	15	83	75	47
Canterbury City	42	13	16	13	73	53	42
Kettering Town	42	14	13	15	74	64	41
Ramsgate Athletic	42	16	8	18	51	59	40
Dover	42	14	10	18	54	59	38
Hinckley Athletic	42	13	9	20	56	81	35
Trowbridge Town	42	13	5	24	68	106	31
Ashford Town	42	11	8	23	60	98	30
Barry Town	42	11	7	24	47	103	29
Deal Town	42	7	13	22	61	127	27
Tunbridge Wells Rangers	42	10	6	26	51	107	26
Gravesend & Northfleet	42	9	7	26	57	101	25
Sittingbourne	42	8	5	29	58	103	21

1965-66

Premier Division

Weymouth	42	22	13	7	70	35	57
Chelmsford City	42	21	12	9	74	50	54
Hereford United	42	21	10	11	81	49	52
Bedford Town	42	23	6	13	80	57	52
Wimbledon	42	20	10	12	80	47	50
Cambridge City	42	19	11	12	67	52	49
Romford	42	21	7	14	87	72	49
Worcester City	42	20	8	14	69	54	48
Yeovil Town	42	17	11	14	91	70	45
Cambridge United	42	18	9	15	72	64	45
King's Lynn	42	18	7	17	75	72	43
Corby Town	42	16	9	17	66	73	41
Wellington Town	42	13	13	16	65	70	39
Nuneaton Borough	42	15	8	19	60	74	38
Folkestone Town	42	14	9	19	53	75	37
Guildford City	42	14	8	20	70	84	36
Poole Town	42	14	7	21	61	75	35
Cheltenham Town	42	13	9	20	69	99	35
Dartford	42	13	7	22	62	69	33
Rugby Town	42	11	10	21	67	95	32
Tonbridge	42	11	6	25	63	101	28
Margate	42	8	10	24	66	111	26

First Division

Barnet	46	30	9	7	114	49	69
Hillingdon Borough	46	27	10	9	101	46	64
Burton Albion	46	28	8	10	121	60	64
Bath City	46	25	13	8	88	50	63
Hastings United	46	25	10	11	104	59	60
Wisbech Town	46	25	9	12	98	54	59
Canterbury City	46	25	8	13	89	66	58
Stevenage Town	46	23	9	14	86	49	55
Kettering Town	46	22	9	15	77	74	53
Merthyr Tydfil	46	22	6	18	95	68	50
Dunstable Town	46	15	14	17	76	72	44
Crawley Town	46	17	10	19	72	71	44
Bexley United	46	20	4	22	65	71	44
Trowbridge Town	46	16	11	19	79	81	43
Dover	46	17	8	21	59	62	42
Barry Town	46	16	10	20	72	94	42
Gravesend & Northfleet	46	16	9	21	84	86	41
Gloucester City	46	14	12	20	75	98	40
Sittingbourne	46	11	12	23	77	121	34
Ramsgate Athletic	46	9	15	22	35	76	33
Hinckley Athletic	46	10	12	24	59	93	32
Tunbridge Wells Rangers	46	12	8	26	47	88	32
Ashford Town	46	9	10	27	44	92	28
Deal Town	46	3	4	39	29	165	10

1966-67

Premier Division

Romford	42	22	8	12	80	60	52
Nuneaton Borough	42	21	9	12	82	54	51
Weymouth	42	18	14	10	64	40	50
Wimbledon	42	19	11	12	88	60	49
Barnet	42	18	13	11	86	66	49
Guildford City	42	19	10	13	65	51	48
Wellington Town	42	20	7	15	70	67	47
Cambridge United	42	16	13	13	75	67	45
Chelmsford City	42	15	15	12	66	59	45
Hereford United	42	16	12	14	79	61	44
King's Lynn	42	15	14	13	78	72	44
Cambridge City	42	15	13	14	66	70	43
Cheltenham Town	42	16	11	15	60	71	43
Yeovil Town	42	14	14	14	66	72	42
Burton Albion	42	17	5	20	63	71	39
Corby Town	42	15	9	18	60	75	39
Poole Town	42	14	11	17	52	65	39
Hillingdon Borough	42	13	18	49	90	70	35
Bath City	42	11	12	19	51	74	34
Worcester City	42	11	8	23	59	79	30
Bedford Town	42	8	13	21	54	72	29
Folkestone Town	42	6	15	21	44	81	27

First Division

Dover	46	29	12	5	92	35	70
Margate	46	31	7	8	127	54	69
Stevenage Town	46	29	8	9	90	32	66
Hastings United	46	25	16	5	89	45	66
Kettering Town	46	27	9	10	105	62	63
Crawley Town	46	26	8	12	81	48	60
Ramsgate Athletic	46	23	8	15	79	62	54
Dartford	46	19	15	12	92	67	53
Tonbridge	46	21	10	15	91	69	52
Trowbridge Town	46	20	12	14	73	60	52
Ashford Town	46	18	8	20	74	68	44
Merthyr Tydfil	46	17	9	20	81	71	43
Gloucester City	46	18	6	22	69	83	42
Canterbury City	46	17	8	21	57	75	42
Wisbech Town	46	16	9	21	87	93	41
Bexley United	46	13	15	18	53	69	41
Banbury United	46	13	14	19	88	100	40
Rugby Town	46	15	7	24	57	77	37
Dunstable Town	46	14	6	26	55	87	34
Barry Town	46	11	11	24	62	89	33
Gravesend & Northfleet	46	11	9	26	63	106	31
Hinckley Athletic	46	10	8	28	44	100	28
Tunbridge Wells Rangers	46	4	15	27	31	96	23
Sittingbourne	46	5	10	31	44	136	20

1967-68

Premier Division

Chelmsford City	42	25	7	10	85	50	57
Wimbledon	42	24	7	11	85	47	55
Cambridge United	42	20	13	9	73	42	53
Cheltenham Town	42	23	7	12	97	67	53
Guildford City	42	18	13	11	56	43	49
Romford	42	20	8	14	72	60	48
Barnet	42	20	8	14	81	71	48
Margate	42	19	8	15	80	71	46
Wellington Town	42	16	13	13	70	66	45
Hillingdon Borough	42	18	9	155	53	54	45
King's Lynn	42	18	8	16	66	57	44
Yeovil Town	42	16	12	14	45	43	44
Weymouth	42	17	8	17	65	62	42
Hereford United	42	17	7	18	58	62	41
Nuneaton Borough	42	13	14	15	62	64	40
Dover	42	17	6	19	54	56	40
Poole Town	42	13	10	19	55	74	36
Stevenage Town	42	13	9	20	57	75	35
Burton Albion	42	14	6	22	51	73	34
Corby Town	42	7	13	22	40	77	27
Cambridge City	42	10	6	26	51	81	26
Hastings United	42	4	8	30	33	94	16

First Division

Worcester City	42	23	14	5	92	35	60
Kettering Town	42	24	10	8	88	40	58
Bedford Town	42	24	7	11	101	40	55
Rugby Town	42	20	15	7	72	44	55
Dartford	42	23	9	10	70	48	55
Bath City	42	21	12	9	78	51	54
Banbury United	42	22	9	11	79	59	53
Ramsgate Athletic	42	17	7	8	70	37	51
Merthyr Tydfil	42	18	13	11	80	66	49
Tonbridge	42	18	9	15	76	71	45
Canterbury City	42	16	11	15	66	63	43
Ashford Town	42	18	6	18	73	78	42
Brentwood Town	42	16	9	17	63	73	41
Bexley United	42	12	13	17	56	64	37
Trowbridge Town	42	12	11	19	64	70	35
Gloucester City	42	12	9	21	54	68	33
Wisbech Town	42	11	10	21	43	78	32
Crawley Town	42	10	8	24	54	85	28
Folkestone Town	42	10	7	25	49	80	27
Dunstable Town	42	8	10	24	44	94	26
Barry Town	42	7	12	23	36	81	26
Gravesend & Northfleet	42	6	7	29	28	112	19

1968-69

Premier Division

Cambridge United	42	27	5	10	72	39	59
Hillingdon Borough	42	24	10	8	68	47	58
Wimbledon	42	21	12	9	66	48	54
King's Lynn	42	20	9	13	68	60	49
Worcester City	42	19	11	12	53	47	49
Romford	42	18	12	12	58	52	48
Weymouth	42	16	16	11	52	41	47
Yeovil Town	42	16	13	13	52	50	45
Kettering Town	42	18	8	16	51	55	44
Dover	42	17	9	16	66	61	43
Nuneaton Borough	42	17	7	18	74	58	41
Barnet	42	15	10	17	72	66	40
Chelmsford City	42	17	6	19	56	58	40
Hereford United	42	15	9	18	66	62	39
Telford United	42	14	10	18	62	61	38
Poole Town	42	16	6	20	75	76	38
Burton Albion	42	16	5	21	55	71	37
Margate	42	14	7	21	79	90	35
Cheltenham Town	42	15	5	22	55	64	35
Bedford Town	42	11	12	19	46	63	34
Rugby Town	42	10	6	26	38	83	26
Guildford City	42	7	11	24	41	73	25

First Division

Brentwood Town	42	26	12	4	44	37	64
Bath City	42	26	10	6	96	40	62
Gloucester City	42	25	9	8	100	53	59
Crawley Town	42	21	13	8	65	32	55
Corby Town	42	22	6	14	81	65	50
Dartford	42	20	8	14	79	51	48
Ramsgate Athletic	42	19	14	7	72	57	47
Salisbury	42	20	6	16	69	52	46
Cambridge City	42	18	10	14	73	63	46
Banbury United	42	16	12	14	67	72	44
Trowbridge Town	42	15	8	19	70	60	44
Folkestone Town	42	19	5	18	53	59	43
Canterbury City	42	17	7	18	67	63	41
Ashford Town	42	16	8	18	72	73	40
Bexley United	42	15	9	18	62	75	39
Hastings United	42	15	9	18	58	69	39
Wisbech Town	42	11	13	18	57	70	35
Dunstable Town	42	14	6	22	73	99	34
Merthyr Tydfil	42	10	7	25	49	101	27
Barry Town	42	8	10	24	39	78	26
Gravesend & Northfleet	42	8	9	25	51	79	25
Tonbridge	42	2	6	34	36	137	10

1969-70

Premier Division

Cambridge United	42	26	6	10	86	49	58
Yeovil Town	42	25	7	10	78	48	57
Chelmsford City	42	20	11	11	76	58	51
Weymouth	42	18	14	10	59	37	50
Wimbledon	42	19	12	11	64	52	50
Hillingdon Borough	42	19	12	11	56	50	50
Barnet	42	16	15	11	71	54	47
Telford United	42	18	10	14	61	62	46
Brentwood Town	42	16	13	13	61	38	45
Hereford United	42	18	9	15	74	65	45
Bath City	42	18	8	16	63	55	44
King's Lynn	42	16	11	15	72	68	43
Margate	42	17	8	17	70	64	42
Dover	42	15	10	17	51	50	40
Kettering Town	42	18	3	21	64	75	39
Worcester City	42	14	10	18	59	44	38
Romford	42	13	11	18	50	62	37
Poole Town	42	8	19	15	48	57	35
Gloucester City	42	12	9	21	53	73	33
Nuneaton Borough	42	11	10	21	52	74	32
Crawley Town	42	6	15	21	53	101	27
Burton Albion	42	3	9	30	24	82	15

First Division

Bedford Town	42	26	9	7	93	37	61
Cambridge City	42	26	8	8	104	43	60
Dartford	42	24	11	7	33	46	58
Ashford Town	42	19	15	8	71	43	53
Rugby Town	42	20	10	12	82	66	50
Trowbridge Town	42	20	8	14	72	65	48
Hastings United	42	18	11	13	67	51	47
Guildford City	42	19	9	14	68	58	47
Banbury United	42	19	8	15	86	72	46
Cheltenham Town	42	20	5	17	78	81	45
Canterbury City	42	15	13	14	61	57	43
Corby Town	42	14	15	13	58	53	43
Folkestone Town	42	19	5	18	57	55	43
Ramsgate Athletic	42	14	13	15	53	57	41
Salisbury	42	13	13	16	48	53	39
Gravesend & Northfleet	42	13	11	18	62	71	37
Bexley United	42	10	11	21	58	76	31
Dunstable Town	42	11	9	22	52	82	31
Merthyr Tydfil	42	9	11	22	40	80	29
Barry Town	42	11	6	25	39	76	28
Wisbech Town	42	8	9	25	58	116	25
Tonbridge	42	4	10	28	46	101	18

1970-71

Premier Division

Yeovil Town	42	25	7	10	66	31	57
Cambridge City	42	22	11	9	67	38	55
Romford	42	23	9	10	63	42	55
Hereford United	42	23	8	11	71	53	54
Chelmsford City	42	20	11	11	61	32	51
Barnet	42	18	14	10	69	49	50
Bedford Town	42	20	10	12	62	46	50
Wimbledon	42	20	8	14	72	54	48
Worcester City	42	20	8	14	61	46	48
Weymouth	42	14	16	12	64	48	44
Dartford	42	15	12	15	53	51	42
Dover	42	16	9	17	64	63	41
Margate	42	15	10	17	64	70	40
Hillingdon Borough	42	17	6	19	61	68	40
Bath City	42	13	12	17	48	68	38
Nuneaton Borough	42	12	12	18	43	66	36
Telford United	42	13	8	21	64	70	34
Poole Town	42	14	6	22	57	75	34
King's Lynn	42	11	7	24	44	67	29
Ashford Town	42	8	13	21	52	86	29
Kettering Town	42	8	11	23	48	84	27
Gloucester City	42	6	10	26	34	81	21

First Division

Guildford City	38	22	10	6	76	36	54
Merthyr Tydfil	38	19	12	7	52	33	50
Gravesend & Northfleet	38	19	10	9	74	42	48
Folkestone	38	20	8	10	83	53	48
Burton Albion	38	19	10	9	56	37	48
Rugby Town	38	17	14	7	58	40	48
Ramsgate Athletic	38	20	5	13	83	54	45
Trowbridge Town	38	19	7	12	78	55	45
Bexley United	38	17	11	10	57	45	45
Crawley Town	38	15	11	12	84	68	41
Hastings United	38	13	12	13	51	50	38
Banbury United	38	13	11	14	58	53	37
Corby Town	38	14	8	16	57	60	36
Salisbury	38	13	7	18	56	60	33
Cheltenham Town	38	8	15	15	44	58	31
Stevenage Athletic	38	12	7	19	55	79	21
Tonbridge	38	8	8	22	48	83	24
Barry Town	38	9	6	23	35	82	24
Dunstable Town	38	8	4	26	32	81	20
Canterbury City	38	5	4	29	37	105	14

1971-72

Premier Division

Chelmsford City	42	28	6	8	109	46	62
Hereford United	42	24	12	6	68	30	60
Dover	42	20	11	11	67	45	51
Barnet	42	21	7	14	80	57	49
Dartford	42	20	8	14	75	68	48
Weymouth	42	21	5	16	69	43	47
Yeovil Town	42	18	11	13	67	51	47
Hillingdon Borough	42	20	6	16	64	58	46
Margate	42	19	8	15	74	68	46
Wimbledon	42	19	7	16	75	64	45
Romford	42	16	13	13	54	49	45
Guildford City	42	20	5	17	71	65	45
Telford United	42	18	7	17	83	68	43
Nuneaton Borough	42	16	10	16	46	47	42
Bedford Town	42	16	9	17	59	66	41
Worcester City	42	17	7	18	46	57	41
Cambridge City	42	12	14	16	68	71	38
Folkestone	42	14	7	21	58	64	35
Poole Town	42	9	11	22	43	72	29
Bath City	42	11	4	27	45	86	26
Merthyr Tydfil	42	7	8	27	29	93	22
Gravesend & Northfleet	42	5	6	31	30	110	16

First Division (North)

Kettering Town	34	23	6	5	70	27	52
Burton Albion	34	18	13	3	58	27	49
Cheltenham Town	34	20	4	10	72	51	44
Rugby Town	34	18	7	9	52	36	43
Wellingborough Town	34	15	10	9	73	44	40
Stourbridge	34	13	14	7	59	42	40
King's Lynn	34	14	11	9	62	45	39
Corby Town	34	15	9	10	47	35	39
Ilkeston Town	34	14	11	9	44	38	39
Banbury United	34	14	5	15	54	46	33
Bury Town	34	14	5	15	47	44	33
Wealdstone	34	14	5	15	51	58	33
Lockheed Leamington	34	15	3	16	41	52	33
Gloucester City	34	8	8	18	46	61	24
Stevenage Athletic	34	8	8	18	41	69	24
Bletchley	34	7	7	20	36	70	21
Dunstable Town	34	5	7	22	29	75	17
Barry Town	34	1	7	26	22	84	9

First Division (South)

Waterlooville	30	15	9	6	40	22	39
Ramsgate Athletic	30	14	11	5	42	27	39
Maidstone United	30	14	10	6	48	28	38
Crawley Town	30	15	5	10	67	55	35
Metropolitan Police	30	15	3	12	48	41	33
Tonbridge	30	12	9	9	37	34	33
Bexley United	30	14	4	12	52	46	32
Basingstoke Town	30	14	4	12	37	36	32
Andover	30	11	9	10	32	34	31
Ashford Town	30	12	4	14	43	48	28
Salisbury	30	10	7	13	45	44	27
Winchester City	30	10	7	13	40	47	27
Hastings United	30	10	7	13	28	42	27
Trowbridge Town	30	8	7	15	41	49	23
Canterbury City	30	7	8	15	39	56	22
Woodford Town	30	4	6	20	22	52	14

1972-73

Premier Division

Team	P	W	D	L	F	A	Pts
Kettering Town	42	20	17	5	74	44	57
Yeovil Town	42	21	14	7	67	61	56
Dover	42	23	9	10	61	68	55
Chelmsford City	42	23	7	12	75	43	53
Worcester City	42	20	13	9	68	47	53
Weymouth	42	20	12	10	72	51	52
Margate	42	17	15	10	80	60	49
Bedford Town	42	16	15	11	43	36	47
Nuneaton Borough	42	16	14	12	51	41	46
Telford United	42	12	20	10	57	47	44
Cambridge City	42	14	15	13	64	53	43
Wimbledon	42	14	14	14	50	50	42
Barnet	42	15	11	16	60	59	41
Romford	42	17	5	20	51	65	39
Hillingdon Borough	42	16	6	20	52	58	38
Dartford	42	12	11	19	49	63	35
Folkestone	42	11	11	20	41	72	33
Guildford City	42	10	11	21	59	84	31
Ramsgate	42	9	13	20	35	61	31
Poole Town	42	10	10	22	50	88	30
Burton Albion	42	9	7	26	43	81	25
Waterlooville	42	4	16	22	33	63	24

First Division (North)

Team	P	W	D	L	F	A	Pts
Grantham	42	29	8	5	113	41	66
Atherstone Town	42	23	11	8	82	48	57
Cheltenham Town	42	24	8	10	87	47	56
Rugby Town	42	20	10	12	60	47	50
Kidderminster Harriers	42	19	12	11	67	56	50
Merthyr Tydfil	42	17	12	13	51	40	46
Corby Town	42	14	16	12	62	56	44
Stourbridge	42	16	11	15	70	64	43
Gloucester City	42	18	7	17	55	64	43
Bromsgrove Rovers	42	17	8	17	63	54	42
Redditch United	42	18	6	18	58	59	42
Banbury United	42	18	5	19	60	53	41
Wellingborough Town	42	17	7	18	58	71	41
King's Lynn	42	14	12	16	45	49	40
Lockheed Leamington	42	13	12	17	51	58	38
Enderby Town	42	12	14	16	50	61	38
Stevenage Athletic	42	12	13	17	50	63	37
Tamworth	42	14	8	20	45	65	36
Bury Town	42	13	9	20	52	69	35
Barry Town	42	11	10	21	45	71	32
Ilkeston Town	42	9	6	27	35	68	24
Bedworth United	42	10	3	29	42	94	23

First Division (South)

Team	P	W	D	L	F	A	Pts
Maidstone United	42	25	12	5	90	38	62
Tonbridge	42	26	7	9	70	44	59
Ashford Town	42	24	7	11	90	40	55
Bideford	42	19	14	9	70	43	52
Minehead	42	20	12	10	65	47	52
Gravesend & Northfleet	42	22	7	13	81	55	51
Bath City	42	18	11	13	56	54	47
Wealdstone	42	16	12	14	81	61	44
Bletchley Town	42	14	13	15	54	51	41
Hastings United	42	14	13	15	53	53	41
Andover	42	15	11	16	62	70	41
Canterbury City	42	14	12	16	51	59	40
Basingstoke Town	42	14	12	16	48	57	40
Crawley Town	42	14	11	17	59	76	39
Metropolitan Police	42	15	8	19	82	75	38
Trowbridge Town	42	15	8	19	65	77	38
Bexley United	42	12	14	16	54	64	38
Salisbury	42	14	10	18	49	60	38
Bognor Regis Town	42	12	9	21	41	66	33
Dorchester Town	42	10	12	20	47	73	32
Winchester City	42	7	11	24	41	79	25
Dunstable Town	42	4	10	28	38	105	18

1973-74

Team	P	W	D	L	F	A	Pts
Dartford	42	22	13	7	67	37	57
Grantham	42	18	13	11	70	49	49
Chelmsford City	42	19	10	13	62	49	48
Kettering Town	42	16	16	10	62	51	48
Maidstone United	42	16	14	12	54	43	46
Yeovil Town	42	13	20	9	45	39	46
Weymouth	42	19	7	16	60	41	45
Barnet	42	18	9	15	55	46	45
Nuneaton Borough	42	13	19	10	54	47	45
Cambridge City	42	15	12	15	45	54	42
Atherstone Town	42	16	9	17	61	59	41
Wimbledon	42	15	11	16	50	56	41
Telford United	42	12	16	14	51	57	40
Dover	42	11	17	14	41	46	39
Tonbridge	42	12	15	15	38	45	39
Romford	42	11	17	14	39	52	39
Margate	42	15	8	19	56	63	38
Guildford City	42	13	11	18	48	67	37
Worcester City	42	11	14	17	53	67	36
Bedford Town	42	11	14	17	38	51	36
Folkestone	42	11	12	19	56	65	34
Hillingdon Borough	42	9	15	18	44	65	33

First Division (North)

Team	P	W	D	L	F	A	Pts
Stourbridge	42	29	11	2	103	36	69
Burton Albion	42	27	9	6	88	32	63
Cheltenham Town	42	24	8	10	75	51	56
AP Leamington	42	21	12	9	82	45	54
Enderby Town	42	19	14	9	60	36	52
Witney Town	42	20	10	12	69	55	50
Stevenage Athletic	42	19	11	12	65	46	49
Banbury United	42	19	11	12	69	57	49
King's Lynn	42	19	10	13	65	50	48
Kidderminster Harriers	42	15	14	13	67	53	44
Merthyr Tydfil	42	16	12	14	70	61	44
Redditch United	42	14	11	17	56	73	39
Bromsgrove Rovers	42	14	10	18	54	61	38
Bedworth United	42	14	10	18	50	77	38
Tamworth	42	13	11	18	42	51	37
Corby Town	42	11	11	19	40	57	35
Bletchley Town	42	10	15	17	47	71	35
Barry Town	42	10	8	24	53	85	29
Bury Town	42	10	6	26	57	84	26
Gloucester City	42	10	6	26	52	81	26
Wellingborough Town	42	7	9	26	42	87	23
Dunstable Town	42	5	11	26	26	83	21

First Division (South)

Team	P	W	D	L	F	A	Pts
Wealdstone	38	26	7	5	75	35	59
Bath City	38	20	8	10	55	34	48
Waterlooville	38	16	15	7	55	38	47
Minehead	38	16	15	7	69	52	47
Bideford	38	17	12	9	61	51	46
Poole Town	38	18	9	11	67	47	45
Bexley United	38	18	7	13	50	42	43
Hastings United	38	16	9	13	45	36	41
Basingstoke Town	38	14	11	13	55	44	39
Gravesend & Northfleet	38	13	13	12	58	52	39
Bognor Regis Town	38	13	12	13	48	54	38
Ashford Town	38	14	8	16	41	42	36
Ramsgate	38	13	9	16	46	44	35
Dorchester Town	38	10	13	15	40	48	33
Canterbury City	38	12	17	37	46	30	
Trowbridge Town	38	8	14	16	44	61	30
Salisbury	38	10	9	19	40	60	29
Metropolitan Police	38	11	18	37	61	29	
Andover	38	11	3	24	38	70	25
Crawley Town	38	6	9	23	35	79	21

1974-75

Premier Division

Wimbledon	42	25	7	10	63	33	57
Nuneaton Borough	42	23	8	11	56	37	54
Yeovil Town	42	21	9	12	64	34	51
Kettering Town	42	20	10	12	73	41	50
Burton Albion	42	18	13	11	54	48	49
Bath City	42	20	8	14	63	50	48
Margate	42	17	12	13	64	64	46
Wealdstone	42	17	11	14	62	61	45
Telford United	42	16	13	13	55	56	45
Chelmsford City	42	16	12	14	62	51	44
Grantham	42	16	11	15	70	62	43
Dover	42	15	13	14	43	53	43
Maidstone United	42	15	12	15	52	50	42
Atherstone Town	42	14	14	14	48	53	42
Weymouth	42	13	13	16	66	58	39
Stourbridge	42	13	12	17	56	70	38
Cambridge	42	11	14	17	51	56	36
Tonbridge	42	11	12	19	44	66	34
Romford	42	10	13	19	46	62	33
Dartford	42	9	13	20	52	70	31
Barnet	42	10	9	23	44	76	29
Guildford & Dorking United	42	10	5	27	45	82	25

First Division (North)

Bedford Town	42	28	9	5	85	33	65
Dunstable Town	42	25	8	9	105	61	58
AP Leamington	42	25	7	10	68	48	57
Redditch United	42	22	12	8	76	40	56
Worcester City	42	24	8	10	84	50	56
Cheltenham Town	42	21	9	12	72	53	51
Tamworth	42	21	8	13	74	53	50
King's Lynn	42	19	10	13	71	64	48
Enderby Town	42	17	12	13	61	48	46
Banbury United	42	18	10	14	52	51	46
Stevenage Athletic	42	16	13	13	62	48	45
Bromsgrove Rovers	42	18	9	15	63	52	45
Merthyr Tydfil	42	11	15	16	53	64	37
Witney Town	42	16	4	22	57	76	36
Corby Town	42	11	13	18	60	57	35
Kidderminster Harriers	42	12	11	19	50	66	35
Gloucester City	42	13	8	21	55	75	34
Wellingborough Town	42	9	13	20	42	61	31
Barry Town	42	10	10	22	49	73	30
Bedworth United	42	9	9	24	60	91	27
Milton Keynes City	42	7	5	30	48	100	19
Bury Town	42	5	7	30	36	119	17

First Division (South)

Gravesend & Northfleet	38	24	12	2	70	30	60
Hillingdon Borough	38	22	8	8	87	45	52
Minehead	38	21	9	8	74	33	51
Ramsgate	38	19	11	8	70	37	49
Bexley United	38	19	7	12	61	44	45
Waterlooville	38	17	11	10	67	49	45
Ashford Town	38	16	12	10	64	55	44
Basingstoke Town	38	16	11	11	64	50	43
Canterbury City	38	16	9	13	54	43	41
Hastings United	38	13	14	11	54	45	40
Poole Town	38	11	13	14	50	60	35
Metropolitan Police	38	11	13	14	54	66	35
Folkestone & Shepway	38	10	14	14	53	57	34
Andover	38	12	8	18	52	71	32
Bognor Regis Town	38	10	11	17	49	64	31
Salisbury	38	9	11	18	45	66	29
Trowbridge Town	38	10	9	19	48	76	29
Bideford	38	10	8	20	40	71	28
Dorchester Town	38	8	10	20	40	63	26
Crawley Town	38	3	5	30	31	102	11

1975-76

Premier Division

Wimbledon	42	26	10	6	74	29	62
Yeovil Town	42	21	12	9	68	35	54
Atherstone Town	42	18	15	9	56	55	51
Maidstone United	42	17	16	9	52	39	50
Nuneaton Borough	42	16	18	8	41	33	50
Gravesend & Northfleet	42	16	18	8	49	47	50
Grantham	42	15	14	13	56	47	44
Dunstable Town	42	17	9	16	52	43	43
Bedford Town	42	13	17	12	55	51	43
Burton Albion	42	17	9	16	52	53	43
Margate	42	15	12	15	62	60	42
Hillingdon Borough	42	13	14	15	61	54	40
Telford United	42	14	12	16	54	51	40
Chelmsford City	42	13	14	15	52	57	40
Kettering Town	42	11	17	14	48	52	39
Bath City	42	11	16	15	62	57	38
Weymouth	42	13	9	20	51	67	35
Dover	42	8	18	16	51	60	34
Wealdstone	42	12	9	21	61	82	33
Tonbridge AFC	42	11	11	20	45	70	33
Cambridge City	42	8	15	19	41	67	31
Stourbridge	42	10	9	23	38	72	29

First Division (North)

Redditch United	42	29	11	2	101	39	69
AP Leamington	42	27	10	5	85	31	64
Witney Town	42	24	9	9	66	40	57
Worcester City	42	24	8	10	90	49	56
Cheltenham Town	42	20	10	12	87	55	50
Barry Town	42	19	10	13	52	47	48
King's Lynn	42	17	14	11	52	48	48
Tamworth	42	18	11	13	65	43	47
Barnet	42	15	12	15	56	56	42
Oswestry Town	42	16	8	18	63	71	40
Enderby Town	42	16	6	20	48	51	38
Banbury United	42	15	8	19	58	67	38
Merthyr Tydfil	42	11	15	16	59	67	37
Bromsgrove Rovers	42	13	11	18	49	65	37
Milton Keynes City	42	15	6	21	51	63	36
Bury Town	42	12	11	19	52	72	35
Gloucester City	42	13	9	20	49	78	35
Kidderminster Harriers	42	13	8	21	54	70	34
Bedworth United	42	8	18	16	41	66	34
Corby Town	42	11	10	21	50	65	32
Wellingborough Town	42	9	11	22	42	68	29
Stevenage Athletic	42	6	6	30	46	105	18

First Division (South)

Minehead	38	27	8	3	102	35	62
Dartford	38	26	4	8	84	46	56
Romford	38	21	9	8	66	37	51
Salisbury	38	17	11	10	73	53	45
Hastings United	38	15	15	8	67	51	45
Poole United	38	20	2	16	57	57	42
Bexley United	38	14	13	11	62	53	41
Waterlooville	38	13	13	12	62	54	39
Basingstoke Town	38	13	12	13	69	71	38
Ashford Town	38	14	8	16	67	73	36
Canterbury City	38	11	13	14	53	60	35
Folkestone & Shepway	38	10	14	14	36	51	34
Metropolitan Police	38	9	14	15	46	58	32
Trowbridge Town	38	11	10	17	48	75	32
Guildford & Dorking United	38	9	13	16	43	50	31
Bognor Regis Town	38	6	17	15	44	72	29
Ramsgate	38	9	10	19	57	76	28
Crawley Town	38	9	10	19	46	66	28
Andover	38	9	10	19	42	62	28
Dorchester Town	38	11	6	21	45	69	28

1976-77

Premier Division

Wimbledon	42	28	7	7	64	22	63
Minehead	42	23	12	7	73	39	58
Kettering Town	42	20	16	6	66	46	56
Bath City	42	20	15	7	51	30	55
Nuneaton Borough	42	20	11	11	52	35	51
Bedford Town	42	17	14	11	54	47	48
Yeovil Town	42	15	16	11	54	42	46
Dover	42	13	16	13	46	43	42
Grantham	42	14	12	16	55	50	40
Maidstone United	42	13	14	15	46	50	40
Gravesend & Northfleet	42	13	13	16	38	43	39
AP Leamington	42	12	15	15	44	53	39
Redditch United	42	12	14	16	45	54	38
Wealdstone	42	13	12	17	54	66	38
Hillingdon Borough	42	14	10	18	45	59	38
Atherstone Town	42	14	9	19	41	49	37
Weymouth	42	16	5	21	53	73	37
Dartford	42	13	10	19	52	57	36
Telford United	42	11	12	19	36	50	34
Chelmsford City	42	9	13	20	56	68	31
Burton Albion	42	10	10	22	41	52	30
Margate	42	9	10	23	47	85	28

First Division (North)

Worcester City	38	32	5	1	97	22	69
Cheltenham Town	38	23	8	7	85	35	54
Witney Town	38	21	8	9	48	31	50
Bromsgrove Rovers	38	20	8	10	61	37	48
Barry Town	38	19	8	11	62	45	46
Cambridge City	38	17	10	11	68	43	44
Stourbridge	38	17	9	12	48	35	43
Kidderminster Harriers	38	17	6	15	74	65	40
Banbury United	38	15	10	13	51	47	40
Gloucester City	38	18	4	16	70	81	40
Enderby Town	38	15	9	14	50	44	39
King's Lynn	38	13	11	14	47	53	37
Corby Town	38	11	13	14	56	64	35
Tamworth	38	11	13	14	49	58	35
Merthyr Tydfil	38	12	6	20	60	69	30
Oswestry Town	38	8	10	20	30	60	26
Wellingborough Town	38	8	7	23	37	73	23
Dunstable	38	7	7	24	38	84	21
Bedworth United	38	5	10	23	28	68	20
Milton Keynes City	38	7	6	25	31	76	20

First Division (South)

Barnet	34	23	8	3	65	25	54
Hastings United	34	18	11	5	47	18	47
Waterlooville	34	19	6	9	50	25	44
Dorchester Town	34	16	11	7	48	30	43
Salisbury	34	15	11	8	57	39	41
Romford	34	18	5	11	47	32	41
Poole Town	34	17	7	10	40	35	41
Trowbridge Town	34	15	8	11	47	39	38
Crawley Town	34	14	9	11	53	42	37
Folkestone & Shepway	34	12	11	11	39	42	35
Basingstoke Town	34	12	10	12	51	43	34
Canterbury City	34	6	16	12	36	46	28
Bognor Regis Town	34	9	9	16	33	50	27
Tonbridge AFC	34	9	9	16	33	50	27
Metropolitan Police	34	5	12	17	37	61	22
Andover	34	4	11	19	17	49	19
Ashford Town	34	5	8	21	32	65	18
Aylesbury United	34	5	6	23	27	68	16

1977-78

Premier Division

Bath City	42	22	18	2	83	32	62
Weymouth	42	21	16	5	64	36	58
Maidstone United	42	20	11	11	59	41	51
Worcester City	42	20	11	11	67	50	51
Gravesend & Northfleet	42	19	11	12	57	42	49
Kettering Town	42	18	11	13	58	48	47
Barnet	42	18	11	13	63	58	47
Wealdstone	42	16	14	12	54	48	46
Telford United	42	17	11	14	52	45	45
Nuneaton Borough	42	15	14	13	38	36	44
Dartford	42	14	15	13	57	65	43
Yeovil Town	42	14	14	14	57	49	42
Hastings United	42	15	9	18	49	60	39
Cheltenham Town	42	12	14	16	43	52	38
Hillingdon Borough	42	13	9	20	45	54	35
Atherstone Town	42	10	15	17	41	56	35
Redditch United	42	15	5	22	40	55	35
AP Leamington	42	11	13	18	34	57	35
Minehead	42	11	12	19	43	48	34
Dover	42	9	13	20	41	63	31
Bedford Town	42	8	13	21	51	75	29
Grantham	42	11	6	25	40	66	28

First Division (North)

Witney Town	38	20	15	3	54	27	55
Bridgend Town	38	20	9	9	59	45	49
Burton Albion	38	17	11	10	48	32	45
Enderby Town	38	17	10	11	54	44	44
Bromsgrove Rovers	38	16	12	10	56	41	44
Banbury United	38	17	10	11	52	47	44
Kidderminster Harriers	38	16	11	11	58	41	43
Merthyr Tydfil	38	18	6	14	85	62	42
Cambridge City	38	14	12	12	56	45	40
Barry Town	38	14	11	13	58	48	39
Wellingborough Town	38	11	15	12	47	43	37
King's Lynn	38	12	13	13	55	55	37
Gloucester City	38	14	8	16	60	75	36
Corby Town	38	9	17	12	46	48	35
Dunstable Town	38	11	13	14	49	59	35
Stourbridge	38	9	15	14	52	53	33
Tamworth	38	10	11	17	37	48	31
Bedworth United	38	8	14	16	36	58	30
Milton Keynes City	38	5	11	22	26	74	21
Oswestry Town	38	6	8	24	29	85	20

First Division (South)

Margate	38	24	10	4	92	32	58
Dorchester Town	38	23	10	5	67	31	56
Salisbury	38	21	10	7	60	27	52
Waterlooville	38	19	13	6	66	36	51
Romford	38	17	15	6	58	37	49
Aylesbury United	38	20	7	11	56	42	47
Trowbridge Town	38	16	11	11	65	59	43
Chelmsford City	38	15	11	12	58	46	41
Folkestone & Shepway	38	16	9	13	64	56	41
Taunton Town	38	15	10	13	57	54	40
Addlestone	38	14	10	14	57	60	38
Crawley Town	38	14	9	15	61	60	37
Basingstoke Town	38	11	11	16	44	50	33
Tonbridge AFC	38	13	5	20	64	77	31
Ashford Town	38	9	13	16	39	60	31
Hounslow	38	10	10	18	43	62	30
Bognor Regis Town	38	9	8	21	52	69	26
Poole Town	38	8	10	20	43	68	26
Andover	38	4	12	22	30	60	20
Canterbury City	38	2	6	30	31	113	10

1978-79

Premier Division

Worcester City	42	27	11	4	92	33	65
Kettering Town	42	27	7	8	109	43	61
Telford United	42	22	10	10	60	39	54
Maidstone United	42	18	18	6	55	35	54
Bath City	42	17	19	6	59	41	53
Weymouth	42	18	15	9	71	51	51
AP Leamington	42	19	11	12	65	53	49
Redditch United	42	19	10	13	70	57	48
Yeovil Town	42	15	16	11	59	49	46
Witney Town	42	17	10	15	53	52	44
Nuneaton Borough	42	13	17	12	59	50	43
Gravesend & Northfleet	42	15	12	15	56	55	42
Barnet	42	16	10	16	52	64	42
Hillingdon Borough	42	12	16	14	50	41	40
Wealdstone	42	12	12	18	51	59	36
Atherstone Town	42	9	17	16	46	65	35
Dartford	42	10	14	18	40	56	34
Cheltenham Town	42	11	10	21	38	72	32
Margate	42	10	9	23	44	75	29
Dorchester Town	42	7	11	24	46	86	25
Hastings United	42	5	13	24	37	85	23
Bridgend Town	42	6	6	30	39	90	18

First Division (North)

Grantham	38	21	10	7	70	45	52
Merthyr Tydfil	38	22	7	9	90	53	51
Alvechurch	38	20	10	8	70	42	50
Bedford Town	38	19	9	10	74	49	47
King's Lynn	38	17	11	10	57	46	45
Oswestry Town	38	18	8	12	63	43	44
Gloucester City	38	18	8	12	76	59	44
Burton Albion	38	16	10	12	51	40	42
Kidderminster Harriers	38	13	14	11	70	60	40
Bedworth United	38	13	14	11	41	34	40
Tamworth	38	15	8	15	47	45	38
Stourbridge	38	15	7	16	64	61	37
Barry Town	38	14	9	15	51	53	37
Enderby Town	38	14	8	16	46	55	36
Banbury United	38	10	13	15	42	58	33
Wellingborough Town	38	13	6	19	50	71	32
Cambridge City	38	9	20	9	37	62	27
Bromsgrove Rovers	38	6	14	18	33	61	26
Milton Keynes City	38	7	9	22	37	87	23
Corby Town	38	5	6	27	40	85	16

First Division (South)

Dover	40	28	9	3	88	20	65
Folkestone & Shepway	40	22	6	12	84	50	50
Gosport Borough	40	19	11	10	62	47	49
Chelmsford City	40	20	7	13	65	61	47
Minehead	40	16	13	11	58	39	45
Poole Town	40	15	15	10	48	44	45
Hounslow	40	16	12	12	56	45	44
Waterlooville	40	17	10	13	52	43	44
Trowbridge Town	40	15	12	13	65	61	42
Aylesbury United	40	16	9	15	54	52	41
Taunton Town	40	16	9	15	53	51	41
Bognor Regis Town	40	17	7	16	58	58	41
Dunstable	40	18	4	18	57	55	40
Tonbridge AFC	40	15	10	15	43	47	40
Salisbury	40	13	10	17	47	51	36
Basingstoke Town	40	12	11	17	49	62	35
Addlestone	40	12	9	19	56	64	33
Andover	40	12	6	22	47	69	30
Ashford Town	40	10	10	20	28	53	30
Crawley Town	40	9	9	22	44	75	27
Canterbury City	40	6	3	31	31	98	15

1979-80

Midland Division

Bridgend Town	42	28	6	8	85	39	62
Minehead	42	22	15	5	70	42	59
Bedford Town	42	20	12	10	71	42	52
Kidderminster Harriers	42	23	6	13	81	59	52
Merthyr Tydfil	42	20	11	11	70	47	51
Enderby Town	42	21	8	13	62	50	50
Stourbridge	42	19	11	12	67	49	49
Alvechurch	42	17	14	11	78	60	48
Trowbridge Town	42	19	9	14	62	61	47
Bromsgrove Rovers	42	18	10	14	67	56	46
Barry Town	42	15	12	15	64	58	42
King's Lynn	42	15	11	16	48	55	41
Banbury United	42	13	14	15	56	56	40
Taunton Town	42	16	8	18	55	62	40
Witney Town	42	10	19	13	43	45	39
Bedworth United	42	12	15	15	40	42	39
Milton Keynes City	42	15	7	20	46	59	37
Gloucester City	42	10	14	18	55	68	32
Cheltenham Town	42	13	5	24	49	70	31
Wellingborough Town	42	9	7	26	54	106	25
Cambridge City	42	6	9	27	30	73	21
Corby Town	42	5	9	28	40	94	19

Gloucester City had points deducted

Southern Division

Dorchester Town	46	25	12	9	81	53	62
Aylesbury United	46	25	11	10	73	40	61
Dover	46	22	13	11	78	47	57
Gosport Borough	46	21	15	10	70	50	57
Dartford	46	21	14	11	66	45	56
Bognor Regis Town	46	20	15	11	66	38	55
Hillingdon Borough	46	19	16	11	64	41	54
Dunstable	46	17	19	10	93	64	53
Addlestone	46	20	13	13	72	57	53
Hastings United	46	19	15	12	74	65	53
Fareham Town	46	16	16	14	61	53	48
Waterlooville	46	17	12	17	67	64	46
Andover	46	16	13	17	65	65	45
Poole Town	46	16	13	17	49	64	45
Canterbury City	46	15	15	15	57	56	60	44
Hounslow	46	14	14	17	44	57	43
Margate	46	17	8	21	51	62	42
Folkestone & Shepway	46	14	11	21	54	63	39
Ashford Town	46	12	14	20	54	71	38
Crawley Town	46	13	11	22	55	72	37
Chelmsford City	46	9	18	19	47	69	36
Basingstoke Town	46	9	15	22	48	79	33
Salisbury	46	10	12	24	47	59	32
Tonbridge AFC	46	3	9	34	30	128	15

1980-81

Midland Division

Alvechurch	42	26	9	7	76	40	61
Bedford Town	42	25	11	6	63	32	61
Trowbridge Town	42	24	9	9	69	39	57
Kidderminster Harriers	42	23	9	10	67	41	55
Barry Town	42	21	9	12	60	40	51
Stourbridge	42	17	16	9	75	49	50
Enderby Town	42	21	8	13	71	47	50
Cheltenham Town	42	18	12	12	70	59	48
Bromsgrove Rovers	42	19	9	14	65	50	47
Corby Town	42	19	7	16	69	58	45
Bridgend Town	42	19	7	16	74	64	45
Minehead	42	19	7	16	54	60	45
Gloucester City	42	19	6	17	82	72	44
Merthyr Tydfil	42	15	12	15	60	50	42
Bedworth United	42	14	12	16	49	46	40
Banbury United	42	11	11	20	51	65	33
Taunton Town	42	10	9	23	48	68	29
Cambridge City	42	8	12	22	46	87	28
Witney Town	42	9	9	24	44	65	27
Wellingborough Town	42	10	7	25	43	91	27
Redditch United	42	11	4	27	54	92	26
Milton Keynes City	42	3	7	32	28	103	13

Southern Division

Dartford	46	26	14	6	76	39	66
Bognor Regis Town	46	25	13	8	95	43	63
Hastings United	46	24	14	8	87	43	62
Gosport Borough	46	24	12	10	84	52	60
Waterlooville	46	19	21	6	67	50	59
Dorchester Town	46	21	13	12	84	56	55
Dover	46	22	10	14	70	50	54
Poole Town	46	19	14	13	70	56	52
Addlestone & Weybridge	46	21	9	16	66	57	51
Dunstable	46	19	13	14	73	68	51
Aylesbury United	46	20	10	16	66	60	50
Hounslow	46	17	13	16	65	55	47
Hillingdon Borough	46	16	15	15	50	49	47
Basingstoke Town	46	16	14	16	69	58	46
Crawley Town	46	18	4	24	64	78	40
Ashford Town	46	12	15	19	55	76	39
Tonbridge AFC	46	12	15	19	44	68	39
Chelmsford City	46	13	12	21	54	78	38
Canterbury City	46	12	13	21	40	59	37
Salisbury	46	14	8	24	57	76	36
Folkestone	46	11	11	24	47	65	33
Margate	46	11	7	28	65	117	29
Fareham Town	46	5	18	23	31	73	28
Andover	46	6	10	30	41	94	22

1982-83

Premier Division

AP Leamington	38	25	4	9	78	50	79
Kidderminster Harriers	38	23	7	8	69	40	76
Welling United	38	21	6	11	63	40	69
Chelmsford City	38	16	11	11	57	40	59
Bedworth United	38	16	11	11	47	39	59
Dartford	38	16	8	14	48	38	56
Gosport Borough	38	14	13	11	47	43	55
Fareham Town	38	16	7	15	73	82	55
Dorchester Town	38	14	12	12	52	50	54
Gravesend & Northfleet	38	14	12	12	49	50	54
Gloucester City	38	13	12	13	61	57	51
Witney Town	38	12	13	13	60	48	47
Alvechurch	38	13	8	17	60	66	47
Stourbridge	38	12	11	15	48	54	47
Corby Town	38	12	11	15	58	67	47
Hastings United	38	11	11	16	48	61	44
Enderby Town	38	11	9	18	44	62	42
Waterlooville	38	10	9	19	62	83	39
Poole Town	38	9	9	20	57	73	36
Addlestone & Weybridge	38	5	10	23	24	62	25

Witney Town had 2 points deducted for fielding an ineligible player

1981-82

Midland Division

Nuneaton Borough	42	27	11	4	88	32	65
Alvechurch	42	26	10	6	79	34	62
Kidderminster Harriers	42	22	12	8	71	40	56
Stourbridge	42	21	10	11	69	47	52
Gloucester City	42	21	9	12	64	48	51
Bedworth United	42	20	10	12	59	40	50
Enderby Town	42	20	10	12	79	66	50
Witney Town	42	19	8	15	71	49	46
Barry Town	42	16	14	12	59	46	46
Corby Town	42	19	8	15	70	59	46
Merthyr Tydfil	42	16	12	14	63	54	44
Wellingborough Town	42	15	12	15	50	45	42
Bridgend Town	42	13	13	16	50	62	39
Bromsgrove Rovers	42	15	8	19	57	63	38
Bedford Town	42	12	13	17	45	54	37
Cheltenham Town	42	11	14	17	65	68	36
Taunton Town	42	12	8	22	46	76	32
Banbury United	42	11	8	23	63	91	30
Minehead	42	12	6	24	38	69	30
Cambridge City	42	10	8	24	38	80	28
Milton Keynes City	42	6	11	25	34	70	23
Redditch United	42	8	5	29	37	103	21

Midland Division

Cheltenham Town	32	22	5	5	65	29	71
Sutton Coldfield Town	32	21	7	4	62	24	70
Forest Green Rovers	32	21	3	8	68	32	66
Merthyr Tydfil	32	17	7	8	64	45	58
Willenhall Town	32	17	6	9	74	49	57
Oldbury United	32	16	6	10	52	49	54
Banbury United	32	15	3	14	59	55	48
Bridgend Town	32	12	11	9	46	37	47
Wellingborough Town	32	13	7	12	49	37	46
Bromsgrove Rovers	32	13	5	14	47	47	44
Dudley Town	32	12	7	13	40	45	43
Bridgwater Town	32	12	6	14	42	43	42
Aylesbury United	32	12	5	15	37	51	41
Redditch United	32	8	6	18	51	73	30
Taunton Town	32	5	7	20	30	64	22
Minehead	32	5	7	20	24	62	22
Milton Keynes City	32	0	4	28	22	90	4

Southern Division

Wealdstone	46	32	8	6	100	32	72
Hastings United	46	31	9	6	79	34	71
Dorchester Town	46	21	18	7	76	41	60
Gosport Borough	46	26	8	12	76	45	60
Fareham Town	46	20	14	12	58	48	54
Poole Town	46	19	15	12	92	63	53
Waterlooville	46	22	9	15	75	53	53
Welling United	46	19	13	14	70	48	51
Addlestone & Weybridge	46	17	17	12	71	53	51
Chelmsford City	46	20	11	15	64	53	51
Aylesbury United	46	19	12	15	79	61	50
Basingstoke Town	46	18	12	16	75	61	48
Dover	46	19	8	19	61	63	46
Ashford Town	46	16	14	16	52	56	46
Tonbridge AFC	46	19	7	20	62	70	45
Dunstable	46	18	8	20	63	68	44
Salisbury	46	16	10	20	64	81	42
Hounslow	46	15	11	20	59	83	41
Hillingdon Borough	46	14	10	22	46	58	38
Canterbury City	46	10	16	20	49	78	36
Crawley Town	46	9	12	25	46	81	30
Folkestone	46	10	6	30	49	101	26
Andover	46	4	11	31	39	100	19
Thanet United	46	5	7	34	37	110	17

Southern Division

Fisher Athletic	34	23	5	6	79	34	74
Folkestone	34	22	6	6	79	41	72
RS Southampton	34	21	7	6	66	30	70
Dunstable	34	19	5	10	57	39	62
Hillingdon Borough	34	14	11	9	41	30	53
Salisbury	34	14	10	10	59	49	52
Crawley Town	34	14	9	11	51	43	51
Ashford Town	34	13	10	11	51	41	49
Tonbridge AFC	34	14	5	15	57	57	47
Hounslow	34	11	12	11	46	47	45
Canterbury City	34	12	9	13	52	63	45
Cambridge City	34	12	5	17	56	63	41
Dover	34	11	7	16	35	52	40
Thanet United	34	10	5	19	30	61	35
Basingstoke Town	34	8	10	16	37	56	34
Woodford Town	34	6	9	19	29	57	27
Andover	34	6	8	20	28	53	26
Erith & Belvedere	34	5	9	20	26	62	24

1983-84

Premier Division

Dartford	38	23	9	6	67	32	78
Fisher Athletic	38	22	9	7	80	42	75
Chelmsford City	38	19	9	10	67	45	66
Gravesend & Northfleet	38	18	9	11	50	38	63
Witney Town	38	18	6	14	75	50	60
King's Lynn	38	18	6	14	42	45	60
Folkestone	38	16	9	13	60	56	57
Cheltenham Town	38	16	7	15	63	56	55
Gloucester City	38	13	15	10	55	50	54
Hastings United	38	15	9	14	55	57	54
Bedworth United	38	15	9	14	51	55	54
Welling United	38	15	7	16	61	61	52
AP Leamington	38	14	9	15	73	83	51
Corby Town	38	12	14	12	55	54	50
Fareham Town	38	13	11	14	65	70	50
Alvechurch	38	12	12	14	56	62	48
Sutton Coldfield Town	38	10	14	14	49	53	44
Gosport Borough	38	6	15	17	31	64	33
Dorchester Town	38	4	8	26	40	69	20
Stourbridge	38	4	7	27	30	82	19

Midland Division

Willenhall Town	38	27	4	7	100	44	85
Shepshed Charterhouse	38	25	5	8	88	37	80
Bromsgrove Rovers	38	20	8	10	73	43	68
Dudley Town	38	18	13	7	71	43	67
Aylesbury United	38	17	15	6	62	35	66
Moor Green	38	18	12	8	63	44	66
Rushden Town	38	17	12	9	68	42	63
Merthyr Tydfil	38	18	8	12	63	44	62
Redditch United	38	17	9	12	67	67	60
VS Rugby	38	15	12	11	68	51	57
Forest Green Rovers	38	15	12	11	67	51	57
Bridgnorth Town	38	16	9	13	64	52	57
Leicester United	38	12	9	17	58	58	45
Oldbury United	38	10	13	15	53	51	43
Coventry Sporting	38	11	7	20	40	67	40
Bridgwater Town	38	10	8	20	39	65	38
Wellingborough Town	38	7	9	22	43	80	30
Banbury United	38	6	11	21	37	78	29
Milton Keynes City	38	3	9	26	31	110	18
Tamworth	38	2	7	29	25	118	13

Southern Division

RS Southampton	38	26	6	6	83	35	84
Crawley Town	38	22	9	7	68	28	75
Basingstoke Town	38	20	9	9	54	36	69
Tonbridge AFC	38	20	9	9	61	44	69
Addlestone & Weybridge	38	19	11	8	58	34	68
Poole Town	38	20	7	11	68	42	67
Hillingdon Borough	38	18	11	9	43	20	65
Ashford Town	38	19	5	14	65	47	62
Salisbury	38	17	8	13	61	48	59
Cambridge City	38	13	9	16	43	53	48
Canterbury City	38	12	9	17	44	52	45
Waterlooville	38	12	9	17	56	69	45
Dover Athletic	38	12	9	17	51	74	45
Chatham Town	38	11	10	17	46	56	43
Andover	38	12	6	20	35	54	42
Erith & Belvedere	38	11	9	18	43	68	42
Dunstable	38	10	8	20	38	65	38
Thanet United	38	9	8	21	40	65	35
Woodford Town	38	7	8	23	30	69	29
Hounslow	38	4	12	22	30	58	24

1984-85

Premier Division

Cheltenham Town	38	24	5	9	83	41	77
King's Lynn	38	23	6	9	73	48	75
Crawley Town	38	22	8	8	76	52	74
Willenhall Town	38	20	8	10	57	38	68
RS Southampton	38	21	4	13	76	52	67
Welling United	38	18	11	9	55	38	65
Folkestone	38	19	6	13	70	54	63
Fisher Athletic	38	19	5	14	67	57	62
Chelmsford City	38	17	10	11	52	50	61
Shepshed Charterhouse	38	18	5	15	67	50	59
Corby Town	38	15	6	17	56	54	51
Bedworth United	38	14	8	16	48	52	50
Gravesend & Northfleet	38	12	12	14	46	46	48
Fareham Town	38	13	8	17	52	55	47
Alvechurch	38	11	7	20	53	59	40
Hastings United	38	11	7	20	46	71	40
Witney Town	38	9	12	17	51	58	39
Gloucester City	38	10	6	22	49	74	36
Trowbridge	38	10	5	23	45	83	35
AP Leamington	38	2	5	31	22	112	11

Midland Division

Dudley Town	34	21	8	5	70	36	71
Aylesbury United	34	20	7	7	62	30	67
Hednesford Town	34	18	7	9	58	42	61
Moor Green	34	17	9	8	63	43	60
VS Rugby	34	17	9	8	59	41	60
Bromsgrove Rovers	34	16	10	8	53	42	58
Stourbridge	34	15	11	8	52	45	56
Redditch United	34	12	11	11	68	57	47
Sutton Coldfield Town	34	13	6	15	50	56	45
Bridgnorth Town	34	13	5	16	67	65	44
Coventry Sporting	34	11	9	14	45	52	42
Merthyr Tydfil	34	10	11	13	43	46	41
Rushden Town	34	10	7	17	42	52	37
Forest Green Rovers	34	9	10	15	49	65	37
Wellingborough Town	34	10	7	17	39	63	37
Oldbury United	34	10	6	18	52	66	36
Banbury United	34	9	5	20	33	59	32
Leicester United	34	3	6	25	17	62	15

Southern Division

Basingstoke Town	38	24	9	5	61	22	81
Gosport Borough	38	22	6	10	78	41	72
Poole Town	38	20	12	6	69	38	72
Hillingdon	38	19	10	9	51	23	67
Thanet United	38	19	9	10	63	47	66
Salisbury	38	19	5	14	55	54	62
Sheppey United	38	18	6	14	49	45	60
Addlestone & Weybridge	38	16	9	13	68	54	57
Waterlooville	38	15	10	13	71	63	55
Canterbury City	38	15	7	16	61	64	52
Woodford Town	38	13	13	12	46	53	52
Tonbridge AFC	38	16	3	19	59	62	51
Andover	38	15	5	18	42	54	50
Dorchester Town	38	13	7	18	45	60	46
Cambridge City	38	11	11	16	59	71	44
Chatham Town	38	12	8	18	44	66	44
Ashford Town	38	10	9	19	54	69	69
Dunstable	38	8	10	20	35	56	64
Dover Athletic	38	7	7	24	39	78	28
Erith & Belvedere	38	6	8	24	36	65	26

1985-86

Premier Division

Welling United	38	29	6	3	95	31	93
Chelmsford City	38	20	10	8	68	41	70
Fisher Athletic	38	20	7	11	67	45	67
Alvechurch	38	19	9	10	71	56	66
Worcester City	38	19	9	10	64	50	66
Crawley Town	38	18	5	15	76	59	59
Shepshed Charterhouse	38	19	1	18	51	52	58
Aylesbury United	38	14	10	14	52	49	52
Folkestone	38	14	10	14	56	56	52
Bedworth United	38	14	8	16	44	49	50
Willenhall Town	38	12	13	13	51	44	49
Dudley Town	38	15	4	19	58	62	49
Corby Town	38	14	7	17	61	67	49
King's Lynn	38	12	10	16	39	42	46
Basingstoke Town	38	13	4	21	36	67	43
RS Southampton	38	11	9	18	44	61	42
Witney Town	38	11	6	21	44	74	39
Gosport Borough	38	10	8	20	42	66	38
Fareham Town	38	8	13	17	40	62	37
Gravesend & Northfleet	38	9	9	20	29	55	36

Midland Division

Bromsgrove Rovers	40	29	5	6	95	44	92
Redditch United	40	23	6	11	70	42	75
Merthyr Tydfil	40	21	10	9	60	40	73
VS Rugby	40	17	14	9	41	31	65
Stourbridge	40	15	14	11	62	49	59
Rusden Town	40	17	7	16	69	74	58
Bilston Town	40	15	12	13	60	48	57
Bridgnorth Town	40	13	18	9	56	45	57
Gloucester City	40	15	12	13	61	57	57
Grantham	40	16	7	17	46	59	55
Wellingborough Town	40	15	9	16	56	56	54
Sutton Coldfield Town	40	13	14	13	60	45	53
Hednesford Town	40	14	9	17	67	70	51
Forest Green Rovers	40	14	9	17	52	56	51
Mile Oak Rovers	40	14	8	18	56	73	50
Leicester United	40	13	10	17	41	48	49
Banbury United	40	13	8	19	38	55	47
Coventry Sporting	40	10	15	15	42	48	45
Moor Green	40	12	6	22	63	91	42
Leamington	40	10	6	24	40	77	36
Oldbury United	40	8	7	25	50	87	31

Southern Division

Cambridge City	40	23	11	6	87	41	80
Salisbury	40	24	8	8	84	51	80
Hastings Town	40	23	9	8	83	51	78
Dover Athletic	40	23	6	11	89	53	75
Corinthian	40	20	9	11	79	45	69
Tonbridge AFC	40	17	13	10	65	51	64
Dunstable	40	17	11	12	70	61	62
Ruislip	40	17	6	17	67	66	57
Erith & Belvedere	40	14	12	14	35	40	54
Waterlooville	40	16	6	18	52	58	54
Burnham & Hillingdon	40	16	6	18	44	59	54
Canterbury City	40	13	13	14	58	58	52
Trowbridge Town	40	13	13	14	57	63	52
Sheppey United	40	14	10	16	43	53	52
Thanet United	40	13	7	20	58	63	46
Woodford Town	40	12	10	18	49	62	46
Poole Town	40	12	7	21	55	63	43
Ashford Town	40	10	12	18	45	65	42
Chatham Town	40	8	15	17	53	70	39
Andover	40	10	8	22	52	92	38
Dorchester Town	40	5	8	27	35	94	23

1986-87

Premier Division

Fisher Athletic	42	25	11	6	72	29	86
Bromsgrove Rovers	42	24	11	7	82	41	83
Aylesbury United	42	24	11	7	72	40	83
Dartford	42	19	12	11	76	43	69
Chelmsford City	42	17	13	12	48	45	64
Cambridge City	42	14	20	8	68	52	62
Redditch United	42	16	14	12	59	54	62
Alvechurch	42	18	8	16	66	62	62
Corby Town	42	14	17	11	65	51	59
Worcester City	42	16	11	15	62	55	59
Shepshed Charterhouse	42	16	10	16	59	59	58
Bedworth United	42	15	12	15	55	51	57
Crawley Town	42	14	11	17	59	60	53
Fareham Town	42	11	17	14	58	49	50
Willenhall Town	42	13	11	18	48	57	50
Basingstoke Town	42	12	12	18	53	78	48
Witney Town	42	12	12	18	29	56	48
Gosport Borough	42	11	13	18	42	57	46
Salisbury	42	12	7	23	52	82	43
King's Lynn	42	9	13	20	48	72	40
Dudley Town	42	9	9	24	39	76	36
Folkestone	42	8	11	23	36	79	35

Midland Division

VS Rugby	38	25	5	8	81	43	80
Leicester United	38	26	1	11	89	49	79
Merthyr Tydfil	38	23	6	9	95	54	75
Moor Green	38	22	6	10	73	55	72
Halesowen Town	38	19	12	7	72	50	69
Hednesford Town	38	21	5	12	84	56	68
Gloucester City	38	19	5	14	77	59	62
Coventry Sporting	38	17	8	13	55	54	59
Forest Green Rovers	38	16	9	13	65	53	57
Stourbridge	38	16	7	15	56	56	55
Grantham	38	15	9	14	74	54	54
Banbury United	38	14	7	17	55	65	49
Buckingham Town	38	13	9	16	55	59	48
Bridgnorth Town	38	12	9	17	59	63	45
Wellingborough Town	38	13	6	19	55	76	45
Mile Oak Rovers	38	11	10	17	50	63	43
Sutton Coldfield Town	38	8	10	20	56	78	34
Bilston Town	38	8	7	23	37	76	31
Leamington	38	4	13	21	37	80	25
Rushden Town	38	1	10	27	42	124	13

Southern Division

Dorchester Town	38	23	8	7	83	42	77
Ashford Town	38	23	7	8	63	32	76
Woodford Town	38	22	6	10	72	44	72
Hastings Town	38	20	10	8	74	54	70
Dover Athletic	38	20	6	12	66	43	66
Gravesend & Northfleet	38	18	7	13	67	46	61
Tonbridge AFC	38	16	10	12	73	67	58
Erith & Belvedere	38	15	12	11	57	50	57
Chatham Town	38	16	9	13	53	46	57
Thanet United	38	14	14	10	56	50	56
Waterlooville	38	16	8	14	66	65	56
Trowbridge Town	38	15	9	14	77	65	54
Dunstable	38	13	9	16	60	57	48
Corinthian	38	11	12	15	56	65	45
Sheppey United	38	9	12	17	43	65	39
Andover	38	9	9	20	51	80	36
Burnham & Hillingdon	38	7	11	20	32	62	32
Poole Town	38	8	6	24	50	90	30
Ruislip	38	6	12	20	35	75	30
Canterbury City	38	8	5	25	46	82	29

1987-88

Premier Division

Team	P	W	D	L	F	A	Pts
Aylesbury United	42	27	8	7	79	35	89
Dartford	42	27	8	7	79	39	89
Cambridge City	42	24	8	10	84	43	80
Bromsgrove Rovers	42	22	11	9	65	39	77
Worcester City	42	22	6	14	58	48	72
Crawley Town	42	17	14	11	73	63	65
Alvechurch	42	17	13	12	54	52	64
Leicester United	42	15	14	13	68	59	59
Fareham Town	42	16	11	15	51	59	59
Corby Town	42	16	8	18	61	64	56
Dorchester Town	42	14	14	14	51	57	56
Ashford Town	42	12	16	14	45	54	52
Shepshed Charterhouse	42	13	11	18	53	62	50
Bedworth United	42	12	14	16	49	64	50
Gosport Borough	42	10	17	15	39	49	47
Burton Albion	42	11	14	17	62	74	47
VS Rugby	42	10	16	16	52	57	46
Redditch United	42	10	13	19	55	63	43
Chelmsford City	42	11	10	21	60	75	43
Willenhall Town	42	9	12	21	39	76	39
Nuneaton Borough	42	8	13	21	58	77	37
Witney Town	42	8	11	23	45	71	35

Midland Division

Team	P	W	D	L	F	A	Pts
Merthyr Tydfil	42	30	4	8	102	40	94
Moor Green	42	26	8	8	91	49	86
Grantham Town	42	27	4	11	97	53	85
Atherstone United	42	22	10	10	93	56	76
Sutton Coldfield Town	42	22	6	14	71	47	72
Halesowen Town	42	18	15	9	75	59	69
Gloucester City	42	18	14	10	86	62	68
Dudley Town	42	20	5	17	64	55	65
Forest Green Rovers	42	14	16	12	67	54	58
Banbury United	42	17	7	18	48	46	58
Bridgnorth Town	42	16	7	19	59	75	55
Buckingham Town	42	15	9	18	74	75	54
King's Lynn	42	16	6	20	53	63	54
Wellingborough Town	42	14	10	18	67	70	52
Rushden Town	42	14	9	19	69	85	51
Trowbridge Town	42	14	3	25	53	82	45
Bilston Town	42	12	8	22	52	87	44
Hednesford Town	42	11	10	21	50	81	43
Mile Oak Rovers	42	9	14	19	43	65	41
Coventry Sporting	42	11	8	23	46	83	41
Stourbridge	42	10	10	22	46	79	40
Paget Rangers	42	10	9	23	49	89	39

Southern Division

Team	P	W	D	L	F	A	Pts
Dover Athletic	40	28	10	2	81	28	94
Waterlooville	40	27	10	3	88	33	91
Salisbury	40	24	11	5	71	33	83
Gravesend & Northfleet	40	20	12	8	60	32	72
Thanet United	40	17	13	10	60	38	64
Andover	40	17	13	10	64	58	64
Dunstable	40	17	12	11	78	56	63
Burnham	40	17	10	13	61	45	61
Bury Town	40	17	7	16	80	67	58
Erith & Belvedere	40	16	9	15	52	56	57
Sheppey United	40	14	10	16	58	52	52
Hastings Town	40	14	10	16	62	70	52
Tonbridge AFC	40	14	8	18	51	56	50
Poole Town	40	13	10	17	69	70	49
Baldock Town	40	12	12	16	44	53	48
Hounslow	40	11	8	21	41	76	41
Folkestone	40	9	11	20	47	76	38
Corinthian	40	9	10	21	49	67	37
Ruislip	40	5	13	22	33	80	28
Canterbury City	40	7	6	27	33	87	27
Chatham Town	40	7	5	28	39	88	26

1988-89

Premier Division

Team	P	W	D	L	F	A	Pts
Merthyr Tydfil	42	26	7	9	104	58	85
Dartford	42	25	7	10	79	33	82
VS Rugby	42	24	7	11	64	43	79
Worcester City	42	20	13	9	72	49	73
Cambridge City	42	20	10	12	72	51	70
Dover Athletic	42	19	12	11	65	47	69
Gosport Borough	42	18	12	12	73	57	66
Burton Albion	42	18	10	14	79	68	64
Bath City	42	15	13	14	66	51	59
Bromsgrove Rovers	42	14	16	12	68	56	59
Wealdstone	42	16	10	16	60	53	59
Crawley Town	42	14	16	12	61	56	59
Dorchester Town	42	14	16	12	56	61	59
Alvechurch	42	16	8	18	56	59	56
Moor Green	42	14	13	15	58	70	55
Corby Town	42	14	11	17	55	59	53
Waterlooville	42	13	13	16	61	63	52
Ashford Town	42	13	13	16	59	76	52
Fareham Town	42	15	6	21	43	68	51
Leicester United	42	6	11	25	46	84	29
Redditch United	42	5	7	30	36	105	22
Bedworth United	42	4	7	31	36	102	19

Midland Division

Team	P	W	D	L	F	A	Pts
Gloucester City	42	28	8	6	95	37	92
Atherstone United	42	26	9	7	85	38	87
Tamworth	42	26	9	7	85	45	87
Halesowen Town	42	25	10	7	85	42	85
Grantham Town	42	23	11	8	66	37	80
Nuneaton Borough	42	19	9	14	71	58	66
Rushden Town	42	19	8	15	71	50	65
Spalding United	42	17	13	12	72	64	64
Dudley Town	42	16	13	13	73	62	61
Sutton Coldfield Town	42	18	7	17	56	56	61
Willenhall Town	42	16	12	14	65	71	60
Forest Green Rovers	42	12	16	14	64	67	52
Bilston Town	42	15	7	20	63	71	52
Ashtree Highfield	42	12	15	15	57	62	51
Hednesford Town	42	12	15	15	49	57	51
Banbury United	42	10	14	18	53	74	44
Bridgnorth Town	42	12	7	23	59	77	43
Stourbridge	42	11	10	21	37	65	43
King's Lynn	42	7	13	22	31	67	34
Coventry Sporting	42	6	13	23	39	91	31
Wellingborough Town	42	5	15	22	39	72	30
Mile Oak Rovers	42	5	10	27	46	98	25

Southern Division

Team	P	W	D	L	F	A	Pts
Chelmsford City	42	30	5	7	106	38	95
Gravesend & Northfleet	42	27	6	9	70	40	87
Poole Town	42	24	11	7	98	48	83
Bury Town	42	25	7	10	75	34	82
Burnham	42	22	13	7	78	47	79
Baldock Town	42	23	5	14	69	40	74
Hastings Town	42	21	11	10	75	48	74
Hounslow	42	21	6	15	75	60	69
Salisbury	42	20	5	17	79	58	65
Trowbridge Town	42	19	7	16	59	52	64
Folkestone	42	17	8	17	62	65	59
Corinthian	42	13	13	16	59	69	52
Canterbury City	42	14	8	20	52	60	50
Witney Town	42	13	11	18	61	71	50
Dunstable	42	11	14	17	42	57	47
Buckingham Town	42	12	10	20	56	79	46
Erith & Belvedere	42	11	10	21	48	63	43
Andover	42	11	9	22	56	90	42
Sheppey United	42	10	8	24	50	90	38
Thanet United	42	7	15	20	47	95	36
Tonbridge AFC	42	7	6	29	50	98	27
Ruislip	42	6	8	28	47	112	26

1989-90

Premier Division

Team	P	W	D	L	F	A	Pts
Dover Athletic	42	32	6	4	87	27	102
Bath City	42	30	8	4	81	28	98
Dartford	42	26	9	7	80	35	87
Burton Albion	42	20	12	10	64	40	72
VS Rugby	42	19	12	11	51	35	69
Atherstone United	42	19	10	13	60	52	67
Gravesend & Northfleet	42	18	12	12	44	50	66
Cambridge City	42	17	11	14	76	56	62
Gloucester City	42	17	11	14	80	68	62
Bromsgrove Rovers	42	17	10	15	56	48	61
Moor Green	42	18	7	17	62	59	61
Wealdstone	42	16	9	17	55	54	57
Dorchester Town	42	16	7	19	52	67	55
Worcester City	42	15	10	17	62	63	54
Crawley Town	42	13	12	17	53	57	51
Waterlooville	42	13	10	19	63	81	49
Weymouth	42	11	13	18	50	70	46
Chelmsford City	42	11	10	21	52	72	43
Ashford Town	42	10	7	25	43	75	37
Corby Town	42	10	6	26	57	77	36
Alvechurch	42	7	5	30	46	95	26
Gosport Borough	42	6	5	31	28	93	23

Midland Division

Team	P	W	D	L	F	A	Pts
Halesowen Town	42	28	8	6	100	49	92
Rushden Town	42	28	5	9	82	39	89
Nuneaton Borough	42	26	7	9	81	47	85
Tamworth	42	22	8	12	82	70	74
Barry Town	42	21	8	13	67	53	71
Spalding United	42	20	7	15	73	63	67
Sutton Coldfield Town	42	18	10	14	72	69	64
Stourbridge	42	17	12	13	73	61	63
Dudley Town	42	18	9	15	69	64	63
Stroud	42	16	13	13	75	62	61
Leicester United	42	17	5	20	66	77	56
Bridgnorth Town	42	13	14	15	68	73	53
King's Lynn	42	16	5	21	57	69	53
Grantham Town	42	14	10	18	57	63	52
Bedworth United	42	14	9	19	50	60	51
Hednesford Town	42	11	14	17	50	62	47
Bilston Town	42	11	14	17	40	54	47
Redditch United	42	11	13	18	57	64	46
Racing Club Warwick	42	11	11	20	45	66	44
Willenhall Town	42	9	9	24	37	66	36
Banbury United	42	9	9	24	46	83	34
Sandwell Borough	42	6	12	24	46	79	30

Southern Division

Team	P	W	D	L	F	A	Pts
Bashley	42	25	7	10	80	47	82
Poole Town	42	23	8	11	85	60	77
Buckingham Town	42	22	10	10	67	46	76
Dunstable	42	20	14	8	56	38	74
Salisbury	42	21	9	12	72	50	72
Hythe Town	42	20	12	10	69	48	72
Trowbridge Town	42	20	9	13	79	64	69
Hastings Town	42	20	9	13	64	54	69
Bury Town	42	18	12	12	76	62	66
Baldock Town	42	18	11	13	69	52	65
Burnham	42	17	11	14	77	52	62
Fareham Town	42	14	14	14	49	53	56
Yate Town	42	16	6	20	53	52	54
Witney Town	42	16	6	20	54	56	54
Canterbury City	42	14	10	18	52	52	52
Margate	42	12	15	15	46	45	51
Folkestone	42	14	9	19	61	83	51
Andover	42	13	11	18	54	70	50
Hounslow	42	11	5	26	39	82	38
Erith & Belvedere	42	8	11	23	34	73	35
Corinthian	42	6	10	26	44	93	28
Sheppey United	42	6	7	29	35	83	25

1990-91

Premier Division

Team	P	W	D	L	F	A	Pts
Farnborough Town	42	26	7	9	79	43	85
Gloucester City	42	23	14	5	86	49	83
Cambridge City	42	21	14	7	63	43	77
Dover Athletic	42	21	11	10	56	37	74
Bromsgrove Rovers	42	20	11	11	68	49	71
Worcester City	42	18	12	12	55	42	66
Burton Albion	42	15	15	12	59	48	60
Halesowen Town	42	17	9	16	73	67	60
VS Rugby	42	16	11	15	56	46	59
Bashley	42	15	12	15	56	52	57
Dorchester Town	42	15	12	15	47	54	57
Wealdstone	42	16	8	18	57	58	56
Dartford	42	15	9	18	61	64	54
Rushden Town	42	14	11	17	64	66	53
Atherstone United	42	14	10	18	55	58	52
Moor Green	42	15	6	21	64	75	51
Poole Town	42	12	13	17	56	69	49
Chelmsford City	42	11	15	16	37	68	48
Crawley Town	42	12	12	18	45	67	48
Waterlooville	42	11	13	18	51	70	46
Gravesend & Northfleet	42	9	7	26	46	91	34
Weymouth	42	4	12	26	50	88	24

Midland Division

Team	P	W	D	L	F	A	Pts
Stourbridge	42	28	6	8	80	48	90
Corby Town	42	27	4	11	99	48	85
Hednesford Town	42	25	7	10	79	47	82
Tamworth	42	25	5	12	84	45	80
Nuneaton Borough	42	21	11	10	74	51	70
Barry Town	42	20	7	15	61	48	67
Newport AFC	42	19	6	17	54	46	63
King's Lynn	42	17	9	16	53	62	60
Grantham Town	42	17	7	18	62	56	56
Redditch United	42	16	10	16	66	75	58
Hinckley Town	42	16	9	17	72	68	57
Sutton Coldfield Town	42	15	11	16	56	65	56
Bedworth United	42	15	9	18	57	73	54
Bilston Town	42	14	9	19	69	79	51
Leicester United	42	14	10	18	65	77	51
Racing Club Warwick	42	12	13	17	56	65	49
Bridgnorth Town	42	13	9	20	62	74	48
Stroud	42	11	14	17	51	64	47
Dudley Town	42	11	13	18	48	73	46
Alvechurch	42	10	8	24	54	92	38
Willenhall Town	42	10	10	22	58	69	37
Spalding United	42	8	9	25	35	70	33

Southern Division

Team	P	W	D	L	F	A	Pts
Buckingham Town	40	25	8	7	73	38	83
Trowbridge Town	40	22	12	6	67	31	78
Salisbury	40	22	11	7	63	39	77
Baldock Town	40	21	9	10	66	52	72
Ashford Town	40	22	5	13	82	52	71
Yate Town	40	21	8	11	76	48	71
Hastings Town	40	18	11	11	66	46	65
Hythe Town	40	17	9	14	55	44	59
Andover	40	16	6	18	69	76	54
Margate	40	14	11	15	52	55	53
Burnham	40	12	16	12	57	49	52
Bury Town	40	15	5	20	58	74	50
Sudbury Town	40	13	10	17	60	68	49
Newport IOW	40	13	9	18	56	62	48
Gosport Borough	40	12	11	17	47	58	47
Witney Town	40	12	11	17	57	75	47
Dunstable	40	9	15	16	48	63	42
Canterbury City	40	12	6	22	60	83	42
Erith & Belvedere	40	10	6	24	46	73	36
Fareham Town	40	9	9	22	46	74	36
Corinthian	40	5	12	23	34	78	27

1991-92

Premier Division

Bromsgrove Rovers	42	27	9	6	78	34	90
Dover Athletic	42	23	15	4	66	30	84
VS Rugby	42	23	11	8	70	44	80
Bashley	42	22	8	12	70	44	74
Cambridge City	42	18	14	10	71	53	68
Dartford	42	17	15	10	62	45	66
Trowbridge Town	42	17	10	15	69	51	61
Halesowen Town	42	15	15	12	61	49	60
Moor Green	42	15	11	16	61	59	56
Burton Albion	42	15	10	17	59	61	55
Dorchester Town	42	14	13	15	66	73	55
Gloucester City	42	15	9	18	67	70	54
Atherstone United	42	15	8	19	54	66	53
Corby Town	42	13	12	17	66	81	51
Waterlooville	42	13	11	18	43	56	50
Worcester City	42	12	13	17	56	59	49
Crawley Town	42	12	12	18	62	67	48
Chelmsford City	42	12	12	18	49	56	48
Wealdstone	42	13	7	22	52	69	46
Poole Town	42	10	13	19	46	77	43
Fisher Athletic	42	9	11	22	53	89	38
Gravesend & Northfleet	42	8	9	25	39	87	33

Midland Division

Solihull Borough	42	29	10	3	92	40	97
Hednesford Town	42	26	13	3	81	37	91
Sutton Coldfield Town	42	21	11	10	71	51	74
Barry Town	42	21	6	15	88	56	69
Bedworth United	42	16	15	11	67	63	63
Nuneaton Borough	42	17	11	14	68	53	62
Tamworth	42	16	12	14	66	52	60
Rushden Town	42	16	12	14	69	63	60
Stourbridge	42	17	8	17	85	62	59
Newport AFC	42	15	13	14	72	60	58
Yate Town	42	14	15	13	65	64	57
Bilston Town	42	15	10	17	56	67	55
Grantham Town	42	11	17	14	59	55	50
King's Lynn	42	13	11	18	61	68	50
Hinckley Town	42	14	8	20	61	87	50
Leicester United	42	12	13	17	56	63	49
Bridgnorth Town	42	12	12	18	61	74	48
Racing Club Warwick	42	11	14	17	45	61	47
Stroud	42	14	4	24	66	88	46
Redditch United	42	12	8	22	52	92	44
Alvechurch	42	11	10	21	54	88	43
Dudley Town	42	8	9	25	41	92	33

Southern Division

Hastings Town	42	28	7	7	80	37	91
Weymouth	42	22	12	8	64	35	78
Havant Town	42	21	12	9	67	46	75
Braintree Town	42	21	8	13	77	58	71
Buckingham Town	42	19	15	8	57	26	69
Andover	42	18	10	14	73	68	64
Ashford Town	42	17	12	13	66	57	63
Sudbury Town	42	18	9	15	70	66	63
Sittingbourne	42	19	10	13	63	41	61
Burnham	42	15	14	13	57	55	59
Baldock Town	42	16	10	16	62	67	58
Salisbury	42	13	16	13	67	51	55
Hythe Town	42	15	10	17	61	62	55
Margate	42	13	16	13	49	56	55
Newport IOW	42	13	10	19	58	63	49
Dunstable	42	12	12	18	55	67	48
Bury Town	42	14	4	24	52	94	46
Witney Town	42	11	12	19	55	76	45
Fareham Town	42	12	8	22	45	71	44
Erith & Belvedere	42	11	10	21	44	67	43
Canterbury City	42	8	14	20	43	69	38
Gosport Borough	42	6	9	27	32	65	27

1992-93

Premier Division

Dover Athletic	40	25	11	4	65	23	86
Cheltenham Town	40	21	10	9	76	40	73
Corby Town	40	20	12	8	68	43	72
Hednesford Town	40	21	7	12	72	52	70
Trowbridge Town	40	18	8	14	70	66	62
Crawley Town	40	16	12	12	68	59	60
Solihull Borough	40	17	9	14	68	59	60
Burton Albion	40	16	11	13	53	50	59
Bashley	40	18	8	14	60	60	59
Halesowen Town	40	15	11	14	67	54	56
Waterlooville	40	15	9	16	59	62	54
Chelmsford City	40	15	9	16	59	69	54
Gloucester City	40	14	11	15	66	68	53
Cambridge City	40	14	10	16	62	73	52
Atherstone United	40	13	14	13	56	60	50
Hastings Town	40	13	11	16	50	55	50
Worcester City	40	12	9	19	45	62	45
Dorchester Town	40	12	6	22	52	74	42
Moor Green	40	10	6	24	58	79	36
VS Rugby	40	10	6	24	40	63	36
Weymouth	40	5	10	25	39	82	23

Bashley had 3 points deducted

Midland Division

Nuneaton Borough	42	29	5	8	102	45	92
Gresley Rovers	42	27	6	9	94	55	87
Rushden & Diamonds	42	25	10	7	85	41	85
Barri	42	26	5	11	82	49	83
Newport AFC	42	23	8	11	73	58	77
Bedworth United	42	22	8	12	72	55	74
Stourbridge	42	17	9	16	93	79	60
Sutton Coldfield Town	42	17	9	16	82	78	60
Redditch United	42	18	6	18	75	79	60
Tamworth	42	16	11	15	65	51	59
Weston-super-Mare	42	17	7	18	79	86	58
Leicester United	42	16	9	17	67	67	57
Grantham Town	42	16	9	17	60	73	57
Bilston Town	42	15	10	17	74	69	55
Evesham United	42	15	8	19	67	83	53
Bridgnorth Town	42	15	7	20	61	68	52
Dudley Town	42	14	8	20	60	75	50
Yate Town	42	15	5	22	63	81	50
Forest Green Rovers	42	12	6	24	61	97	42
Hinckley Athletic	42	9	11	22	56	89	37
King's Lynn	42	10	6	26	45	90	36
Racing Club Warwick	42	3	7	32	40	88	16

Southern Division

Sittingbourne	42	26	12	4	102	43	90
Salisbury	42	27	7	8	87	50	88
Witney Town	42	25	9	8	77	37	84
Gravesend & Northfleet	42	25	4	13	99	63	79
Havant Town	42	23	6	13	78	55	75
Sudbury Town	42	20	11	11	89	54	71
Erith & Belvedere	42	22	5	15	73	66	71
Ashford Town	42	20	8	14	91	66	68
Braintree Town	42	20	6	16	95	65	66
Margate	42	19	7	16	65	58	64
Wealdstone	42	18	7	17	75	69	61
Buckingham Town	42	16	11	15	61	58	59
Baldock Town	42	15	9	18	59	63	54
Poole Town	42	15	7	20	61	69	52
Fareham Town	42	14	8	20	67	65	50
Burnham	42	14	8	20	53	77	50
Canterbury City	42	12	10	20	54	76	46
Newport IOW	42	9	16	17	44	56	43
Fisher Athletic	42	8	9	25	38	98	33
Andover	42	7	9	26	42	99	30
Dunstable	42	5	14	23	42	92	29
Bury Town	42	8	5	29	46	119	29

1993-94

Premier Division

Team	P	W	D	L	F	A	Pts
Farnborough Town	42	25	7	10	74	44	82
Cheltenham Town	42	21	12	9	67	38	75
Halesowen Town	42	21	11	10	69	46	74
Atherstone United	42	22	7	13	57	43	73
Crawley Town	42	21	10	11	56	42	73
Chelmsford City	42	21	7	14	74	59	70
Trowbridge Town	42	16	17	9	52	41	65
Sittingbourne	42	17	13	12	65	48	64
Corby Town	42	17	8	17	52	56	59
Gloucester City	42	17	6	19	55	60	57
Burton Albion	42	15	11	10	57	49	56
Hastings Town	42	16	7	19	51	60	55
Hednesford Town	42	15	9	18	67	66	54
Gresley Rovers	42	14	11	17	61	72	53
Worcester City	42	14	9	19	61	70	51
Solihull Borough	42	13	11	18	52	57	50
Cambridge City	42	13	11	18	50	60	50
Dorchester Town	42	12	11	19	38	51	47
Moor Green	42	11	10	21	49	66	43
Waterlooville	42	11	10	21	47	69	43
Bashley	42	11	10	21	47	80	43
Nuneaton Borough	42	11	8	23	42	66	41

Midland Division

Team	P	W	D	L	F	A	Pts
Rushden & Diamonds	42	29	11	2	109	37	98
VS Rugby	42	28	8	6	98	41	92
Weston-super-Mare	42	27	10	5	94	39	91
Newport AFC	42	26	9	7	84	37	87
Clevedon Town	42	24	10	8	75	46	82
Redditch United	42	19	11	12	79	62	68
Tamworth	42	19	7	16	82	68	64
Bilston Town	42	16	10	16	65	73	58
Stourbridge	42	17	6	19	71	75	57
Evesham United	42	16	8	18	50	60	56
Grantham Town	42	16	6	20	77	73	54
Bridgnorth Town	42	15	6	21	56	68	51
Racing Club Warwick	42	13	12	17	53	66	51
Dudley Town	42	13	10	19	64	61	49
Forest Green Rangers	42	12	12	18	61	84	48
Sutton Coldfield Town	42	12	8	22	53	75	44
Bedworth United	42	12	7	23	62	81	43
Hinckley Town	42	11	10	21	44	71	43
Leicester United	42	11	9	22	34	73	42
King's Lynn	42	9	11	22	47	72	38
Yate Town	42	10	6	26	48	86	36
Armitage	42	8	11	23	45	103	35

Southern Division

Team	P	W	D	L	F	A	Pts
Gravesend & Northfleet	42	27	11	4	87	24	92
Sudbury Town	42	27	8	7	98	47	89
Witney Town	42	27	8	7	69	36	89
Salisbury City	42	26	10	6	90	39	88
Havant Town	42	27	4	11	101	41	85
Ashford Town	42	24	13	5	93	46	85
Baldock Town	42	26	7	9	76	40	85
Newport IOW	42	22	8	12	74	51	74
Margate	42	20	8	14	76	58	68
Weymouth	42	18	9	15	71	65	63
Tonbridge	42	19	5	18	59	62	62
Buckingham Town	42	14	14	14	43	42	56
Braintree Town	42	16	7	19	72	84	55
Fareham Town	42	12	12	18	54	75	48
Poole Town	42	13	6	23	54	86	45
Burnham	42	10	9	23	53	92	39
Fisher 93	42	9	10	23	52	81	37
Dunstable	42	9	7	26	50	91	34
Erith & Belvedere	42	9	5	28	40	72	32
Canterbury City	42	8	7	27	35	80	31
Wealdstone	42	6	7	29	45	95	25
Bury Town	42	3	5	34	36	121	14

1994-95

Premier Division

Team	P	W	D	L	F	A	Pts
Hednesford Town	42	28	9	5	99	49	93
Cheltenham Town	42	25	11	6	87	39	86
Burton Albion	42	20	15	7	55	39	75
Gloucester City	42	22	8	12	76	48	74
Rushden & Diamonds	42	19	11	12	99	65	68
Dorchester Town	42	19	10	13	84	61	67
Leek Town	42	19	10	13	72	60	67
Gresley Rovers	42	17	12	13	70	63	63
Cambridge City	42	18	8	16	60	55	62
Worcester City	42	14	15	13	46	34	57
Crawley Town	42	15	10	17	64	71	55
Hastings Town	42	13	14	15	55	57	53
Halesowen Town	42	14	10	18	81	80	52
Gravesend & Northfleet	42	16	13	16	38	55	52
Chelmsford City	42	14	6	22	56	60	48
Atherstone United	42	12	12	18	51	67	48
VS Rugby	42	11	14	17	49	61	47
Sudbury Town	42	12	10	20	50	77	46
Solihull Borough	42	10	15	17	39	65	45
Sittingbourne	42	11	10	21	51	73	43
Trowbridge Town	42	9	13	20	43	69	40
Corby Town	42	4	10	28	36	113	21

Corby Town had 1 point deducted for fielding ineligible players

Midland Division

Team	P	W	D	L	F	A	Pts
Newport AFC	42	29	8	5	106	39	95
Ilkeston Town	42	25	6	11	101	75	81
Tamworth	42	24	8	10	98	70	80
Moor Green	42	23	8	11	105	63	77
Bridgnorth Town	42	22	10	10	75	49	76
Buckingham Town	42	20	14	8	55	37	74
Nuneaton Borough	42	19	11	12	76	55	68
Rothwell Town	42	19	7	16	71	71	64
King's Lynn	42	18	8	16	76	64	62
Racing Club Warwick	42	17	11	14	68	63	62
Dudley Town	42	17	10	15	65	69	61
Bilston Town	42	17	8	17	73	64	59
Bedworth United	42	17	7	18	64	68	58
Evesham United	42	14	10	18	57	56	52
Hinckley Town	42	14	0	18	61	76	52
Stourbridge	42	15	7	20	59	77	52
Sutton Coldfield Town	42	12	10	20	62	72	46
Forest Green Rovers	42	11	13	18	56	76	46
Redditch United	42	8	14	20	47	64	38
Leicester United	42	10	8	24	51	99	38
Grantham Town	42	8	9	25	55	93	33
Armitage	42	2	5	35	35	116	11

Southern Division

Team	P	W	D	L	F	A	Pts
Salisbury City	42	30	7	5	88	37	97
Baldock Town	42	28	10	4	92	44	94
Havant Town	42	25	10	7	81	34	85
Waterlooville	42	24	8	10	77	36	80
Ashford Town	42	21	12	9	106	72	75
Weston-super-Mare	42	18	13	11	82	54	67
Bashley	42	18	11	13	62	49	65
Weymouth	42	16	13	13	60	55	61
Newport IOW	42	17	10	15	67	67	61
Witney Town	42	14	14	14	57	57	56
Clevedon Town	42	14	13	15	73	64	55
Tonbridge Angels	42	14	12	16	74	87	54
Margate	42	15	7	20	60	72	52
Braintree Town	42	12	13	17	64	71	49
Wealdstone	42	13	8	21	76	94	47
Yate Town	42	11	13	18	57	75	46
Fisher 93	42	9	16	17	54	70	43
Bury Town	42	11	8	23	59	86	41
Erith & Belvedere	42	10	9	23	49	94	39
Poole Town	42	10	8	24	53	79	38
Fareham Town	42	10	8	24	46	91	38
Burnham	42	7	7	28	40	89	28

1995-96

Premier Division

Team	P	W	D	L	F	A	Pts
Rushden & Diamonds	42	29	7	6	99	41	94
Halesowen Town	42	27	11	4	70	36	92
Cheltenham Town	42	21	11	10	76	57	74
Gloucester City	42	21	8	13	65	47	71
Gresley Rovers	42	20	10	12	70	58	70
Worcester City	42	19	12	11	61	43	69
Merthyr Tydfil	42	19	6	17	67	59	63
Hastings Town	42	16	13	13	68	56	61
Crawley Town	42	15	13	14	57	56	58
Sudbury Town	42	15	10	17	69	71	55
Gravesend & Northfleet	42	15	10	17	60	62	55
Chelmsford City	42	13	16	13	46	53	55
Dorchester Town	42	15	8	19	62	57	53
Newport AFC	42	13	13	16	53	59	52
Salisbury City	42	14	10	18	57	69	52
Burton Albion	42	13	12	17	55	56	51
Atherstone United	42	12	12	18	58	75	48
Baldock Town	42	11	14	17	51	56	47
Cambridge City	42	12	10	20	56	68	46
Ilkeston Town	42	11	10	21	53	87	43
Stafford Rangers	42	11	4	27	58	90	37
VS Rugby	42	5	10	27	37	92	25

Midland Division

Team	P	W	D	L	F	A	Pts
Nuneaton Borough	42	30	5	7	82	35	95
King's Lynn	42	27	5	10	85	43	84
Bedworth United	42	24	10	8	76	42	81
Moor Green	42	22	8	12	81	47	74
Paget Rangers	42	21	9	12	70	45	72
Tamworth	42	22	3	17	97	64	69
Solihull Borough	42	19	9	14	77	64	66
Rothwell Town	42	17	14	11	79	62	65
Buckingham Town	42	18	9	15	74	62	63
Dudley Town	42	15	16	11	83	66	61
Stourbridge	42	17	8	17	60	63	59
Bilston Town	42	16	9	17	61	62	57
Sutton Coldfield Town	42	16	9	17	62	67	57
Grantham Town	42	17	5	20	71	83	56
Redditch United	42	14	11	17	57	77	53
Leicester United	42	13	13	16	58	72	52
Hinckley Town	42	14	7	21	62	83	49
Racing Club Warwick	42	10	13	19	67	90	43
Evesham United	42	11	6	25	59	94	39
Corby Town	42	9	7	26	52	95	34
Bury Town	42	8	8	26	57	95	32
Bridgnorth Town	42	7	6	29	53	112	27

Bedworth United 1 point deducted, King's Lynn had 2 points deducted

Southern Division

Team	P	W	D	L	F	A	Pts
Sittingbourne	42	28	4	10	102	44	88
Ashford Town	42	25	9	8	75	44	84
Waterlooville	42	24	8	10	87	44	80
Newport IOW	42	24	6	12	75	58	78
Braintree Town	42	24	8	10	93	70	77
Weymouth	42	24	4	14	75	55	76
Havant Town	42	23	11	8	73	42	74
Forest Green Rovers	42	22	8	12	85	55	74
Trowbridge Town	42	18	8	16	86	51	62
Yate Town	42	17	8	17	85	71	59
Margate	42	18	5	19	68	62	59
Witney Town	42	16	11	15	60	54	59
Weston-super-Mare	42	16	9	17	78	68	57
Cinderford Town	42	16	8	18	74	77	56
Fisher 93	42	14	13	15	58	59	55
Bashley	42	14	11	17	63	61	53
Clevedon Town	42	15	6	21	70	80	51
Tonbridge Angels	42	13	10	19	58	79	49
Fleet Town	42	14	5	23	58	79	47
Fareham Town	42	12	5	25	71	97	41
Erith & Belvedere	42	4	4	34	38	111	16
Poole Town	42	0	1	41	17	188	1

Braintree Town 3 points deducted, Havant Town had 6 points deducted

1996-97

Premier Division

Team	P	W	D	L	F	A	Pts
Gresley Rovers	42	25	10	7	75	40	85
Cheltenham Town	42	21	11	10	76	44	74
Gloucester City	42	21	10	11	81	56	73
Halesowen Town	42	21	10	11	77	54	73
King's Lynn	42	20	8	14	65	61	68
Burton Albion	42	18	12	12	70	53	66
Nuneaton Borough	42	19	9	14	61	52	66
Sittingbourne	42	19	7	16	76	65	64
Merthyr Tydfil	42	17	9	16	69	61	60
Worcester City	42	15	14	13	52	50	59
Atherstone United	42	15	13	14	46	47	58
Salisbury City	42	15	13	14	57	66	58
Sudbury Town	42	16	7	19	72	72	55
Gravesend & Northfleet	42	16	7	19	63	73	55
Dorchester Town	42	14	9	19	62	66	51
Hastings Town	42	12	15	15	49	60	51
Crawley Town	42	13	8	21	49	67	47
Cambridge City	42	11	13	18	57	65	46
Ashford Town	42	9	18	15	53	79	45
Baldock Town	42	11	8	23	52	90	41
Newport AFC	42	9	13	20	40	60	40
Chelmsford City	42	6	14	22	49	70	32

Midland Division

Team	P	W	D	L	F	A	Pts
Tamworth	40	30	7	3	90	28	97
Rothwell Town	40	20	11	9	82	54	71
Ilkeston Town	40	19	13	8	76	50	70
Grantham Town	40	22	4	14	65	46	70
Bedworth United	40	18	11	11	77	41	65
Solihull Borough	40	19	8	13	84	62	65
Bilston Town	40	18	10	12	74	57	64
Moor Green	40	18	7	15	88	68	61
Stafford Rangers	40	17	9	14	68	62	60
Raunds Town	40	16	11	13	61	66	59
Racing Club Warwick	40	16	10	14	70	72	58
Shepshed Dynamo	40	14	12	14	64	65	54
Redditch United	40	15	8	17	56	59	53
Paget Rangers	40	13	9	18	42	55	48
Dudley Town	40	12	10	18	70	89	46
Hinckley Town	40	11	11	18	39	63	44
Stourbridge	40	10	9	21	61	81	39
Evesham United	40	9	12	19	55	77	39
VS Rugby	40	9	9	22	49	81	36
Corby Town	40	8	8	24	49	88	32
Sutton Coldfield Town	40	7	9	24	29	85	30

Leicester United FC closed down and their record was expunged from the League table.

Southern Division

Team	P	W	D	L	F	A	Pts
Forest Green Rovers	42	27	10	5	87	40	91
St Leonards Stamcroft	42	26	9	7	95	48	87
Havant Town	42	23	10	9	81	49	79
Weston-super-Mare	42	21	13	8	82	43	76
Margate	42	21	9	12	70	47	72
Witney Town	42	20	11	11	71	42	71
Weymouth	42	20	10	12	82	51	70
Tonbridge Angels	42	17	15	10	56	44	66
Newport IOW	42	15	15	12	73	58	60
Fisher Athletic (London)	42	18	6	18	77	77	60
Clevedon Town	42	17	9	16	75	76	60
Fareham Town	42	14	12	16	53	70	54
Bashley	42	15	8	19	73	84	53
Dartford	42	14	10	18	59	64	52
Waterlooville	42	14	9	19	58	67	51
Cirencester Town	42	12	12	18	50	68	48
Cinderford Town	42	13	7	22	64	76	46
Trowbridge Town	42	11	11	20	50	61	44
Yate Town	42	12	8	22	55	87	44
Fleet Town	42	12	6	24	47	91	42
Erith & Belvedere	42	9	10	23	60	95	37
Buckingham Town	42	2	8	32	27	107	14

1997-98

Premier Division

Forest Green Rovers	42	27	8	7	93	55	89
Merthyr Tydfil	42	24	12	6	80	42	84
Burton Albion	42	21	8	13	64	43	71
Dorchester Town	42	19	13	10	63	38	70
Halesowen Town	42	18	15	9	70	38	69
Bath City	42	19	12	11	72	51	69
Worcester City	42	19	12	11	54	44	69
King's Lynn	42	18	11	13	64	65	65
Atherstone United	42	17	12	13	55	49	63
Crawley Town	42	17	8	17	63	60	59
Gloucester City	42	16	11	15	57	57	59
Nuneaton Borough	42	17	6	19	68	61	57
Cambridge City	42	16	8	18	62	70	56
Hastings Town	42	14	12	16	67	70	54
Tamworth	42	14	11	17	68	65	53
Rothwell Town	42	11	16	15	55	73	49
Gresley Rovers	42	14	6	22	59	77	48
Salisbury City	42	12	12	18	53	72	48
Bromsgrove Rovers	42	13	6	23	67	85	45
Sittingbourne	42	12	8	22	47	66	44
Ashford Town	42	8	5	29	34	85	29
St Leonards Stamcroft	42	5	10	27	48	97	25

Midland Division

Grantham Town	40	30	4	6	87	39	94
Ilkeston Town	40	29	6	5	123	39	93
Solihull Borough	40	22	9	9	81	48	75
Raunds Town	40	20	8	12	73	44	68
Wisbech Town	40	20	7	13	79	57	67
Moor Green	40	20	7	13	72	55	67
Bilston Town	40	20	5	15	69	57	65
Blakenall	40	17	13	10	66	55	64
Stafford Rangers	40	18	6	16	57	56	60
Redditch United	40	16	11	13	59	41	59
Stourbridge	40	16	9	15	57	55	57
Hinckley United	40	15	11	14	59	56	56
Brackley Town	40	15	7	18	45	57	52
Bedworth United	40	15	5	20	50	73	50
Racing Club Warwick	40	11	9	20	49	56	42
Shepshed Dynamo	40	9	14	17	55	74	41
Sutton Coldfield Town	40	9	12	19	42	68	39
Paget Rangers	40	9	12	19	40	75	39
VS Rugby	40	8	12	20	53	93	36
Evesham United	40	7	9	24	47	94	30
Corby Town	40	2	8	30	41	112	14

Southern Division

Weymouth	42	32	2	8	107	48	98
Chelmsford City	42	29	8	5	86	39	95
Bashley	42	29	4	9	101	59	91
Newport IOW	42	25	9	8	72	34	84
Fisher Athletic (London)	42	25	5	12	87	50	80
Margate	42	23	8	11	71	42	77
Newport AFC	42	21	6	15	83	65	69
Witney Town	42	20	9	13	74	58	69
Clevedon Town	42	20	7	15	57	55	67
Waterlooville	42	17	7	18	69	64	58
Dartford	42	17	7	18	60	60	58
Havant Town	42	13	14	16	65	70	53
Fleet Town	42	16	5	21	63	83	53
Tonbridge Angels	42	14	10	18	49	55	52
Trowbridge Town	42	14	6	22	55	69	48
Erith & Belvedere	42	11	13	18	47	68	46
Fareham Town	42	12	9	21	75	87	45
Cirencester Town	42	12	7	23	63	88	43
Weston-super-Mare	42	12	5	25	49	86	41
Baldock Town	42	10	5	27	53	81	35
Cinderford Town	42	6	5	31	40	112	23
Yate Town	42	5	7	30	44	97	22

1998-99

Premier Division

Nuneaton Borough	42	27	9	6	91	33	90
Boston United	42	17	16	9	69	51	67
Ilkeston Town	42	18	13	11	72	59	67
Bath City	42	18	11	13	70	44	65
Hastings Town	42	18	11	13	57	49	65
Gloucester City	42	18	11	13	57	52	65
Worcester City	42	18	9	15	58	54	63
Halesowen Town	42	17	11	14	72	60	62
Tamworth	42	19	5	18	62	67	62
King's Lynn	42	17	10	15	53	46	61
Crawley Town	42	17	10	15	57	58	61
Salisbury City	42	16	12	14	56	61	60
Burton Albion	42	17	7	18	58	52	58
Weymouth	42	14	14	14	56	55	56
Merthyr Tydfil	42	15	8	19	52	62	53
Atherstone United	42	12	14	16	47	52	50
Grantham Town	42	14	8	20	51	58	50
Dorchester Town	42	11	15	16	49	63	48
Rothwell Town	42	13	9	20	47	67	48
Cambridge City	42	11	12	19	47	68	45
Gresley Rovers	42	12	8	22	49	73	44
Bromsgrove Rovers	42	8	7	27	38	84	31

Hastings Town resigned from the League

Midland Division

Clevedon Town	42	28	8	6	83	35	92
Newport AFC	42	26	7	9	92	51	85
Redditch United	42	22	12	8	81	45	75
Hinckley United	42	20	12	10	58	40	72
Stafford Rangers	42	21	8	13	92	60	71
Bilston Town	42	20	11	11	79	69	71
Solihull Borough	42	19	12	11	76	53	69
Moor Green	42	20	7	15	71	61	64
Blakenall	42	17	14	11	65	54	65
Shepshed Dynamo	42	17	12	13	62	54	63
Sutton Coldfield Town	42	17	8	17	46	57	59
Stourbridge	42	16	10	16	60	55	58
Evesham United	42	16	9	17	63	63	57
Wisbech Town	42	16	9	17	59	66	57
Weston-super-Mare	42	15	10	17	59	56	55
Bedworth United	42	15	9	18	63	52	54
Cinderford Town	42	13	8	21	61	74	47
Stamford AFC	42	13	7	22	60	75	46
Paget Rangers	42	11	12	19	49	58	45
VS Rugby	42	12	9	21	53	74	45
Racing Club Warwick	42	5	8	29	38	93	23
Bloxwich Town	42	1	2	39	26	151	5

Southern Division

Havant & Waterlooville	42	29	7	6	86	32	94
Margate	42	27	8	7	84	33	89
Folkestone Invicta	42	26	8	8	92	47	86
Newport IOW	42	23	7	12	68	40	76
Chelmsford City	42	20	12	10	91	51	72
Raunds Town	42	19	13	10	87	50	70
Ashford Town	42	17	12	13	59	54	63
Baldock Town	42	17	9	16	60	59	60
Fisher Athletic (London)	42	16	11	15	58	54	59
Bashley	42	17	7	18	74	77	58
Witney Town	42	15	12	15	56	48	57
Cirencester Town	42	16	8	18	61	66	56
Sittingbourne	42	11	18	12	53	56	54
Dartford	42	14	10	18	48	53	52
Erith & Belvedere	42	15	7	20	48	64	52
Tonbridge Angels	42	12	15	15	48	59	51
St Leonards	42	14	8	20	57	72	50
Fleet Town	42	11	11	19	54	72	47
Corby Town	42	10	10	22	48	73	40
Yate Town	42	10	7	25	37	79	37
Andover	42	6	10	26	50	115	28
Brackley Town	42	6	8	28	41	105	26

1999-2000

Premier Division

	P	W	D	L	F	A	Pts
Boston United	42	27	11	4	102	39	92
Burton Albion	42	23	9	10	73	43	78
Margate	42	23	8	11	64	43	77
Bath City	42	19	15	8	70	49	72
King's Lynn	42	19	14	9	59	43	71
Tamworth	42	20	10	12	80	51	70
Newport County	42	16	18	8	67	50	66
Clevedon Town	42	18	9	15	52	52	63
Ilkeston Town	42	16	12	14	77	69	60
Weymouth	42	14	16	12	60	51	58
Halesowen Town	42	14	14	14	52	54	56
Crawley Town	42	15	8	19	68	82	53
Havant & Waterlooville	42	13	13	16	63	68	52
Cambridge City	42	14	10	18	52	66	52
Worcester City	42	13	11	18	60	66	50
Salisbury City	42	14	8	20	70	84	50
Merthyr Tydfil	42	13	9	20	51	63	48
Dorchester Town	42	10	17	15	56	65	47
Grantham Town	42	14	5	23	63	76	47
Gloucester City	42	8	14	20	40	82	38
Rothwell Town	42	5	14	23	48	85	29
Atherstone United	42	5	13	24	30	76	28

Eastern Division

	P	W	D	L	F	A	Pts
Fisher Athletic (London)	42	31	5	6	107	42	98
Folkestone Invicta	42	30	7	5	101	39	97
Newport IOW	42	25	7	10	74	40	82
Chelmsford City	42	24	8	10	74	38	80
Hastings Town	42	22	9	11	76	56	75
Ashford Town	42	21	9	12	70	49	72
Tonbridge Angels	42	20	10	12	82	60	70
Dartford	42	17	6	19	52	58	57
Burnham	42	15	9	18	55	64	54
Baldock Town	42	14	10	18	57	69	52
Erith & Belvedere	42	14	9	19	62	68	51
Witney Town	42	13	11	18	48	60	50
VS Rugby	42	13	11	18	58	79	50
Wisbech Town	42	14	7	21	58	66	49
Spalding United	42	14	6	22	52	71	48
Sittingbourne	42	13	7	22	48	75	46
Stamford	42	9	18	15	50	62	45
St Leonards	42	11	12	19	67	81	45
Raunds Town	42	11	12	19	44	63	45
Bashley	42	12	7	23	56	95	43
Corby Town	42	11	12	19	56	62	42
Fleet Town	42	8	8	26	54	104	32

Corby Town had 3 points deducted for fielding an ineligible player
Raunds Town gave notice to withdraw and take the place of the 2nd relegated Club. They then unsuccessfully sought re-election

Western Division

	P	W	D	L	F	A	Pts
Stafford Rangers	42	29	6	7	107	47	93
Moor Green	42	26	12	4	85	33	90
Hinckley United	42	25	12	5	89	47	87
Tiverton Town	42	26	7	9	91	44	85
Solihull Borough	42	20	11	11	85	66	71
Blakenall	42	19	12	11	70	46	69
Cirencester Town	42	20	8	14	72	64	68
Bilston Town	42	16	18	8	66	52	66
Cinderford Town	42	17	11	14	62	64	62
Redditch United	42	17	10	15	73	65	61
Gresley Rovers	42	14	15	13	54	49	57
Weston-super-Mare	42	16	9	17	55	55	57
Sutton Coldfield Town	42	13	17	12	49	52	56
Evesham Town	42	13	12	17	69	61	51
Bedworth Town	42	13	10	19	52	71	49
Rocester	42	12	12	18	63	78	48
Bromsgrove Rovers	42	13	7	22	59	72	46
Shepshed Dynamo	42	12	7	23	46	66	43
Paget Rangers	42	11	4	27	44	82	37
Racing Club Warwick	42	7	14	21	41	82	35
Stourbridge	42	10	3	29	45	101	33
Yate Town	42	3	3	36	28	108	12

2000-2001

Premier Division

	P	W	D	L	F	A	Pts
Margate	42	28	7	7	75	27	91
Burton Albion	42	25	13	4	76	36	88
King's Lynn	42	18	11	13	67	58	65
Welling United	42	17	13	12	59	55	64
Weymouth	42	17	12	13	69	51	63
Havant & Waterlooville	42	18	9	15	65	53	63
Stafford Rangers	42	18	9	15	70	59	63
Worcester City	42	18	8	16	52	53	62
Moor Green	42	18	8	16	49	53	62
Newport County	42	17	10	15	70	61	61
Crawley Town	42	17	10	15	61	54	61
Tamworth	42	17	8	17	58	55	59
Salisbury City	42	17	8	17	64	69	59
Ilkeston Town	42	16	11	15	51	61	59
Bath City	42	15	13	14	67	68	55
Cambridge City	42	13	13	11	18	56	59	50
Folkestone Invicta	42	14	6	22	49	74	48
Merthyr Tydfil	42	11	13	18	49	62	46
Clevedon Town	42	11	7	24	61	74	40
Fisher Athletic (London)	42	12	6	24	51	85	39
Dorchester Town	42	10	8	24	40	70	38
Halesowen Town	42	8	13	21	47	69	37

Bath City and Fisher Athletic (London) both had 3 points deducted

Eastern Division

	P	W	D	L	F	A	Pts
Newport IOW	42	28	10	4	91	30	94
Chelmsford City	42	27	9	6	102	45	90
Grantham Town	42	25	11	6	100	47	86
Histon	42	23	11	8	84	53	80
Baldock Town	42	23	10	9	81	44	79
Hastings Town	42	22	10	10	72	50	76
Stamford	42	20	11	11	69	59	71
Tonbridge Angels	42	18	11	13	79	58	65
Langney Sports	42	19	8	15	75	55	65
Rothwell Town	42	20	5	17	86	74	62
Corby Town	42	14	10	18	64	92	52
Ashford Town	42	15	4	23	53	83	49
Banbury United	42	12	11	19	57	54	47
Witney Town	42	12	11	19	55	71	47
Bashley	42	10	14	18	57	71	44
Dartford	42	11	11	20	49	67	44
Burnham	42	10	14	18	39	65	43
Wisbech Town	42	10	9	23	45	89	39
St Leonards	42	9	10	23	55	87	37
Erith & Belvedere	42	10	7	25	49	92	37
Sittingbourne	42	8	9	25	41	79	33
Spalding United	42	7	12	23	35	73	33

Burnham had 1 point deducted, Rothwell Town had 3 points deducted

Western Division

	P	W	D	L	F	A	Pts
Hinckley United	42	30	8	4	102	38	98
Tiverton Town	42	28	7	7	97	36	91
Bilston Town	42	27	9	6	88	48	90
Evesham United	42	27	5	10	86	46	86
Mangotsfield United	42	25	9	8	91	45	84
Solihull Borough	42	22	12	8	73	43	78
Redditch United	42	17	13	12	76	69	64
Weston-super-Mare	42	17	10	15	68	58	61
Atherstone United	42	16	11	15	64	58	59
Rochester	42	18	5	19	57	77	59
Cirencester Town	42	14	15	13	65	74	57
Rugby United	42	13	10	19	51	68	49
Gloucester City	42	12	11	19	76	86	47
Blakenall	42	13	10	19	54	64	46
Shepshed Dynamo	42	12	9	21	56	73	45
Bedworth United	42	12	9	21	38	60	45
Racing Club Warwick	42	13	6	23	46	77	45
Gresley Rovers	42	11	8	23	46	65	41
Cinderford Town	42	11	8	23	56	84	41
Sutton Coldfield Town	42	7	14	21	45	66	35
Paget Rovers	42	9	4	29	38	93	31
Bromsgrove Rovers	42	7	9	26	49	92	30

Blakenall had 3 points deducted

2001-2002

Premier Division

Team	P	W	D	L	F	A	Pts
Kettering Town	42	27	6	9	80	41	87
Tamworth	42	24	13	5	81	41	85
Havant & Waterlooville	42	22	9	11	74	50	75
Crawley Town	42	21	10	11	67	48	73
Newport County	42	19	9	14	61	48	66
Tiverton Town	42	17	10	15	70	63	61
Moor Green	42	18	7	17	64	62	61
Worcester City	42	16	12	14	65	54	60
Stafford Rangers	42	17	9	16	70	62	60
Ilkeston Town	42	14	16	12	58	61	58
Weymouth United	42	15	11	16	59	67	56
Hinckley Town	42	14	13	15	64	62	55
Folkestone Invicta	42	14	12	16	51	61	54
Cambridge City	42	12	16	14	60	70	52
Welling United	42	13	12	17	69	66	51
Hednesford Town	42	15	6	21	59	70	51
Bath City	42	13	11	18	56	65	50
Chelmsford City	42	13	11	18	63	75	50
Newport IOW	42	12	12	18	38	61	48
King's Lynn	42	11	13	18	44	57	46
Merthyr Tydfil	42	12	8	22	53	71	44
Salisbury City	42	6	8	28	36	87	26

Eastern Division

Team	P	W	D	L	F	A	Pts
Hastings Town	42	29	8	5	85	38	95
Grantham Town	42	29	6	7	99	43	93
Dorchester Town	42	26	10	6	81	36	88
Histon	42	23	8	11	83	49	77
Stamford	42	24	4	14	76	61	76
Fisher Athletic (London)	42	20	10	12	83	56	70
Eastbourne Borough	42	21	6	15	63	46	69
Dartford	42	18	5	19	62	66	59
Erith & Belvedere	42	18	3	21	75	79	57
Bashley	42	15	11	16	71	63	56
Burnham	42	15	10	17	52	54	55
Rugby United	42	16	6	20	55	67	54
Rothwell Town	42	14	8	20	46	66	50
Ashford Town	42	14	6	22	58	78	48
Banbury United	42	13	9	20	53	66	47
Chatham Town	42	13	8	21	56	87	47
Sittingbourne	42	14	4	24	46	69	46
Spalding	42	13	6	23	72	84	45
Tonbridge Angels	42	13	6	23	65	80	45
St Leonards	42	14	3	25	52	88	45
Corby Town	42	10	13	19	54	82	43
Wisbech Town	42	11	8	23	56	84	41

Western Division

Team	P	W	D	L	F	A	Pts
Halesowen Town	40	27	9	4	85	24	90
Chippenham Town	40	26	9	5	81	28	87
Weston-super-Mare	40	22	10	8	70	38	76
Solihull Borough	40	20	11	9	75	42	71
Gresley Rovers	40	19	9	12	59	50	66
Sutton Coldfield Town	40	17	11	12	53	46	62
Mangotsfield United	40	17	10	13	74	54	61
Stourport Swifts	40	18	6	16	59	59	60
Atherstone United	40	16	8	16	61	59	56
Clevedon Town	40	15	11	14	57	58	56
Bedworth United	40	16	7	17	59	63	55
Evesham United	40	16	7	17	54	70	55
Cirencester Town	40	17	3	20	64	69	54
Gloucester City	40	14	10	16	48	63	52
Cinderford Town	40	14	9	17	54	67	51
Shepshed Dynamo	40	10	10	20	64	84	40
Bilston Town	40	11	7	22	50	72	40
Redditch United	40	11	6	23	47	77	39
Swindon Supermarine	40	11	4	25	52	76	37
Racing Club Warwick	40	8	11	21	38	63	35
Rocester	40	5	12	23	33	75	27

2002-2003

Premier Division

Team	P	W	D	L	F	A	Pts
Tamworth	42	26	10	6	73	32	88
Stafford Rangers	42	21	12	9	76	40	75
Dover Athletic	42	19	14	9	42	35	71
Tiverton Town	42	19	12	11	60	43	69
Chippenham Town	42	17	17	8	59	37	68
Worcester City	42	18	13	11	60	39	67
Crawley Town	42	17	13	12	64	51	64
Havant & Waterlooville	42	15	15	12	67	64	60
Chelmsford City	42	15	12	15	65	63	57
Newport County	42	15	11	16	53	52	56
Hednesford Town	42	14	13	15	59	60	55
Moor Green	42	13	14	15	49	58	53
Hinckley Town	42	12	16	14	61	64	52
Bath City	42	13	13	16	50	61	52
Welling United	42	13	12	17	55	58	51
Grantham Town	42	14	9	19	59	65	51
Weymouth	42	12	15	15	44	62	51
Cambridge City	42	13	10	19	54	56	49
Halesowen Town	42	12	13	17	52	63	49
Hastings United	42	10	13	19	44	57	43
Ilkeston Town	42	10	10	22	54	92	40
Folkestone Invicta	42	7	7	28	57	105	28

Eastern Division

Team	P	W	D	L	F	A	Pts
Dorchester Town	42	28	9	5	114	40	93
Eastbourne Borough	42	29	6	7	92	33	93
Stamford	42	27	6	9	80	39	87
Salisbury City	42	27	8	7	81	42	86
Bashley	42	23	12	7	90	44	81
King's Lynn	42	24	7	11	98	62	79
Rothwell Town	42	22	10	10	77	52	76
Banbury United	42	21	11	10	75	50	74
Tonbridge Angels	42	20	11	11	71	55	71
Histon	42	20	7	15	99	62	67
Ashford Town	42	18	9	15	63	57	63
Sittingbourne	42	15	8	19	57	69	53
Burnham	42	15	7	20	62	79	52
Fisher Athletic	42	15	5	22	57	80	50
Chatham Town	42	14	5	23	54	84	47
Newport IOW	42	12	6	24	53	87	42
Dartford	42	11	8	23	48	78	41
Erith & Belvedere	42	11	6	25	65	96	39
Corby Town	42	9	11	22	49	84	38
Fleet Town	42	8	8	26	34	80	32
Spalding United	42	4	6	32	40	108	18
St. Leonards	42	4	4	34	38	116	16

Western Division

Team	P	W	D	L	F	A	Pts
Merthyr Tydfil	42	28	8	6	78	32	92
Weston-super-Mare	42	26	7	9	77	42	85
Bromsgrove Rovers	42	23	7	12	73	41	76
Solihull Borough	42	21	13	8	77	48	76
Gloucester City	42	22	9	11	87	58	75
Mangotsfield United	42	21	10	11	106	53	73
Redditch United	42	22	6	14	76	42	72
Rugby United	42	20	9	13	58	43	69
Gresley Rovers	42	19	10	13	63	54	67
Taunton Town	42	20	7	15	76	78	67
Sutton Coldfield Town	42	18	10	14	63	53	64
Evesham United	42	19	6	17	76	72	63
Clevedon Town	42	14	13	15	54	60	55
Cirencester Town	42	15	7	20	62	82	52
Cinderford Town	42	13	12	17	50	67	51
Shepshed Dynamo	42	12	6	24	48	76	42
Stourport Swifts	42	10	11	21	48	66	41
Bedworth United	42	11	7	24	46	74	40
Swindon Supermarine	42	11	5	26	52	85	38
Atherstone United	42	9	10	23	45	78	37
Rocester	42	9	10	23	34	74	37
Racing Club Warwick	42	3	9	30	33	104	18

2003-2004

Premier Division

Crawley Town	42	25	9	8	77	43	84
Weymouth	42	20	12	10	76	47	72
Stafford Rangers	42	19	11	12	55	43	68
Nuneaton Borough	42	17	15	10	65	49	66
Worcester City	42	18	9	15	71	50	63
Hinckley United	42	15	14	13	55	46	59
Newport County	42	15	14	13	52	50	59
Cambridge City	42	14	15	13	54	53	57
Welling United	42	16	8	18	56	58	56
Weston-super-Mare	42	14	13	15	52	52	55
Eastbourne Borough	42	14	13	15	48	56	55
Havant & Waterlooville	42	15	10	17	59	70	55
Moor Green	42	14	12	16	42	54	54
Merthyr Tydfil	42	13	14	15	60	66	53
Tiverton Town	42	12	15	15	63	64	51
Bath City	42	13	12	17	49	57	51
Dorchester Town	42	14	9	19	56	69	51
Chelmsford City	42	11	16	15	46	53	49
Dover Athletic	42	12	13	17	50	59	49
Hednesford Town	42	12	12	18	56	69	48
Chippenham Town	42	10	17	15	51	63	47
Grantham Town	42	10	15	17	45	67	45

Eastern Division

King's Lynn	42	28	7	7	90	35	91
Histon	42	26	10	6	96	41	88
Tonbridge Angels	42	27	7	8	82	46	88
* Eastleigh	42	27	4	11	88	40	82
Folkestone Invicta	42	20	15	7	91	45	75
Salisbury City	42	21	11	10	73	45	74
Stamford	42	20	11	11	63	45	71
Banbury United	42	19	10	13	65	57	67
Burgess Hill Town	42	19	7	16	67	54	64
Sittingbourne	42	18	8	16	61	55	62
Bashley	42	18	7	17	66	58	61
Ashford Town	42	15	9	18	51	53	54
Chatham Town	42	13	10	19	49	67	49
Fisher Athletic	42	13	10	19	61	81	49
Corby Town	42	12	9	21	44	75	45
Dartford	42	13	6	23	48	81	45
* Burnham	42	12	11	19	52	76	44
Hastings United	42	12	7	23	60	91	43
Newport IOW	42	11	7	24	42	69	40
Rothwell Town	42	9	11	22	30	47	38
Erith & Belvedere	42	7	10	25	45	84	31
Fleet Town	42	5	7	30	35	114	22

* Eastleigh and Burnham both had 3 points deducted.

Western Division

Redditch United	40	25	9	6	75	30	84
Gloucester City	40	24	7	9	77	46	79
Cirencester Town	40	24	4	12	73	40	76
Halesowen Town	40	20	13	7	64	40	73
Rugby United	40	21	8	11	57	40	71
Team Bath	40	21	6	13	62	41	69
Solihull Borough	40	19	9	12	50	31	66
Sutton Coldfield	40	16	15	9	52	38	63
Bromsgrove Rovers	40	16	11	13	60	48	59
Ilkeston Town	40	16	10	14	58	59	58
Clevedon Town	40	16	5	19	55	59	53
Gresley Rovers	40	15	7	18	52	60	52
Mangotsfield United	40	14	8	18	70	70	50
Evesham United	40	15	5	20	56	57	50
Taunton Town	40	14	8	18	50	55	50
Yate Town	40	11	9	20	51	79	42
Swindon Supermarine	40	10	9	21	41	69	39
Stourport Swifts	40	9	11	20	43	62	38
Bedworth United	40	8	12	20	39	61	36
Cinderford Town	40	7	9	24	50	94	30
Shepshed Dynamo	40	5	13	22	31	87	28

2004-2005

Premier Division

Histon	42	24	6	12	93	57	78
Chippenham Town	42	22	9	11	81	55	75
Merthyr Tydfil	42	19	14	9	62	47	71
Hednesford Town	42	20	10	12	68	40	70
Bedford Town	42	19	12	11	70	52	69
Bath City	42	19	12	11	57	43	69
Cirencester Town	42	19	11	12	63	52	68
Tiverton Town	42	18	13	11	70	55	67
Halesowen Town	42	19	9	14	64	52	66
Aylesbury United	42	20	3	19	67	66	63
King's Lynn	42	19	4	19	78	69	61
Chesham United	42	18	5	19	84	82	59
Grantham Town	42	17	7	18	57	55	58
Team Bath	42	14	12	16	54	68	54
Gloucester City	42	12	17	13	63	61	53
Rugby United	42	13	12	17	48	60	51
Banbury United	42	13	9	20	56	69	48
Hitchin Town	42	13	9	20	55	77	48
Hemel Hempstead Town	42	11	10	21	60	88	43
Dunstable Town	42	11	6	25	56	98	39
Stamford	42	6	18	18	40	60	36
Solihull Borough	42	10	4	28	45	85	34

Eastern Division

Fisher Athletic	42	30	6	6	96	41	96
East Thurrock United	42	25	12	5	92	38	87
Maldon Town	42	27	6	9	92	51	87
Uxbridge	42	26	7	9	87	37	85
Wivenhoe Town	42	21	11	10	74	49	74
Barking & East Ham United	42	20	10	12	63	37	70
Boreham Wood	42	19	9	14	80	61	66
Barton Rovers	42	20	4	18	76	72	64
Waltham Forest	42	16	9	17	68	61	57
Leighton Town	42	13	15	14	57	59	54
Chatham Town	42	15	9	18	53	63	54
Wingate & Finchley	42	15	8	19	60	75	53
Arlesey Town	42	14	10	18	53	67	52
Beaconsfield SYCOB	42	12	12	18	54	65	48
Harlow Town	42	13	8	21	53	65	47
Dartford	42	11	13	18	58	75	46
Aveley	42	12	9	21	57	69	45
Berkhamsted Town	42	15	7	20	66	101	45
Sittingbourne	42	10	12	20	53	70	42
Great Wakering Rovers	42	9	11	22	45	78	38
Erith & Belvedere	42	11	7	24	56	92	37
Tilbury	42	6	9	27	41	108	27

Berkhamsted Town had 7 points deducted.
Erith & Belvedere had 3 points deducted.

Western Division

Mangotsfield United	42	24	11	7	89	49	83
Yate Town	42	24	9	9	83	40	81
Evesham United	42	23	10	9	66	31	79
Clevedon Town	42	24	6	12	82	49	78
Bromsgrove Rovers	42	19	15	8	60	42	72
Ashford Town (Middlesex)	42	17	13	12	63	46	64
Brackley Town	42	18	10	14	69	53	64
Paulton Rovers	42	18	7	17	62	61	61
Burnham	42	17	7	18	64	64	58
Rothwell Town	42	16	10	16	57	57	58
Thame United	42	17	6	19	58	69	57
Corby Town	42	14	12	16	52	62	54
Marlow	42	13	14	15	58	67	53
Stourport Swifts	42	15	7	20	62	63	52
Bedworth United	42	15	7	20	51	60	52
Cinderford Town	42	13	12	17	50	64	51
Taunton Town	42	14	8	20	66	75	50
Sutton Coldfield	42	16	11	15	54	61	48
Swindon Supermarine	42	12	12	18	43	60	48
Bracknell Town	42	10	13	19	53	75	43
Oxford City	42	11	8	23	49	71	41
Egham Town	42	6	4	32	25	97	22

Sutton Coldfield had 11 points deducted.

2005-2006

Premier Division

Salisbury City	42	30	5	7	83	27	95
Bath City	42	25	8	9	66	33	83
King's Lynn	42	25	7	10	73	41	82
Chippenham Town	42	22	11	9	69	45	77
Bedford Town	42	22	10	10	69	53	76
Yate Town	42	21	5	16	78	74	68
Banbury United	42	17	11	14	66	61	62
Halesowen Town	42	15	15	12	54	45	60
Merthyr Tydfil	42	17	9	16	62	58	60
Mangotsfield United	42	15	13	14	67	67	58
Grantham Town	42	15	11	16	49	49	56
Tiverton Town	42	14	10	18	69	65	52
Gloucester City	42	14	10	18	57	60	52
Hitchin Town	42	13	12	17	59	76	51
Rugby Town	42	13	11	18	58	66	50
Cheshunt	42	13	9	20	57	70	48
Team Bath	42	14	6	22	55	68	48
Cirencester Town	42	14	4	24	49	68	46
Northwood	42	12	6	24	53	88	42
Evesham United	42	9	14	19	46	58	41
Aylesbury United	42	9	12	21	43	69	39
Chesham United	42	9	9	24	43	84	36

Eastern Division

Boreham Wood	42	24	12	6	84	41	84
Corby Town	42	25	9	8	63	33	84
Enfield Town	42	24	9	9	75	43	81
Stamford	42	20	10	12	73	53	70
Barking & East Ham United	42	20	10	12	63	47	70
Wivenhoe Town	42	17	11	14	56	54	62
Dartford	42	16	13	13	65	57	61
Waltham Forest	42	17	8	17	64	66	59
Harlow Town	42	14	16	12	57	56	58
Arlesey Town	42	15	11	16	58	65	56
Rothwell Town	42	13	14	15	48	53	53
Wingate & Finchley	42	13	14	15	57	64	53
Great Wakering Rovers	42	13	12	17	65	67	51
Uxbridge	42	13	11	18	62	64	50
Potters Bar Town	42	13	11	18	60	66	50
Enfield	42	13	11	18	52	64	50
Chatham Town	42	13	10	19	51	57	49
Sittingbourne	42	12	12	18	53	69	48
Barton Rovers	42	13	8	21	59	73	47
Aveley	42	11	13	18	51	70	46
Ilford	42	8	17	17	35	59	41
Berkhamsted Town	42	8	12	22	51	81	36

Western Division

Clevedon Town	42	28	6	8	86	45	90
Ashford Town (Middlesex)	42	24	8	10	84	50	80
Brackley Town	42	23	9	10	71	34	78
Hemel Hempstead Town	42	22	9	11	86	47	75
Swindon Supermarine	42	22	9	11	70	47	75
Marlow	42	22	6	14	62	59	72
Sutton Coldfield Town	42	21	6	15	91	62	69
Leighton Town	42	19	8	15	55	48	65
Willenhall Town	42	17	12	13	78	61	63
Rushall Olympic	42	17	11	14	73	57	62
Bromsgrove Rovers	42	17	11	14	65	50	62
Solihull Borough	42	15	13	14	50	51	58
Beaconsfield SYCOB	42	14	13	15	60	66	55
Burnham	42	16	5	21	58	71	53
Cinderford Town	42	14	9	19	71	79	51
Bedworth United	42	14	9	19	46	57	51
Paulton Rovers	42	12	10	20	55	76	46
Taunton Town	42	12	9	21	67	81	45
Bracknell Town	42	12	6	24	53	77	42
Stourport Swifts	42	9	14	19	55	80	41
Dunstable Town	42	8	12	22	45	91	36
Thame United	42	4	5	33	30	122	17

FOOTBALL CONFERENCE

1979-80

Altrincham	38	24	8	6	79	35	56
Weymouth	38	22	10	6	73	37	54
Worcester City	38	19	11	8	53	36	49
Boston United	38	16	13	9	52	43	45
Gravesend & Northfleet	38	17	10	11	49	44	44
Maidstone United	38	16	11	11	54	37	43
Kettering Town	38	15	13	10	55	50	43
Northwich Victoria	38	16	10	12	50	38	42
Bangor City	38	14	14	10	41	46	42
Nuneaton Borough	38	13	13	12	58	44	39
Scarborough	38	12	15	11	47	38	39
Yeovil Town	38	13	10	15	46	49	36
Telford United	38	13	8	17	52	60	34
Barrow	38	14	6	18	47	55	34
Wealdstone	38	9	15	14	42	54	33
Bath City	38	10	12	16	43	69	32
Barnet	38	10	10	18	32	48	30
AP Leamington	38	7	11	20	32	63	25
Stafford Rangers	38	6	10	22	41	57	22
Redditch United	38	5	8	25	26	69	18

1980-81

Altrincham	38	23	8	7	72	41	54
Kettering Town	38	21	9	8	66	37	51
Scarborough	38	17	13	8	49	29	47
Northwich Victoria	38	17	11	10	53	40	45
Weymouth	38	19	6	13	54	40	44
Bath City	38	16	10	12	51	32	42
Maidstone United	38	16	9	13	64	53	41
Boston United	38	16	9	13	63	58	41
Barrow	38	15	8	15	50	49	38
Frickley Athletic	38	15	8	15	61	62	38
Stafford Rangers	38	11	15	12	56	56	37
Worcester City	38	14	7	17	47	54	35
Telford United	38	13	9	16	47	59	35
Yeovil Town	38	14	6	18	60	64	34
Gravesend & Northfleet	38	13	8	17	48	55	34
AP Leamington	38	10	11	17	47	66	31
Barnet	38	12	7	19	39	64	31
Nuneaton Borough	38	10	9	19	49	65	29
Wealdstone	38	9	11	18	37	56	29
Bangor City	38	6	12	20	35	68	24

1981-82

Runcorn	42	28	9	5	75	37	93
Enfield	42	26	8	8	90	46	86
Telford United	42	23	8	11	70	51	77
Worcester City	42	21	8	13	70	60	71
Dagenham	42	19	12	11	69	51	69
Northwich Victoria	42	20	9	13	56	46	69
Scarborough	42	19	11	12	65	52	68
Barrow	42	18	11	13	59	50	65
Weymouth	42	18	9	15	56	47	63
Boston United	42	17	11	14	61	57	62
Altrincham	42	14	13	15	66	56	55
Bath City	42	15	10	17	50	57	55
Yeovil Town	42	14	11	17	56	68	53
Stafford Rangers	42	12	16	14	48	47	52
Frickley Athletic	42	14	10	18	47	60	52
Maidstone United	42	11	15	16	55	59	48
Trowbridge Town	42	12	11	19	38	54	47
Barnet	42	9	14	19	36	52	41
Kettering Town	42	9	13	20	64	76	40
Gravesend & Northfleet	42	10	10	22	51	69	40
Dartford	42	10	9	23	47	69	39
AP Leamington	42	4	10	28	40	105	22

1982-83

Team	P	W	D	L	F	A	Pts
Enfield	42	25	9	8	95	48	84
Maidstone United	42	25	8	9	83	34	83
Wealdstone	42	22	13	7	80	41	79
Runcorn	42	22	8	12	73	53	74
Boston United	42	20	12	10	77	57	72
Telford United	42	20	11	11	69	48	71
Weymouth	42	20	10	12	63	48	70
Northwich Victoria	42	18	10	14	68	63	64
Scarborough	42	17	12	13	71	58	63
Bath City	42	17	9	16	58	55	60
Nuneaton Borough	42	15	13	14	57	60	58
Altrincham	42	15	10	17	62	56	55
Bangor City	42	14	13	15	71	77	55
Dagenham	42	12	15	15	60	65	51
Barnet	42	16	3	23	55	78	51
Frickley Athletic	42	12	13	17	66	77	49
Worcester City	42	12	10	20	58	87	46
Trowbridge Town	42	12	7	23	56	88	43
Kettering Town	42	11	7	24	69	99	40
Yeovil Town	42	11	7	24	63	99	40
Barrow	42	8	12	22	46	74	36
Stafford Rangers	42	5	14	23	40	75	29

1983-84

Team	P	W	D	L	F	A	Pts
Maidstone United	42	23	13	6	71	34	70
Nuneaton Borough	42	24	11	7	70	40	69
Altrincham	42	23	9	10	64	39	65
Wealdstone	42	21	14	7	75	36	62
Runcorn	42	20	13	9	61	45	62
Bath City	42	17	12	13	60	48	53
Northwich Victoria	42	16	14	12	54	47	51
Worcester City	42	15	13	14	64	55	49
Barnet	42	16	10	16	55	58	49
Kidderminster Harriers	42	14	14	14	54	61	49
Telford United	42	17	11	14	50	58	49
Frickley Athletic	42	17	10	15	68	56	48
Scarborough	42	14	16	12	52	55	48
Enfield	42	14	9	19	61	58	43
Weymouth	42	13	8	21	54	65	42
Gateshead	42	12	13	17	59	73	42
Boston United	42	13	12	17	66	80	41
Dagenham	42	14	8	20	57	69	40
Kettering Town	42	12	9	21	53	67	37
Yeovil Town	42	12	8	22	55	77	35
Bangor City	42	10	6	26	54	82	29
Trowbridge Town	42	5	7	30	33	87	19

2 points awarded for a Home win, 3 points awarded for an Away win, 1 point awarded for any Draw

1984-85

Team	P	W	D	L	F	A	Pts
Wealdstone	42	20	10	12	64	54	62
Nuneaton Borough	42	19	14	9	85	53	58
Dartford	42	17	13	12	57	48	57
Bath City	42	21	9	12	52	49	57
Altrincham	42	21	6	15	63	47	56
Scarborough	42	17	13	12	69	62	54
Enfield	42	17	13	12	84	61	53
Kidderminster Harriers	42	17	8	17	79	77	51
Northwich Victoria	42	16	11	15	50	46	50
Telford United	42	15	14	13	59	54	49
Frickley Athletic	42	18	7	17	65	71	49
Kettering Town	42	15	12	15	68	59	48
Maidstone United	42	15	13	14	58	51	48
Runcorn	42	13	15	14	48	47	48
Barnet	42	15	11	16	59	52	47
Weymouth	42	15	13	14	70	66	45
Boston United	42	15	10	17	69	69	45
Barrow	42	11	16	15	47	57	43
Dagenham	42	13	10	19	47	67	41
Worcester City	42	12	9	21	55	84	38
Gateshead	42	9	12	21	51	82	33
Yeovil Town	42	6	11	25	44	87	25

2 points awarded for a Home win, 3 points awarded for an Away win, 1 point awarded for any Draw.   Gateshead had 1 point deducted

1985-86

Team	P	W	D	L	F	A	Pts
Enfield	42	27	10	5	94	47	76
Frickley Athletic	42	25	10	7	78	50	69
Kidderminster Harriers	42	24	7	11	99	62	67
Altrincham	42	22	11	9	70	49	63
Weymouth	42	19	15	8	75	60	61
Runcorn	42	19	14	9	70	44	60
Stafford Rangers	42	19	13	10	61	54	60
Telford United	42	18	10	14	68	66	51
Kettering Town	42	15	15	12	55	53	49
Wealdstone	42	16	9	17	57	56	47
Cheltenham Town	42	16	11	15	69	69	46
Bath City	42	13	11	18	53	54	45
Boston United	42	16	7	19	66	76	44
Barnet	42	13	11	18	56	60	41
Scarborough	42	13	11	18	54	66	40
Northwich Victoria	42	10	12	20	42	54	37
Maidstone United	42	9	16	17	57	66	36
Nuneaton Borough	42	13	5	24	58	73	36
Dagenham	42	10	12	20	48	66	36
Wycombe Wanderers	42	10	13	19	55	84	36
Dartford	42	8	9	25	51	82	26
Barrow	42	7	8	27	41	86	24

2 points awarded for a Home win; 3 points awarded for an Away win; 1 point awarded for any Draw

1986-87

Team	P	W	D	L	F	A	Pts
Scarborough	42	27	10	5	64	33	91
Barnet	42	25	10	7	86	39	85
Maidstone United	42	21	10	11	71	48	73
Enfield	42	21	7	14	66	47	70
Altrincham	42	18	15	9	66	53	69
Boston United	42	21	6	15	82	74	69
Sutton United	42	19	11	12	81	51	68
Runcorn	42	18	13	11	71	58	67
Telford United	42	18	10	14	69	59	64
Bath City	42	17	12	13	63	62	63
Cheltenham Town	42	16	13	13	64	50	61
Kidderminster Harriers	42	17	4	21	77	81	55
Stafford Rangers	42	14	11	17	58	60	53
Weymouth	42	13	12	17	68	77	51
Dagenham	42	14	7	21	56	72	49
Kettering Town	42	12	11	19	54	66	47
Northwich Victoria	42	10	14	18	53	69	44
Nuneaton Borough	42	10	14	18	48	73	44
Wealdstone	42	11	10	21	50	70	43
Welling United	42	10	10	22	61	84	40
Frickley Athletic	42	7	11	24	47	82	32
Gateshead	42	6	13	23	48	95	31

1987-88

Team	P	W	D	L	F	A	Pts
Lincoln City	42	24	10	8	86	48	82
Barnet	42	23	11	8	93	45	80
Kettering Town	42	22	9	11	68	48	75
Runcorn	42	21	11	10	68	47	74
Telford United	42	20	10	12	65	50	70
Stafford Rangers	42	20	9	13	79	58	69
Kidderminster Harriers	42	18	15	9	75	66	69
Sutton United	42	16	18	8	77	54	66
Maidstone United	42	18	9	15	79	64	63
Weymouth	42	18	9	15	53	43	63
Macclesfield Town	42	18	9	15	64	62	63
Enfield	42	15	10	17	68	78	55
Cheltenham Town	42	11	20	11	64	67	53
Altrincham	42	14	10	18	59	59	52
Fisher Athletic	42	13	13	16	58	61	52
Boston United	42	14	7	21	60	75	49
Northwich Victoria	42	10	17	15	46	57	47
Wycombe Wanderers	42	11	13	18	50	76	46
Welling United	42	11	9	22	50	72	42
Bath City	42	9	10	23	48	76	37
Wealdstone	42	5	17	20	39	76	32
Dagenham	42	5	6	31	37	104	21

1988-89

Maidstone United	40	25	9	6	92	46	84
Kettering Town	40	23	7	10	56	39	76
Boston United	40	22	8	10	61	51	74
Wycombe Wanderers	40	20	11	9	68	52	71
Kidderminster Harriers	40	21	6	13	68	57	69
Runcorn	40	19	8	13	77	53	65
Macclesfield Town	40	17	10	13	63	57	61
Barnet	40	18	7	15	64	69	61
Yeovil Town	40	15	11	14	68	67	56
Northwich Victoria	40	14	11	15	64	65	53
Welling United	40	14	11	15	45	46	53
Sutton United	40	12	15	13	64	54	51
Enfield	40	14	8	18	62	67	50
Altrincham	40	13	10	17	51	61	49
Cheltenham Town	40	12	12	16	55	58	48
Telford United	40	13	9	18	37	43	48
Chorley	40	13	6	21	57	71	45
Fisher Athletic	40	10	11	19	55	65	41
Stafford Rangers	40	11	7	22	49	74	40
Aylesbury United	40	9	9	22	43	71	36
Weymouth	40	7	10	23	37	70	31
Newport County	29	4	7	18	31	62	19

Newport County expelled from League – their record was deleted.

1989-90

Darlington	42	26	9	7	76	25	87
Barnet	42	26	7	9	81	41	85
Runcorn	42	19	13	10	79	62	70
Macclesfield Town	42	17	15	10	56	41	66
Kettering Town	42	18	12	12	66	53	66
Welling United	42	18	10	14	62	50	64
Yeovil Town	42	17	12	13	62	54	63
Sutton United	42	19	6	17	68	64	63
Merthyr Tydfil	42	16	14	12	67	63	62
Wycombe Wanderers	42	17	10	15	64	56	61
Cheltenham Town	42	16	11	15	58	60	59
Telford United	42	15	13	14	56	63	58
Kidderminster Harriers	42	15	9	18	64	67	54
Barrow	42	12	16	14	51	67	52
Northwich Victoria	42	15	5	22	51	67	50
Altrincham	42	12	13	17	49	48	49
Stafford Rangers	42	12	12	18	50	62	48
Boston United	42	13	8	21	48	67	47
Fisher Athletic	42	13	7	22	55	78	46
Chorley	42	13	6	23	42	67	45
Farnborough Town	42	10	12	20	60	73	42
Enfield	42	10	6	26	52	89	36

1990-91

Barnet	42	26	9	7	103	52	87
Colchester United	42	25	10	7	68	35	85
Altrincham	42	23	13	6	87	46	82
Kettering Town	42	23	11	8	67	45	80
Wycombe Wanderers	42	21	11	10	75	46	74
Telford United	42	20	7	15	62	52	67
Macclesfield Town	42	17	12	13	63	52	63
Runcorn	42	16	10	16	69	67	58
Merthyr Tydfil	42	16	9	17	62	61	57
Barrow	42	15	12	15	59	65	57
Welling United	42	13	15	14	55	57	54
Northwich Victoria	42	13	13	16	65	75	52
Kidderminster Harrier	42	14	10	18	56	67	52
Yeovil Town	42	13	11	18	58	58	50
Stafford Rangers	42	12	14	16	48	51	50
Cheltenham Town	42	12	12	18	54	72	48
Gateshead	42	14	6	22	52	92	48
Boston United	42	12	11	19	55	69	47
Slough Town	42	13	6	23	51	80	45
Bath City	42	10	12	20	55	61	42
Sutton United	42	10	9	23	62	82	39
Fisher Athletic	42	5	15	22	38	79	30

1991-92

Colchester United	42	28	10	4	98	40	94
Wycombe Wanderers	42	30	4	8	84	35	94
Kettering Town	42	20	13	9	72	50	73
Merthyr Tydfil	42	18	14	10	59	56	68
Farnborough Town	42	18	13	12	68	53	66
Telford United	42	19	7	16	62	66	64
Redbridge Forest	42	18	9	15	69	56	63
Boston United	42	18	9	15	71	66	63
Bath City	42	16	12	14	54	51	60
Witton Albion	42	16	10	16	63	60	58
Northwich Victoria	42	16	6	20	63	58	54
Welling United	42	14	12	16	69	79	54
Macclesfield Town	42	13	13	16	50	50	52
Gateshead	42	12	13	18	49	57	48
Yeovil Town	42	11	14	17	40	49	47
Runcorn	42	11	13	18	50	63	46
Stafford Rangers	42	10	16	16	41	59	46
Altrincham	42	11	12	19	61	82	45
Kidderminster Harriers	42	12	9	21	56	77	45
Slough Town	42	13	6	23	56	82	45
Cheltenham Town	42	10	13	19	56	83	43
Barrow	42	8	14	20	52	72	38

1992-93

Wycombe Wanderers	42	24	11	7	84	37	83
Bromsgrove Rovers	42	18	14	10	67	49	68
Dagenham & Redbridge	42	19	11	12	75	47	67
Yeovil Town	42	18	12	12	59	49	66
Slough Town	42	18	11	13	60	55	65
Stafford Rangers	42	18	10	14	55	47	64
Bath City	42	15	14	13	53	46	59
Woking	42	17	8	17	58	62	59
Kidderminster Harriers	42	14	16	12	60	60	58
Altrincham	42	15	13	14	49	52	58
Northwich Victoria	42	16	8	18	68	55	56
Stalybridge Celtic	42	13	17	12	48	55	56
Kettering Town	42	14	13	15	61	63	55
Gateshead	42	14	10	18	53	56	52
Telford United	42	14	10	18	55	60	52
Merthyr Tydfil	42	14	10	18	51	79	52
Witton Albion	42	11	17	14	62	65	50
Macclesfield	42	12	13	17	40	50	49
Runcorn	42	13	10	19	58	76	49
Welling United	42	12	12	18	57	72	48
Farnborough Town	42	12	11	19	68	87	47
Boston United	42	9	13	20	50	69	40

Dagenham & Redbridge had 1 point deducted

1993-94

Kidderminster Harriers	42	22	9	11	63	35	75
Kettering Town	42	18	15	8	46	24	72
Woking	42	18	13	11	58	58	67
Southport	42	18	12	12	57	51	66
Runcorn	42	14	19	9	63	57	61
Dagenham & Redbridge	42	15	14	13	62	54	59
Macclesfield Town	42	16	11	15	48	49	59
Dover Athletic	42	17	7	18	48	49	58
Stafford Rangers	42	14	15	13	56	52	57
Altrincham	42	16	9	17	41	42	57
Gateshead	42	15	12	15	45	53	57
Bath City	42	13	17	12	47	38	56
Halifax Town	42	13	16	13	55	49	55
Stalybridge Celtic	42	14	12	16	54	55	54
Northwich Victoria	42	11	19	12	44	45	52
Welling United	42	13	12	17	47	49	51
Telford United	42	13	12	17	41	49	51
Bromsgrove Rovers	42	12	15	15	54	66	51
Yeovil Town	42	14	9	19	49	62	51
Merthyr Tydfil	42	12	15	15	60	61	49
Slough Town	42	11	14	17	44	58	47
Witton Albion	42	7	13	22	37	63	44

Merthyr Tydfil had 2 points deducted

1994-95

	P	W	D	L	F	A	Pts
Macclesfield Town	42	24	8	10	70	40	80
Woking	42	21	12	9	76	54	75
Southport	42	21	9	12	68	50	72
Altrincham Town	42	20	8	14	77	60	68
Stevenage Borough	42	20	7	15	68	49	67
Kettering Town	42	19	10	13	73	56	67
Gateshead	42	19	10	13	61	53	67
Halifax Town	42	17	12	13	68	54	63
Runcorn	42	16	10	16	59	71	58
Northwich Victoria	42	14	15	13	77	66	57
Kidderminster Harriers	42	16	9	17	63	61	57
Bath City	42	15	12	15	55	56	57
Bromsgrove Rovers	42	14	13	15	66	69	55
Farnborough Town	42	15	10	17	45	64	55
Dagenham & Redbridge	42	13	13	16	56	69	52
Dover Athletic	42	11	16	15	48	55	49
Welling United	42	13	10	19	57	74	49
Stalybridge Celtic	42	11	14	17	52	72	47
Telford United	42	10	16	16	53	62	46
Merthyr Tydfil	42	11	11	20	53	63	44
Stafford Rangers	42	9	11	22	53	79	38
Yeovil Town	42	8	14	20	50	71	37

Yeovil Town had 1 point deducted for fielding an ineligible player

1995-96

	P	W	D	L	F	A	Pts
Stevenage Borough	42	27	10	5	101	44	91
Woking	42	25	8	9	83	54	83
Hednesford Town	42	23	7	12	71	46	76
Macclesfield Town	42	22	9	11	66	49	75
Gateshead	42	18	13	11	58	46	67
Southport	42	18	12	12	77	64	66
Kidderminster Harriers	42	18	10	14	78	66	64
Northwich Victoria	42	16	12	14	72	64	60
Morecambe	42	17	8	17	78	72	59
Farnborough Town	42	15	14	13	63	58	59
Bromsgrove Rovers	42	15	14	13	59	57	59
Altrincham	42	15	13	14	59	64	58
Telford United	42	15	10	17	51	56	55
Stalybridge Celtic	42	16	7	19	59	68	55
Halifax Town	42	13	13	16	49	63	52
Kettering Town	42	13	9	20	68	84	48
Slough Town	42	13	8	21	63	76	47
Bath City	42	13	7	22	45	66	46
Welling United	42	10	15	17	42	53	45
Dover Athletic	42	11	7	24	51	74	40
Runcorn	42	9	8	25	48	87	35
Dagenham & Redbridge	42	7	12	23	43	73	33

1996-97

	P	W	D	L	F	A	Pts
Macclesfield Town	42	27	9	6	80	30	90
Kidderminster Harriers	42	26	7	9	84	42	85
Stevenage Borough	42	24	10	8	87	53	82
Morecambe	42	19	9	14	69	56	66
Woking	42	18	10	14	71	63	64
Northwich Victoria	42	17	12	13	61	54	63
Farnborough Town	42	16	13	13	58	53	61
Hednesford Town	42	16	12	14	52	50	60
Telford United	42	16	10	16	46	56	58
Gateshead	42	15	11	16	59	63	56
Southport	42	15	10	17	51	61	55
Rushden & Diamonds	42	14	11	17	61	63	53
Stalybridge Celtic	42	14	10	18	53	58	52
Kettering Town	42	14	9	19	53	62	51
Hayes	42	12	14	16	54	55	50
Slough Town	42	12	14	16	62	65	50
Dover Athletic	42	12	14	16	57	68	50
Welling United	42	13	9	20	50	60	48
Halifax Town	42	12	12	18	55	74	48
Bath City	42	12	11	19	53	80	47
Bromsgrove Rovers	42	12	5	25	41	67	41
Altrincham	42	9	12	21	49	73	39

1997-98

	P	W	D	L	F	A	Pts
Halifax Town	42	25	12	5	74	43	87
Cheltenham Town	42	23	9	10	63	43	78
Woking	42	22	8	12	72	46	74
Rushden & Diamonds	42	23	5	14	79	57	74
Morecambe	42	21	10	11	77	64	73
Hereford United	42	18	13	11	56	49	67
Hednesford Town	42	18	12	12	59	50	66
Slough Town	42	18	10	14	58	49	64
Northwich Victoria	42	15	15	12	63	59	60
Welling United	42	17	9	16	64	62	60
Yeovil Town	42	17	8	17	73	63	59
Hayes	42	16	10	16	62	52	58
Dover Athletic	42	15	10	17	60	70	55
Kettering Town	42	13	13	16	53	60	52
Stevenage Borough	42	13	12	17	59	63	51
Southport	42	13	11	18	56	58	50
Kidderminster Harriers	42	11	14	17	56	63	49
Farnborough Town	42	12	8	22	56	70	44
Leek Town	42	10	14	18	52	67	44
Telford United	42	10	12	20	53	76	42
Gateshead	42	8	11	23	51	87	35
Stalybridge Celtic	42	7	8	27	48	93	29

1998-99

	P	W	D	L	F	A	Pts
Cheltenham Town	42	22	14	6	71	36	80
Kettering Town	42	22	10	10	58	37	76
Hayes	42	22	8	12	63	50	74
Rushden & Diamonds	42	20	12	10	71	42	72
Yeovil Town	42	20	11	11	68	54	71
Stevenage Borough	42	17	17	8	62	45	68
Northwich Victoria	42	19	9	14	60	51	66
Kingstonian	42	17	13	12	50	49	64
Woking	42	18	9	15	51	45	62
Hednesford Town	42	15	16	11	49	44	61
Dover Athletic	42	15	13	14	54	48	58
Forest Green Rovers	42	15	13	14	55	50	58
Hereford United	42	15	10	17	49	46	55
Morecambe	42	15	8	19	60	76	53
Kidderminster Harriers	42	14	9	19	56	52	51
Doncaster Rovers	42	12	12	18	51	55	48
Telford United	42	10	16	16	44	60	46
Southport	42	10	15	17	47	59	45
Barrow	42	11	10	21	40	63	43
Welling United	42	9	14	19	44	65	41
Leek Town	42	8	8	26	48	76	32
Farnborough United	42	7	11	24	41	89	32

1999-2000

	P	W	D	L	F	A	Pts
Kidderminster Harriers	42	26	7	9	75	40	85
Rushden & Diamonds	42	21	13	8	71	42	76
Morecambe	42	18	16	8	70	48	70
Scarborough	42	19	12	11	60	35	69
Kingstonian	42	20	7	15	58	44	67
Dover Athletic	42	18	12	12	65	56	66
Yeovil Town	42	18	10	14	60	63	64
Hereford United	42	15	14	13	61	52	59
Southport	42	15	13	14	55	56	58
Stevenage Borough	42	16	9	17	60	54	57
Hayes	42	16	8	18	57	58	56
Doncaster Rovers	42	15	9	18	46	48	54
Kettering Town	42	12	16	14	44	50	52
Woking	42	13	13	16	45	53	52
Nuneaton Borough	42	12	15	15	49	53	51
Telford United	42	14	9	19	56	66	51
Hednesford Town	42	15	6	21	45	68	51
Northwich Victoria	42	13	12	17	53	78	51
Forest Green Rovers	42	13	8	21	54	63	47
Welling United	42	13	8	21	54	66	47
Altrincham	42	9	19	14	51	60	46
Sutton United	42	8	10	24	39	75	34

2000-2001

Rushden & Diamonds	42	25	11	6	78	36	86
Yeovil Town	42	24	8	10	73	50	80
Dagenham & Redbridge	42	23	8	11	71	54	77
Southport	42	20	9	13	58	46	69
Leigh RMI	42	19	11	12	63	57	68
Telford United	42	19	8	15	51	51	65
Stevenage Borough	42	15	18	9	71	61	63
Chester City	42	16	14	12	49	43	62
Doncaster Rovers	42	15	13	14	47	43	58
Scarborough	42	14	16	12	56	54	58
Hereford United	42	14	15	13	60	46	57
Boston United	42	13	17	12	74	63	56
Nuneaton Borough	42	13	15	14	60	60	54
Woking	42	13	15	14	52	57	54
Dover Athletic	42	14	11	17	54	56	53
Forest Green Rovers	42	11	15	16	43	54	48
Northwich Victoria	42	11	13	18	49	67	46
Hayes	42	12	10	20	44	71	46
Morecambe	42	11	12	19	64	66	45
Kettering Town	42	11	10	21	46	62	43
Kingstonian	42	8	10	24	47	73	34
Hednesford Town	42	5	13	24	46	86	28

2001-2002

Boston United	42	25	9	8	84	42	84
Dagenham & Redbridge	42	24	12	6	70	47	84
Yeovil Town	42	19	13	10	66	53	70
Doncaster Rovers	42	18	13	11	68	46	67
Barnet	42	19	10	13	64	48	67
Morecambe	42	17	11	14	63	67	62
Farnborough Town	42	18	7	17	66	54	61
Margate	42	14	16	12	59	53	58
Telford United	42	14	15	13	63	58	57
Nuneaton Borough	42	16	9	17	57	57	57
Stevenage Borough	42	15	10	17	57	60	55
Scarborough	42	14	14	14	55	63	55
Northwich Victoria	42	16	7	19	57	70	55
Chester City	42	15	9	18	54	51	54
Southport	42	13	14	15	53	49	53
Leigh RMI	42	15	8	19	56	58	53
Hereford United	42	14	10	18	50	53	52
Forest Green Rovers	42	12	15	15	54	76	51
Woking	42	13	9	20	59	70	48
Hayes	42	13	5	24	53	80	44
Stalybridge Celtic	42	11	10	21	40	69	43
Dover Athletic	42	11	6	25	41	65	39

2002-2003

Yeovil Town	42	28	11	3	100	37	95
Morecambe	42	23	9	10	86	42	78
Doncaster Rovers	42	22	12	8	73	47	78
Chester City	42	21	12	9	59	31	75
Dagenham & Redbridge	42	21	9	12	71	59	72
Hereford United	42	19	7	16	64	51	64
Scarborough	42	18	10	14	63	54	64
Halifax Town	42	18	10	14	50	51	64
Forest Green Rovers	42	17	8	17	61	62	59
Margate	42	15	11	16	60	66	56
Barnet	42	13	14	15	65	68	53
Stevenage Borough	42	14	10	18	61	55	52
Farnborough Town	42	13	12	17	57	56	51
Northwich Victoria	42	13	12	17	66	72	51
Telford United	42	14	7	21	54	69	49
Burton Albion	42	13	10	19	52	77	49
Gravesend & Northfleet	42	12	12	18	62	73	48
Leigh RMI	42	14	6	22	44	71	48
Woking	42	11	14	17	52	81	47
Nuneaton Borough	42	13	7	22	51	78	46
Southport	42	11	12	19	54	69	45
Kettering Town	42	8	7	27	37	73	31

2003-2004

Chester City	42	27	11	4	85	34	92
Hereford United	42	28	7	7	103	44	91
Shrewsbury Town	42	20	14	8	67	42	74
Barnet	42	19	14	9	60	46	71
Aldershot Town	42	20	10	12	80	67	70
Exeter City	42	19	12	11	71	57	69
Morecambe	42	20	7	15	66	66	67
Stevenage Borough	42	18	9	15	58	52	63
Woking	42	15	16	11	65	52	61
Accrington Stanley	42	15	13	14	68	61	58
Gravesend & Northfleet	42	14	15	13	69	66	57
Telford United	42	15	10	17	49	51	55
Dagenham & Redbridge	42	15	9	18	59	64	54
Burton Albion	42	15	7	20	57	59	51
Scarborough	42	12	15	15	51	54	51
Margate	42	14	9	19	56	64	51
Tamworth	42	13	10	19	49	68	49
Forest Green Rovers	42	12	12	18	58	80	48
Halifax Town	42	12	8	22	43	65	44
Farnborough Town	42	10	9	23	53	74	39
Leigh RMI	42	7	8	27	46	97	29
Northwich Victoria	42	4	11	27	30	80	23

Burton Albion had 1 point deducted.

2004-2005

Conference National

Barnet	42	26	8	8	90	44	86
Hereford United	42	21	11	10	68	41	74
Carlisle United	42	20	13	9	74	37	73
Aldershot Town	42	21	10	11	68	52	73
Stevenage Borough	42	22	6	14	65	52	72
Exeter City	42	20	11	11	71	50	71
Morecambe	42	19	14	9	69	50	71
Woking	42	18	14	10	58	45	68
Halifax Town	42	19	9	14	74	56	66
Accrington Stanley	42	18	11	13	72	58	65
Dagenham & Redbridge	42	19	8	15	68	60	65
Crawley Town	42	16	9	17	50	50	57
Scarborough	42	14	14	14	60	46	56
Gravesend & Northfleet	42	13	11	18	58	64	50
Tamworth	42	14	11	17	53	63	50
Burton Albion	42	13	11	18	50	66	50
York City	42	11	10	21	39	66	43
Canvey Island	42	9	15	18	53	65	42
Northwich Victoria	42	14	10	18	58	72	42
Forest Green Rovers	42	6	15	21	41	81	33
Farnborough Town	42	6	11	25	35	89	29
Leigh RMI	42	4	6	32	31	98	18

Northwich Victoria had 10 points deducted.
Tamworth had 3 points deducted.

Conference North

Southport	42	25	9	8	83	45	84
Nuneaton Borough	42	25	6	11	68	45	81
Droylsden	42	24	7	11	82	52	79
Kettering Town	42	21	7	14	56	50	70
Altrincham	42	19	12	11	66	46	69
Harrogate Town	42	19	11	12	62	49	68
Worcester City	42	16	12	14	59	53	60
Stafford Rangers	42	14	17	11	52	44	59
Redditch United	42	18	8	16	65	59	59
Hucknall Town	42	15	14	13	59	57	59
Gainsborough Trinity	42	16	9	17	55	55	57
Hinckley United	42	15	11	16	55	62	56
Lancaster City	42	14	12	16	51	59	54
Alfreton Town	42	15	8	19	53	55	53
Vauxhall Motors	42	14	11	17	48	57	53
Barrow	42	14	10	18	50	64	52
Worksop Town	42	16	12	14	59	59	50
Moor Green	42	13	10	19	55	64	49
Stalybridge Celtic	42	12	12	18	52	70	48
Runcorn FC Halton	42	10	12	20	44	63	42
Ashton United	42	8	9	25	46	79	33
Bradford Park Avenue	42	5	9	28	37	70	24

Worksop Town had 10 points deducted.
Redditch United had 3 points deducted.

Conference South

	P	W	D	L	F	A	Pts
Grays Athletic	42	30	8	4	118	31	98
Cambridge City	42	23	6	13	60	44	75
Thurrock	42	21	6	15	61	56	69
Lewes	42	18	11	13	73	64	65
Eastbourne Borough	42	18	10	14	65	47	64
Basingstoke Town	42	19	6	17	57	52	63
Weymouth	42	17	11	14	62	59	62
Dorchester Town	42	17	11	14	77	81	62
Bognor Regis Town	42	17	9	16	70	65	60
Bishop's Stortford	42	17	8	17	70	66	59
Weston-super-Mare	42	15	13	14	55	60	58
Hayes	42	15	11	16	55	57	56
Havant & Waterlooville	42	16	7	19	64	69	55
St. Albans City	42	16	6	20	64	76	54
Sutton United	42	14	11	17	60	71	53
Welling United	42	15	7	20	64	68	52
Hornchurch	42	17	10	15	71	63	51
Newport County	42	13	11	18	56	61	50
Carshalton Athletic	42	13	9	20	44	72	48
Maidenhead United	42	12	10	20	54	81	46
Margate	42	12	8	22	54	75	34
Redbridge	42	11	3	28	50	86	33

Hornchurch and Margate had 10 points deducted.
Redbridge had 3 points deducted.

2005-2006

Conference National

	P	W	D	L	F	A	Pts
Accrington Stanley	42	28	7	7	76	45	91
Hereford United	42	22	14	6	59	33	80
Grays Athletic	42	21	13	8	94	55	76
Halifax Town	42	21	12	9	55	40	75
Morecambe	42	22	8	12	68	41	74
Stevenage Borough	42	19	12	11	62	47	69
Exeter City	42	18	9	15	65	48	63
York City	42	17	12	13	63	48	63
Burton Albion	42	16	12	14	50	52	60
Dagenham & Redbridge	42	16	10	16	63	59	58
Woking	42	14	14	14	58	47	56
Cambridge United	42	15	10	17	51	57	55
Aldershot Town	42	16	6	20	61	74	54
Canvey Island	42	13	12	17	47	58	51
Kidderminster Harriers	42	13	11	18	39	55	50
Gravesend & Northfleet	42	13	10	19	45	57	49
Crawley Town	42	12	11	19	48	55	47
Southport	42	10	10	22	36	68	40
Forest Green Rovers	42	8	14	20	49	62	38
Tamworth	42	8	14	20	32	63	38
Scarborough	42	9	10	23	40	66	37
Altrincham	42	10	11	21	40	71	23

Altrincham had 18 points deducted for fielding an ineligible player but
were not relegated after Canvey Island withdrew from the League and
Scarborough were relegated for a breach of the rules.

Conference North

	P	W	D	L	F	A	Pts
Northwich Victoria	42	29	5	8	97	49	92
Stafford Rangers	42	25	10	7	68	34	85
Nuneaton Borough	42	22	11	9	68	43	77
Droylsden	42	20	12	10	80	56	72
Harrogate Town	42	22	5	15	66	56	71
Kettering Town	42	19	10	13	63	49	67
Stalybridge Celtic	42	19	9	14	74	54	66
Worcester City	42	16	14	12	58	46	62
Moor Green	42	15	16	11	67	64	61
Hinckley United	42	14	16	12	60	55	58
Hyde United (P)	42	15	11	16	68	61	56
Hucknall Town	42	14	13	15	56	55	55
Workington (P)	42	14	13	15	60	62	55
Barrow	42	12	11	19	62	67	47
Lancaster City	42	12	11	19	52	66	47
Gainsborough Trinity	42	11	13	18	45	65	46
Alfreton Town	42	10	15	17	46	58	45
Vauxhall Motors	42	12	7	23	50	71	43
Worksop Town	42	10	11	21	46	71	41
Redditch United	42	9	12	21	53	78	39
Leigh RMI	42	9	13	20	45	79	39
Hednesford Town	42	7	14	21	42	87	35

Leigh RMI had 1 point deducted.

Conference South

	P	W	D	L	F	A	Pts
Weymouth	42	30	4	8	80	34	90
St. Albans City	42	27	5	10	94	47	86
Farnborough Town	42	23	9	10	65	41	78
Lewes	42	21	10	11	78	57	73
Histon	42	21	8	13	70	56	71
Havant & Waterlooville	42	21	10	11	64	48	70
Cambridge City	42	20	10	12	78	46	67
Eastleigh	42	21	3	18	65	58	66
Welling United	42	16	17	9	58	44	65
Thurrock	42	16	10	16	60	60	58
Dorchester Town	42	16	7	19	60	72	55
Bognor Regis Town	42	12	13	17	54	55	49
Sutton United	42	13	10	19	48	61	49
Weston-super-Mare	42	14	7	21	57	88	49
Bishop's Stortford	42	11	15	16	55	63	48
Yeading	42	13	8	21	47	62	47
Eastbourne Borough	42	10	16	16	51	61	46
Newport County	42	12	8	22	50	67	44
Basingstoke Town	42	12	8	22	47	72	44
Hayes	42	11	9	22	47	60	42
Carshalton Athletic	42	8	16	18	42	68	40
Maidenhead United	42	8	9	25	49	99	31

Weymouth had 4 points deducted.
Havant & Waterlooville and Cambridge City had 3 points deducted.
Maidenhead United had 2 points deducted.

ISTHMIAN LEAGUE

1905-06

London Caledonians	10	7	1	2	25	8	15
Clapton	10	6	1	3	11	13	13
Casuals	10	3	4	3	14	14	10
Civil Service	10	4	1	5	16	20	9
Ealing Association	10	3	2	5	15	19	8
Ilford	10	1	3	6	5	12	5

1906-07

Ilford	10	8	2	0	26	9	18
London Caledonians	10	6	0	4	19	14	12
Clapton	10	4	3	3	18	11	11
Civil Service	10	3	1	6	11	19	7
Ealing Association	10	3	1	6	12	22	7
Casuals	10	2	1	7	15	26	5

1907-08

London Caledonians	10	5	2	3	20	15	12
Clapton	10	4	3	3	24	14	11
Ilford	10	5	1	4	28	22	11
Oxford City	10	5	1	4	20	20	11
Dulwich Hamlet	10	3	2	5	15	18	8
West Norwood	10	3	1	6	13	31	7

1908-09

Bromley	18	11	1	6	42	29	23
Leytonstone	18	9	4	5	43	31	22
Ilford	18	9	4	5	37	36	22
Dulwich Hamlet	18	9	2	7	39	30	20
Clapton	18	8	4	6	34	32	20
Oxford City	18	6	4	8	29	32	16
Nunhead	18	7	2	9	31	35	16
Shepherd's Bush	18	6	3	9	26	44	15
London Caledonians	18	4	6	8	25	34	14
West Norwood	18	5	2	11	40	43	12

1909-10

Bromley	18	11	4	3	32	10	26
Clapton	18	10	4	4	56	19	24
Nunhead	18	10	4	4	49	26	24
Ilford	18	10	3	5	31	17	23
Dulwich Hamlet	18	8	4	6	26	26	20
Leytonstone	18	7	3	8	44	46	17
Oxford City	18	5	4	9	28	45	14
London Caledonians	18	5	3	10	19	40	13
West Norwood	18	5	2	11	28	54	12
Shepherd's Bush	18	2	3	13	23	55	7

1910-11

Clapton	18	11	4	3	39	19	26
Leytonstone	18	12	1	5	47	30	25
Dulwich Hamlet	18	8	5	5	28	22	21
Oxford City	18	7	4	7	32	43	18
Ilford	18	8	1	9	41	32	17
Shepherd's Bush	18	7	3	8	31	27	17
Bromley	18	8	4	6	32	27	16
Nunhead	18	5	4	9	32	36	14
West Norwood	18	4	5	9	24	43	13
London Caledonians	18	3	3	12	18	45	9

Bromley had 4 points deducted

1911-12

London Caledonians	20	11	7	2	39	25	29
Ilford	20	11	3	6	37	24	25
Nunhead	20	10	5	5	36	30	25
Dulwich Hamlet	20	8	5	7	33	23	21
West Norwood	20	9	3	8	38	38	21
Clapton	20	7	5	8	37	37	19
Woking	20	7	5	8	38	41	19
Shepherd's Bush	20	5	6	9	39	49	16
Leytonstone	20	5	6	9	28	38	16
Oxford City	20	5	5	10	33	36	15
Tunbridge Wells	20	5	4	11	23	40	14

1912-13

London Caledonians	20	14	5	1	38	12	33
Leytonstone	20	12	3	5	45	20	27
Nunhead	20	12	3	5	36	23	27
Clapton ·	20	7	7	6	23	20	21
Dulwich Hamlet	20	8	4	8	34	28	20
Woking	20	7	5	8	33	40	19
Oxford City	20	6	6	8	23	39	18
Ilford	20	6	5	9	27	37	17
Shepherd's Bush	20	5	5	10	26	38	15
Tunbridge Wells	20	5	4	11	22	36	14
West Norwood	20	3	3	14	23	37	9

1913-14

London Caledonians	20	12	6	2	55	23	30
Nunhead	20	11	6	3	49	27	28
Ilford	20	11	4	5	52	35	26
Dulwich Hamlet	20	10	4	6	34	22	24
New Crusaders	20	10	3	7	40	30	23
Oxford City	20	10	0	10	42	42	20
Leytonstone	20	8	4	8	29	32	20
Clapton	20	8	3	9	29	27	19
Shepherd's Bush	20	7	2	11	24	46	16
West Norwood	20	4	3	13	27	47	11
Woking	20	1	1	18	11	61	3

1919

Leytonstone	8	5	1	2	21	7	11
Ilford	8	4	2	2	22	16	10
Dulwich Hamlet	8	3	2	3	19	17	8
Nunhead	8	3	2	3	18	19	8
Clapton	8	0	3	5	14	35	3

1919-20

Dulwich Hamlet	22	15	3	4	58	16	33
Nunhead	22	14	5	3	48	26	33
Tufnell Park	22	12	4	6	45	32	28
Ilford	22	13	1	8	63	42	27
Oxford City	22	12	3	7	63	51	27
London Caledonians	22	10	3	9	32	30	23
Leytonstone	22	8	3	11	50	43	19
Clapton	22	8	3	11	38	44	19
Civil Service	22	7	4	11	35	40	18
Woking	22	6	3	13	36	42	15
West Norwood	22	5	4	13	19	53	14
Casuals	22	3	2	17	20	88	8

1920-21

Ilford	22	16	4	2	70	24	36
London Caledonians	22	13	5	4	45	17	31
Tufnell Park	22	14	3	5	43	24	31
Nunhead	22	12	5	5	53	33	29
Dulwich Hamlet	22	11	6	5	60	30	28
Oxford City	22	12	3	7	56	38	27
Leytonstone	22	8	6	8	36	29	22
Clapton	22	7	7	8	33	52	21
Civil Service	22	3	7	12	28	45	13
Woking	22	3	5	14	16	43	11
Casuals	22	3	3	16	31	87	9
West Norwood	22	2	2	18	18	67	6

1921-22

Ilford	26	17	4	5	66	34	38
Dulwich Hamlet	26	14	8	4	65	24	36
London Caledonians	26	16	4	6	41	21	36
Nunhead	26	12	5	9	65	41	29
Clapton	26	13	3	10	51	46	29
Tufnell Park	26	10	7	9	44	39	27
Oxford City	26	18	2	12	48	47	26
Wycombe Wanderers	26	18	2	12	61	64	26
Civil Service	26	9	8	9	60	48	26
Woking	26	10	6	10	39	49	26
Leytonstone	26	9	6	11	41	48	24
West Norwood	26	8	5	13	43	57	21
Wimbledon	26	7	4	15	52	56	18
Casuals	26	0	2	24	25	107	2

1922-23

Clapton	26	15	7	4	51	33	37
Nunhead	26	15	5	6	52	32	35
London Caledonians	26	13	7	6	43	26	33
Ilford	26	11	7	8	57	38	29
Casuals	26	12	5	9	68	51	29
Civil Service	26	9	10	7	39	36	28
Wycombe Wanderers	26	11	4	11	61	61	26
Dulwich Hamlet	26	9	7	10	60	44	25
Leytonstone	26	9	7	10	45	56	25
Tufnell Park	26	9	5	12	41	45	23
Wimbledon	26	10	2	14	49	50	22
Woking	26	7	6	13	42	67	20
Oxford City	26	6	5	15	45	68	17
West Norwood	26	5	5	16	25	71	15

1923-24

St Albans City	26	17	5	4	72	38	39
Dulwich Hamlet	26	15	6	5	49	28	36
Clapton	26	14	5	7	73	50	33
Wycombe Wanderers	26	14	5	7	88	65	33
London Caledonians	26	14	3	9	53	49	31
Civil Service	26	12	5	9	52	47	29
Casuals	26	13	1	12	65	54	27
Ilford	26	9	6	11	56	59	24
Nunhead	26	8	8	10	41	46	24
Wimbledon	26	8	4	14	43	62	20
Tufnell Park	26	8	2	16	38	53	18
Woking	26	5	8	13	31	62	18
Oxford City	27	7	2	17	53	74	16
Leytonstone	26	6	4	16	41	68	16

1924-25

London Caledonians	26	18	5	3	76	36	41
Clapton	26	19	1	6	64	34	39
St Albans City	26	16	2	8	69	39	34
Tufnell Park	26	11	4	11	47	41	26
Ilford	26	11	4	11	46	42	26
Leytonstone	26	12	2	12	55	63	26
The Casuals	26	12	1	13	55	58	25
Wycombe Wanderers	26	11	2	13	58	61	24
Civil Service	26	10	4	12	52	64	24
Nunhead	26	9	5	12	45	43	23
Wimbledon	26	10	2	14	50	54	22
Dulwich Hamlet	26	8	5	13	42	57	21
Oxford City	26	9	2	15	38	71	20
Woking	26	5	3	18	33	67	13

1925-26

Dulwich Hamlet	26	20	1	5	80	49	41
London Caledonians	26	18	1	7	81	44	37
Clapton	26	14	4	8	64	50	32
Wycombe Wanderers	26	14	3	9	97	83	31
St Albans City	26	12	6	8	76	54	30
Nunhead	26	13	4	9	49	43	30
Ilford	26	13	2	11	81	70	28
Leytonstone	26	12	1	13	75	63	25
Woking	26	8	6	12	56	73	22
Tufnell Park	26	8	5	13	36	53	21
The Casuals	26	8	4	14	48	61	20
Wimbledon	26	9	1	16	61	77	19
Oxford City	26	8	1	17	48	76	17
Civil Service	26	5	1	20	43	99	11

1926-27

St Albans City	26	20	1	5	96	34	41
Ilford	26	18	0	9	76	57	34
Wimbledon	26	15	3	8	72	45	33
Nunhead	26	11	8	7	51	33	30
Woking	26	12	6	8	68	60	30
London Caledonians	26	11	7	8	58	47	29
Clapton	26	11	4	11	58	60	26
Leytonstone	26	11	1	14	54	78	23
Dulwich Hamlet	26	9	4	13	60	58	22
Wycombe Wanderers	26	10	2	14	59	86	22
Tufnell Park	26	8	4	14	45	55	20
Oxford City	26	7	5	14	46	72	19
The Casuals	26	8	3	15	37	78	19
Civil Service	26	6	4	16	48	65	16

1927-28

St Albans City	26	15	5	6	86	50	35
London Caledonians	26	12	9	5	63	38	33
Ilford	26	14	4	8	72	54	32
Woking	26	13	5	8	72	56	31
Nunhead	26	13	2	11	57	54	28
Wimbledon	26	12	3	11	57	48	27
Leytonstone	26	13	1	12	53	56	27
Clapton	26	8	10	8	52	47	26
Dulwich Hamlet	26	8	9	9	56	49	25
The Casuals	26	8	8	10	54	58	24
Wycombe Wanderers	26	9	5	12	60	69	23
Oxford City	26	7	7	12	36	57	21
Civil Service	26	8	4	14	38	76	20
Tufnell Park	26	4	4	18	38	82	12

1928-29

Nunhead	26	15	6	5	47	35	36
London Caledonians	26	15	4	7	65	33	34
Dulwich Hamlet	26	14	6	6	65	34	34
Wimbledon	26	9	10	7	66	54	28
Ilford	26	12	3	11	67	52	27
Clapton	26	11	5	10	60	55	27
Tufnell Park	26	11	5	10	58	55	27
St Albans City	26	12	3	11	63	69	27
Leytonstone	26	11	3	12	56	79	25
Wycombe Wanderers	26	10	3	13	58	60	23
Oxford City	26	10	3	13	61	71	23
The Casuals	26	8	5	13	49	60	21
Woking	26	8	3	15	39	65	19
Civil Service	26	4	5	17	39	71	13

1929-30

Nunhead	26	19	3	4	69	36	41
Dulwich Hamlet	26	15	6	5	74	39	36
Kingstonian	26	15	4	7	57	37	34
Ilford	26	16	1	9	84	60	33
Woking	26	11	5	10	66	65	27
Wimbledon	26	11	2	13	64	66	24
Wycombe Wanderers	26	10	4	12	49	52	24
The Casuals	26	8	7	11	50	51	23
Oxford City	26	10	3	13	45	60	23
St Albans City	26	9	4	13	54	77	22
Clapton	26	8	4	14	47	57	20
London Caledonians	26	8	3	15	49	69	19
Leytonstone	26	8	3	15	48	68	19
Tufnell Park	26	6	7	13	35	54	19

1930-31

Wimbledon	26	18	6	2	69	37	42
Dulwich Hamlet	26	12	9	5	51	39	33
Wycombe Wanderers	26	12	6	8	67	45	30
The Casuals	26	12	6	8	71	56	30
St Albans City	26	11	7	8	67	66	29
Ilford	26	10	6	10	70	62	26
Oxford City	26	10	5	11	43	48	25
London Caledonians	26	8	8	10	43	53	24
Kingstonian	26	10	4	12	49	64	24
Tufnell Park	26	9	5	12	45	61	23
Nunhead	26	9	4	13	49	54	22
Woking	26	9	4	13	56	63	22
Clapton	26	7	4	15	62	75	18
Leytonstone	26	6	4	16	46	65	16

1931-32

Wimbledon	26	17	2	7	60	35	36
Ilford	26	13	9	4	71	45	35
Dulwich Hamlet	26	15	3	8	69	43	33
Wycombe Wanderers	26	14	5	7	72	50	33
Oxford City	26	15	2	9	63	49	32
Kingstonian	26	13	3	10	71	50	29
Tufnell Park	26	9	7	10	50	48	25
Nunhead	26	9	7	10	54	61	25
The Casuals	26	10	4	12	59	65	24
Clapton	26	9	5	12	50	57	23
Leytonstone	26	9	3	14	36	61	21
St Albans City	26	8	4	14	57	78	20
Woking	26	6	5	15	44	64	17
London Caledonians	26	2	7	17	24	74	11

1932-33

Dulwich Hamlet	26	15	6	5	71	45	36
Leytonstone	26	16	4	6	66	43	36
Kingstonian	26	15	2	9	77	49	32
Ilford	26	14	0	12	60	58	28
The Casuals	26	12	2	12	48	36	26
Tufnell Park	26	11	3	12	51	51	25
St Albans City	26	12	1	13	57	63	25
Clapton	26	10	5	11	51	65	25
Oxford City	26	9	6	11	49	54	24
Woking	26	10	4	12	53	61	24
Wycombe Wanderers	26	10	4	12	47	56	24
Nunhead	26	8	6	12	42	50	22
Wimbledon	26	8	5	13	55	67	21
London Caledonians	26	5	6	15	35	64	16

1933-34

Kingstonian	26	15	7	4	80	42	37
Dulwich Hamlet	26	15	5	6	68	36	35
Wimbledon	26	13	7	6	62	35	33
Tufnell Park	26	14	5	7	55	50	33
Ilford	26	15	2	9	60	56	32
The Casuals	26	13	5	8	47	32	31
Leytonstone	26	13	3	10	55	48	29
Nunhead	26	10	5	11	48	44	25
London Caledonians	26	7	8	11	29	51	22
Wycombe Wanderers	26	9	2	15	57	60	20
St Albans City	26	8	4	14	44	75	20
Oxford City	26	7	4	15	45	57	18
Clapton	26	5	6	15	35	62	16
Woking	26	6	1	19	43	81	13

1934-35

Wimbledon	26	14	7	5	63	30	35
Oxford City	26	14	4	8	69	50	32
Leytonstone	26	15	2	9	49	36	32
Dulwich Hamlet	26	11	7	8	66	45	29
Tufnell Park	26	11	7	8	53	44	29
Kingstonian	26	11	6	9	44	40	28
Nunhead	26	10	7	9	35	34	27
London Caledonians	26	9	7	10	40	41	25
St Albans City	26	9	6	11	61	80	24
Ilford	26	9	6	11	40	56	24
Clapton	26	7	7	12	46	48	21
Woking	26	9	3	14	44	63	21
Wycombe Wanderers	26	7	6	13	51	69	20
The Casuals	26	6	5	15	37	57	17

1935-36

Wimbledon	26	19	2	5	82	29	40
The Casuals	26	14	5	7	60	45	33
Ilford	26	13	3	10	67	47	29
Dulwich Hamlet	26	10	8	8	64	47	28
Nunhead	26	11	6	9	51	40	28
Wycombe Wanderers	26	13	2	11	60	68	28
Clapton	26	11	5	10	42	46	27
Oxford City	26	11	4	11	60	58	26
St Albans City	26	11	2	13	59	64	24
Woking	26	9	4	13	43	62	22
Tufnell Park	26	9	3	14	42	61	21
London Caledonians	26	9	3	14	35	52	21
Kingstonian	26	9	2	15	43	56	20
Leytonstone	26	7	3	16	34	67	17

1936-37

Kingstonian	26	18	3	5	63	43	39
Nunhead	26	17	3	6	77	32	37
Leytonstone	26	16	4	6	71	42	36
Ilford	26	14	5	7	86	39	33
Dulwich Hamlet	26	12	6	8	64	48	30
Wycombe Wanderers	26	10	5	11	55	52	25
Wimbledon	26	9	7	10	52	53	25
Clapton	26	10	5	11	42	51	25
The Casuals	26	10	3	13	46	58	23
Woking	26	9	4	13	53	69	22
Oxford City	26	8	5	13	56	89	21
St Albans City	26	7	5	14	44	62	19
Tufnell Park	26	4	7	15	43	74	15
London Caledonians	26	5	4	17	26	66	14

1937-38

Leytonstone	26	17	6	3	72	34	40
Ilford	26	17	3	6	70	39	37
Tufnell Park	26	15	2	9	62	47	32
Nunhead	26	14	3	9	52	44	31
Wycombe Wanderers	26	12	5	9	69	55	29
Dulwich Hamlet	26	13	3	10	57	46	29
Kingstonian	26	12	4	10	51	48	28
Clapton	26	9	6	11	49	53	24
Wimbledon	26	10	3	13	62	49	23
London Caledonians	26	9	4	13	44	55	22
Oxford City	26	7	7	12	35	71	21
The Casuals	26	8	3	15	51	74	19
Woking	26	7	2	17	41	72	16
St Albans City	26	4	5	17	31	60	13

1938-39

Leytonstone	26	18	4	4	68	32	40
Ilford	26	17	4	5	68	32	38
Kingstonian	26	17	3	6	62	39	37
Dulwich Hamlet	26	15	5	6	60	32	35
Wimbledon	26	14	3	9	88	56	31
Nunhead	26	11	6	9	54	44	28
The Casuals	26	11	6	9	54	51	28
Clapton	26	12	2	12	69	61	26
Wycombe Wanderers	26	10	6	10	62	62	26
St Albans City	26	8	5	13	44	50	21
Woking	26	9	2	15	35	56	20
Oxford City	26	4	4	18	44	84	12
Tufnell Park	26	4	4	18	33	87	12
London Caledonians	26	3	4	19	26	81	10

1945-46

Walthamstow Avenue	26	21	0	5	100	31	42
Oxford City	26	17	6	3	91	40	40
Romford	26	15	3	8	83	59	33
Dulwich Hamlet	26	14	2	10	63	59	30
Tufnell Park	26	12	4	10	70	55	28
Woking	26	10	7	9	56	54	27
Ilford	26	12	2	12	56	71	26
Leytonstone	26	11	3	12	61	75	25
Wycombe Wanderers	26	9	3	14	80	88	21
Wimbledon	26	7	6	13	52	72	20
Corinthian Casuals	26	8	4	14	58	83	20
Clapton	26	8	3	15	51	62	19
St Albans City	26	6	6	14	48	85	18
Kingstonian	26	6	3	17	48	86	15

1946-47

Leytonstone	26	19	2	5	92	36	40
Dulwich Hamlet	26	17	3	6	78	46	37
Romford	26	13	8	5	76	52	34
Walthamstow Avenue	26	13	4	9	64	37	30
Oxford City	26	12	6	8	70	51	30
Kingstonian	26	12	4	10	54	57	28
Wycombe Wanderers	26	9	8	9	62	62	26
Wimbledon	26	10	5	11	68	64	25
Ilford	26	7	7	12	66	78	21
Tufnell Park	26	8	5	13	45	69	21
Woking	26	7	7	12	34	62	21
Clapton	26	6	8	12	41	59	20
St Albans City	26	7	5	14	47	79	19
Corinthian Casuals	26	4	4	18	36	80	12

1947-48

Leytonstone	26	19	1	6	87	38	39
Kingstonian	26	16	6	4	74	39	38
Walthamstow Avenue	26	17	3	6	61	37	37
Dulwich Hamlet	26	17	2	7	71	39	36
Wimbledon	26	13	6	7	66	40	32
Romford	26	14	1	11	53	47	29
Oxford City	26	10	5	11	50	68	25
Woking	26	10	3	13	63	55	23
Ilford	26	7	8	11	51	59	22
St Albans City	26	9	2	15	43	56	20
Wycombe Wanderers	26	7	5	14	51	65	19
Tufnell Park	26	7	4	15	38	83	18
Clapton	26	5	4	17	35	69	14
Corinthian Casuals	26	5	2	19	33	81	12

1948-49

Dulwich Hamlet	26	15	6	5	60	31	36
Walthamstow Avenue	26	16	4	6	65	38	36
Wimbledon	26	15	4	7	64	41	34
Ilford	26	14	3	9	56	36	31
Oxford City	26	13	5	8	48	34	31
Leytonstone	26	12	6	8	49	41	30
Woking	26	14	1	11	64	59	29
Romford	26	11	3	12	47	54	25
Kingstonian	26	10	4	12	43	47	24
Corinthian Casuals	26	11	2	13	47	59	24
Wycombe Wanderers	26	11	2	13	49	61	24
St Albans City	26	6	6	14	40	60	16
Clapton	26	5	5	16	32	61	15
Tufnell Park	26	1	5	20	28	70	7

St Albans City had 2 points deducted

1949-50

Leytonstone	26	17	5	4	77	31	39
Wimbledon	26	18	2	6	72	51	38
Kingstonian	26	16	3	7	59	39	35
Walthamstow Avenue	26	14	6	6	73	42	34
Dulwich Hamlet	26	14	3	9	60	47	31
St Albans City	26	12	3	11	59	45	27
Woking	26	10	6	10	60	71	26
Wycombe Wanderers	26	9	7	10	51	52	25
Romford	26	10	4	12	45	49	24
Ilford	26	10	4	12	46	53	24
Clapton	26	8	6	12	51	59	22
Oxford City	26	6	6	14	35	54	18
Corinthian Casuals	26	4	5	17	41	69	13
Tufnell Park	26	3	2	21	24	91	8

1950-51

Leytonstone	26	20	3	3	72	26	43
Walthamstow Avenue	26	15	4	7	57	37	34
Romford	26	15	3	8	58	49	33
Wimbledon	26	13	5	8	58	39	31
Dulwich Hamlet	26	14	2	10	54	43	30
Woking	26	11	6	9	65	55	28
Ilford	26	12	4	10	44	45	28
Corinthian Casuals	26	13	0	13	62	60	26
St Albans City	26	11	4	11	32	36	26
Kingstonian	26	9	4	13	46	54	22
Wycombe Wanderers	26	8	3	15	46	64	19
Oxford City	26	7	4	15	47	65	18
Clapton	26	6	5	15	29	50	17
Tufnell Park Edmonton	26	4	1	21	24	73	9

1951-52

Leytonstone	26	13	9	4	63	36	35
Wimbledon	26	16	3	7	65	44	35
Walthamstow Avenue	26	15	4	7	71	43	34
Romford	26	14	4	8	64	42	32
Kingstonian	26	11	7	8	62	48	29
Wycombe Wanderers	26	12	5	9	64	59	29
Woking	26	11	5	10	60	71	27
Dulwich Hamlet	26	11	4	11	60	53	26
Corinthian Casuals	26	11	4	11	55	66	26
St Albans City	26	9	7	10	48	53	25
Ilford	26	8	5	13	32	47	21
Clapton	26	9	2	15	50	59	20
Oxford City	26	6	3	17	50	72	15
Tufnell Park Edmonton	26	2	6	18	25	73	10

1952-53

Walthamstow Avenue	28	19	6	3	53	25	44
Bromley	28	17	4	7	71	35	38
Leytonstone	28	14	6	8	60	38	34
Wimbledon	28	14	5	9	68	37	33
Kingstonian	28	13	6	9	62	50	32
Dulwich Hamlet	28	15	2	11	62	52	32
Romford	28	12	8	8	62	52	32
Wycombe Wanderers	28	14	2	12	54	62	30
St Albans City	28	11	6	11	43	57	28
Barking	28	9	7	12	42	51	25
Ilford	28	10	4	14	59	57	24
Woking	28	10	4	14	57	72	24
Corinthian Casuals	28	7	9	12	45	56	23
Oxford City	28	5	2	21	37	87	12
Clapton	28	2	5	21	27	71	9

1953-54

Bromley	28	18	3	7	76	45	39
Walthamstow Avenue	28	13	7	8	55	30	33
Wycombe Wanderers	28	15	3	10	65	44	33
Ilford	28	11	10	7	48	44	32
Corinthian Casuals	28	12	7	9	59	44	31
Woking	28	13	4	11	54	58	30
Leytonstone	28	12	5	11	58	48	29
St Albans City	28	11	6	11	54	55	28
Dulwich Hamlet	28	11	6	11	55	57	28
Romford	28	11	5	12	57	54	27
Clapton	28	11	5	12	42	56	27
Barking	28	11	2	15	59	84	24
Kingstonian	28	8	7	13	59	71	23
Wimbledon	28	7	8	13	43	59	22
Oxford City	28	4	6	18	49	84	14

1954-55

Walthamstow Avenue	28	21	1	6	80	38	43
St Albans City	28	18	3	7	61	41	39
Bromley	28	18	2	8	66	34	38
Wycombe Wanderers	28	16	3	9	68	43	35
Ilford	28	13	5	10	64	46	31
Barking	28	15	1	12	55	51	31
Woking	28	12	3	13	75	79	27
Kingstonian	28	10	7	11	47	57	27
Leytonstone	28	10	4	14	35	51	24
Oxford City	28	10	3	15	43	74	23
Clapton	28	9	4	15	41	50	22
Wimbledon	28	10	2	16	48	62	22
Corinthian Casuals	28	9	3	16	50	65	21
Dulwich Hamlet	28	7	5	16	48	60	19
Romford	28	4	10	14	43	73	18

1955-56

Wycombe Wanderers	28	19	5	4	82	36	43
Bromley	28	12	7	9	54	43	31
Leytonstone	28	12	7	9	50	44	31
Woking	28	14	3	11	62	60	31
Barking	28	12	7	9	41	45	31
Kingstonian	28	12	6	10	67	64	30
Walthamstow Avenue	28	13	3	12	61	45	29
Ilford	28	10	8	10	44	52	28
Oxford City	28	10	7	11	48	55	27
Clapton	28	9	8	11	45	48	26
Wimbledon	28	12	2	14	51	62	26
Corinthian Casuals	28	9	7	12	56	56	25
Dulwich Hamlet	28	9	6	13	55	67	24
Romford	28	9	6	13	42	55	24
St Albans City	28	2	10	16	36	62	14

1956-57

Wycombe Wanderers	30	18	6	6	86	53	42
Woking	30	20	1	9	104	47	41
Bromley	30	16	5	9	78	60	37
Oxford City	30	16	3	11	65	57	35
Ilford	30	12	8	10	59	65	32
Tooting & Mitcham United	30	10	11	9	53	48	31
Kingstonian	30	11	9	10	72	77	31
Walthamstow Avenue	30	11	8	11	48	46	30
Dulwich Hamlet	30	13	3	14	65	54	29
St Albans City	30	13	3	14	62	71	29
Leytonstone	30	11	6	13	50	50	28
Clapton	30	9	9	12	48	59	27
Wimbledon	30	10	5	15	47	66	25
Romford	30	10	5	15	53	81	25
Barking	30	7	6	17	48	72	20
Corinthian Casuals	30	7	4	19	46	78	18

1957-58

Tooting & Mitcham United	30	20	6	4	79	33	46
Wycombe Wanderers	30	19	4	7	78	42	42
Walthamstow Avenue	30	17	5	8	63	35	39
Bromley	30	13	9	8	66	51	35
Oxford City	30	13	6	11	59	48	32
Leytonstone	30	13	6	11	49	48	32
Wimbledon	30	15	2	13	64	66	32
Corinthian Casuals	30	12	8	10	62	68	32
Woking	30	12	7	11	70	58	31
Barking	30	10	6	14	49	61	26
St Albans City	30	11	3	16	56	76	25
Clapton	30	8	9	13	42	65	25
Kingstonian	30	7	8	15	45	66	22
Dulwich Hamlet	30	7	7	16	49	64	21
Ilford	30	8	4	18	46	70	20
Romford	30	6	8	16	45	71	20

1958-59

Wimbledon	30	22	3	5	91	38	47
Dulwich Hamlet	30	18	5	7	68	44	41
Wycombe Wanderers	30	18	4	8	93	50	40
Oxford City	30	17	4	9	87	58	38
Walthamstow Avenue	30	16	5	9	59	40	37
Tooting & Mitcham United	30	15	4	11	84	55	34
Barking	30	14	2	14	59	53	30
Woking	30	12	6	12	66	66	30
Bromley	30	11	7	12	56	55	29
Clapton	30	10	6	14	55	67	26
Ilford	30	10	6	14	46	67	26
Kingstonian	30	9	4	17	54	72	22
St Albans City	30	8	6	16	53	89	22
Leytonstone	30	7	6	17	40	87	20
Romford	30	7	5	18	54	76	19
Corinthian Casuals	30	7	5	18	44	92	19

1959-60

Tooting & Mitcham United	30	17	8	5	75	43	42
Wycombe Wanderers	30	19	3	8	84	46	41
Wimbledon	30	18	3	9	66	36	39
Kingstonian	30	18	3	9	76	51	39
Corinthian Casuals	30	18	1	11	69	61	37
Bromley	30	15	6	9	75	46	36
Dulwich Hamlet	30	14	6	10	65	47	34
Walthamstow Avenue	30	11	11	8	48	38	33
Oxford City	30	10	10	10	57	57	30
Leytonstone	30	10	8	12	43	46	28
Woking	30	10	6	14	54	61	26
St Albans City	30	10	6	14	50	65	26
Maidstone United	30	10	5	15	53	60	25
Barking	30	7	4	19	30	75	18
Ilford	30	5	6	19	34	86	16
Clapton	30	3	4	23	32	92	10

1960-61

Bromley	30	20	6	4	89	42	46
Walthamstow Avenue	30	20	5	5	87	38	45
Wimbledon	30	18	6	6	72	43	42
Dulwich Hamlet	30	17	4	9	71	59	35
Maidstone United	30	14	8	8	63	39	36
Leytonstone	30	15	6	9	46	34	36
Tooting & Mitcham United	30	14	3	13	69	51	31
Wycombe Wanderers	30	12	5	13	63	61	29
St Albans City	30	12	4	14	45	72	28
Oxford City	30	10	7	13	59	59	27
Corinthian Casuals	30	9	9	12	49	59	27
Kingstonian	30	10	6	14	55	61	26
Woking	30	10	6	14	58	71	26
Ilford	30	5	8	17	30	69	18
Barking	30	3	8	19	30	76	14
Clapton	30	3	5	22	25	77	11

1961-62

Wimbledon	30	19	6	5	68	24	44
Leytonstone	30	17	7	6	61	44	41
Walthamstow Avenue	30	14	8	8	51	31	36
Kingstonian	30	15	5	10	65	48	35
Tooting & Mitcham United	30	12	10	8	62	47	34
Oxford City	30	12	9	9	56	49	33
Wycombe Wanderers	30	12	7	11	57	51	31
Corinthian Casuals	30	12	7	11	45	51	31
St Albans City	30	10	9	11	55	55	29
Woking	30	9	9	12	51	60	27
Dulwich Hamlet	30	11	4	15	55	66	26
Barking	30	9	8	13	40	64	26
Ilford	30	7	10	13	50	59	24
Bromley	30	10	4	16	49	69	24
Clapton	30	6	8	16	45	67	20
Maidstone United	30	6	7	17	34	59	19

1962-63

Wimbledon	30	19	8	3	84	33	46
Kingstonian	30	18	8	4	79	37	44
Tooting & Mitcham United	30	17	8	5	65	37	42
Ilford	30	19	3	8	70	44	41
Walthamstow Avenue	30	14	7	9	51	44	35
Maidstone United	30	13	8	9	56	45	34
Bromley	30	12	10	8	57	51	34
Leytonstone	30	12	7	11	48	50	31
Wycombe Wanderers	30	10	10	10	56	61	30
St Albans City	30	11	5	14	54	49	27
Barking	30	8	10	12	39	50	26
Oxford City	30	8	9	13	55	64	25
Woking	30	8	6	16	42	66	22
Clapton	30	7	4	19	30	71	18
Dulwich Hamlet	30	4	5	21	30	71	13
Corinthian Casuals	30	4	4	22	28	71	12

1963-64

Wimbledon	38	27	6	5	87	44	60
Hendon	38	25	4	9	124	38	54
Kingstonian	38	24	4	10	100	62	52
Sutton United	38	23	5	10	99	64	51
Enfield	38	20	10	8	96	56	50
Oxford City	38	20	8	10	90	55	48
Tooting & Mitcham United	38	19	8	11	78	51	46
St Albans City	38	14	12	12	62	63	40
Ilford	38	16	8	14	75	79	40
Maidstone United	38	15	8	15	65	71	38
Walthamstow Avenue	38	15	6	17	70	66	36
Leytonstone	38	14	8	16	66	71	36
Wycombe Wanderers	38	13	6	19	74	80	32
Hitchin Town	38	14	4	20	67	100	32
Bromley	38	11	8	19	64	75	30
Barking	38	10	9	19	46	69	29
Woking	38	10	9	19	48	88	29
Corinthian Casuals	38	10	4	24	52	92	24
Dulwich Hamlet	38	6	12	20	47	97	24
Clapton	38	2	5	31	31	120	9

1964-65

Hendon	38	28	7	3	123	49	63
Enfield	38	29	5	4	98	35	63
Kingstonian	38	24	8	6	86	44	56
Leytonstone	38	24	5	9	115	62	53
Oxford City	38	20	7	11	76	51	47
St Albans City	38	18	9	11	63	43	45
Sutton United	38	17	11	10	74	57	45
Wealdstone	38	19	6	13	93	68	44
Bromley	38	14	11	13	71	80	39
Tooting & Mitcham United	38	15	7	16	71	66	37
Hitchin Town	38	13	9	16	61	66	35
Walthamstow Avenue	38	15	5	18	63	82	35
Wycombe Wanderers	38	13	7	18	70	85	33
Corinthian Casuals	38	13	7	18	56	77	33
Barking	38	10	8	20	58	80	28
Ilford	38	8	8	22	43	89	24
Maidstone United	38	8	6	24	49	86	22
Dulwich Hamlet	38	8	5	25	45	79	21
Clapton	38	8	3	27	43	91	19
Woking	38	7	4	27	45	113	18

Hendon beat Enfield in a play-off to decide the Championship

1965-66

Leytonstone	38	27	7	4	98	33	63
Hendon	38	27	5	6	111	55	59
Enfield	38	24	8	6	104	54	56
Wycombe Wanderers	38	25	6	7	100	65	56
Kingstonian	38	24	5	9	94	55	53
Wealdstone	38	20	6	12	90	64	46
Maidstone United	38	19	6	13	74	61	44
St Albans City	38	19	5	14	57	56	43
Sutton United	38	17	7	14	83	72	41
Tooting & Mitcham United	38	16	7	15	65	58	39
Corinthian Casuals	38	17	5	16	74	67	39
Woking	38	12	10	16	60	83	34
Walthamstow Avenue	38	12	9	17	81	75	33
Oxford City	38	10	9	19	49	72	29
Barking	38	10	7	21	51	72	27
Bromley	38	10	5	23	69	101	25
Ilford	38	7	10	21	50	84	24
Hitchin Town	38	6	8	24	57	118	20
Clapton	38	5	6	27	46	103	16
Dulwich Hamlet	38	5	5	28	30	95	15

1966-67

Sutton United	38	26	7	5	89	33	59
Walthamstow Avenue	38	22	12	4	89	47	56
Wycombe Wanderers	38	23	8	7	92	54	54
Enfield	38	25	2	11	87	33	52
Hendon	38	20	9	9	64	37	49
Tooting & Mitcham United	38	19	10	9	76	60	48
Leytonstone	38	19	9	10	67	38	47
St Albans City	38	16	12	10	59	45	44
Kingstonian	38	18	8	12	60	49	44
Oxford City	38	15	9	14	74	61	39
Woking	38	13	10	15	65	71	36
Wealdstone	38	13	8	17	72	73	34
Barking	38	11	12	15	56	61	34
Bromley	38	12	7	19	50	67	31
Clapton	38	10	8	20	49	92	28
Ilford	38	8	10	20	43	77	26
Corinthian Casuals	38	9	7	22	45	68	25
Maidstone United	38	6	10	22	43	90	22
Hitchin Town	38	8	6	24	39	89	22
Dulwich Hamlet	38	3	4	31	33	107	10

1967-68

Enfield	38	28	8	2	85	22	64
Sutton United	38	22	11	5	89	27	55
Hendon	38	23	6	9	90	36	52
Leytonstone	38	21	10	7	78	41	52
St Albans City	38	20	8	10	78	41	48
Walthamstow Avenue	38	19	9	10	81	64	47
Wealdstone	38	19	8	11	80	45	46
Tooting & Mitcham United	38	19	5	14	57	45	43
Barking	38	17	8	13	75	57	42
Oxford City	38	17	4	17	59	58	38
Kingstonian	38	14	10	14	56	61	38
Hitchin Town	38	14	9	15	61	73	37
Bromley	38	12	10	16	58	80	34
Wycombe Wanderers	38	13	5	20	73	85	31
Dulwich Hamlet	38	10	7	21	39	66	27
Clapton	38	10	7	21	51	88	27
Woking	38	8	8	22	50	90	24
Corinthian Casuals	38	7	10	21	40	80	24
Ilford	38	7	7	24	41	77	21
Maidstone United	38	3	4	31	26	131	10

1968-69

Enfield	38	27	7	4	103	28	61
Hitchin Town	38	23	10	5	67	41	56
Sutton United	38	22	9	7	83	29	53
Wycombe Wanderers	38	23	6	9	70	37	52
Wealdstone	38	20	11	7	73	48	51
Hendon	38	22	5	11	69	47	49
St Albans City	38	17	13	8	75	44	47
Barking	38	20	7	11	69	46	47
Oxford City	38	18	8	12	76	64	44
Tooting & Mitcham United	38	16	10	12	68	55	42
Leytonstone	38	18	4	16	71	53	40
Kingstonian	38	15	8	15	62	56	38
Walthamstow Avenue	38	10	10	18	47	71	30
Maidstone United	38	10	8	20	47	75	28
Clapton	38	10	7	21	52	76	27
Woking	38	8	7	23	45	77	23
Bromley	38	8	7	23	52	95	23
Dulwich Hamlet	38	6	9	23	31	77	21
Ilford	38	6	8	24	33	77	20
Corinthian Casuals	38	2	4	32	23	120	8

1969-70

Enfield	38	27	8	3	91	26	62
Wycombe Wanderers	38	25	11	2	85	24	61
Sutton United	38	24	9	5	75	35	57
Barking	38	21	9	8	93	47	51
Hendon	38	19	12	7	77	44	50
St Albans City	38	21	8	9	69	40	50
Hitchin Town	38	19	10	9	71	40	48
Tooting & Mitcham United	38	19	5	14	88	62	43
Leytonstone	38	17	7	14	57	41	41
Wealdstone	38	15	10	13	53	48	40
Oxford City	38	15	7	16	61	78	37
Kingstonian	38	13	9	16	55	57	35
Ilford	38	8	15	15	42	73	31
Dulwich Hamlet	38	8	12	18	46	66	28
Woking	38	10	7	21	46	69	27
Walthamstow Avenue	38	11	5	22	52	81	27
Clapton	38	9	7	22	45	87	25
Maidstone United	38	7	8	23	48	84	22
Corinthian Casuals	38	6	3	29	30	99	15
Bromley	38	3	4	31	28	111	10

1970-71

Wycombe Wanderers	38	28	6	4	93	32	62
Sutton United	38	29	3	6	76	35	61
St Albans City	38	23	10	5	87	26	56
Enfield	38	24	7	7	67	24	55
Ilford	38	21	7	10	74	51	49
Hendon	38	18	11	9	81	37	47
Barking	38	20	4	14	89	59	44
Leytonstone	38	17	10	11	68	50	44
Woking	38	18	6	14	57	50	42
Walthamstow Avenue	38	14	11	13	63	52	39
Oxford City	38	13	10	15	51	48	36
Hitchin Town	38	12	9	17	46	60	33
Wealdstone	38	12	8	18	45	64	32
Tooting & Mitcham United	38	11	9	18	44	66	31
Kingstonian	38	11	8	19	53	71	30
Bromley	38	10	6	22	34	77	26
Dulwich Hamlet	38	7	10	21	30	66	24
Maidstone United	38	7	6	25	42	84	20
Clapton	38	5	7	26	33	101	17
Corinthian Casuals	38	2	8	28	23	103	12

1971-72

Wycombe Wanderers	40	31	3	6	102	20	65
Enfield	40	26	8	6	90	41	60
Walton & Hersham	40	24	8	8	69	25	56
Hendon	40	23	10	7	79	35	56
Bishop's Stortford	40	24	5	11	61	37	53
Sutton United	40	21	10	9	77	43	52
St Albans City	40	23	4	13	74	47	50
Ilford	40	17	11	12	62	52	45
Barking	40	20	4	16	65	61	44
Hitchin Town	40	17	10	13	68	66	44
Bromley	40	16	10	14	67	64	42
Hayes	40	14	12	14	50	48	40
Oxford City	40	13	9	18	67	74	35
Woking	40	11	10	19	52	58	32
Kingstonian	40	10	12	18	49	59	32
Walthamstow Avenue	40	12	8	20	58	71	32
Leytonstone	40	11	8	21	48	68	30
Tooting & Mitcham United	40	6	9	25	38	93	21
Clapton	40	7	7	26	45	118	21
Dulwich Hamlet	40	4	12	24	35	81	20
Corinthian Casuals	40	3	4	33	21	116	10

Second Division

Dagenham	30	22	4	4	68	23	70
Slough Town	30	18	6	6	46	23	60
Hertford Town	30	17	5	8	46	29	56
Chesham Town	30	16	6	8	61	43	54
Aveley	30	16	5	9	50	28	53
Tilbury	30	14	5	11	47	36	47
Maidenhead United	30	12	11	7	36	30	47
Horsham	30	12	9	9	47	35	45
Harwich & Parkeston	30	11	9	10	46	41	42
Staines Town	30	10	8	12	34	41	38
Carshalton Athletic	30	8	8	14	34	51	32
Hampton	30	6	10	14	33	51	28
Harlow Town	30	6	9	15	33	48	27
Finchley	30	6	7	17	29	52	25
Southall	30	3	10	17	17	52	19
Wokingham Town	30	3	8	19	30	74	17

1972-73

Hendon	42	34	6	2	88	18	74
Walton & Hersham	42	25	11	6	60	25	61
Leatherhead	42	23	10	9	76	32	56
Wycombe Wanderers	42	25	6	11	66	32	56
Walthamstow Avenue	42	20	12	10	66	48	52
Tooting & Mitcham United	42	20	11	11	73	39	51
Sutton United	42	21	9	12	69	48	51
Kingstonian	42	20	10	12	60	49	50
Enfield	42	20	8	14	90	54	48
Bishop's Stortford	42	18	12	12	58	51	48
Hayes	42	19	8	15	69	42	46
Dulwich Hamlet	42	18	9	15	59	52	45
Ilford	42	18	9	15	61	59	45
Leytonstone	42	17	11	14	55	54	45
Woking	42	18	8	16	61	56	44
Hitchin Town	42	15	9	18	52	64	39
Barking	42	8	7	27	45	88	23
St Albans City	42	5	12	25	34	76	22
Oxford City	42	6	7	29	30	101	19
Bromley	42	4	10	28	31	70	18
Clapton	42	3	11	28	31	100	17
Corinthian Casuals	42	3	8	31	30	106	14

1973-74

First Division

Wycombe Wanderers	42	27	9	6	96	34	90
Hendon	42	25	13	4	63	20	88
Bishop's Stortford	42	26	9	7	78	26	87
Dulwich Hamlet	42	22	11	9	71	38	77
Leatherhead	42	23	6	13	81	44	75
Walton & Hersham	42	20	12	10	68	50	72
Woking	42	22	6	14	63	55	72
Leytonstone	42	20	9	13	63	44	69
Ilford	42	20	8	14	60	44	68
Hayes	42	17	14	11	65	43	65
Oxford City	42	15	16	11	45	47	61
Sutton United	42	13	16	13	51	52	55
Hitchin Town	42	15	10	17	68	73	55
Barking	42	14	12	16	57	58	54
Kingstonian	42	12	15	15	47	46	51
Tooting & Mitcham United	42	14	9	19	57	62	51
Enfield	42	13	11	18	50	57	50
Walthamstow Avenue	42	11	13	18	46	62	46
Bromley	42	7	9	26	37	81	30
Clapton	42	8	3	31	36	128	27
St Albans City	42	4	7	31	30	92	19
Corinthian Casuals	42	3	4	35	31	107	13

1974-75

First Division

Wycombe Wanderers	42	28	11	3	93	30	95
Enfield	42	29	8	5	78	26	95
Dagenham	42	28	5	9	95	44	89
Tooting & Mitcham United	42	25	9	8	78	46	84
Dulwich Hamlet	42	24	10	8	75	38	82
Leatherhead	42	23	10	9	83	42	79
Ilford	42	23	10	9	98	51	79
Oxford City	42	17	9	16	63	56	60
Slough Town	42	17	6	19	68	52	57
Sutton United	42	17	6	19	68	63	57
Bishop's Stortford	42	17	6	19	56	64	57
Hitchin Town	42	15	10	17	57	71	55
Hendon	42	15	7	20	59	74	52
Walthamstow Avenue	42	13	9	20	56	62	48
Woking	42	12	10	20	53	73	46
Hayes	42	10	14	18	52	66	44
Barking	42	12	8	22	57	81	44
Leytonstone	42	12	7	23	42	61	43
Kingstonian	42	13	4	25	48	73	43
Clapton	42	12	4	26	46	96	40
Walton & Hersham	42	9	4	29	37	108	31
Bromley	42	6	3	33	25	110	21

Second Division

Staines Town	34	23	2	9	65	23	71
Southall	34	20	3	11	55	41	63
Tilbury	34	19	5	10	64	36	60
Harwich & Parkeston	34	18	4	12	52	44	58
Chesham United	34	17	6	11	59	39	57
St Albans City	34	15	11	8	42	37	56
Harlow Town	34	16	6	12	53	47	54
Horsham	34	16	5	13	59	49	53
Maidenhead United	34	13	7	14	38	40	46
Hampton	34	12	7	15	44	42	43
Croydon	34	11	10	13	48	55	43
Hertford Town	34	10	7	17	35	52	37
Boreham Wood	34	7	15	12	41	49	36
Wokingham Town	34	10	6	18	32	43	36
Finchley	34	9	9	16	36	53	36
Carshalton Athletic	34	9	9	16	38	58	36
Aveley	34	9	7	18	34	63	34
Corinthian Casuals	34	8	9	17	35	59	33

Tilbury had 2 points deducted

1975-76

First Division

Enfield	42	26	9	7	83	38	87
Wycombe Wanderers	42	24	10	8	71	41	82
Dagenham	42	25	6	11	89	55	81
Ilford	42	22	10	10	58	39	76
Dulwich Hamlet	42	22	5	15	67	41	71
Hendon	42	20	11	11	60	41	71
Tooting & Mitcham United	42	19	11	12	73	49	68
Leatherhead	42	19	10	13	63	53	67
Staines Town	42	19	9	14	46	37	66
Slough Town	42	17	12	13	58	45	63
Sutton United	42	17	11	14	71	60	62
Bishop's Stortford	42	15	12	15	51	47	57
Walthamstow Avenue	42	14	11	17	47	60	53
Woking	42	14	9	19	58	62	51
Barking	42	15	6	21	57	70	51
Hitchin Town	42	13	11	18	45	57	50
Hayes	42	10	19	13	44	48	49
Kingstonian	42	13	8	21	53	87	47
Southall & Ealing Borough	42	11	9	22	56	69	42
Leytonstone	42	10	10	22	41	63	40
Oxford City	42	9	8	25	29	65	35
Clapton	42	3	3	36	19	112	12

Second Division

Tilbury	42	32	6	4	97	30	102
Croydon	42	28	14	0	81	27	98
Carshalton Athletic	42	28	6	8	75	37	90
Chesham United	42	21	12	9	91	51	75
Harwich & Parkeston	42	21	11	10	78	56	74
Hampton	42	21	9	12	72	52	72
St Albans City	42	18	12	12	59	48	66
Boreham Wood	42	17	12	13	68	50	63
Harrow Borough	42	15	12	15	71	74	57
Hornchurch	42	15	11	16	61	61	56
Horsham	42	14	13	15	60	55	55
Wembley	42	14	13	15	51	54	55
Wokingham Town	42	13	16	13	45	52	55
Walton & Hersham	42	14	12	16	61	56	54
Finchley	42	14	11	17	52	53	53
Bromley	42	11	11	20	64	86	44
Aveley	42	11	9	22	34	51	42
Harlow Town	42	11	9	22	50	73	42
Maidenhead United	42	6	17	19	32	65	35
Ware	42	7	12	23	50	95	33
Hertford Town	42	5	9	28	32	87	24
Corinthian Casuals	42	4	7	31	42	113	19

1976-77

First Division

Enfield	42	24	12	6	63	34	84
Wycombe Wanderers	42	25	8	9	71	34	83
Dagenham	42	23	10	9	80	39	79
Hendon	42	19	10	13	60	48	67
Tilbury	42	18	13	11	57	49	67
Tooting & Mitcham	42	18	10	14	85	72	64
Walthamstow Avenue	42	19	7	16	61	55	64
Slough Town	42	18	9	15	51	46	63
Hitchin Town	42	19	6	17	60	66	63
Leatherhead	42	18	7	17	61	47	61
Staines Town	42	16	13	13	52	48	61
Leytonstone	42	16	11	15	59	57	59
Barking	42	16	9	17	63	61	57
Southall & Ealing Borough	42	15	8	19	52	64	53
Croydon	42	13	10	19	38	52	49
Sutton United	42	14	7	21	40	55	49
Kingstonian	42	13	7	22	45	60	46
Hayes	42	12	10	20	49	69	46
Woking	42	11	12	19	47	61	45
Bishop's Stortford	42	11	11	20	51	71	44
Dulwich Hamlet	42	11	8	23	52	68	41
Ilford	42	10	8	24	32	73	38

Second Division

Boreham Wood	42	35	4	5	80	26	103
Carshalton Athletic	42	25	12	5	80	33	87
Harwich & Parkeston	42	23	8	11	93	61	77
Wembley	42	23	8	11	82	58	77
Harrow Borough	42	21	12	9	78	44	75
Horsham	42	23	5	14	67	56	74
Bromley	42	20	10	12	71	46	70
Oxford City	42	20	8	14	73	55	68
Hampton	42	20	8	14	62	45	68
Wokingham Town	42	16	14	12	60	44	62
Hornchurch	42	18	7	17	62	53	61
Chesham United	42	17	10	15	63	66	61
St Albans City	42	16	12	14	59	53	60
Walton & Hersham	42	17	9	16	57	56	60
Aveley	42	14	8	20	49	62	50
Corinthian Casuals	42	13	6	23	52	75	45
Harlow Town	42	11	8	23	39	77	41
Hertford Town	42	9	9	24	45	80	36
Maidenhead United	42	8	8	26	36	73	32
Clapton	42	7	9	28	43	87	30
Finchley	42	5	13	24	36	82	28
Ware	42	5	8	29	43	98	23

1977-78

Premier Division

Enfield	42	35	5	2	96	27	110
Dagenham	42	24	7	11	78	55	79
Wycombe Wanderers	42	22	9	11	66	41	75
Tooting & Mitcham United	42	22	8	12	64	49	74
Hitchin Town	42	20	9	13	69	53	69
Sutton United	42	18	12	12	66	57	66
Leatherhead	42	18	11	13	62	48	65
Croydon	42	18	10	14	61	52	64
Walthamstow Avenue	42	17	12	13	64	61	63
Barking	42	17	7	18	76	66	58
Carshalton Athletic	42	15	11	16	60	62	56
Hayes	42	15	11	16	46	53	56
Hendon	42	16	7	19	57	55	55
Woking	42	14	11	17	62	62	53
Boreham Wood	42	15	8	19	48	65	53
Slough Town	42	14	8	20	52	69	0
Staines Town	42	12	13	17	46	60	49
Tilbury	42	11	12	19	57	68	45
Kingstonian	42	8	13	21	43	65	37
Leytonstone	42	7	15	20	44	71	36
Southall & Ealing Borough	42	6	15	21	43	74	33
Bishop's Stortford	42	7	8	27	36	83	29

First Division

Dulwich Hamlet	42	28	9	5	91	25	93
Oxford City	42	26	5	11	85	44	83
Bromley	42	23	13	6	74	41	82
Walton & Hersham	42	22	11	9	69	41	77
Ilford	42	21	14	7	57	47	77
St Albans City	42	22	10	10	83	46	76
Wokingham Town	42	19	12	11	69	48	69
Harlow Town	42	19	8	15	63	49	65
Harrow Borough	42	17	10	15	59	54	61
Maidenhead United	42	16	13	13	55	54	61
Hertford Town	42	15	14	13	57	51	59
Chesham United	42	14	13	15	69	70	55
Hampton	42	13	13	16	49	53	52
Harwich & Parkeston	42	12	13	17	68	79	49
Wembley	42	15	3	24	56	82	48
Horsham	42	12	10	20	41	57	46
Finchley	42	11	13	18	41	68	46
Aveley	42	13	7	22	47	75	46
Ware	42	8	13	21	61	95	37
Clapton	42	10	6	26	46	78	36
Hornchurch	42	8	10	24	47	81	34
Corinthian Casuals	42	3	10	29	40	88	19

Second Division

Team	P	W	D	L	F	A	Pts
Epsom & Ewell	32	21	5	6	65	34	68
Metropolitan Police	32	19	6	7	53	30	63
Farnborough Town	32	19	4	9	68	40	61
Molesey	32	17	8	7	47	27	59
Egham Town	32	15	9	8	52	34	54
Tring Town	32	14	11	7	62	32	53
Letchworth Garden City	32	14	11	7	67	48	53
Lewes	32	13	7	12	52	51	46
Rainham Town	32	13	6	13	42	50	45
Worthing	32	11	9	12	40	45	42
Eastbourne United	32	10	8	14	40	50	38
Cheshunt	32	9	6	17	43	60	33
Feltham	32	7	9	16	30	49	30
Camberley Town	32	6	11	15	32	49	29
Hemel Hempstead	32	6	9	17	33	50	27
Epping Town	32	7	6	19	37	64	27
Willesden	32	7	3	22	38	88	24

Second Division

Team	P	W	D	L	F	A	Pts
Farnborough Town	34	26	3	5	77	34	81
Camberley Town	34	21	8	5	71	32	71
Molesey	34	19	11	4	55	33	68
Lewes	34	19	6	9	66	50	63
Feltham	34	16	7	11	47	36	55
Letchworth Garden City	34	14	10	10	56	48	52
Eastbourne United	34	16	4	14	47	45	52
Hemel Hempstead	34	13	11	10	46	37	50
Epping Town	34	14	7	13	49	44	49
Rainham Town	34	13	10	11	42	41	49
Cheshunt	34	11	8	15	43	49	41
Hungerford Town	34	11	8	15	48	58	41
Worthing	34	9	8	17	40	50	35
Hornchurch	34	9	8	17	39	62	35
Egham Town	34	7	12	15	48	54	33
Tring Town	34	6	8	20	33	56	26
Willesden	34	6	8	20	41	77	26
Corinthian Casuals	34	4	7	23	23	65	19

1978-79

Premier Division

Team	P	W	D	L	F	A	Pts
Barking	42	28	9	5	92	50	93
Dagenham	42	25	6	11	83	63	81
Enfield	42	22	11	9	69	37	77
Dulwich Hamlet	42	21	13	8	69	39	76
Slough Town	42	20	12	10	61	44	72
Wycombe Wanderers	42	20	9	13	59	44	69
Woking	42	18	14	10	79	59	68
Croydon	42	19	9	14	61	51	66
Hendon	42	16	14	12	55	48	62
Leatherhead	42	17	9	16	57	45	60
Sutton United	42	17	9	16	62	51	60
Tooting & Mitcham United	42	15	14	13	52	52	59
Walthamstow Avenue	42	15	6	21	61	69	51
Tilbury	42	13	1	18	60	76	50
Boreham Wood	42	13	10	19	50	67	49
Hitchin Town	42	12	11	19	59	71	47
Carshalton Athletic	42	10	16	16	49	69	46
Hayes	42	9	18	15	45	58	45
Oxford City	42	12	7	23	50	80	43
Staines Town	42	6	16	20	40	64	34
Leytonstone	42	8	7	27	36	75	31
Kingstonian	42	3	15	24	35	72	24

First Division

Team	P	W	D	L	F	A	Pts
Harlow Town	42	31	7	4	93	32	100
Harrow Borough	42	26	8	8	85	49	86
Maidenhead United	42	25	6	11	72	50	81
Bishop's Stortford	42	22	11	9	68	40	77
Horsham	42	23	7	12	63	47	76
Hertford Town	42	21	11	10	62	41	74
Harwich & Parkeston	42	22	5	15	90	57	71
Bromley	42	18	12	12	76	50	66
Hampton	42	17	11	14	59	47	62
Epsom & Ewell	42	18	7	17	69	41	61
Wembley	42	15	14	13	57	57	59
Aveley	42	17	6	19	57	67	57
Wokingham Town	42	17	8	17	64	68	56
Clapton	42	15	8	19	67	80	53
Metropolitan Police	42	12	13	17	58	55	49
Walton & Hersham	42	12	9	21	47	71	45
Ilford	42	13	5	24	48	80	44
Ware	42	11	10	21	46	69	43
Chesham United	42	11	9	22	46	66	42
Finchley	42	7	15	20	43	75	36
St Albans City	42	7	7	28	43	90	28
Southall & Ealing Borough	42	5	5	32	41	114	20

Wokingham Town had 3 points deducted

1979-80

Premier Division

Team	P	W	D	L	F	A	Pts
Enfield	42	25	9	8	74	32	84
Walthamstow Avenue	42	24	9	9	87	48	81
Dulwich Hamlet	42	21	16	5	66	37	79
Sutton United	42	20	13	9	67	40	73
Dagenham	42	20	13	9	82	56	73
Tooting & Mitcham United	42	21	6	15	62	59	69
Barking	42	19	10	13	72	51	67
Harrow Borough	42	17	15	10	64	51	66
Woking	42	17	13	12	78	59	64
Wycombe Wanderers	42	17	13	12	72	53	64
Harlow Town	42	14	12	16	55	61	54
Hitchin Town	42	13	15	14	55	69	54
Hendon	42	12	13	17	50	57	49
Slough Town	42	13	10	19	54	71	49
Boreham Wood	42	13	10	19	50	69	49
Staines Town	42	14	6	22	46	67	48
Hayes	42	12	9	21	48	68	45
Leatherhead	42	11	11	20	51	60	44
Carshalton Athletic	42	12	7	23	48	78	43
Croydon	42	10	10	22	33	56	40
Oxford City	42	10	9	23	49	87	39
Tilbury	42	7	11	24	41	90	30

Tilbury had 2 points deducted

First Division

Team	P	W	D	L	F	A	Pts
Leytonstone & Ilford	42	31	6	5	83	35	99
Bromley	42	24	10	8	93	44	82
Maidenhead United	42	24	8	10	81	46	80
Bishop's Stortford	42	24	8	10	74	47	80
Kingstonian	42	22	8	12	59	44	74
Chesham United	42	18	13	11	68	56	67
St Albans City	42	17	13	12	65	47	64
Farnborough Town	42	19	7	16	70	57	64
Epsom & Ewell	42	18	7	17	62	57	61
Camberley Town	42	16	10	16	43	38	58
Walton & Hersham	42	15	12	15	61	50	57
Wembley	42	16	8	18	46	52	56
Wokingham Town	42	14	11	17	45	49	53
Hertford Town	42	13	11	18	71	74	50
Aveley	42	12	13	17	45	55	49
Hampton	42	14	7	21	57	74	49
Finchley	42	13	9	20	44	59	48
Metropolitan Police	42	13	8	21	46	67	47
Ware	42	11	12	19	45	61	45
Clapton	42	14	3	25	48	77	45
Harwich & Parkeston	42	11	6	25	51	84	38
Horsham	42	6	4	32	29	113	22

Harwich & Parkeston had 1 point deducted

Second Division

	P	W	D	L	F	A	Pts
Billericay Town	36	31	3	2	100	18	96
Lewes	36	24	7	5	82	33	79
Hungerford Town	36	21	8	7	78	36	71
Eastbourne United	36	21	6	9	77	45	69
Letchworth Garden City	36	21	6	9	63	32	69
Hornchurch	36	21	6	9	66	39	69
Molesey	36	15	9	12	67	60	54
Barton Rovers	36	15	7	14	49	49	52
Worthing	36	14	9	13	58	54	51
Cheshunt	36	13	7	16	47	52	46
Rainham Town	36	12	7	17	54	65	43
Egham Town	36	11	9	16	47	53	42
Southall & Ealing Borough	36	11	6	19	43	69	39
Feltham	36	8	11	17	23	49	35
Tring Town	36	7	13	16	38	55	34
Epping Town	36	10	4	22	44	69	34
Willesden	36	9	6	21	32	83	33
Hemel Hempstead	36	4	9	23	33	72	21
Corinthian Casuals	36	6	3	27	24	92	21

Second Division

	P	W	D	L	F	A	Pts
Feltham	38	24	10	4	65	30	82
Hornchurch	38	25	6	7	74	35	81
Hungerford Town	38	23	10	5	84	29	79
Barton Rovers	38	19	11	8	61	25	68
Worthing	38	19	11	8	74	43	68
Cheshunt	38	19	11	8	57	33	68
Letchworth Garden City	38	18	7	13	49	40	61
Southall	38	14	11	13	48	52	53
Dorking Town	38	13	12	13	47	45	51
Horsham	38	16	3	19	47	47	51
Hemel Hempstead	38	14	7	17	47	54	49
Egham Town	38	13	9	16	45	62	48
Harwich & Parkeston	38	12	11	15	57	58	47
Rainham Town	38	11	13	14	44	45	46
Epping Town	38	12	7	19	37	50	43
Eastbourne United	38	11	10	17	59	75	43
Willesden	38	11	8	19	57	68	41
Tring Town	38	11	6	21	40	71	39
Molesey	38	4	9	25	31	83	21
Corinthian Casuals	38	1	8	29	17	95	11

1980-81

Premier Division

	P	W	D	L	F	A	Pts
Slough Town	42	23	13	6	73	34	82
Enfield	42	23	11	8	81	43	80
Wycombe Wanderers	42	22	9	11	76	49	75
Leytonstone & Ilford	42	19	12	11	78	57	69
Sutton United	42	19	12	11	82	65	69
Hendon	42	18	10	14	66	58	64
Dagenham	42	17	11	14	79	66	62
Hayes	42	18	8	16	45	50	62
Harrow Borough	42	16	11	15	57	52	59
Bromley	42	16	9	17	63	69	57
Staines Town	42	15	9	18	60	61	54
Tooting & Mitcham United	42	15	8	19	49	53	53
Hitchin Town	42	14	10	18	64	62	52
Croydon	42	12	15	15	51	51	51
Dulwich Hamlet	42	13	12	17	62	67	51
Leatherhead	42	12	14	16	36	50	50
Carshalton Athletic	42	14	8	20	57	82	50
Barking	42	13	12	17	58	72	49
Harlow Town	42	11	15	16	53	66	48
Walthamstow Avenue	42	13	7	22	50	81	46
Boreham Wood	42	10	13	19	46	69	43
Woking	42	11	7	24	40	69	37

Barking had 1 point deducted
Woking had 3 points deducted

First Division

	P	W	D	L	F	A	Pts
Bishop's Stortford	42	30	6	6	84	28	96
Billericay Town	42	29	6	7	67	34	93
Epsom & Ewell	42	24	12	6	80	36	84
Farnborough Town	42	23	11	8	75	39	80
St Albans City	42	24	5	13	85	61	77
Kingstonian	42	20	9	13	63	52	66
Oxford City	42	18	9	15	71	48	63
Wokingham Town	42	16	15	11	70	56	63
Metropolitan Police	42	18	7	17	61	58	61
Chesham United	42	17	7	18	64	64	58
Lewes	42	17	7	18	72	83	58
Maidenhead United	42	16	7	19	58	62	55
Walton & Hersham	42	12	15	15	46	53	51
Hertford Town	42	13	11	18	46	65	50
Hampton	42	12	13	17	46	53	49
Aveley	42	13	9	20	54	55	48
Wembley	42	13	8	21	47	61	47
Clapton	42	12	8	22	53	86	44
Ware	42	9	13	20	50	69	40
Tilbury	42	10	8	24	42	84	35
Camberley Town	42	8	7	27	42	88	31
Finchley	42	6	11	25	36	77	29

Kingstonian and Tilbury both had 3 points deducted

1981-82

Premier Division

	P	W	D	L	F	A	Pts
Leytonstone & Ilford	42	26	5	11	91	52	83
Sutton United	42	22	9	11	72	49	75
Wycombe Wanderers	42	21	10	11	63	48	73
Staines Town	42	21	9	12	58	45	72
Walthamstow Avenue	42	21	7	14	81	62	70
Harrow Borough	42	18	13	11	77	55	67
Tooting & Mitcham United	42	19	10	13	58	47	67
Slough Town	42	17	13	12	64	54	64
Leatherhead	42	16	12	14	57	52	60
Hayes	42	16	10	16	58	52	58
Croydon	42	16	9	17	59	57	57
Barking	42	14	14	14	53	51	56
Hendon	42	13	13	16	56	65	52
Dulwich Hamlet	42	14	10	18	47	59	52
Bishop's Stortford	42	15	5	22	50	70	50
Carshalton Athletic	42	14	8	20	58	86	50
Billericay Town	42	11	16	15	41	50	49
Hitchin Town	42	12	11	19	56	77	47
Bromley	42	13	7	22	63	79	46
Woking	42	11	13	18	57	75	46
Harlow Town	42	10	11	21	50	73	41
Boreham Wood	42	8	13	21	47	58	37

First Division

	P	W	D	L	F	A	Pts
Wokingham Town	40	29	5	6	86	30	92
Bognor Regis Town	40	23	10	7	65	34	79
Metropolitan Police	40	22	11	7	75	48	77
Oxford City	40	21	11	8	82	47	74
Feltham	40	20	8	12	65	49	68
Lewes	40	19	7	14	73	66	64
Hertford Town	40	16	10	14	62	54	58
Wembley	40	14	15	11	69	55	57
Farnborough Town	40	15	11	14	71	57	56
Epsom & Ewell	40	16	8	16	52	44	56
Kingstonian	40	16	7	17	57	56	55
Hampton	40	15	9	16	52	52	54
Hornchurch	40	13	15	12	42	50	54
Aveley	40	14	10	16	46	58	54
St Albans City	40	14	9	17	55	55	51
Maidenhead United	40	11	10	19	49	70	43
Tilbury	40	9	15	16	49	66	42
Walton & Hersham	40	10	11	19	43	65	41
Chesham United	40	9	9	22	41	71	36
Clapton	40	9	7	24	44	75	34
Ware	40	5	2	33	29	105	17

Second Division

	P	W	D	L	F	A	Pts
Worthing	40	29	6	5	95	25	93
Cheshunt	40	25	7	8	79	33	82
Hungerford Town	40	22	10	8	89	42	74
Barton Rovers	40	22	8	10	65	32	74
Windsor & Eton	40	22	6	12	69	49	72
Corinthian Casuals	40	19	12	9	67	50	69
Harwich & Parkeston	40	19	12	9	64	47	69
Letchworth Garden City	40	15	11	14	67	55	56
Dorking Town	40	13	17	10	52	44	56
Hemel Hempstead	40	15	9	16	54	49	54
Basildon United	40	16	5	19	64	51	53
Finchley	40	14	9	17	57	68	51
Southall	40	12	14	14	36	42	50
Epping Town	40	12	11	17	48	62	47
Molesey	40	13	7	20	61	73	46
Egham Town	40	11	9	20	56	64	42
Rainham Town	40	11	9	20	53	83	42
Tring Town	40	9	13	18	49	78	40
Eastbourne United	40	9	12	19	51	73	39
Horsham	40	10	9	21	42	79	39
Camberley Town	40	3	2	35	21	140	11

Hungerford Town had 2 points deducted

Second Division

	P	W	D	L	F	A	Pts
Clapton	42	30	4	8	96	46	94
Windsor & Eton	42	27	7	8	98	43	88
Barton Rovers	42	26	6	10	86	48	84
Leyton Wingate	42	25	8	9	111	41	83
Basildon United	42	23	13	6	92	42	82
Uxbridge	42	22	12	8	80	42	78
Hungerford Town	42	22	10	10	82	39	76
Corinthian Casuals	42	23	6	13	95	48	75
Egham Town	42	21	8	13	77	67	71
Tring Town	42	20	10	12	86	59	70
Letchworth Garden City	42	18	13	11	68	53	66
Southall	42	18	7	17	81	80	61
Molesey	42	17	9	16	73	56	60
Dorking Town	42	15	9	18	56	75	54
Hemel Hempstead	42	12	14	16	53	59	50
Rainham Town	42	14	4	24	57	94	46
Eastbourne United	42	10	6	26	54	104	36
Epping Town	42	6	8	28	29	89	26
Ware	42	6	6	30	34	97	24
Finchley	42	4	12	26	28	92	24
Horsham	42	5	7	30	32	106	22
Harwich & Parkeston	42	5	7	30	42	130	22

Letchworth Garden City had 1 point deducted

1982-83

Premier Division

	P	W	D	L	F	A	Pts
Wycombe Wanderers	42	26	7	9	79	47	85
Leytonstone & Ilford	42	24	9	9	71	39	81
Harrow Borough	42	24	7	11	91	58	79
Hayes	42	23	9	10	63	41	78
Sutton United	42	20	8	14	96	71	68
Dulwich Hamlet	42	18	14	10	59	52	68
Slough Town	42	18	13	11	73	36	67
Bognor Regis Town	42	19	8	15	53	48	65
Tooting & Mitcham United	42	18	9	15	65	62	63
Billericay Town	42	17	10	15	54	51	61
Croydon	42	17	9	16	68	58	60
Hendon	42	18	6	18	68	61	60
Bishop's Stortford	42	17	9	16	61	58	60
Barking	42	14	14	14	47	55	56
Bromley	42	14	12	16	51	50	54
Carshalton Athletic	42	15	9	18	58	60	54
Wokingham Town	42	13	9	20	37	51	48
Walthamstow Avenue	42	12	11	19	48	64	47
Staines Town	42	12	11	19	62	79	47
Hitchin Town	42	11	9	22	49	77	42
Woking	42	6	6	30	30	79	24
Leatherhead	42	4	5	33	35	121	17

Premier Division

	P	W	D	L	F	A	Pts
Harrow Borough	42	25	13	4	73	42	88
Worthing	42	20	11	11	89	72	71
Slough Town	42	20	9	13	73	56	69
Sutton United	42	18	12	12	67	45	66
Hayes	42	17	13	12	56	41	64
Hitchin Town	42	16	15	11	58	57	63
Wycombe Wanderers	42	16	14	12	63	52	62
Wokingham Town	42	18	10	14	78	55	61
Hendon	42	17	10	15	62	51	61
Dulwich Hamlet	42	16	11	15	61	64	59
Bishop's Stortford	42	15	13	14	56	57	58
Harlow Town	42	15	11	16	64	70	56
Bognor Regis Town	42	14	13	15	62	69	55
Staines Town	42	15	9	18	63	72	54
Billericay Town	42	15	8	19	53	73	53
Barking	42	13	13	16	60	64	52
Croydon	42	14	10	18	52	58	52
Walthamstow Avenue	42	13	10	19	53	67	49
Leytonstone & Ilford	42	13	9	20	54	67	48
Carshalton Athletic	42	11	10	21	59	72	43
Tooting & Mitcham United	42	10	13	19	50	63	43
Bromley	42	7	11	24	33	72	32

Wokingham Town had 3 points deducted

First Division

	P	W	D	L	F	A	Pts
Worthing	40	25	6	9	76	39	81
Harlow Town	40	21	11	8	84	55	74
Farnborough Town	40	20	13	7	69	39	73
Hertford Town	40	20	11	9	70	61	71
Oxford City	40	19	13	8	70	49	70
Boreham Wood	40	21	6	13	62	42	69
Metropolitan Police	40	19	9	12	77	57	66
Walton & Hersham	40	17	6	17	65	59	57
Hampton	40	15	10	15	62	60	55
Wembley	40	14	10	16	62	61	52
Aveley	40	15	7	18	52	62	52
Kingstonian	40	13	12	15	53	53	51
Tilbury	40	12	10	18	41	47	46
Feltham	40	11	12	17	45	54	45
Chesham United	40	13	6	21	43	70	45
Epsom & Ewell	40	10	14	16	44	49	44
Lewes	40	12	8	20	47	71	44
Cheshunt	40	10	13	17	41	49	43
Hornchurch	40	11	8	21	45	74	41
Maidenhead United	40	10	10	20	57	87	40
St Albans City	40	10	9	21	52	79	37

St Albans City had 2 points deducted

First Division

	P	W	D	L	F	A	Pts
Windsor & Eton	42	26	7	9	89	44	85
Epsom & Ewell	42	23	9	10	73	51	78
Wembley	42	21	11	10	65	32	74
Maidenhead United	42	22	8	12	67	42	74
Boreham Wood	42	22	7	13	74	43	73
Farnborough Town	42	18	12	12	78	60	66
Hampton	42	18	12	12	65	49	66
Metropolitan Police	42	20	5	17	79	64	65
Chesham United	42	18	8	16	64	57	62
Tilbury	42	17	10	15	54	64	61
Leatherhead	42	15	10	17	67	56	55
Aveley	42	15	10	17	49	53	55
Woking	42	16	7	19	66	73	55
Hertford Town	42	15	9	18	56	73	54
Oxford City	42	14	9	19	57	56	51
Lewes	42	13	12	17	49	65	51
Walton & Hersham	42	13	10	19	52	70	49
Hornchurch	42	13	10	19	43	65	49
Kingstonian	42	13	9	20	47	67	48
Clapton	42	12	11	19	49	67	47
Cheshunt	42	12	8	22	45	64	44
Feltham	42	7	4	31	31	106	25

Second Division

Basildon United	42	30	7	5	88	27	97
St Albans City	42	29	9	5	100	46	96
Leyton Wingate	42	29	4	9	97	41	91
Tring Town	42	23	11	8	89	44	80
Corinthian Casuals	42	23	11	8	75	47	80
Hungerford Town	42	21	12	9	94	47	75
Uxbridge	42	18	15	9	61	36	69
Grays Athletic	42	20	9	13	72	57	69
Dorking	42	21	5	16	66	54	68
Southall	42	20	8	14	79	60	65
Egham Town	42	16	15	11	59	49	63
Epping Town	42	15	16	11	61	50	61
Molesey	42	13	14	15	59	68	53
Barton Rovers	42	15	8	19	54	64	53
Letchworth Garden City	42	15	7	20	48	66	52
Newbury Town	42	14	5	23	60	82	47
Hemel Hempstead	42	12	9	21	63	69	45
Rainham Town	42	7	5	30	38	114	26
Finchley	42	5	9	28	28	78	24
Eastbourne United	42	7	3	32	36	98	24
Ware	42	6	6	30	48	114	24
Horsham	42	7	4	31	40	104	23

Southall had 2 points deducted
Horsham had 3 points deducted

1984-85

Premier Division

Sutton United	42	23	15	4	115	55	84
Worthing	42	24	8	10	89	59	80
Wycombe Wanderers	42	24	6	12	68	46	78
Wokingham Town	42	20	13	9	74	54	73
Windsor & Eton	42	19	10	13	65	55	67
Bognor Regis Town	42	20	6	16	67	58	66
Dulwich Hamlet	42	16	17	9	82	57	65
Harrow Borough	42	18	8	16	70	56	62
Hayes	42	17	8	17	60	56	59
Tooting & Mitcham United	42	16	11	15	64	66	59
Walthamstow Avenue	42	15	11	16	64	65	56
Croydon	42	15	12	15	62	63	54
Epsom & Ewell	42	13	14	15	65	62	53
Slough Town	42	13	12	17	69	74	51
Carshalton Athletic	42	14	8	20	55	68	50
Bishop's Stortford	42	12	12	18	48	67	48
Hendon	42	9	19	14	62	65	46
Billericay Town	42	11	14	17	53	74	46
Barking	42	13	7	22	43	75	46
Hitchin Town	42	10	15	17	55	70	45
Leytonstone & Ilford	42	11	10	21	37	72	43
Harlow Town	42	5	12	25	45	95	27

Billercay Town had 1 point deducted
Croydon had 3 points deducted

First Division

Farnborough Town	42	26	8	8	101	45	86
Kingstonian	42	23	10	9	67	39	79
Leatherhead	42	23	10	9	109	61	76
Chesham United	42	22	8	12	78	46	74
Wembley	42	20	10	12	59	40	70
St Albans City	42	19	10	13	79	60	67
Tilbury	42	18	13	11	86	68	67
Bromley	42	18	9	15	71	64	63
Hampton	42	17	11	14	75	62	62
Staines Town	42	16	11	15	59	53	59
Maidenhead United	42	17	8	17	65	64	59
Walton & Hersham	42	16	8	18	60	69	55
Aveley	42	16	7	19	62	78	55
Oxford City	42	14	12	16	62	53	54
Lewes	42	15	9	18	70	72	54
Basildon United	42	15	8	19	55	61	53
Boreham Wood	42	15	7	20	72	83	52
Hornchurch	42	15	6	21	55	74	51
Woking	42	15	6	21	60	91	51
Metropolitan Police	42	10	12	20	65	92	42
Clapton	42	5	11	26	50	124	26
Hertford Town	42	5	10	27	36	97	25

Walton & Hersham had 1 point deducted
Leatherhead had 3 points deducted

Second Division North

Leyton Wingate	38	24	9	5	98	50	81
Finchley	38	24	8	6	66	31	79
Heybridge Swifts	38	22	9	7	71	33	75
Stevenage Borough	38	23	6	9	79	49	75
Saffron Walden Town	38	22	8	8	73	31	74
Tring Town	38	19	11	8	76	41	68
Chalfont St Peter	38	17	10	11	72	41	61
Flackwell Heath	38	16	11	11	54	40	59
Berkhamsted Town	38	15	12	11	50	42	57
Letchworth Garden City	38	17	6	15	66	69	57
Royston Town	38	13	9	16	47	77	48
Cheshunt	38	14	5	19	52	57	47
Marlow	38	13	6	19	64	81	45
Hemel Hempstead	38	11	7	20	49	65	40
Barton Rovers	38	9	8	21	40	62	35
Wolverton Town	38	9	8	21	38	77	35
Kingsbury Town	38	9	7	22	53	72	34
Harefield United	38	7	9	22	51	81	30
Haringey Borough	38	6	12	20	38	79	30
Ware	38	7	5	26	40	100	26

Finchley had 1 point deducted
The record of Epping Town was expunged

Second Division South

Grays Athletic	36	24	9	3	84	25	81
Uxbridge	36	22	10	4	81	20	76
Molesey	36	20	5	11	62	42	65
Hungerford Town	36	18	9	9	71	49	63
Whyteleafe	36	17	10	9	66	34	61
Egham Town	36	17	7	12	54	42	58
Southall	36	18	3	15	54	57	57
Bracknell Town	36	15	7	14	54	48	52
Banstead Athletic	36	14	8	14	63	70	50
Horsham	36	13	10	13	44	39	49
Ruislip Manor	36	13	10	13	48	49	49
Dorking	36	12	11	13	45	50	47
Rainham Town	36	12	8	16	58	61	44
Feltham	36	10	13	13	44	58	43
Camberley Town	36	10	12	14	44	54	42
Eastbourne United	36	10	9	17	66	72	39
Petersfield Town	36	9	5	22	41	80	32
Newbury Town	36	8	7	21	35	69	16
Chertsey Town	36	2	3	31	23	118	6

Chertsey Town had 3 points deducted
Newbury Town had 15 points deducted

1985-86

Premier Division

Sutton United	42	29	8	5	109	39	95
Yeovil Town	42	28	7	7	92	48	91
Farnborough Town	42	23	8	11	90	50	77
Croydon	42	23	7	12	70	50	76
Harrow Borough	42	21	8	13	76	66	71
Slough Town	42	18	8	16	66	68	62
Bishop's Stortford	42	17	10	15	55	61	61
Kingstonian	42	15	15	12	57	56	60
Dulwich Hamlet	42	17	9	16	64	79	60
Wokingham Town	42	16	10	16	67	64	58
Windsor & Eton	42	17	7	18	58	75	58
Tooting & Mitcham United	42	14	11	17	65	76	53
Walthamstow Avenue	42	12	14	16	69	70	50
Worthing	42	13	10	19	72	82	49
Bognor Regis Town	42	15	6	21	63	70	48
Hayes	42	10	17	15	36	42	47
Hitchin Town	42	11	14	17	53	69	47
Barking	42	11	13	18	45	55	46
Hendon	42	10	13	19	59	77	43
Carshalton Athletic	42	9	13	20	56	79	40
Billericay Town	42	9	12	21	59	78	39
Epsom & Ewell	42	8	12	22	63	90	36

Bognor Regis Town had 3 points deducted

First Division

Team	P	W	D	L	F	A	Pts
St Albans City	42	23	11	8	92	61	80
Bromley	42	24	8	10	68	41	80
Wembley	42	22	12	8	59	30	78
Oxford City	42	22	11	9	75	51	77
Hampton	42	21	11	10	63	45	74
Leyton Wingate	42	21	10	11	77	56	73
Uxbridge	42	20	8	14	64	49	68
Staines Town	42	18	10	14	69	66	64
Boreham Wood	42	15	16	11	62	54	61
Walton & Hersham	42	16	10	16	68	71	58
Lewes	42	16	8	18	61	75	56
Leytonstone & Ilford	42	13	15	14	57	67	54
Finchley	42	12	17	13	61	59	53
Grays Athletic	42	13	11	18	69	75	50
Leatherhead	42	14	8	20	62	68	50
Tilbury	42	13	11	18	60	66	50
Maidenhead United	42	13	7	22	61	67	46
Basildon United	42	12	9	21	52	72	45
Hornchurch	42	11	11	20	44	59	44
Chesham United	42	12	6	24	51	87	42
Harlow Town	42	8	14	20	53	70	38
Aveley	42	8	6	28	59	98	30

Second Division North

Team	P	W	D	L	F	A	Pts
Stevenage Borough	38	26	6	6	71	24	84
Kingsbury Town	38	25	8	5	84	35	83
Heybridge Swifts	38	20	8	10	65	46	68
Cheshunt	38	18	10	10	60	40	64
Hertford Town	38	17	7	14	60	50	58
Chalfont St Peter	38	15	11	12	53	50	56
Tring Town	38	14	13	11	58	46	55
Royston Town	38	13	13	12	59	57	52
Saffron Walden Town	38	13	12	13	61	65	51
Berkhamsted Town	38	14	8	16	45	52	50
Haringey Borough	38	14	7	17	49	51	49
Letchworth Garden City	38	13	8	17	46	52	47
Rainham Town	38	14	4	20	54	91	46
Hemel Hempstead	38	12	9	17	50	66	45
Ware	38	11	11	16	56	61	44
Vauxhall Motors	38	11	10	17	58	62	43
Barton Rovers	38	12	7	19	50	60	43
Harefield United	38	9	12	17	56	72	39
Clapton	38	10	7	21	51	90	37
Wolverton Town	38	8	11	19	42	58	35

Second Division South

Team	P	W	D	L	F	A	Pts
Southwick	38	25	8	5	86	34	83
Bracknell Town	38	24	9	5	80	23	81
Woking	38	23	9	6	94	45	78
Newbury Town	38	22	7	9	86	53	73
Whyteleafe	38	21	10	7	61	41	73
Molesey	38	21	8	9	59	39	71
Metropolitan Police	38	20	6	12	72	48	66
Southall	38	19	7	12	76	58	64
Dorking	38	18	10	10	70	57	64
Feltham	38	16	7	15	65	60	55
Banstead Athletic	38	15	8	15	60	66	53
Petersfield United	38	12	9	17	61	71	45
Hungerford Town	38	11	6	21	57	78	39
Flackwell Heath	38	11	6	21	46	72	39
Eastbourne United	38	9	8	21	51	81	35
Camberley Town	38	9	7	22	53	64	34
Egham Town	38	7	8	23	41	83	29
Horsham	38	6	10	22	33	74	28
Ruislip Manor	38	5	12	21	44	87	27
Marlow	38	6	5	27	47	108	23

1986-87

Premier Division

Team	P	W	D	L	F	A	Pts
Wycombe Wanderers	42	32	5	5	103	32	101
Yeovil Town	42	28	8	6	71	27	92
Slough Town	42	23	8	11	70	44	77
Hendon	42	22	7	13	67	53	73
Bognor Regis Town	42	20	10	12	85	61	70
Harrow Borough	42	20	10	12	68	44	70
Croydon	42	18	10	14	51	48	64
Barking	42	16	14	12	76	56	62
Farnborough Town	42	17	11	14	66	72	62
Bishop's Stortford	42	15	15	12	62	57	60
Bromley	42	16	11	15	63	72	59
Kingstonian	42	16	9	17	58	50	57
Windsor & Eton	42	13	15	14	47	52	54
St Albans City	42	14	9	19	61	70	51
Carshalton Athletic	42	13	9	20	55	68	48
Wokingham Town	42	14	6	22	47	61	48
Hayes	42	12	12	18	45	68	48
Dulwich Hamlet	42	12	10	20	62	71	46
Tooting & Mitcham United	42	12	9	21	51	53	45
Hitchin Town	42	13	5	24	56	69	44
Worthing	42	8	9	25	58	107	33
Walthamstow Avenue	42	4	6	32	36	113	18

First Division

Team	P	W	D	L	F	A	Pts
Leytonstone & Ilford	42	30	5	7	78	29	95
Leyton Wingate	42	23	13	6	68	31	82
Bracknell Town	42	24	9	9	92	48	81
Southwick	42	23	7	12	80	66	76
Wembley	42	21	9	12	61	47	72
Grays Athletic	42	19	10	13	76	64	67
Kingsbury Town	42	20	7	15	69	67	67
Boreham Wood	42	20	6	16	59	52	66
Uxbridge	42	18	9	15	60	59	63
Leatherhead	42	17	11	14	45	48	62
Hampton	42	18	5	19	57	55	59
Basildon United	42	16	10	16	58	60	58
Billericay Town	42	14	12	16	57	52	54
Staines Town	42	13	13	16	40	51	52
Lewes	42	15	6	21	55	65	51
Stevenage Borough	42	12	11	19	61	67	47
Oxford City	42	11	10	21	64	72	43
Walton & Hersham	42	11	10	21	53	74	43
Tilbury	42	12	7	23	46	70	43
Epsom & Ewell	42	12	7	23	44	68	43
Maidenhead United	42	11	4	27	44	76	37
Finchley	42	6	11	25	44	90	29

Second Division North

Team	P	W	D	L	F	A	Pts
Chesham United	42	28	6	8	81	48	90
Wolverton Town	42	23	14	5	74	32	83
Haringey Borough	42	22	13	7	86	40	79
Heybridge Swifts	42	21	11	10	81	54	74
Aveley	42	19	13	10	68	50	70
Letchworth Garden City	42	19	11	12	77	62	68
Barton Rovers	42	18	11	13	49	39	65
Tring Town	42	19	7	16	69	49	64
Collier Row	42	19	5	18	67	65	62
Ware	42	17	8	17	51	50	59
Saffron Walden Town	42	14	14	14	56	54	56
Wivenhoe Town	42	15	11	16	61	61	56
Vauxhall Motors	42	15	10	17	61	57	55
Hornchurch	42	13	16	13	60	60	55
Hertford Town	42	14	13	15	52	53	55
Berkhamsted Town	42	12	16	14	62	64	52
Harlow Town	42	13	11	18	45	55	50
Rainham Town	42	12	11	19	53	70	47
Clapton	42	10	11	21	45	63	41
Hemel Hempstead	42	9	12	21	48	77	39
Royston Town	42	4	12	26	37	109	24
Cheshunt	42	5	6	31	43	114	21

Second Division South

Woking	40	27	7	6	110	32	88
Marlow	40	28	4	8	78	36	88
Dorking	40	24	12	4	78	30	84
Feltham	40	25	3	12	79	34	78
Ruislip Manor	40	22	10	8	85	47	76
Chertsey Town	40	18	11	11	56	44	65
Metropolitan Police	40	16	13	11	70	61	61
Chalfont St Peter	40	17	10	13	60	55	61
Hungerford Town	40	14	14	12	55	48	56
Harefield United	40	14	14	12	53	47	56
Eastbourne United	40	15	10	15	72	59	55
Whyteleafe	40	12	15	13	52	63	51
Horsham	40	14	8	18	54	61	50
Egham Town	40	14	6	20	45	77	48
Camberley Town	40	13	3	24	62	89	42
Flackwell Heath	40	9	11	20	34	63	38
Banstead Athletic	40	7	15	18	44	61	36
Petersfield United	40	9	8	23	45	84	34
Molesey	40	7	12	21	37	89	33
Newbury Town	40	6	14	20	51	83	32
Southall	40	6	6	28	28	85	24

Second Division North

Wivenhoe Town	42	26	10	6	105	42	88
Collier Row	42	22	13	7	71	39	79
Tilbury	42	18	15	9	61	40	69
Berkhamsted Town	42	19	12	11	71	53	69
Harlow Town	42	17	16	9	67	36	67
Ware	42	17	15	10	63	58	66
Witham Town	42	17	14	11	69	47	65
Vauxhall Motors	42	16	17	9	56	42	65
Heybridge Swifts	42	17	13	12	56	50	64
Tring Town	42	18	6	18	69	67	60
Letchworth Garden City	42	18	5	19	59	64	59
Finchley	42	16	10	16	67	54	58
Clapton	42	14	15	13	50	62	57
Hornchurch	42	13	15	14	56	65	54
Barton Rovers	42	13	10	19	43	60	49
Rainham Town	42	12	12	18	63	66	48
Royston Town	42	13	8	21	49	70	47
Saffron Waldon Town	42	13	7	22	34	67	46
Hemel Hempstead	42	11	12	19	38	71	45
Haringey Borough	42	11	8	23	54	78	41
Aveley	42	8	13	21	42	65	37
Hertford Town	42	8	4	30	45	92	28

Second Division South

Chalfont St Peter	42	26	9	7	81	35	87
Metropolitan Police	42	23	17	2	80	32	86
Dorking	42	25	11	6	86	39	86
Feltham	42	21	12	9	74	41	75
Epsom & Ewell	42	21	11	10	71	49	74
Chertsey Town	42	22	7	13	63	47	73
Whyteleafe	42	20	11	11	84	55	71
Hungerford Town	42	21	7	14	66	54	70
Ruislip Manor	42	21	5	16	74	57	68
Yeading	42	19	10	13	83	56	67
Maidenhead United	42	18	12	12	69	54	66
Eastbourne United	42	18	10	14	67	57	64
Harefield Town	42	18	6	18	59	60	60
Egham Town	42	12	12	18	45	55	48
Horsham	42	12	10	20	45	66	46
Southall	42	13	7	22	45	72	46
Molesey	42	11	11	20	42	63	44
Newbury Town	42	8	13	21	40	81	37
Camberley Town	42	9	9	24	51	94	36
Flackwell Heath	42	6	8	28	42	96	26
Banstead Athletic	42	6	7	29	34	81	25
Petersfield United	42	6	7	29	45	102	25

1987-88

Premier Division

Yeovil Town	42	24	9	9	66	34	81
Bromley	42	23	7	12	68	40	76
Slough Town	42	21	9	12	67	41	72
Leytonstone & Ilford	42	20	11	11	59	43	71
Wokingham Town	42	21	7	14	62	52	70
Hayes	42	20	9	13	62	48	69
Windsor & Eton	42	16	17	9	59	43	65
Farnborough Town	42	17	11	14	63	60	62
Carshalton Athletic	42	16	13	13	49	41	61
Hendon	42	16	12	14	62	58	60
Tooting & Mitcham United	42	15	14	13	57	59	59
Harrow Borough	42	15	11	16	53	58	56
Bishop's Stortford	42	15	10	17	55	58	55
Kingstonian	42	14	12	16	47	53	54
St Albans City	42	15	6	21	60	69	51
Bognor Regis Town	42	14	9	19	41	57	51
Leyton Wingate	42	14	8	20	58	64	50
Croydon	42	11	13	18	40	52	46
Barking	42	11	12	19	44	57	45
Dulwich Hamlet	42	10	11	21	46	64	41
Hitchin Town	42	10	8	24	46	79	38
Basingstoke Town	42	6	17	19	37	71	35

First Division

Marlow	42	32	5	5	100	44	101
Grays Athletic	42	30	10	2	74	25	100
Woking	42	25	7	10	91	52	82
Boreham Wood	42	21	9	12	65	45	72
Staines Town	42	19	11	12	71	48	68
Wembley	42	18	11	13	54	46	65
Basildon United	42	18	9	15	65	58	63
Walton & Hersham	42	15	16	11	53	44	61
Hampton	42	17	10	15	59	54	61
Leatherhead	42	16	11	15	64	53	59
Southwick	42	13	12	17	59	63	51
Oxford City	42	13	12	17	70	77	51
Worthing	42	14	8	20	67	73	50
Kingsbury Town	42	11	17	14	62	69	50
Walthamstow Avenue	42	13	11	18	53	63	50
Lewes	42	12	13	17	83	77	49
Uxbridge	42	11	16	15	41	47	49
Chesham United	42	12	10	20	69	77	46
Bracknell Town	42	12	9	21	54	80	45
Billericay Town	42	11	11	20	58	88	44
Stevenage Borough	42	11	9	22	36	64	42
Wolverton Town	42	3	3	36	23	124	12

1988-89

Premier Division

Leytonstone & Ilford	42	26	11	5	76	36	89
Farnborough Town	42	24	9	9	85	61	81
Slough Town	42	24	6	12	72	42	78
Carshalton Athletic	42	19	15	8	59	36	72
Grays Athletic	42	19	13	10	62	47	70
Kingstonian	42	19	11	12	54	37	68
Bishop's Stortford	42	20	6	16	70	56	66
Hayes	42	18	12	12	6	47	66
Bognor Regis Town	42	17	11	14	38	49	62
Barking	42	16	13	13	49	45	61
Wokingham Town	42	15	11	16	60	54	56
Hendon	42	13	17	12	51	68	56
Windsor & Eton	42	14	13	15	52	50	55
Bromley	42	13	15	14	61	48	54
Leyton Wingate	42	13	15	14	55	56	54
Dulwich Hamlet	42	12	12	18	58	57	48
St Albans City	42	12	9	21	51	59	45
Dagenham	42	11	12	19	53	68	45
Harrow Borough	42	9	13	20	53	75	40
Marlow	42	9	11	22	48	83	38
Tooting & Mitcham United	42	10	6	26	41	81	36
Croydon	42	4	9	29	27	81	21

First Division

Staines Town	40	26	9	5	79	29	87
Basingstoke Town	40	25	8	7	85	36	83
Woking	40	24	10	6	72	30	82
Hitchin Town	40	21	11	8	60	32	74
Wivenhoe Town	40	22	6	12	62	44	72
Lewes	40	21	8	11	72	54	71
Walton & Hersham	40	21	7	12	56	36	70
Kingsbury Town	40	20	7	13	65	41	67
Uxbridge	40	19	7	14	60	54	64
Wembley	40	18	6	16	45	58	60
Boreham Wood	40	16	9	15	57	52	57
Leatherhead	40	14	8	18	56	58	50
Metropolitan Police	40	13	9	18	52	68	48
Chesham United	40	12	9	19	54	67	45
Southwick	40	9	15	16	44	58	42
Chalfont St Peter	40	11	9	20	56	82	42
Hampton	40	7	14	19	37	62	35
Worthing	40	8	10	22	49	80	32
Collier Row	40	8	7	25	37	82	31
Bracknell Town	40	8	6	26	38	70	30
Basildon Town	40	6	7	27	34	77	25

Worthing had 2 points deducted.

Second Division North

Harlow Town	42	27	9	6	83	38	90
Purfleet	42	22	12	8	60	42	78
Tring Town	42	22	10	10	65	44	76
Stevenage Borough	42	20	13	9	84	55	73
Heybridge Swifts	42	21	9	12	64	43	72
Billericay Town	42	19	11	12	65	52	68
Clapton	42	18	11	13	65	56	65
Barton Rovers	42	18	11	13	58	50	65
Aveley	42	18	10	14	54	52	64
Hertford Town	42	16	13	13	62	49	59
Ware	42	17	8	17	60	65	59
Hemel Hempstead	42	16	10	16	55	58	58
Witham Town	42	16	7	19	69	67	55
Vauxhall Motors	42	15	9	18	53	57	54
Berkhamsted Town	42	14	10	18	57	70	52
Hornchurch	42	11	16	15	59	61	49
Tilbury	42	13	10	19	53	60	49
Royston Town	42	12	7	23	46	72	43
Rainham Town	42	9	15	18	49	62	42
Saffron Walden Town	42	8	16	18	54	72	40
Letchworth Garden City	42	4	18	20	34	71	30
Wolverton Town	42	5	7	30	42	95	13

Hertford Town 2 points deducted, Wolverton Town 9 points deducted.

Second Division South

Dorking	40	32	4	4	109	35	100
Whyteleafe	40	25	9	6	86	41	84
Finchley	40	21	9	10	70	45	72
Molesey	40	19	13	8	58	42	70
Harefield United	40	19	7	14	56	45	64
Hungerford Town	40	17	13	10	55	45	64
Ruislip Manor	40	16	9	15	56	43	57
Feltham	40	16	9	15	58	53	57
Epsom & Ewell	40	16	8	16	55	55	56
Egham Town	40	16	7	17	54	58	55
Eastbourne United	40	15	9	16	68	61	54
Chertsey Town	40	13	14	13	55	58	53
Flackwell Heath	40	13	11	16	51	49	50
Camberley Town	40	15	5	20	51	71	50
Yeading	40	13	9	18	47	63	46
Banstead Athletic	40	12	8	20	50	65	44
Maidenhead United	40	10	13	17	44	61	43
Southall	40	11	10	19	41	73	43
Newbury Town	40	11	8	21	47	65	41
Horsham	40	7	14	19	36	68	35
Petersfield United	40	5	7	28	36	87	22

Yeading had 2 points deducted.

1989-90

Premier Division

Slough Town	42	27	11	4	85	38	92
Wokingham Town	42	26	11	5	67	34	89
Aylesbury United	42	25	9	8	86	30	84
Kingstonian	42	24	9	9	87	51	81
Grays Athletic	42	19	13	10	59	44	70
Dagenham	42	17	15	10	54	43	66
Leyton Wingate	42	20	6	16	54	48	66
Basingstoke Town	42	18	9	15	65	55	63
Bishop's Stortford	42	19	6	17	60	59	63
Carshalton Athletic	42	19	5	18	63	59	59
Redbridge Forest	42	16	11	15	65	62	59
Hendon	42	15	10	17	54	63	55
Windsor & Eton	42	13	15	14	51	47	54
Hayes	42	14	11	17	61	59	53
St Albans City	42	13	10	19	49	59	49
Staines Town	42	14	6	22	53	69	48
Marlow	42	11	13	18	42	59	46
Harrow Borough	42	11	10	21	51	79	43
Bognor Regis Town	42	9	14	19	37	67	41
Barking	42	7	11	24	53	86	32
Bromley	42	7	11	24	32	69	32
Dulwich Hamlet	42	6	8	28	32	80	26

Carshalton Athletic had 3 points deducted.

First Division

Wivenhoe Town	42	31	7	4	94	36	100
Woking	42	30	8	4	102	29	98
Southwick	42	23	15	4	68	30	84
Hitchin Town	42	22	13	7	60	30	79
Walton & Hersham	42	20	10	12	68	50	70
Dorking	42	19	12	11	66	41	69
Boreham Wood	42	17	13	12	60	59	64
Harlow Town	42	16	13	13	60	53	61
Metropolitan Police	42	16	11	15	54	59	59
Chesham United	42	15	12	15	46	49	57
Chalfont St Peter	42	14	13	15	50	59	55
Tooting & Mitcham United	42	14	13	15	42	51	55
Worthing	42	15	8	19	56	63	53
Whyteleafe	42	11	16	15	50	65	49
Lewes	42	12	11	19	55	65	47
Wembley	42	11	10	21	57	68	43
Croydon	42	9	16	17	43	57	43
Uxbridge	42	11	10	21	52	75	43
Hampton	42	8	13	21	28	51	37
Leatherhead	42	7	10	25	34	77	31
Purfleet	42	7	8	27	33	78	29
Kingsbury Town	42	8	10	24	45	78	25

Kingsbury Town had 9 points deducted

Second Division North

Heybridge Swifts	42	26	9	7	79	29	87
Aveley	42	23	16	3	68	24	85
Hertford Town	42	24	11	7	92	51	83
Stevenage Borough	42	21	16	5	70	31	79
Barton Rovers	42	22	6	14	60	45	72
Tilbury	42	20	9	13	68	54	69
Basildon United	42	13	20	9	50	44	59
Collier Row	42	15	13	14	43	45	58
Royston Town	42	15	11	16	63	72	56
Saffron Walden Town	42	15	11	16	60	73	56
Vauxhall Motors	42	14	13	15	54	55	55
Clapton	42	13	16	13	50	46	54
Ware	42	14	11	17	53	59	53
Hemel Hempstead	42	12	15	15	58	50	51
Billericay Town	42	13	11	18	49	58	50
Hornchurch	42	12	12	18	49	64	48
Berkhamsted Town	42	9	16	17	44	68	43
Finchley	42	11	10	21	50	75	43
Tring Town	42	10	9	23	48	70	39
Witham Town	42	8	14	20	44	56	38
Rainham Town	42	9	11	22	48	75	38
Letchworth Garden City	42	7	12	23	30	68	33

Clapton had 1 point deducted

Second Division South

Yeading	40	29	4	7	86	37	91
Molesey	40	24	11	5	76	30	83
Abingdon Town	40	22	9	9	64	39	75
Ruislip Manor	40	20	12	8	60	32	72
Maidenhead United	40	20	12	8	66	39	72
Southall	40	22	5	13	56	33	71
Newbury Town	40	21	7	12	50	36	70
Flackwell Heath	40	16	11	13	69	65	59
Hungerford Town	40	14	16	10	54	51	58
Egham Town	40	12	14	14	39	38	50
Banstead Athletic	40	14	8	18	46	47	50
Harefield United	40	13	9	18	44	46	48
Chertsey Town	40	13	9	18	53	58	48
Epsom & Ewell	40	13	9	18	49	54	48
Malden Vale	40	13	7	20	36	67	46
Eastbourne United	40	11	10	19	47	65	43
Camberley Town	40	11	9	20	44	66	42
Feltham	40	11	7	22	47	80	40
Bracknell Town	40	10	9	21	40	57	39
Petersfield United	40	10	8	22	48	93	38
Horsham	40	4	8	28	29	70	20

Second Division North

Stevenage Borough	42	34	5	3	122	29	107
Vauxhall Motors	42	24	10	8	82	50	82
Billericay Town	42	22	8	12	70	41	74
Ware	42	22	8	12	78	51	74
Berkhamsted Town	42	19	11	12	60	51	68
Witham Town	42	19	10	13	70	59	67
Purfleet	42	17	14	11	68	57	65
Rainham Town	42	19	7	16	57	46	64
Hemel Hempstead	42	16	14	12	62	56	62
Barton Rovers	42	17	10	15	61	58	61
Saffron Walden Town	42	16	13	13	72	77	61
Collier Row	42	16	11	15	63	63	59
Kingsbury Town	42	17	8	17	64	72	59
Edgware Town	42	17	7	18	73	65	58
Hertford Town	42	16	10	16	69	70	58
Royston Town	42	14	15	13	78	62	57
Tilbury	42	14	6	22	70	79	48
Basildon United	42	11	10	21	61	90	43
Hornchurch	42	10	9	23	53	87	39
Clapton	42	9	10	23	54	93	34
Finchley	42	6	7	29	50	112	24
Tring Town	42	1	9	32	30	99	12

Finchley had 1 point deducted
Clapton had 3 points deducted

1990-91

Premier Division

Redbridge Forest	42	29	6	7	74	43	93
Enfield	42	26	11	5	83	30	89
Aylesbury United	42	24	11	7	90	47	83
Woking	42	24	10	8	84	39	82
Kingstonian	42	21	12	9	86	57	75
Grays Athletic	42	20	8	14	66	53	68
Marlow	42	18	13	11	72	49	67
Hayes	42	20	5	17	60	57	65
Carshalton Athletic	42	19	7	16	80	67	64
Wivenhoe Town	42	16	11	15	69	66	59
Wokingham Town	42	15	13	14	58	54	58
Windsor & Eton	42	15	10	17	48	63	55
Bishop's Stortford	42	14	12	16	54	49	54
Dagenham	42	13	11	18	62	68	50
Hendon	42	12	10	20	48	62	46
St Albans City	42	11	12	19	60	74	45
Bognor Regis Town	42	12	8	22	44	71	44
Basingstoke Town	42	12	7	23	57	95	43
Staines Town	42	10	10	22	46	79	39
Harrow Borough	42	10	8	24	57	84	38
Barking	42	8	10	24	41	85	34
Leyton Wingate	42	7	7	28	44	91	28

Staines Town had 1 point deducted

First Division

Chesham United	42	27	8	7	102	37	89
Bromley	42	22	14	6	62	37	80
Yeading	42	23	8	11	75	45	77
Aveley	42	21	9	12	76	43	72
Hitchin Town	42	21	9	12	78	50	72
Tooting & Mitcham United	42	20	12	10	71	48	72
Walton & Hersham	42	21	8	13	73	48	71
Molesey	42	22	5	15	65	46	71
Whyteleafe	42	21	6	15	62	53	69
Dorking	42	20	5	17	78	67	65
Chalfont St Peter	42	19	5	18	56	63	62
Dulwich Hamlet	42	16	11	15	67	54	59
Harlow Town	42	17	8	17	73	64	59
Boreham Wood	42	15	8	19	46	53	53
Wembley	42	13	12	17	62	59	51
Uxbridge	42	15	5	22	45	61	50
Croydon	42	15	5	22	44	85	50
Heybridge Swifts	42	13	10	19	46	59	49
Southwick	42	13	8	21	49	75	47
Lewes	42	10	8	24	49	82	38
Metropolitan Police	42	9	6	27	55	76	33
Worthing	42	2	4	36	28	157	10

Second Division South

Abingdon Town	42	29	7	6	95	28	94
Maidenhead United	42	28	8	6	85	33	92
Egham Town	42	27	6	9	100	46	87
Malden Vale	42	26	5	11	72	44	83
Ruislip Manor	42	25	5	12	93	44	80
Southall	42	23	10	9	84	43	79
Harefield United	42	23	10	9	81	56	79
Newbury Town	42	23	8	11	71	45	77
Hungerford Town	42	16	13	13	84	69	61
Leatherhead	42	17	9	16	82	55	60
Banstead Athletic	42	15	13	14	58	62	58
Hampton	42	14	15	13	62	43	57
Epsom & Ewell	42	15	12	15	49	50	57
Chertsey Town	42	15	9	18	76	72	54
Horsham	42	14	7	21	58	67	49
Flackwell Heath	42	11	11	20	56	78	44
Bracknell Town	42	11	7	24	60	97	40
Feltham	42	10	8	24	45	80	38
Cove	42	10	7	25	51	94	37
Eastbourne United	42	10	7	25	53	109	37
Petersfield United	42	6	3	33	35	119	21
Camberley Town	42	1	6	35	27	143	9

1991-92

Premier Division

Woking	42	30	7	5	96	25	97
Enfield	42	24	7	11	59	45	79
Sutton United	42	19	13	10	88	51	70
Chesham United	42	20	10	12	67	48	70
Wokingham Town	42	19	10	13	73	58	67
Marlow	42	20	7	15	56	50	67
Aylesbury United	42	16	17	9	69	46	65
Carshalton Athletic	42	18	8	16	64	67	62
Dagenham	42	15	16	11	70	59	61
Kingstonian	42	17	8	17	71	65	59
Windsor & Eton	42	15	11	16	56	56	56
Bromley	42	14	12	16	51	57	54
St Albans City	42	14	11	17	66	70	53
Basingstoke Town	42	14	11	17	56	65	53
Grays Athletic	42	14	11	17	53	68	53
Wivenhoe Town	42	16	4	22	56	81	52
Hendon	42	13	9	20	59	73	48
Harrow Borough	42	11	13	18	58	78	46
Hayes	42	10	14	18	52	63	44
Staines Town	42	11	10	21	43	73	43
Bognor Regis Town	42	9	11	22	51	89	38
Bishop's Stortford	42	7	12	23	41	68	33

First Division

Stevenage Borough	40	30	6	4	95	37	96
Yeading	40	24	10	6	83	34	82
Dulwich Hamlet	40	22	9	9	71	40	75
Boreham Wood	40	22	7	11	65	40	73
Wembley	40	21	6	13	54	43	69
Abingdon Town	40	19	8	13	60	47	65
Tooting & Mitcham United	40	16	13	11	57	45	61
Hitchin Town	40	17	10	13	55	45	61
Walton & Hersham	40	15	13	12	62	50	58
Molesey	40	16	9	15	55	61	57
Dorking	40	16	7	17	68	65	55
Barking	40	14	11	15	51	54	53
Chalfont St Peter	40	15	6	19	62	70	51
Leyton Wingate	40	13	11	16	53	56	50
Uxbridge	40	13	8	19	47	62	47
Maidenhead United	40	13	7	20	52	61	46
Harlow Town	40	11	9	20	50	70	42
Croydon	40	11	6	23	44	68	39
Heybridge Swifts	40	8	9	23	33	71	33
Whyteleafe	40	7	10	23	42	78	31
Aveley	40	8	3	29	33	95	27

Second Division

Purfleet	42	27	8	7	97	48	89
Lewes	42	23	14	5	74	36	83
Billericay Town	42	24	8	10	75	44	80
Leatherhead	42	23	6	13	68	40	75
Ruislip Manor	42	20	9	13	74	51	69
Egham Town	42	19	12	11	81	62	69
Metropolitan Police	42	20	9	13	76	58	69
Saffron Walden Town	42	19	11	12	86	67	68
Hemel Hempstead	42	18	10	14	63	50	64
Hungerford Town	42	18	7	17	53	58	61
Barton Rovers	42	17	8	17	61	64	59
Worthing	42	17	8	17	67	72	59
Witham Town	42	16	11	15	56	61	59
Banstead Athletic	42	16	10	16	69	58	58
Malden Vale	42	15	12	15	63	48	57
Rainham Town	42	14	13	15	53	48	55
Ware	42	14	9	19	58	62	51
Berkhamsted Town	42	13	11	18	56	57	50
Harefield United	42	11	7	24	47	66	40
Southall	42	8	7	27	39	93	31
Southwick	42	6	2	34	29	115	20
Newbury Town	42	4	8	30	30	117	20

Third Division

Edgware Town	40	30	3	7	106	44	93
Chertsey Town	40	29	4	7	115	44	91
Tilbury	40	26	9	5	84	40	87
Hampton	40	26	5	9	93	35	83
Horsham	40	23	8	9	92	51	77
Cove	40	21	9	10	74	49	72
Flackwell Heath	40	19	12	9	78	50	69
Thame United	40	19	7	14	73	46	64
Epsom & Ewell	40	17	11	12	55	50	62
Collier Row	40	17	9	14	67	59	60
Royston Town	40	17	7	16	59	58	58
Kingsbury Town	40	12	10	18	54	61	46
Hertford Town	40	12	10	18	55	73	46
Petersfield United	40	12	9	19	45	67	45
Camberley Town	40	11	8	21	52	69	41
Feltham & Hounslow	40	11	2	22	53	78	40
Bracknell Town	40	10	7	23	48	90	37
Hornchurch	40	8	7	25	40	87	31
Tring Town	40	9	4	27	35	94	31
Clapton	40	9	3	28	47	92	30
Eastbourne United	40	5	5	30	34	121	20

1992-93

Premier Division

Chesham United	42	30	8	4	104	34	98
St Albans City	42	28	9	5	103	50	93
Enfield	42	25	6	11	94	48	81
Carshalton Athletic	42	22	10	10	96	56	76
Sutton United	42	18	14	10	74	57	68
Grays Athletic	42	18	11	13	61	64	65
Stevenage Borough	42	18	8	16	62	60	62
Harrow Borough	42	16	14	12	59	60	62
Hayes	42	16	13	13	64	59	61
Aylesbury United	42	18	6	18	70	77	60
Hendon	42	12	18	12	52	54	54
Basingstoke Town	42	12	17	13	49	45	53
Kingstonian	42	14	10	18	59	58	52
Dulwich Hamlet	42	12	14	16	52	66	50
Marlow	42	12	11	19	72	73	47
Wokingham Town	42	11	13	18	62	67	46
Bromley	42	11	13	18	51	72	46
Wivenhoe Town	42	13	7	22	41	75	46
Yeading	42	11	12	19	58	66	45
Staines Town	42	10	13	19	59	77	43
Windsor & Eton	42	8	7	27	40	90	31
Bognor Regis Town	42	5	10	27	46	106	25

First Division

Hitchin Town	40	25	7	8	67	29	82
Molesey	40	23	11	6	81	38	80
Dorking	40	23	9	8	73	40	78
Purfleet	40	19	12	9	67	42	69
Bishop's Stortford	40	19	10	11	63	42	67
Abingdon Town	40	17	13	10	65	47	64
Tooting & Mitcham United	40	17	12	11	68	46	63
Billericay Town	40	18	6	16	67	61	60
Wembley	40	14	15	11	44	34	57
Walton & Hersham	40	14	12	14	58	54	54
Boreham Wood	40	12	14	14	44	43	50
Maidenhead United	40	10	18	12	45	50	48
Leyton	40	11	14	15	56	61	47
Whyteleafe	40	12	10	18	63	71	46
Uxbridge	40	11	13	16	50	59	46
Heybridge Swifts	40	11	9	20	47	65	42
Croydon	40	11	9	20	54	82	42
Chalfont St Peter	40	7	17	16	48	70	38
Barking	40	10	8	22	42	80	38
Lewes	40	9	10	21	34	80	37
Aveley	40	9	7	24	45	87	34

Second Division

Worthing	42	28	7	7	105	50	91
Ruislip Manor	42	25	12	5	78	33	87
Berkhamsted Town	42	24	8	10	77	55	80
Hemel Hempstead	42	22	12	8	84	52	78
Metropolitan Police	42	22	6	14	84	51	72
Malden Vale	42	20	9	13	78	54	69
Chertsey Town	42	20	7	15	84	60	67
Saffron Walden Town	42	19	10	13	63	49	67
Newbury Town	42	14	18	10	53	51	60
Hampton	42	16	11	15	59	59	59
Edgware Town	42	16	10	16	84	75	58
Egham Town	42	16	9	17	60	71	57
Banstead Athletic	42	14	13	15	67	52	55
Leatherhead	42	14	11	17	66	61	53
Ware	42	12	11	19	68	76	47
Witham Town	42	10	16	16	54	65	46
Tilbury	42	12	8	22	55	101	44
Barton Rovers	42	9	14	19	40	66	41
Hungerford Town	42	11	8	23	37	93	41
Rainham Town	42	9	10	23	56	80	37
Harefield United	42	10	7	25	37	72	37
Southall	42	7	7	28	43	106	28

Third Division

Aldershot Town	38	28	8	2	90	35	92
Thame United	38	21	11	6	84	38	74
Collier Row	38	21	11	6	68	30	74
Leighton Town	38	21	10	7	89	47	73
Cove	38	21	8	9	69	42	71
Northwood	38	19	11	8	84	68	68
Royston Town	38	17	8	13	59	42	59
East Thurrock United	38	17	7	14	69	58	58
Kingsbury Town	38	15	9	14	62	59	54
Hertford Town	38	14	10	14	61	64	52
Flackwell Heath	38	15	6	17	82	76	51
Tring Town	38	12	11	15	59	63	47
Hornchurch	38	11	13	14	53	52	46
Horsham	38	12	7	19	63	72	43
Epsom & Ewell	38	10	11	17	52	67	41
Bracknell Town	38	7	13	18	52	94	34
Clapton	38	8	7	23	46	74	31
Camberley Town	38	8	7	23	37	72	31
Petersfield United	38	6	12	20	36	90	30
Feltham & Hounslow	38	5	4	29	47	119	19

Second Division

Newbury Town	42	32	7	3	115	36	103
Chertsey Town	42	33	3	6	121	48	102
Aldershot Town	42	30	7	5	78	27	97
Barton Rovers	42	25	8	9	68	37	83
Witham Town	42	21	10	11	68	51	73
Malden Vale	42	20	10	12	70	49	70
Thame United	42	19	12	11	87	51	69
Metropolitan Police	42	20	9	13	75	54	69
Banstead Athletic	42	19	9	14	56	53	66
Aveley	42	19	5	18	60	66	62
Edgware Town	42	16	10	16	88	75	58
Saffron Walden Town	42	17	7	18	61	62	58
Hemel Hempstead	42	14	11	17	47	43	53
Egham Town	42	14	8	20	48	65	50
Ware	42	14	7	21	48	76	49
Hungerford Town	42	13	7	22	56	66	46
Tilbury	42	13	3	26	59	81	42
Hampton	42	12	5	25	42	70	41
Leatherhead	42	10	6	26	46	92	36
Lewes	42	8	11	24	38	85	34
Collier Row	42	7	8	27	37	88	29
Rainham Town	42	4	2	36	24	116	14

Third Division

Bracknell Town	40	25	8	7	78	29	83
Cheshunt	40	23	12	5	62	34	81
Oxford City	40	24	6	10	94	55	78
Harlow Town	40	22	11	7	61	36	77
Southall	40	17	12	11	66	53	63
Camberley Town	40	18	7	15	56	50	61
Hertford Town	40	18	6	16	67	65	60
Royston Town	40	15	11	14	44	41	56
Northwood	40	15	11	14	78	77	56
Epsom & Ewell	40	15	9	16	63	62	54
Harefield United	40	12	15	13	45	55	51
Cove	40	15	6	19	59	74	51
Kingsbury Town	40	12	14	14	57	54	50
Feltham & Hounslow	40	14	7	19	60	63	49
Leighton Town	40	12	11	17	51	64	47
East Thurrock Town	40	10	15	15	65	64	45
Clapton	40	12	9	19	51	65	45
Hornchurch	40	12	8	20	42	60	44
Tring Town	40	10	11	19	48	64	41
Flackwell Heath	40	9	11	20	44	83	38
Horsham	40	6	8	26	43	86	26

1993-94

Premier Division

Stevenage Borough	42	31	4	7	88	39	97
Enfield	42	28	8	6	80	28	92
Marlow	42	25	7	10	90	67	82
Chesham United	42	24	8	10	73	45	80
Sutton United	42	23	10	9	77	31	79
Carshalton Athletic	42	22	7	13	81	53	73
St Albans City	42	21	10	11	81	54	73
Hitchin Town	42	21	7	14	81	56	70
Harrow Borough	42	18	11	13	54	56	65
Kingstonian	42	18	9	15	101	64	63
Hendon	42	18	9	15	61	51	63
Aylesbury United	42	17	7	18	64	67	58
Hayes	42	15	8	19	63	72	53
Grays Athletic	42	15	5	22	56	69	50
Bromley	42	14	7	21	56	69	49
Dulwich Hamlet	42	13	8	21	52	74	47
Yeading	42	11	13	18	58	66	46
Molesey	42	11	11	20	44	62	44
Wokingham Town	42	11	6	25	38	67	39
Dorking	42	9	4	29	58	104	31
Basingstoke Town	42	5	12	25	38	86	27
Wivenhoe Town	42	5	3	34	38	152	18

First Division

Bishop's Stortford	42	24	13	5	83	31	85
Purfleet	42	22	12	8	70	44	78
Walton & Hersham	42	22	11	9	81	53	77
Tooting & Mitcham United	42	21	12	9	66	37	75
Heybridge Swifts	42	20	11	11	72	45	71
Billericay Town	42	20	11	11	70	51	71
Abingdon Town	42	20	10	12	61	50	70
Worthing	42	19	11	12	79	46	68
Leyton	42	20	8	14	88	66	68
Boreham Wood	42	17	15	10	69	50	66
Staines Town	42	18	9	15	85	56	63
Bognor Regis Town	42	15	14	13	57	48	59
Wembley	42	16	10	16	66	52	58
Barking	42	15	11	16	63	69	56
Uxbridge	42	15	8	19	57	58	53
Whyteleafe	42	15	6	21	71	90	51
Maidenhead United	42	12	13	17	52	48	49
Berkhamsted Town	42	12	9	21	65	77	45
Ruislip Manor	42	10	8	24	42	79	38
Chalfont St Peter	42	7	10	25	40	79	31
Windsor & Eton	42	8	7	27	47	94	31
Croydon	42	3	3	36	37	198	12

1994-95

Premier Division

Enfield	42	26	9	5	106	43	93
Slough Town	42	22	13	7	82	56	79
Hayes	42	20	14	8	66	47	74
Aylesbury United	42	21	6	15	86	59	69
Hitchin Town	42	18	12	12	68	59	66
Bromley	42	18	11	13	76	67	65
St Albans City	42	17	13	12	96	81	64
Molesey	42	18	8	16	65	61	62
Yeading	42	14	15	13	60	59	57
Harrow Borough	42	17	6	19	64	67	57
Dulwich Hamlet	42	16	9	17	70	82	57
Carshalton Athletic	42	16	9	17	69	84	57
Kingstonian	42	16	8	18	62	57	56
Walton & Hersham	42	14	11	17	75	73	53
Sutton United	42	13	12	17	74	69	51
Purfleet	42	13	12	17	76	90	51
Hendon	42	12	14	16	57	65	50
Grays Athletic	42	11	16	15	57	61	49
Bishop's Stortford	42	12	11	19	53	76	47
Chesham United	42	12	9	21	60	87	45
Marlow	42	10	9	23	52	84	39
Wokingham Town	42	6	9	27	39	86	27

First Division

Boreham Wood	42	31	5	6	90	38	98
Worthing	42	21	13	8	93	49	76
Chertsey Town	42	21	11	10	109	57	74
Aldershot Town	42	23	5	14	80	53	74
Billericay Town	42	20	9	13	68	52	69
Staines Town	42	17	12	13	83	65	63
Basingstoke Town	42	17	10	15	81	71	61
Tooting & Mitcham United	42	15	14	13	58	48	59
Wembley	42	16	11	15	70	61	59
Abingdon Town	42	16	11	15	67	69	59
Whyteleafe	42	17	7	18	70	78	58
Maidenhead United	42	15	12	15	73	76	57
Uxbridge	42	15	11	16	54	62	56
Leyton	42	15	10	17	67	66	55
Barking	42	16	7	19	74	77	55
Heybridge Swifts	42	16	6	20	73	78	54
Ruislip Manor	42	14	11	17	70	75	53
Bognor Regis Town	42	13	14	15	57	63	53
Berkhamsted Town	42	14	10	18	54	70	52
Newbury Town	42	12	15	15	58	71	51
Wivenhoe Town	42	8	7	27	47	94	31
Dorking	42	3	3	36	40	163	12

Second Division

Thame United	42	30	3	9	97	49	93
Barton Rovers	42	25	7	10	93	51	82
Oxford City	42	24	8	10	86	47	80
Bracknell Town	42	23	9	10	86	47	78
Metropolitan Police	42	19	12	11	81	65	69
Hampton	42	20	9	13	79	74	69
Croydon	42	20	5	17	85	65	65
Banstead Athletic	42	18	10	14	73	59	64
Saffron Walden Town	42	17	13	12	64	59	64
Chalfont St Peter	42	17	12	13	67	54	63
Witham Town	42	18	9	15	75	64	63
Leatherhead	42	16	12	14	71	75	60
Edgware Town	42	16	10	16	70	66	58
Tilbury	42	15	9	18	62	82	54
Cheshunt	42	13	13	16	66	81	52
Ware	42	14	7	21	61	81	49
Egham Town	42	11	14	17	60	65	47
Hemel Hempstead	42	10	11	21	45	76	41
Hungerford Town	42	11	7	24	55	81	40
Windsor & Eton	42	10	8	24	58	84	38
Aveley	42	9	5	28	48	95	32
Malden Vale	42	5	9	28	46	108	24

Third Division

Collier Row	40	30	5	5	86	23	95
Canvey Island	40	28	4	8	88	42	88
Bedford Town	40	22	11	7	90	50	77
Northwood	40	22	8	10	80	47	74
Horsham	40	22	6	12	84	61	72
Southall	40	21	8	11	87	59	71
Leighton Town	40	20	8	12	66	43	68
Camberley Town	40	19	8	13	59	39	65
Kingsbury Town	40	18	11	1	72	54	65
Hornchurch	40	17	8	15	64	63	59
Clapton	40	14	11	15	69	61	53
Tring Town	40	13	12	15	68	69	51
East Thurrock United	40	14	8	18	60	79	50
Epsom & Ewell	40	13	10	17	58	62	49
Harlow Town	40	13	8	19	53	83	47
Harefield United	40	12	8	20	51	79	44
Hertford Town	40	11	10	19	56	78	43
Feltham & Hounslow	40	13	4	23	64	87	43
Flackwell Heath	40	8	4	28	50	99	28
Lewes	40	6	5	29	34	104	23
Cove	40	3	5	32	37	94	14

1995-96

Premier Division

Hayes	42	24	14	4	76	32	86
Enfield	42	26	8	8	78	35	86
Boreham Wood	42	24	11	7	69	29	83
Yeovil Town	42	23	11	8	83	51	80
Dulwich Hamlet	42	23	11	8	85	59	80
Carshalton Athletic	42	22	8	12	68	49	74
St Albans City	42	20	12	10	70	41	72
Kingstonian	42	20	11	11	62	38	71
Harrow Borough	42	19	10	13	70	56	67
Sutton United	42	17	14	11	71	56	65
Aylesbury United	42	17	12	13	71	58	63
Bishop's Stortford	42	16	9	17	61	62	57
Yeading	42	11	14	17	48	60	47
Hendon	42	12	10	20	52	65	46
Chertsey Town	42	13	6	23	45	71	45
Purfleet	42	12	8	22	48	67	44
Grays Athletic	42	11	11	20	43	63	44
Hitchin Town	42	10	10	22	41	74	40
Bromley	42	10	7	25	52	91	37
Molesey	42	9	9	24	46	81	36
Walton & Hersham	42	9	7	26	42	79	34
Worthing	42	4	7	31	42	106	19

First Division

Oxford City	42	28	7	7	98	60	91
Heybridge Swifts	42	27	7	8	97	43	88
Staines Town	42	23	11	8	82	59	80
Leyton Pennant	42	22	7	13	77	57	73
Aldershot Town	42	21	9	12	81	46	72
Billericay Town	42	19	9	14	58	58	66
Bognor Regis Town	42	18	11	13	71	53	65
Marlow	42	19	5	18	72	75	62
Basingstoke Town	42	16	13	13	70	60	61
Uxbridge	42	16	12	14	46	49	60
Wokingham Town	42	16	10	16	62	65	58
Chesham United	42	15	12	15	51	44	57
Thame United	42	14	13	15	64	73	55
Maidenhead United	42	12	14	16	50	63	50
Whyteleafe	42	12	13	17	71	81	49
Abingdon Town	42	13	9	20	63	80	48
Barton Rovers	42	12	10	20	69	87	46
Berkhamsted Town	42	11	11	20	52	68	44
Tooting & Mitcham United	42	11	10	21	45	64	43
Ruislip Manor	42	11	9	22	55	77	42
Wembley	42	11	8	23	49	66	41
Barking	42	4	12	26	35	90	24

Second Division

Canvey Island	40	25	12	3	91	36	87
Croydon	40	25	6	9	78	42	81
Hampton	40	23	10	7	74	44	79
Banstead Athletic	40	21	11	8	72	36	74
Collier Row	40	21	11	8	73	41	74
Wivenhoe Town	40	21	8	11	82	57	71
Metropolitan Police	40	18	10	12	57	45	64
Bedford Town	40	18	10	12	69	59	64
Bracknell Town	40	18	8	14	69	50	62
Edgware Town	40	16	9	15	72	67	57
Tilbury	40	12	11	17	52	62	47
Ware	40	13	8	19	55	80	47
Chalfont St Peter	40	11	13	16	58	63	46
Leatherhead	40	12	10	18	71	77	46
Saffron Walden Town	40	11	12	17	56	58	45
Cheshunt	40	10	12	18	56	90	42
Hemel Hempstead	40	10	10	20	46	62	40
Egham Town	40	12	3	25	42	74	39
Witham Town	40	8	10	22	35	68	34
Hungerford Town	40	9	7	24	44	79	34
Dorking	40	8	5	27	44	104	29

Third Division

Horsham	40	29	5	6	95	40	92
Leighton Town	40	28	5	7	95	34	89
Windsor & Eton	40	27	6	7	117	46	87
Wealdstone	40	23	8	9	104	39	77
Harlow Town	40	22	10	8	85	62	76
Northwood	40	20	9	11	76	56	69
Epsom & Ewell	40	18	14	8	95	57	68
Kingsbury Town	40	15	16	9	61	48	61
East Thurrock United	40	17	8	15	61	50	59
Aveley	40	16	10	14	62	53	58
Wingate & Finchley	40	16	7	17	74	70	55
Lewes	40	14	7	19	56	72	49
Flackwell Heath	40	14	5	21	60	84	47
Hornchurch	40	11	8	21	55	77	41
Harefield United	40	11	7	22	49	89	40
Tring Town	40	10	8	22	40	78	38
Camberley Town	40	9	9	22	45	81	36
Hertford Town	40	10	5	25	72	103	35
Cove	40	8	10	22	37	89	34
Clapton	40	9	6	25	48	89	33
Southall	40	9	5	26	34	104	32

1996-97

Premier Division

Yeovil Town	42	31	8	3	83	34	101
Enfield	42	28	11	3	91	29	98
Sutton United	42	18	13	11	87	70	67
Dagenham & Redbridge	42	18	11	13	57	43	65
Yeading	42	17	14	11	58	47	65
St Albans City	42	18	11	13	65	55	65
Aylesbury United	42	18	11	13	64	54	65
Purfleet	42	17	11	14	67	63	62
Heybridge Swifts	42	16	14	12	62	62	62
Boreham Wood	42	15	13	14	56	52	58
Kingstonian	42	16	8	18	79	79	56
Dulwich Hamlet	42	14	13	15	57	57	55
Carshalton Athletic	42	14	11	17	51	56	53
Hitchin Town	42	15	7	20	67	73	52
Oxford City	42	14	10	18	67	83	52
Hendon	42	13	12	17	53	59	51
Harrow Borough	42	12	14	16	58	62	50
Bromley	42	13	9	20	67	72	48
Bishop's Stortford	42	10	13	19	43	64	43
Staines Town	42	10	8	24	46	71	38
Grays Athletic	42	8	9	25	43	78	33
Chertsey Town	42	8	7	27	40	98	31

First Division

Chesham United	42	27	6	9	80	46	87
Basingstoke Town	42	22	13	7	81	38	79
Walton & Hersham	42	21	13	8	67	41	76
Hampton	42	21	12	9	62	39	75
Billericay Town	42	21	12	9	69	49	75
Bognor Regis Town	42	21	9	12	63	44	72
Aldershot Town	42	19	14	9	67	45	71
Uxbridge	42	15	17	10	65	48	62
Whyteleafe	42	18	7	17	71	68	61
Molesey	42	17	9	16	50	53	60
Abingdon Town	42	15	11	16	44	42	56
Leyton Pennant	42	14	12	16	71	72	54
Maidenhead United	42	15	10	17	57	57	52
Wokingham Town	42	14	10	18	41	45	52
Thame United	42	13	10	19	57	69	49
Worthing	42	11	11	20	58	77	44
Barton Rovers	42	11	11	20	61	58	44
Croydon	42	11	10	21	40	57	43
Berkhamsted Town	42	11	9	22	47	66	42
Canvey Island	42	9	14	19	52	71	41
Marlow	42	11	6	25	41	84	39
Tooting & Mitcham United	42	8	8	26	40	85	32

Maidenhead United had 3 points deducted

Second Division

Collier Row & Romford	42	28	12	2	93	33	96
Leatherhead	42	30	5	7	116	45	95
Wembley	42	23	11	8	92	45	80
Barking	42	22	13	7	69	40	79
Horsham	42	22	11	9	78	48	77
Edgware Town	42	20	14	8	74	50	74
Bedford Town	42	21	8	13	77	43	71
Banstead Athletic	42	21	5	16	75	52	68
Windsor & Eton	42	17	13	12	65	62	64
Leighton Town	42	17	12	13	64	52	63
Bracknell Town	42	17	9	16	78	71	60
Wivenhoe Town	42	17	9	16	69	62	60
Chalfont St Peter	42	14	13	15	53	61	55
Hungerford Town	42	14	13	15	68	77	55
Metropolitan Police	42	14	7	21	72	75	49
Tilbury	42	14	7	21	68	77	49
Witham Town	42	11	10	21	39	67	43
Egham Town	42	10	9	23	47	86	39
Cheshunt	42	9	3	30	37	101	30
Ware	42	7	8	27	44	80	29
Dorking	42	7	6	29	40	100	27
Hemel Hempstead	42	5	6	31	34	125	21

Third Division

Wealdstone	32	24	3	5	72	24	75
Braintree Town	32	23	5	4	99	29	74
Northwood	32	18	10	4	60	31	64
Harlow Town	32	19	4	9	60	41	61
Aveley	32	17	6	9	64	39	57
East Thurrock United	32	16	6	10	58	51	54
Camberley Town	32	15	6	11	55	44	51
Wingate & Finchley	32	11	7	14	52	63	40
Hornchurch	32	11	6	15	35	51	39
Clapton	32	11	6	15	31	49	39
Lewes	32	10	8	14	45	53	38
Kingsbury Town	32	11	4	17	41	54	37
Hertford Town	32	10	6	16	55	65	36
Epsom & Ewell	32	8	5	19	62	78	29
Flackwell Heath	32	8	5	19	36	71	29
Tring Town	32	7	3	22	33	74	24
Southall	32	6	4	22	28	69	22

1997-98

Premier Division

Kingstonian	42	25	12	5	84	35	87
Boreham Wood	42	23	11	8	81	42	80
Sutton United	42	22	12	8	83	56	78
Dagenham & Redbridge	42	21	10	11	73	50	73
Hendon	42	21	10	11	69	50	73
Heybridge Swifts	42	18	11	13	74	62	65
Enfield	42	18	8	16	66	58	62
Basingstoke Town	42	17	11	14	56	60	62
Walton & Hersham	42	18	6	18	50	70	60
Purfleet	42	15	13	14	57	58	58
St Albans City	42	17	7	18	54	59	58
Harrow Borough	42	15	10	17	60	67	55
Gravesend & Northfleet	42	15	8	19	65	67	53
Chesham United	42	14	10	18	71	70	52
Bromley	42	13	13	16	53	53	52
Dulwich Hamlet	42	13	11	18	56	67	50
Carshalton Athletic	42	13	9	20	54	60	48
Aylesbury United	42	13	8	21	55	70	47
Bishop's Stortford	42	14	5	23	53	69	47
Yeading	42	12	11	19	49	65	47
Hitchin Town	42	8	15	19	45	62	39
Oxford City	42	7	9	26	35	76	30

First Division

Aldershot Town	42	28	8	6	89	36	92
Billericay Town	42	25	6	11	78	44	81
Hampton	42	22	15	5	75	47	81
Maidenhead United	42	25	5	12	76	37	80
Uxbridge	42	23	6	13	66	59	75
Grays Athletic	42	21	10	11	79	49	73
Romford	42	21	8	13	92	59	71
Bognor Regis Town	42	20	9	13	77	45	69
Leatherhead	42	18	11	13	70	51	65
Leyton Pennant	42	17	11	14	66	58	62
Chertsey Town	42	16	13	13	83	70	61
Worthing	42	17	6	19	64	71	57
Berkhamsted Town	42	15	8	19	59	69	53
Staines Town	42	13	10	19	54	74	49
Croydon	42	13	10	19	47	64	49
Barton Rovers	42	11	13	18	53	72	46
Wembley	42	10	15	17	38	61	45
Molesey	42	10	11	21	47	65	41
Whyteleafe	42	10	10	22	48	83	40
Wokingham Town	42	7	10	25	41	74	31
Abingdon Town	42	9	4	29	47	101	31
Thame United	42	7	9	25	33	96	30

Second Division

Canvey Island	42	30	8	4	116	41	98
Braintree Town	42	29	11	2	117	45	98
Wealdstone	42	24	11	7	81	46	83
Bedford Town	42	22	12	8	55	25	78
Metropolitan Police	42	21	8	13	80	65	71
Wivenhoe Town	42	18	12	12	84	66	66
Edgware Town	42	18	10	14	81	65	64
Chalfont St Peter	42	17	13	12	63	60	64
Northwood	42	17	11	14	65	69	62
Windsor & Eton	42	17	7	18	75	72	58
Tooting & Mitcham United	42	16	9	17	58	56	57
Barking	42	15	12	15	62	75	57
Banstead Athletic	42	15	9	18	60	63	54
Marlow	42	16	5	21	64	78	53
Horsham	42	13	9	20	67	75	48
Bracknell Town	42	13	8	21	68	93	47
Leighton Town	42	13	6	23	45	78	45
Hungerford Town	42	11	11	20	66	77	44
Witham Town	42	9	13	20	55	68	40
Tilbury	42	9	12	21	57	88	39
Egham Town	42	9	5	28	47	101	32
Cheshunt	42	4	10	28	31	90	32

Third Division

Hemel Hempstead	38	27	6	5	86	28	87
Hertford Town	38	26	5	7	77	31	83
Harlow Town	38	24	11	3	81	43	83
Camberley Town	38	24	7	7	93	43	79
Ford United	38	23	9	6	90	34	78
East Thurrock United	38	23	7	8	70	40	76
Epsom & Ewell	38	17	6	15	69	57	57
Ware	38	17	6	15	69	57	57
Aveley	38	16	7	15	65	57	55
Corinthian Casuals	38	16	6	16	59	57	54
Hornchurch	38	12	9	17	55	68	45
Clapton	38	13	6	19	46	61	45
Flackwell Heath	38	12	9	17	50	76	45
Croydon Athletic	38	12	7	19	58	63	43
Tring Town	38	12	7	19	51	69	43
Southall	38	10	6	22	41	85	46
Dorking	38	9	6	23	49	94	33
Wingate & Finchley	38	7	8	23	46	80	29
Lewes	38	7	5	26	34	88	26
Kingsbury Town	38	5	3	30	35	93	18

1998-99

Premier Division

Sutton United	42	27	7	8	89	39	88
Aylesbury United	42	23	8	11	67	38	77
Dagenham & Redbridge	42	20	13	9	71	44	73
Purfleet	42	22	7	13	71	54	73
Enfield	42	21	9	12	73	49	72
St Albans City	42	17	17	8	71	52	68
Aldershot Town	42	16	14	12	83	48	62
Basingstoke Town	42	17	10	15	63	53	61
Harrow Borough	42	17	9	16	72	66	60
Gravesend & Northfleet	42	18	6	18	54	53	60
Slough Town	42	16	11	15	60	53	59
Billericay Town	42	15	13	14	54	56	58
Hendon	42	16	9	17	70	71	57
Boreham Wood	42	14	15	13	59	63	57
Chesham United	42	15	9	18	58	79	54
Dulwich Hamlet	42	14	8	20	53	63	50
Heybridge Swifts	42	13	9	20	51	85	48
Walton & Hersham	42	12	7	23	50	77	43
Hampton	42	10	12	20	41	71	42
Carshalton Athletic	42	10	10	22	47	82	40
Bishops Stortford	42	9	10	23	49	90	37
Bromley	42	8	11	23	50	72	35

First Division

Canvey Island	42	28	6	8	76	41	90
Hitchin Town	42	25	10	7	75	38	85
Wealdstone	42	26	6	10	75	48	84
Braintree Town	42	20	10	12	75	48	70
Bognor Regis Town	42	20	8	14	63	44	68
Grays Athletic	42	19	11	12	56	42	68
Oxford City	42	16	14	12	58	51	62
Croydon	42	16	13	13	53	53	61
Chertsey Town	42	14	14	12	57	57	58
Romford	42	14	15	13	58	63	57
Maidenhead United	42	13	15	14	50	46	54
Worthing	42	13	13	16	47	61	52
Leyton Pennant	42	13	12	17	62	70	51
Uxbridge	42	13	11	18	54	51	50
Barton Rovers	42	11	15	16	43	49	48
Yeading	42	12	10	20	51	55	46
Leatherhead	42	12	9	21	48	59	45
Whyteleafe	42	13	6	23	51	72	45
Staines Town	42	10	15	17	33	57	45
Molesey	42	8	20	14	35	52	44
Wembley	42	10	10	22	36	71	40
Berkhamsted Town	42	10	7	25	53	81	37

Second Division

Bedford Town	42	29	7	6	89	31	94
Harlow Town	42	27	8	7	100	47	89
Thame United	42	26	8	8	89	50	86
Hemel Hempstead	42	21	12	9	90	50	75
Windsor & Eton	42	22	6	14	87	55	72
Banstead Athletic	42	21	8	13	83	62	71
Northwood	42	20	7	15	67	68	67
Tooting & Mitcham United	42	19	9	14	63	62	66
Chalfont St Peter	42	16	12	14	70	71	60
Metropolitan Police	42	17	8	17	61	58	59
Leighton Town	42	16	10	16	60	64	58
Horsham	42	17	6	19	74	67	57
Marlow	42	16	9	17	72	68	57
Edgware Town	42	14	10	18	65	68	52
Witham Town	42	12	15	15	64	64	51
Hungerford Town	42	13	12	17	59	61	51
Wivenhoe Town	42	14	8	20	71	83	50
Wokingham Town	42	14	4	24	44	79	46
Barking	42	10	11	21	50	75	41
Hertford Town	42	11	2	29	44	96	35
Bracknell Town	42	7	10	25	48	92	31
Abingdon Town	42	6	6	30	48	124	24

Third Division

Ford United	38	27	5	6	110	42	86
Wingate & Finchley	38	25	5	8	79	38	80
Cheshunt	38	23	10	5	70	41	79
Lewes	38	25	3	10	86	45	78
Epsom & Ewell	38	19	5	14	61	51	62
Ware	38	19	4	15	79	60	61
Tilbury	38	17	8	13	74	52	59
Croydon Athletic	38	16	10	12	82	59	58
East Thurrock United	38	15	13	10	74	56	58
Egham Town	38	16	8	14	65	58	56
Corinthian Casuals	38	16	7	15	70	71	55
Southall	38	14	9	15	68	66	51
Camberley Town	38	14	8	16	66	77	50
Aveley	38	12	7	19	50	67	43
Flackwell Heath	38	11	9	18	59	70	42
Hornchurch	38	10	9	19	48	73	39
Clapton	38	11	6	21	48	89	39
Dorking	38	8	7	23	52	98	31
Kingsbury Town	38	6	3	29	40	98	21
Tring Town	38	5	6	27	38	108	21

1999-2000

Premier Division

Dagenham & Redbridge	42	32	5	5	97	35	101
Aldershot Town	42	24	5	13	71	51	77
Chesham United	42	20	10	12	64	50	70
Purfleet	42	18	15	9	70	48	69
Canvey Island	42	21	6	15	70	53	69
St Albans City	42	19	10	13	75	55	67
Billericay Town	42	18	12	12	62	62	66
Hendon	42	18	8	16	61	64	62
Slough Town	42	17	9	16	61	59	60
Dulwich Hamlet	42	17	5	20	62	68	56
Gravesend & Northfleet	42	15	10	17	66	67	55
Farnborough Town	42	14	11	17	52	55	53
Hampton & Richmond Borough	42	13	13	16	49	57	52
Enfield	42	13	11	18	64	68	50
Heybridge Swifts	42	13	11	18	57	65	50
Hitchin Town	42	13	11	18	59	72	50
Carshalton Athletic	42	12	12	18	55	65	48
Basingstoke Town	42	13	9	20	56	71	48
Harrow Borough	42	14	6	22	54	70	48
Aylesbury United	42	13	9	20	64	81	48
Boreham Wood	42	11	10	21	44	71	43
Walton & Hersham	42	11	8	23	44	70	41

First Division

Croydon	42	25	9	8	85	47	84
Grays Athletic	42	21	12	9	80	44	75
Maidenhead United	42	20	15	7	72	45	75
Thame United	42	20	13	9	61	38	73
Worthing	42	19	12	11	80	60	69
Staines Town	42	19	12	11	63	52	69
Whyteleafe	42	20	9	13	60	49	69
Bedford Town	42	17	12	13	59	52	63
Bromley	42	17	9	16	63	65	60
Uxbridge	42	15	13	14	60	44	58
Bishop's Stortford	42	16	10	16	57	62	58
Barton Rovers	42	16	8	18	64	83	56
Oxford City	42	17	4	21	57	55	55
Braintree Town	42	15	10	17	65	74	55
Yeading	42	12	18	12	53	54	54
Wealdstone	42	13	12	17	51	58	51
Bognor Regis Town	42	12	13	17	47	53	49
Harlow Town	42	11	13	18	62	76	46
Romford	42	12	9	21	51	70	45
Leatherhead	42	9	13	20	47	70	40
Chertsey Town	42	9	5	28	50	84	32
Leyton Pennant	42	7	9	26	34	85	30

Second Division

Hemel Hempstead	42	31	8	3	98	27	101
Northwood	42	29	9	4	109	40	96
Ford United	42	28	8	6	108	41	92
Berkhamsted Town	42	22	8	12	75	52	74
Windsor & Eton	42	20	13	9	73	53	73
Wivenhoe Town	42	20	9	13	61	47	69
Barking	42	18	13	11	70	51	67
Marlow	42	20	4	18	86	66	64
Metropolitan Police	42	18	7	17	75	71	61
Banstead Athletic	42	16	11	15	55	56	59
Tooting & Mitcham United	42	16	7	19	72	74	55
Wokingham Town	42	15	9	18	58	80	54
Wembley	42	14	11	17	47	53	53
Edgware Town	42	13	11	18	72	71	50
Hungerford Town	42	13	10	19	61	78	49
Cheshunt	42	12	12	18	53	65	48
Horsham	42	13	8	21	66	81	47
Leighton Town	42	13	8	21	65	84	47
Molesey	42	10	12	20	54	69	42
Wingate & Finchley	42	11	7	24	54	97	40
Witham Town	42	7	9	26	39	110	30
Chalfont St Peter	42	2	8	32	39	124	14

Third Division

East Thurrock United	40	26	7	7	89	42	85
Great Wakering Rovers	40	25	7	8	81	41	82
Tilbury	40	21	12	7	67	39	75
Hornchurch	40	19	12	9	72	57	69
Croydon Athletic	40	19	11	10	85	52	68
Epsom & Ewell	40	18	12	10	67	46	66
Lewes	40	18	10	12	73	51	64
Bracknell Town	40	15	16	9	81	64	61
Aveley	40	17	10	13	73	64	61
Corinthian Casuals	40	16	10	14	59	51	58
Flackwell Heath	40	17	6	17	74	76	57
Ware	40	16	8	16	74	62	56
Egham Town	40	14	13	13	48	43	55
Hertford Town	40	15	10	15	63	60	55
Abingdon Town	40	10	12	18	48	64	42
Kingsbury Town	40	11	8	21	55	86	41
Camberley Town	40	11	7	22	44	79	40
Tring Town	40	10	9	21	37	64	39
Dorking	40	9	10	21	53	69	37
Clapton	40	9	7	24	50	93	34
Southall	40	3	5	32	33	123	14

2000-2001

Premier Division

Farnborough Town	42	31	6	5	86	27	99
Canvey Island	42	27	8	7	79	41	89
Basingstoke Town	42	22	13	7	73	40	79
Aldershot Town	41	21	11	9	73	39	74
Chesham United	42	22	6	14	78	52	72
Gravesend & Northfleet	42	22	5	15	62	45	71
Heybridge Swifts	42	18	13	11	74	60	67
Billericay Town	41	18	13	10	62	54	67
Hampton & Richmond Borough	42	18	12	12	73	60	66
Hitchin Town	42	18	5	19	72	62	59
Purfleet	42	14	13	15	55	55	55
Hendon	42	16	6	18	62	62	54
Sutton United	41	14	11	16	74	70	53
St Albans City	42	15	5	22	50	69	50
Grays Athletic	42	14	8	20	49	68	50
Maidenhead United	42	15	2	25	47	63	47
Croydon	42	12	10	20	55	77	46
Enfield	42	12	9	21	48	74	45
Harrow Borough	41	10	11	20	61	90	41
Slough Town	42	10	9	23	40	62	39
Carshalton Athletic	42	10	6	26	40	85	36
Dulwich Hamlet	42	4	10	28	33	84	22

First Division

Boreham Wood	42	26	7	9	82	49	85
Bedford Town	42	22	16	4	81	40	82
Braintree Town	42	25	6	11	112	60	81
Bishop's Stortford	42	24	6	12	103	76	78
Thame United	42	22	8	12	86	54	74
Ford United	42	19	12	11	70	58	69
Uxbridge	42	21	5	16	73	55	68
Northwood	42	20	8	14	89	81	68
Whyteleafe	42	20	6	16	62	69	66
Oxford City	42	16	13	13	64	49	61
Harlow Town	42	15	16	11	70	66	61
Worthing	42	16	9	17	69	69	57
Staines Town	42	16	8	18	60	66	56
Aylesbury United	42	17	4	21	65	55	55
Yeading	42	15	9	18	72	74	54
Bognor Regis Town	42	13	11	18	71	71	50
Walton & Hersham	42	14	8	20	59	80	50
Bromley	42	14	6	22	63	86	48
Wealdstone	42	12	9	21	54	73	45
Leatherhead	42	12	4	26	37	87	40
Romford	42	9	4	29	53	113	31
Barton Rovers	42	2	9	31	30	94	15

Second Division

Tooting & Mitcham United	42	26	11	5	92	35	89
Windsor	42	24	10	8	70	40	82
Barking	42	23	13	6	82	54	82
Berkhamsted Town	42	24	8	10	99	49	80
Wivenhoe Town	42	23	11	8	78	52	80
Hemel Hempstead	42	22	10	10	74	44	76
Horsham	42	19	9	14	84	61	66
Chertsey Town	42	18	9	15	59	59	63
Great Wakering Rovers	42	16	13	13	69	59	61
Tilbury	42	18	6	18	61	67	60
Banstead Athletic	42	17	8	17	69	58	59
East Thurrock United	42	16	11	15	72	64	59
Metropolitan Police	42	18	4	20	64	77	58
Marlow	42	15	11	16	62	61	56
Molesey	42	14	9	19	53	61	51
Wembley	42	12	10	20	39	63	46
Hungerford Town	42	11	9	22	40	73	42
Leyton Pennant	42	10	11	21	47	74	41
Cheshunt	42	11	6	25	48	77	39
Edgware Town	42	9	9	24	41	77	36
Leighton Town	42	8	10	24	44	87	34
Wokingham Town	42	3	12	27	39	94	20

Wokingham Town had 1 point deducted

Third Division

Arlesey Town	42	34	6	2	138	37	108
Lewes	41	25	11	5	104	34	86
Ashford Town	42	26	7	9	102	49	85
Flackwell Heath	42	24	10	8	93	51	82
Corinthian Casuals	42	24	10	8	83	50	82
Aveley	42	24	3	15	85	61	75
Epsom & Ewell	42	23	4	15	76	52	73
Witham Town	42	21	9	12	76	57	72
Bracknell Town	41	19	10	12	90	70	67
Croydon Athletic	41	15	12	14	78	63	57
Ware	42	17	6	19	75	76	57
Tring Town	42	16	9	17	60	71	57
Egham Town	42	15	11	16	60	60	56
Hornchurch	42	14	13	15	73	60	55
Wingate & Finchley	42	15	7	20	75	75	52
Kingsbury Town	42	11	8	23	74	100	41
Abingdon Town	42	12	7	23	53	102	40
Dorking	42	10	9	23	59	99	39
Hertford Town	41	9	8	24	57	97	35
Camberley Town	42	8	8	26	53	107	32
Clapton	42	5	9	28	48	121	24
Chalfont St Peter	42	4	1	37	30	150	13

Abingdon Town had 3 points deducted

2001-2002

Premier Division

Gravesend & Northfleet	42	31	6	5	90	33	99
Canvey Island	42	30	5	7	107	41	95
Aldershot Town	42	22	7	13	76	51	73
Braintree Town	42	23	4	15	66	61	73
Purfleet	42	19	15	8	67	44	72
Grays Athletic	42	20	10	12	65	55	70
Chesham United	42	19	10	13	69	53	67
Hendon Town	42	19	5	18	66	54	62
Billericay Town	42	16	13	13	59	60	61
St Albans City	42	16	9	17	71	60	57
Hitchin Town	42	15	10	17	73	81	55
Sutton Albion	42	13	15	14	62	62	54
Heybridge Swifts	42	15	9	18	68	85	54
Kingstonian	42	13	13	16	50	56	52
Boreham Wood	42	15	6	21	49	62	51
Maidenhead United	42	15	5	22	51	63	50
Bedford Town	42	12	12	18	64	69	48
Basingstoke Town	42	11	15	16	50	68	48
Enfield	42	11	9	22	48	77	42
Hampton & Richmond Borough	42	9	13	20	51	71	40
Harrow Borough	42	8	10	24	50	89	34
Croydon	42	7	5	30	36	93	26

First Division

Ford United	42	27	7	8	92	56	88
Bishop's Stortford	42	26	9	7	104	51	87
Aylesbury United	42	23	10	9	96	64	79
Bognor Regis Town	42	20	13	9	74	55	73
Northwood	42	19	11	12	92	64	68
Carshalton Athletic	42	17	16	9	64	53	67
Harlow Town	42	19	9	14	77	65	66
Slough Town	42	17	11	14	68	51	62
Uxbridge	42	18	6	18	68	65	60
Oxford City	42	17	9	16	59	66	60
Thame United	42	15	14	13	75	61	59
Tooting & Mitcham United	42	16	11	15	70	70	59
Walton & Hersham	42	16	10	16	75	70	58
Yeading	42	16	10	16	84	90	58
Worthing	42	15	8	19	69	65	53
Staines Town	42	12	11	19	45	60	47
Dulwich Hamlet	42	11	13	18	64	76	46
Wealdstone	42	11	12	19	60	82	45
Bromley	42	10	11	21	44	74	41
Whyteleafe	42	10	11	21	46	86	41
Barking & East Ham United	42	8	7	27	61	123	31
Windsor & Eton	42	7	5	30	53	93	26

Second Division

Lewes	42	29	9	4	108	31	96
Horsham	42	27	9	6	104	44	90
Berkhamstead Town	42	23	10	9	82	51	79
Arlesey Town	42	23	6	13	89	55	75
Banstead Athletic	42	22	8	12	83	54	74
Leyton Pennant	42	22	8	12	84	60	74
Great Wakering Rovers	42	21	8	13	64	37	71
East Thurrock United	42	21	8	13	67	59	71
Marlow	42	18	13	11	73	63	67
Hemel Hempstead Town	42	18	10	14	82	66	64
Leatherhead	42	17	6	19	72	62	57
Ashford Town	42	15	11	16	58	71	56
Metropolitan Police	42	16	7	19	84	84	55
Barton Rovers	42	15	9	18	54	60	54
Hungerford Town	42	14	9	19	56	75	51
Tilbury	42	15	6	21	55	74	51
Chertsey Town	42	10	14	18	79	112	44
Wembley	42	9	10	23	51	82	37
Molesey	42	10	6	26	40	93	36
Cheshunt	42	7	13	22	51	84	34
Wivenhoe Town	42	8	9	25	55	111	33
Romford	42	4	7	31	42	105	19

Third Division

Croydon Athletic	42	30	5	7	138	41	95
Hornchurch	42	25	11	6	96	46	86
Aveley	42	26	6	10	109	55	84
Bracknell Town	42	25	8	9	96	54	83
Epsom & Ewell	42	20	15	7	79	51	75
Egham Town	42	21	11	10	72	59	74
Wingate & Finchley	42	20	9	13	80	60	69
Dorking	42	18	14	10	77	66	68
Tring Town	42	19	11	12	64	62	68
Corinthian-Casuals	42	18	13	11	69	44	67
Hertford Town	42	20	7	15	88	74	67
Witham Town	42	15	10	17	66	72	55
Ware	42	14	10	18	74	76	52
Chalfont St Peter	42	15	4	23	69	92	49
Wokingham Town	42	14	6	22	79	105	48
Abingdon Town	42	13	7	22	61	75	46
Leighton Town	42	8	12	22	56	95	36
Kingsbury Town	42	8	11	23	58	91	35
Edgware Town	42	9	7	26	65	101	34
Flackwell Heath	42	9	8	25	53	99	32
Clapton	42	9	4	29	45	118	31
Camberley Town	42	7	9	26	37	95	30

2002-2003

Premier Division

Aldershot Town	46	33	6	7	81	36	105
Canvey Island	46	28	8	10	112	56	92
Hendon	46	22	13	11	70	56	79
St. Albans City	46	23	8	15	73	65	77
Basingstoke Town	46	23	7	16	80	60	76
Sutton United	46	22	9	15	77	62	75
Hayes	46	20	13	13	67	54	73
Purfleet	46	19	15	12	68	48	72
Bedford Town	46	21	9	16	66	58	72
Maidenhead United	46	16	17	13	75	63	65
Kingstonian	46	16	17	13	71	64	65
Billericay Town	46	17	11	18	46	44	62
Bishop's Stortford	46	16	11	19	74	72	59
Hitchin Town	46	15	13	18	69	67	58
Ford United	46	15	12	19	78	84	57
Braintree Town	46	14	12	20	59	71	54
Aylesbury United	46	13	15	18	62	75	54
Harrow Borough	46	15	9	22	54	75	54
Grays Athletic	46	14	11	21	53	59	53
Heybridge Swifts	46	13	14	19	52	80	53
Chesham United	46	14	10	22	56	81	52
Boreham Wood	46	11	15	20	50	58	48
Enfield	46	9	11	26	47	101	38
Hampton & Richmond Borough	46	3	14	29	35	86	23

Division One (North)

Northwood	46	28	7	11	109	56	91
Hornchurch	46	25	15	6	85	48	90
Hemel Hempstead Town	46	26	7	13	70	55	85
Slough Town	46	22	14	10	86	59	80
Uxbridge	46	23	10	13	62	41	79
Aveley	46	21	14	11	66	48	77
Berkhamsted Town	46	21	13	12	92	68	76
Thame United	46	20	12	14	84	51	72
Wealdstone	46	21	9	16	85	69	72
Harlow Town	46	20	12	14	66	53	72
Marlow	46	19	10	17	74	63	67
Barking & East Ham United	46	19	9	18	73	76	66
Yeading	46	18	11	17	77	69	65
Great Wakering Rovers	46	17	14	15	64	70	65
Oxford City	46	17	13	16	55	51	64
Arlesey Town	46	17	12	17	69	71	63
East Thurrock United	46	17	10	19	75	79	61
Wingate & Finchley	46	15	11	20	70	74	56
Barton Rovers	46	15	7	24	53	65	52
Tilbury	46	14	7	25	55	96	49
Wivenhoe Town	46	9	11	26	56	94	38
Leyton Pennant	46	9	7	30	38	81	34
Wembley	46	7	11	28	57	111	32
Hertford Town	46	6	6	34	46	119	24

Division One (South)

Carshalton Athletic	46	28	8	10	73	44	92
Bognor Regis Town	46	26	10	10	92	34	88
Lewes	46	24	16	6	106	50	88
Dulwich Hamlet	46	23	12	11	73	49	81
Whyteleafe	46	21	13	12	74	51	76
Bromley	46	21	13	12	70	53	76
Walton & Hersham	46	20	13	13	87	63	73
Horsham	46	21	9	16	80	58	72
Epsom & Ewell	46	19	12	15	67	66	69
Egham Town	46	19	10	17	62	71	67
Tooting & Mitcham United	46	18	9	19	83	78	63
Worthing	46	17	12	17	78	75	63
Windsor & Eton	46	18	9	19	66	65	63
Leatherhead	46	16	13	17	71	66	61
Staines Town	46	14	16	16	57	63	58
Banstead Athletic	46	14	15	17	58	59	57
Ashford Town (Middlesex)	46	14	11	21	47	70	53
Croydon	46	15	8	23	56	87	53
Croydon Athletic	46	13	13	20	52	66	52
Bracknell Town	46	12	16	18	57	74	52
Corinthian Casuals	46	12	14	20	50	68	50
Molesey	46	13	9	24	52	79	48
Metropolitan Police	46	12	10	24	50	76	46
Chertsey Town	46	3	7	36	43	139	16

Division Two

Cheshunt	30	25	3	2	91	29	78
Leyton	30	21	5	4	77	22	68
Flackwell Heath	30	17	3	10	52	44	54
Abingdon Town	30	14	11	5	65	42	53
Hungerford Town	30	12	12	6	49	36	48
Leighton Town	30	14	3	13	61	43	45
Witham Town	30	12	8	10	40	43	44
Ware	30	12	5	13	47	53	41
Clapton	30	12	5	13	40	47	41
Tring Town	30	11	5	14	49	58	38
Kingsbury Town	30	9	11	10	38	48	38
Edgware Town	30	10	3	17	49	65	33
Wokingham Town	30	7	7	16	34	81	28
Dorking	30	6	6	18	49	63	24
Chalfont St. Peter	30	6	5	19	34	63	23
Camberley Town	30	4	4	22	23	61	16

2003-2004

Premier Division

Canvey Island	46	32	8	6	106	42	104
Sutton United	46	25	10	11	94	56	85
Thurrock	46	24	11	11	87	45	83
Hendon	46	25	8	13	68	47	83
* Hornchurch	46	24	11	11	63	35	82
Grays Athletic	46	22	15	9	82	39	81
Carshalton Athletic	46	24	9	13	66	55	81
Hayes	46	21	11	14	56	46	74
Kettering Town	46	20	11	15	63	63	71
Bognor Regis Town	46	20	10	16	69	67	70
Bishop's Stortford	46	20	9	17	78	61	69
Maidenhead United	46	18	9	19	60	68	63
Ford United	46	16	14	16	69	63	62
Basingstoke Town	46	17	9	20	58	64	60
Bedford Town	46	14	13	19	62	63	55
Heybridge Swifts	46	14	11	21	55	51	53
Harrow Borough	46	12	14	20	47	63	50
Kingstonian	46	12	13	21	40	56	49
St. Albans City	46	12	12	22	55	83	48
Hitchin Town	46	13	8	25	55	89	47
Northwood	46	12	9	25	65	95	45
Billericay Town	46	11	11	24	51	66	44
Braintree Town	46	11	6	29	41	88	39
Aylesbury United	46	5	14	27	41	101	29

* Hornchurch had 1 point deducted

Division One (North)

Yeading	46	32	7	7	112	54	103
Leyton	46	29	9	8	90	53	96
Cheshunt	46	27	10	9	119	54	91
Chesham United	46	24	9	13	104	60	81
Dunstable Town	46	23	9	14	86	61	78
Hemel Hempstead Town	46	22	12	12	75	72	78
Wealdstone	46	23	7	16	81	51	76
Arlesey Town	46	23	7	16	95	70	76
Boreham Wood	46	20	13	13	82	59	73
Harlow Town	46	20	10	16	75	51	70
Wingate & Finchley	46	19	13	14	68	63	70
East Thurrock United	46	19	11	16	62	54	68
Uxbridge	46	15	14	17	59	57	59
Aveley	46	15	14	17	67	71	59
Thame United	46	16	9	21	72	83	57
* Waltham Forest	46	15	13	18	62	60	55
Wivenhoe Town	46	15	10	21	79	104	55
Barton Rovers	46	16	6	24	52	80	54
Oxford City	46	14	11	21	55	65	53
Berkhamstead Town	46	12	10	24	66	88	46
Great Wakering Rovers	46	10	13	23	47	97	43
Tilbury	46	10	9	27	56	100	39
Barking & East Ham United	46	8	7	31	37	100	31
Enfield	46	5	7	34	44	138	22

* Waltham Forest had 3 points deducted.

2004-2005

Premier Division

Yeading	42	25	11	6	74	48	86
Billericay Town	42	23	11	8	78	40	80
Eastleigh	42	22	13	7	84	49	79
Braintree Town	42	19	17	6	67	33	74
Leyton	42	21	8	13	71	57	71
Hampton & Richmond	42	21	8	13	64	53	71
Heybridge Swifts	42	18	9	15	76	65	63
Chelmsford City	42	17	11	14	63	58	62
Staines Town	42	17	9	16	59	53	60
Worthing	42	16	11	15	50	45	59
Hendon	42	17	7	18	48	60	58
Salisbury City	42	16	9	17	60	64	57
Slough Town	42	15	10	17	61	66	55
Folkestone Invicta	42	14	10	18	51	53	52
Windsor & Eton	42	12	14	16	48	62	50
Harrow Borough	42	13	10	19	41	54	49
Northwood	42	14	7	21	49	66	49
Wealdstone	42	13	8	21	60	73	47
Cheshunt	42	12	11	19	58	71	47
Tonbridge Angels	42	11	10	21	47	73	43
Dover Athletic	42	10	9	23	50	66	39
Kingstonian	42	7	5	30	43	93	26

Division One (South)

Lewes	46	29	7	10	113	61	94
Worthing	46	26	14	6	87	46	92
Windsor & Eton	46	26	13	7	75	39	91
Slough Town	46	28	6	12	103	63	90
Hampton & Richmond Borough	46	26	11	9	82	45	89
Staines Town	46	26	9	11	85	52	87
Dulwich Hamlet	46	23	15	8	77	57	84
Bromley	46	22	10	14	80	58	76
Walton & Hersham	46	20	14	12	76	55	74
Croydon Athletic	46	20	10	16	70	54	70
Tooting & Mitcham United	46	20	9	17	82	68	69
Ashford Town (Middlesex)	46	18	13	15	69	62	67
Leatherhead	46	19	9	18	83	88	66
Bracknell Town	46	19	6	21	81	87	63
Horsham	46	16	11	19	71	69	59
Marlow	46	16	11	19	50	64	59
Whyteleafe	46	17	4	25	66	93	55
Banstead Athletic	46	15	8	23	56	73	53
Molesey	46	12	6	28	45	84	42
Metropolitan Police	46	9	14	23	58	84	41
Croydon	46	10	10	26	57	88	40
Egham Town	46	8	8	30	55	92	32
Corinthian Casuals	46	6	6	34	48	110	24
Epsom & Ewell	46	5	8	33	40	117	23

Division One

AFC Wimbledon	42	29	10	3	91	33	97
Walton & Hersham	42	28	4	10	69	34	88
Horsham	42	24	6	12	90	61	78
Bromley	42	22	9	11	49	44	75
Metropolitan Police	42	22	8	12	72	51	74
Cray Wanderers	42	19	16	7	95	54	73
Leatherhead	42	20	13	9	73	55	73
Tooting & Mitcham United	42	18	15	9	92	60	69
Whyteleafe	42	20	6	16	60	59	66
Burgess Hill Town	42	19	6	17	73	62	63
Hastings United	42	15	11	16	55	57	56
Croydon Athletic	42	13	16	13	66	65	55
Corinthian-Casuals	42	15	9	18	56	64	54
Bashley	42	13	13	16	68	74	52
Dulwich Hamlet	42	10	14	18	61	64	44
Molesey	42	12	8	22	46	70	44
Banstead Athletic	42	10	10	22	50	64	40
Newport IOW	42	10	10	22	50	88	40
Fleet Town	42	11	5	26	47	86	38
Ashford Town	42	8	12	22	47	85	36
Dorking	42	8	11	23	43	89	35
Croydon	42	5	10	27	37	91	25

Division Two

Leighton Town	42	28	7	7	111	36	91
Dorking	42	27	8	7	87	47	89
Hertford Town	42	24	9	9	74	35	81
Chertsey Town	42	22	9	11	75	53	75
Flackwell Heath	42	22	5	15	71	53	71
Witham Town	42	20	10	12	75	54	70
Kingsbury Town	42	14	11	17	60	64	53
Ware	42	14	10	18	67	60	52
Abingdon Town	42	15	6	21	83	81	51
Camberley Town	42	15	6	21	51	71	51
Wembley	42	13	9	20	46	67	48
Wokingham Town	42	12	7	23	55	94	43
Edgware Town	42	12	6	24	62	88	42
Chalfont St. Peter	42	12	6	24	57	89	42
Clapton	42	8	5	29	47	129	29

Division Two

Ilford	30	22	3	5	62	23	69
Enfield	30	21	3	6	64	33	66
Brook House	30	20	4	6	65	25	64
Hertford Town	30	17	7	6	65	40	58
Witham Town	30	16	3	11	67	53	51
Chertsey Town	30	15	6	9	55	48	51
Abingdon Town	30	13	9	8	65	42	48
Edgware Town	30	12	3	15	40	41	39
Flackwell Heath	30	11	5	14	50	55	38
Ware	30	9	10	11	41	55	37
Chalfont St Peter	30	9	7	14	41	52	34
Camberley Town	30	9	5	16	36	44	32
Wembley	30	8	5	17	41	55	29
Epsom & Ewell	30	8	4	18	41	64	28
Kingsbury Town	30	5	4	21	35	76	19
Clapton	30	3	6	21	20	82	15

2005-2006

Premier Division

	P	W	D	L	F	A	Pts
Braintree Town	42	28	10	4	74	32	94
Heybridge Swifts	42	28	3	11	70	46	87
Fisher Athletic	42	26	7	9	84	46	85
AFC Wimbledon	42	22	11	9	67	36	77
Hampton & Richmond	42	24	3	15	73	54	75
Staines Town	42	20	10	12	74	56	70
Billericay Town	42	19	12	11	69	45	69
Worthing	42	19	10	13	71	60	67
Walton & Hersham	42	19	7	16	55	50	64
Chelmsford City	42	18	10	14	57	62	64
Bromley	42	16	14	12	57	49	62
East Thurrock United	42	18	5	19	60	60	59
Folkestone Invicta	42	16	10	16	47	51	58
Margate	42	11	17	14	49	55	50
Leyton	42	13	9	20	58	61	48
Harrow Borough	42	13	9	20	56	73	48
Slough Town	42	13	8	21	63	75	47
Wealdstone	42	13	5	24	68	82	44
Hendon	42	9	12	21	44	64	39
Maldon Town	42	8	11	23	41	73	35
Windsor & Eton	42	8	8	26	37	75	32
Redbridge	42	3	5	34	28	97	14

Division One

	P	W	D	L	F	A	Pts
Ramsgate	44	24	14	6	84	38	86
Horsham	44	25	11	8	94	55	86
Tonbridge Angels	44	24	8	12	71	48	80
Metropolitan Police	44	24	7	13	72	46	79
Dover Athletic	44	21	14	9	69	46	77
Tooting & Mitcham United	44	22	9	13	93	62	75
Kingstonian	44	20	14	10	82	56	74
Croydon Athletic	44	20	13	11	56	41	73
Bashley	44	20	10	14	63	61	70
Leatherhead	44	18	14	12	64	50	68
Cray Wanderers	44	20	8	16	80	74	68
Hastings United	44	19	10	15	65	58	67
Dulwich Hamlet	44	19	8	17	55	43	65
Fleet Town	44	13	19	12	50	56	58
Walton Casuals	44	16	10	18	68	75	58
Lymington & New Milton	44	12	11	21	61	80	47
Molesey	44	12	10	22	56	79	46
Whyteleafe	44	10	14	20	50	66	44
Burgess Hill Town	44	10	10	24	57	83	40
Banstead Athletic	44	8	13	23	43	71	37
Ashford Town	44	8	11	25	41	81	35
Newport IOW	44	6	11	27	38	97	29
Corinthian Casuals	44	6	9	29	39	85	27

Division Two

	P	W	D	L	F	A	Pts
Ware	30	19	4	7	77	36	61
Witham Town	30	17	7	6	61	30	58
Brook House	30	17	7	6	63	33	58
Flackwell Heath	30	15	7	8	54	49	52
Egham Town	30	15	5	10	39	36	50
Chertsey Town	30	14	7	9	47	37	49
Edgware Town	30	13	5	12	46	41	44
Chalfont St Peter	30	13	2	15	50	53	41
Dorking	30	11	8	11	48	51	41
Croydon	30	11	7	12	43	43	40
Wembley	30	11	6	13	44	43	39
Kingsbury Town	30	9	10	11	32	37	37
Hertford Town	30	7	10	13	35	54	31
Camberley Town	30	5	8	17	31	57	23
Epsom & Ewell	30	5	6	19	32	64	21
Clapton	30	4	9	17	33	71	16

Clapton had 5 points deducted.

NORTHERN PREMIER LEAGUE

1968-69

	P	W	D	L	F	A	Pts
Macclesfield Town	38	27	6	5	82	38	60
Wigan Athletic	38	18	12	8	59	41	48
Morecambe	38	16	14	8	64	37	46
Gainsborough Trinity	38	19	8	11	64	43	46
South Shields	38	19	8	11	78	56	46
Bangor City	38	18	9	11	102	64	45
Hyde United	38	16	10	12	71	65	42
Goole Town	38	15	10	13	80	78	40
Altrincham	38	14	10	14	69	52	38
Fleetwood	38	16	6	16	58	58	38
Gateshead	38	14	9	15	42	48	37
South Liverpool	38	12	13	13	56	66	37
Northwich Victoria	38	16	5	17	59	82	37
Boston United	38	14	8	16	59	65	36
Runcorn	38	12	11	15	59	63	35
Netherfield	38	12	4	22	51	69	28
Scarborough	38	9	10	19	49	68	28
Ashington	38	10	8	20	48	74	28
Chorley	38	8	9	21	46	75	25
Worksop Town	38	6	8	24	34	88	20

1969-70

	P	W	D	L	F	A	Pts
Macclesfield Town	38	22	8	8	72	41	52
Wigan Athletic	38	20	12	6	56	32	52
Boston United	38	21	8	9	65	33	50
Scarborough	38	20	10	8	74	39	50
South Shields	38	19	7	12	66	43	45
Gainsborough Trinity	38	16	11	11	64	49	43
Stafford Rangers	38	16	7	15	59	52	39
Bangor City	38	15	9	14	68	63	39
Northwich Victoria	38	15	8	15	60	66	38
Netherfield	38	14	9	15	56	54	37
Hyde United	38	15	7	16	59	59	37
Altincham	38	14	8	16	62	65	36
Fleetwood	38	13	10	15	53	60	36
Runcorn	38	11	13	14	57	72	35
Morecambe	38	10	13	15	41	51	33
South Liverpool	38	11	11	16	44	55	33
Great Harwood	38	10	9	19	63	92	29
Matlock Town	38	8	12	18	52	67	28
Goole Town	38	10	6	22	50	71	26
Gateshead	38	5	12	21	37	94	22

1970-71

	P	W	D	L	F	A	Pts
Wigan Athletic	42	27	13	2	91	32	67
Stafford Rangers	42	27	7	8	87	51	61
Scarborough	42	23	12	7	83	40	58
Boston United	42	22	12	8	69	31	56
Macclesfield Town	42	23	10	9	84	45	56
Northwich Victoria	42	22	5	15	71	55	49
Bangor City	42	19	10	13	72	61	48
Altrincham	42	19	10	13	80	76	48
South Liverpool	42	15	15	12	67	57	45
Chorley	42	14	14	14	58	61	42
Gainsborough Trinity	42	15	11	16	65	63	41
Morecambe	42	14	11	17	67	79	39
South Shields	42	12	14	16	67	66	38
Bradford Park Avenue	42	15	8	19	54	73	38
Lancaster City	42	12	12	18	53	76	36
Netherfield	42	13	9	20	59	57	35
Matlock Town	42	10	13	19	58	80	33
Fleetwood	42	10	11	21	56	90	31
Great Harwood	42	8	13	21	66	98	29
Runcorn	42	10	5	27	58	84	25
Kirkby Town	42	6	13	23	57	93	25
Goole Town	42	10	4	28	44	98	24

1971-72

Team	P	W	D	L	F	A	Pts
Stafford Rangers	46	30	11	5	91	32	71
Boston United	46	28	13	5	87	37	69
Wigan Athletic	46	27	10	9	70	43	64
Scarborough	46	21	15	10	75	46	57
Northwich Victoria	46	20	14	12	65	59	54
Macclesfield Town	46	18	15	13	61	50	51
Gainsborough Trinity	46	21	9	16	93	79	51
South Shields	46	18	14	14	75	57	50
Bangor City	46	20	8	18	93	74	48
Altrincham	46	18	11	17	72	58	47
Skelmersdale United	46	19	9	18	61	58	47
Matlock Town	46	20	7	19	67	75	47
Chorley	46	17	12	17	66	59	46
Lancaster City	46	15	14	17	84	84	44
Great Harwood	46	15	14	17	60	74	44
Ellesmere Port Town	46	17	9	20	67	71	43
Morecambe	46	15	10	21	51	64	40
Bradford Park Avenue	46	13	13	20	54	71	39
Netherfield	46	16	5	25	51	73	37
Fleetwood	46	11	15	20	43	67	37
South Liverpool	46	12	12	22	61	73	36
Runcorn	46	8	14	24	48	80	30
Goole Town	46	9	10	27	51	97	28
Kirkby Town	46	6	12	28	38	104	24

1972-73

Team	P	W	D	L	F	A	Pts
Boston United	46	27	16	3	88	34	70
Scarborough	46	26	9	11	72	39	61
Wigan Athletic	46	23	14	9	69	38	60
Altrincham	46	22	16	8	75	55	60
Bradford Park Avenue	46	19	17	10	63	50	55
Stafford Rangers	46	20	11	15	63	46	51
Gainsborough Trinity	46	18	13	15	70	50	49
Northwich Victoria	46	17	15	14	74	62	49
Netherfield	46	20	9	17	68	65	49
Macclesfield Town	46	16	16	14	58	47	48
Ellesmere Port Town	46	18	11	17	52	56	47
Skelmersdale United	46	15	16	15	58	59	46
Bangor City	46	16	13	17	70	60	45
Mossley	46	17	11	18	70	73	45
Morecambe	46	17	11	18	62	70	45
Great Harwood	46	14	15	17	63	74	43
South Liverpool	46	12	19	15	47	57	43
Runcorn	46	15	12	19	75	78	42
Goole Town	46	13	13	20	64	73	39
South Shields	46	17	4	25	64	81	38
Matlock Town	46	11	11	24	42	80	33
Lancaster City	46	10	11	25	53	78	31
Barrow	46	12	6	28	52	101	30
Fleetwood	46	5	15	26	31	77	25

1973-74

Team	P	W	D	L	F	A	Pts
Boston United	46	27	11	8	69	32	65
Wigan Athletic	46	28	8	10	96	39	64
Altrincham	46	26	11	9	77	34	63
Stafford Rangers	46	27	9	10	101	43	63
Scarborough	46	22	14	10	62	43	58
South Shields	46	25	6	15	87	48	56
Runcorn	46	21	14	11	72	47	56
Macclesfield Town	46	18	15	13	48	47	51
Bangor City	46	19	11	16	65	56	49
Gainsborough Trinity	46	18	11	17	77	64	47
South Liverpool	46	16	15	15	55	47	47
Skelmersdale United	46	16	13	17	50	59	45
Goole Town	46	14	15	17	60	69	43
Fleetwood	46	14	15	17	48	68	43
Mossley	46	15	11	20	53	65	41
Northwich Victoria	46	14	13	19	68	75	41
Morecambe	46	13	13	20	62	84	39
Buxton	46	14	10	22	45	71	38
Matlock Town	46	11	14	21	50	79	36
Great Harwood	46	10	14	22	52	74	34
Bradford Park Avenue	46	9	15	22	42	84	33
Barrow	46	13	7	26	46	94	33
Lancaster City	46	10	12	24	52	67	32
Netherfield	46	11	5	30	42	88	27

1974-75

Team	P	W	D	L	F	A	Pts
Wigan Athletic	46	33	6	7	94	38	72
Runcorn	46	30	8	8	102	42	68
Altrincham	46	26	12	8	87	43	64
Stafford Rangers	46	25	13	8	81	39	63
Scarborough	46	24	12	10	73	45	60
Mossley	46	23	11	12	78	52	57
Gateshead United	46	22	12	12	74	48	56
Goole Town	46	19	12	15	75	71	50
Northwich Victoria	46	18	12	16	83	71	48
Great Harwood	46	17	14	15	69	66	48
Matlock Town	46	19	8	19	87	79	46
Boston United	46	16	14	16	64	63	46
Morecambe	46	14	15	17	71	87	43
Worksop Town	46	14	14	18	69	66	42
South Liverpool	46	14	14	18	59	71	42
Buxton	46	11	17	18	50	77	39
Macclesfield Town	46	11	14	21	46	62	36
Lancaster City	46	13	10	23	53	76	36
Bangor City	46	13	9	24	56	67	35
Gainsborough Trinity	46	10	15	21	46	79	35
Skelmersdale United	46	13	7	26	63	93	33
Barrow	46	9	15	22	45	72	33
Netherfield	46	12	8	26	42	91	32
Fleetwood	46	5	10	31	26	97	20

1975-76

Team	P	W	D	L	F	A	Pts
Runcorn	46	29	10	7	95	42	68
Stafford Rangers	46	26	15	5	81	41	67
Scarborough	46	26	10	10	84	43	62
Matlock Town	46	26	9	11	96	63	61
Boston United	46	27	6	13	95	58	60
Wigan Athletic	46	21	15	10	61	42	57
Altrincham	46	20	14	12	77	57	54
Bangor City	46	21	12	13	80	70	54
Mossley	46	21	11	14	70	58	53
Goole Town	46	20	13	13	58	49	53
Northwich Victoria	46	17	17	12	79	59	51
Lancaster City	46	18	9	19	61	70	45
Worksop Town	46	17	10	19	63	56	44
Gainsborough Trinity	46	13	17	16	58	69	43
Macclesfield Town	46	15	12	19	50	64	42
Gateshead United	46	17	7	22	64	63	41
Buxton	46	11	13	22	37	62	35
Skelmersdale United	46	12	10	24	45	74	34
Netherfield	46	11	11	24	55	76	33
Morecambe	46	11	11	24	47	67	33
Great Harwood	46	13	7	26	58	86	33
South Liverpool	46	12	9	25	45	78	33
Barrow	46	12	9	25	47	84	33
Fleetwood	46	3	9	34	36	131	15

1976-77

Team	P	W	D	L	F	A	Pts
Boston United	44	27	11	6	82	35	65
Northwich Victoria	44	27	11	6	85	43	65
Matlock Town	44	26	11	7	108	57	63
Bangor City	44	22	11	11	87	52	55
Scarborough	44	21	12	11	77	66	54
Goole Town	44	23	6	15	64	50	52
Lancaster City	44	21	9	14	71	58	51
Gateshead United	44	18	12	14	80	64	48
Mossley	44	17	14	13	74	59	48
Altrincham	44	19	9	16	60	53	47
Stafford Rangers	44	16	14	14	60	55	46
Runcorn	44	15	14	15	57	49	44
Worksop Town	44	16	12	16	50	58	44
Wigan Athletic	44	14	15	15	62	54	43
Morecambe	44	13	11	20	59	75	37
Gainsborough Trinity	44	13	10	21	58	74	36
Great Harwood	44	11	14	19	63	84	36
Buxton	44	11	13	20	48	63	35
Macclesfield Town	44	8	15	21	41	68	31
Frickley Athletic	44	11	8	25	53	93	30
Barrow	44	11	6	27	56	87	28
South Liverpool	44	10	8	26	51	104	28
Netherfield	44	9	8	27	47	92	26

1977-78

Boston United	46	31	9	6	85	35	71
Wigan Athletic	46	25	15	6	83	45	65
Bangor City	46	26	10	10	92	50	62
Scarborough	46	26	10	10	80	39	62
Altrincham	46	22	15	9	84	49	59
Northwich Victoria	46	22	14	10	83	55	50
Stafford Rangers	46	22	13	11	71	41	57
Runcorn	46	19	18	9	70	44	56
Mossley	46	22	11	13	85	73	55
Matlock Town	46	21	12	13	79	60	54
Lancaster City	46	15	14	17	66	82	44
Frickley Athletic	46	15	12	19	77	81	42
Barrow	46	14	12	20	50	61	40
Goole Town	46	15	9	22	60	68	39
Great Harwood	46	13	13	20	66	83	39
Gainsborough Trinity	46	14	10	22	61	74	38
Gateshead	46	16	5	25	65	74	37
Netherfield	46	11	13	22	50	80	35
Workington	46	13	8	25	48	80	34
Worksop Town	46	12	10	24	45	84	34
Morecambe	46	11	11	24	67	92	33
Macclesfield Town	46	12	9	25	60	92	33
Buxton	46	13	6	27	60	95	32
South Liverpool	46	9	7	30	53	111	25

1978-79

Mossley	44	32	5	7	117	48	69
Altrincham	44	25	11	8	93	39	61
Matlock Town	44	24	8	12	100	59	56
Scarborough	44	19	14	11	61	44	52
Southport	44	19	14	11	62	49	52
Boston United	44	17	18	9	40	33	52
Runcorn	44	21	9	14	79	54	51
Stafford Rangers	44	18	14	12	67	41	50
Goole Town	44	17	15	12	56	61	49
Northwich Victoria	44	18	11	15	64	52	47
Lancaster City	44	17	12	15	62	54	46
Bangor City	44	15	14	15	65	66	44
Worksop Town	44	13	14	17	55	67	40
Workington	44	16	7	21	62	74	39
Netherfield	44	13	11	20	39	69	37
Barrow	44	14	9	21	47	78	37
Gainsborough Trinity	44	12	12	20	52	67	36
Morecambe	44	11	13	20	55	65	35
Frickley Athletic	44	13	9	22	58	70	35
South Liverpool	44	12	10	22	48	85	34
Gateshead	44	11	11	22	42	63	33
Buxton	44	11	9	24	50	84	31
Macclesfield Town	44	8	10	26	40	92	26

1979-80

Mossley	42	28	9	5	96	41	65
Witton Albion	42	28	8	6	89	30	64
Frickley Athletic	42	24	13	5	93	48	61
Burton Albion	42	25	6	11	83	42	56
Matlock Town	42	18	17	7	87	53	53
Buxton	42	21	9	12	61	48	51
Worksop Town	42	20	10	12	65	52	50
Macclesfield Town	42	18	11	13	67	53	47
Grantham	42	18	8	16	71	65	44
Marine	42	16	10	16	65	57	42
Goole Town	42	14	13	15	61	63	41
Lancaster City	42	13	13	16	74	77	39
Oswestry Town	42	12	14	16	44	60	38
Gainsborough Trinity	42	14	8	20	64	75	36
Runcorn	42	11	11	20	46	63	33
Gateshead	42	11	11	20	50	77	33
Morecambe	42	10	12	20	40	59	32
Netherfield	42	7	15	20	37	66	29
Southport	42	8	13	21	30	75	29
South Liverpool	42	7	14	21	51	84	28
Workington	42	8	12	22	50	85	28
Tamworth	42	8	9	25	26	77	25

1980-81

Runcorn	42	32	7	3	99	22	71
Mossley	42	24	7	11	95	55	55
Marine	42	22	10	10	60	41	54
Buxton	42	21	7	14	64	50	49
Gainsborough Trinity	42	17	13	12	50	57	47
Burton Albion	42	19	8	15	63	54	46
Witton Albion	42	19	8	15	70	62	46
Goole Town	42	14	16	12	56	50	44
South Liverpool	42	19	6	17	59	64	44
Workington	42	15	13	14	57	48	43
Gateshead	42	12	18	12	65	61	42
Worksop Town	42	15	11	16	66	61	41
Macclesfield Town	42	13	13	16	52	69	39
Grantham	42	14	9	19	57	74	37
Matlock Town	42	12	12	18	57	80	36
Lancaster City	42	13	9	20	48	70	35
Netherfield	42	11	12	19	73	81	34
Oswestry Town	42	13	8	21	54	67	34
King's Lynn	42	8	18	16	46	65	34
Southport	42	11	11	26	42	68	33
Morecambe	42	11	8	23	42	74	30
Tamworth	42	9	12	21	38	76	30

1981-82

Bangor City	42	27	8	7	108	60	62
Mossley	42	24	11	7	76	43	59
Witton Albion	42	22	10	10	75	44	54
Gateshead	42	19	14	9	65	49	52
King's Lynn	42	19	12	11	61	36	50
Grantham	42	18	13	11	65	53	49
Burton Albion	42	19	9	14	71	62	47
Southport	42	16	14	12	63	55	46
Marine	42	17	12	13	64	57	46
Macclesfield Town	42	17	9	16	67	58	43
Workington	42	18	7	17	62	60	43
Worksop Town	42	15	13	14	52	60	43
South Liverpool	42	13	13	16	55	57	39
Goole Town	42	13	13	16	56	60	39
Oswestry Town	42	14	11	17	55	59	39
Buxton	42	14	11	17	48	56	39
Lancaster City	42	13	12	17	47	50	38
Gainsborough Trinity	42	10	13	19	60	69	33
Tamworth	42	10	9	23	31	56	29
Morecambe	42	9	11	22	43	86	29
Matlock Town	42	7	12	23	38	72	26
Netherfield	42	5	9	28	31	91	19

1982-83

Gateshead	42	32	4	6	114	43	100
Mossley	42	25	9	8	77	42	84
Burton Albion	42	24	9	9	81	53	81
Chorley	42	23	11	8	77	49	80
Macclesfield Town	42	24	8	10	71	49	80
Marine	42	17	17	8	81	57	68
Workington	42	19	10	13	71	55	67
Hyde United	42	18	12	12	91	63	66
King's Lynn	42	17	13	12	62	44	64
Matlock Town	42	18	10	14	70	65	64
Witton Albion	42	17	12	13	82	52	63
Buxton	42	17	9	16	60	62	60
Morecambe	42	16	11	15	75	66	59
Grantham	42	15	13	14	49	50	58
Southport	42	11	14	17	58	65	47
Goole Town	42	13	7	22	52	66	46
Gainsborough Trinity	42	11	9	22	60	71	42
Oswestry Town	42	10	8	24	56	99	38
South Liverpool	42	7	15	20	57	91	36
Tamworth	42	7	8	27	44	97	29
Worksop Town	42	5	10	27	50	98	25
Netherfield	42	2	9	31	28	129	15

1983-84

Barrow	42	29	10	3	92	38	97
Matlock Town	42	23	8	11	72	48	77
South Liverpool	42	22	11	9	55	44	77
Grantham	42	20	8	14	64	51	68
Burton Albion	42	17	13	12	61	47	64
Macclesfield Town	42	18	10	14	65	55	64
Rhyl	42	19	6	17	64	55	63
Horwich	42	18	9	15	64	59	63
Gainsborough Trinity	42	17	11	14	82	66	62
Stafford Rangers	42	15	17	10	65	52	62
Hyde United	42	17	8	17	61	63	59
Marine	42	16	10	16	63	68	58
Witton Albion	42	14	14	14	64	57	56
Chorley	42	14	11	17	68	65	53
Workington	42	14	9	19	53	57	51
Southport	42	14	8	20	57	74	50
Worksop Town	42	13	8	21	57	74	47
Goole Town	42	12	10	20	59	80	46
Morecambe	42	11	12	19	59	75	45
Oswestry Town	42	11	8	23	66	97	41
Buxton	42	11	6	25	52	91	39
Mossley	42	9	9	24	47	74	33

Mossley had 3 points deducted

1984-85

Stafford Rangers	42	26	8	8	81	40	86
Macclesfield Town	42	23	13	6	67	39	82
Witton Albion	42	22	8	12	57	39	74
Hyde United	42	21	8	13	68	52	71
Marine	42	18	15	9	59	34	69
Burton Albion	42	18	15	9	70	49	69
Worksop Town	42	19	10	13	68	56	67
Workington	42	18	9	15	59	53	63
Horwich	42	16	14	12	67	50	62
Bangor City	42	17	9	16	70	61	60
Gainsborough Trinity	42	14	14	14	72	73	56
Southport	42	15	9	18	65	66	54
Matlock Town	42	14	9	19	56	66	51
Oswestry Town	42	14	9	19	59	75	51
Mossley	42	14	9	19	45	65	51
Goole Town	42	13	11	18	60	65	50
Rhyl	42	11	14	17	52	63	47
Morecambe	42	11	14	17	51	67	47
Chorley	42	12	10	20	47	63	46
South Liverpool	42	9	15	18	43	71	42
Grantham	42	8	13	21	41	69	36
Buxton	42	8	6	28	38	79	30

Grantham had 1 point deducted

1985-86

Gateshead	42	24	10	8	85	51	82
Marine	42	23	11	8	63	35	80
Morecambe	42	17	17	8	59	39	68
Gainsborough Trinity	42	18	14	10	66	52	68
Burton Albion	42	18	12	12	64	47	66
Southport	42	17	11	14	70	66	62
Worksop Town	42	17	10	15	51	48	61
Workington	42	14	18	10	54	46	59
Macclesfield Town	42	17	8	17	67	65	59
Hyde United	42	14	15	13	63	62	57
Witton Albion	42	15	13	14	56	59	57
Mossley	42	13	16	13	56	60	55
Bangor City	42	13	15	14	51	51	54
Rhyl	42	14	10	18	65	71	52
South Liverpool	42	11	17	14	43	44	50
Horwich	42	15	6	21	53	63	50
Caernarfon Town	42	11	17	14	51	63	50
Oswestry Town	42	12	13	17	51	60	49
Buxton	42	11	12	19	55	76	45
Chorley	42	9	15	18	56	64	42
Matlock Town	42	9	15	18	59	75	42
Goole Town	42	7	11	24	37	78	31

Workington, Witton Albion, Horwich and Goole Town all had 1 point deducted.

1986-87

Macclesfield Town	42	26	10	6	80	47	88
Bangor City	42	25	12	5	74	35	87
Caernarfon Town	42	20	16	6	67	40	76
Marine	42	21	10	11	70	43	73
South Liverpool	42	21	10	11	58	40	73
Morecambe	42	20	12	10	68	49	72
Matlock Town	42	20	10	12	81	67	70
Southport	42	19	11	12	67	49	68
Chorley	42	16	12	14	58	59	60
Mossley	42	15	12	15	57	52	57
Hyde United	42	15	10	17	81	70	55
Burton Albion	42	16	6	20	56	68	54
Buxton	42	13	14	15	71	68	53
Witton Albion	42	15	8	19	68	79	53
Barrow	42	15	7	20	42	57	52
Goole Town	42	13	12	17	58	62	51
Oswestry Town	42	14	8	20	55	83	50
Rhyl	42	10	15	17	56	74	45
Worksop Town	42	9	13	20	56	74	40
Gainsborough Trinity	42	9	10	23	53	77	37
Workington	42	5	14	23	38	70	28
Horwich RMI	42	3	12	27	36	85	20

Workington and Horwich RMI both had 1 point deducted.

1987-88

Premier Division

Chorley	42	26	10	6	78	35	88
Hyde United	42	25	10	7	91	52	85
Caernarfon Town	42	22	10	10	56	34	76
Morecambe	42	19	15	8	61	41	72
Barrow	42	21	8	13	70	41	71
Worksop Town	42	20	11	11	74	55	71
Bangor City	42	20	10	12	71	55	70
Rhyl	42	18	13	11	70	42	67
Marine	42	19	10	13	67	45	67
Frickley Athletic	42	18	11	13	61	55	65
Witton Albion	42	16	12	14	61	47	60
Goole Town	42	17	9	16	71	61	60
Horwich	42	17	9	16	46	42	60
Southport	42	15	12	15	43	48	57
South Liverpool	42	10	19	13	56	64	49
Buxton	42	11	14	17	72	76	47
Mossley	42	11	11	20	54	75	44
Gateshead	42	11	7	24	52	71	40
Matlock Town	42	10	8	24	58	89	38
Gainsborough Trinity	42	8	10	24	38	81	34
Oswestry Town	42	6	10	26	44	101	28
Workington	42	6	3	33	28	113	21

First Division

Fleetwood Town	36	22	7	7	85	45	73
Stalybridge Celtic	36	22	6	8	72	42	72
Leek Town	36	20	10	6	63	38	70
Accrington Stanley	36	21	6	9	71	39	69
Farsley Celtic	36	18	9	9	64	48	60
Droylsden	36	16	10	10	63	48	58
Eastwood Hanley	36	14	12	10	50	37	54
Winsford United	36	15	6	15	59	47	51
Congleton Town	36	12	16	8	43	39	51
Harrogate Town	36	13	9	14	51	50	48
Alfreton Town	36	13	8	15	53	54	47
Radcliffe Borough	36	11	13	12	66	62	46
Irlam Town	36	12	10	14	39	45	46
Penrith	36	11	11	14	46	51	44
Sutton Town	36	11	5	20	51	96	38
Lancaster City	36	10	6	20	45	72	36
Eastwood Town	36	8	10	18	45	65	34
Curzon Ashton	36	8	4	24	43	73	28
Netherfield	36	4	4	28	35	93	16

Congleton Town had 1 point deducted
Farsley Celtic had 3 points deducted

1988-89

Premier Division

Barrow	42	26	9	7	89	35	87
Hyde United	42	24	8	10	77	44	80
Witton Albion	42	22	13	7	67	39	79
Bangor City	42	22	10	10	77	48	76
Marine	42	23	7	12	69	48	76
Goole Town	42	22	7	13	75	60	73
Fleetwood Town	42	19	16	7	53	44	73
Rhyl	42	18	10	14	75	65	64
Frickley Athletic	42	17	10	15	64	53	61
Mossley	42	17	9	16	56	58	60
South Liverpool	42	15	13	14	65	57	58
Caernarfon Town	42	15	10	17	49	53	55
Matlock Town	42	16	5	21	65	73	53
Southport	42	13	12	17	66	52	51
Buxton	42	12	14	16	61	63	50
Morecambe	42	13	9	20	55	60	47
Gainsborough Trinity	42	12	11	19	56	73	47
Shepshed Charterhouse	42	14	8	20	19	80	44
Stalybridge Celtic	42	9	13	20	16	81	40
Horwich	42	7	14	21	12	70	35
Gateshead	42	7	13	22	36	70	34
Worksop Town	42	6	5	31	42	103	23

Morecambe had 1 point deducted
Shepshed Charterhouse had 6 points deducted

First Division

Colne Dynamo	42	30	11	1	102	21	98
Bishop Auckland	42	28	5	9	78	28	89
Leek Town	42	25	11	6	74	41	85
Droylsden	42	25	9	8	84	48	84
Whitley Bay	42	23	6	13	77	49	75
Accrington Stanley	42	21	10	11	81	60	73
Lancaster City	42	21	8	13	76	54	71
Harrogate Town	42	19	7	16	68	61	64
Newtown	42	15	12	15	65	59	57
Congleton Town	42	15	11	16	62	66	56
Workington	42	17	3	22	59	74	54
Eastwood Town	42	14	10	13	55	61	52
Curzon Ashton	42	13	11	18	74	72	50
Farsley Celtic	42	12	13	17	52	73	49
Irlam Town	42	11	14	17	53	63	47
Penrith	42	14	5	23	61	91	47
Radcliffe Borough	42	12	10	20	62	86	46
Eastwood Hanley	42	11	12	10	46	67	45
Winsford United	42	13	6	23	58	93	35
Alfreton Town	42	8	11	23	44	92	35
Netherfield	42	8	9	25	57	90	32
Sutton Town	42	7	6	29	70	109	23

Leek Town and Netherfield both had 1 point deducted
Colne Dynamo had 3 points deducted
Sutton Town had 4 points deducted

1989-90

Premier Division

Colne Dynamoes	42	32	6	4	86	40	102
Gateshead	42	22	10	10	78	58	76
Witton Albion	42	22	7	13	67	39	73
Hyde United	42	21	8	13	73	50	71
South Liverpool	42	20	9	13	89	79	69
Matlock Town	42	18	12	12	61	42	66
Southport	42	17	14	11	54	48	65
Fleetwood Town	42	17	12	13	73	66	63
Marine	42	16	14	12	59	55	62
Bangor City	42	15	15	12	64	58	60
Bishop Auckland	42	17	8	17	72	64	59
Frickley Athletic	42	16	8	18	56	61	56
Horwich	42	15	13	14	66	69	55
Morecambe	42	15	9	18	58	70	54
Gainsborough Trinity	42	16	8	18	59	55	53
Buxton	42	15	8	19	59	72	53
Stalybridge Celtic	42	12	9	21	48	61	45
Mossley	42	11	10	21	61	82	43
Goole Town	42	12	5	25	54	77	41
Shepshed	42	11	7	24	55	82	40
Caernarfon Town	42	10	8	24	56	86	38
Rhyl	42	7	10	25	43	77	30

Rhyl had 1 point deducted
Horwich and Gainsborough Trinity both had 3 points deducted

First Division

Leek Town	42	26	8	8	70	31	86
Droylsden	42	27	6	9	81	46	80
Accrington Stanley	42	22	10	10	80	53	76
Whitley Bay	42	21	11	10	93	59	74
Emley	42	20	9	13	70	42	69
Congleton Town	42	20	12	10	65	53	69
Winsford United	42	18	10	14	65	53	64
Curzon Ashton	42	17	11	14	66	60	62
Harrogate Town	42	17	9	16	68	62	60
Lancaster City	42	15	14	13	73	54	59
Eastwood Town	42	16	11	15	61	64	59
Farsley Celtic	42	17	6	19	71	75	57
Rossendale United	42	15	9	18	73	69	54
Newtown	42	14	12	16	49	62	54
Irlam Town	42	14	11	17	61	66	53
Workington	42	14	8	20	56	64	50
Radcliffe Borough	42	14	7	21	47	63	49
Alfreton Town	42	13	8	21	59	85	47
Worksop Town	42	13	5	24	56	95	44
Netherfield	42	11	6	25	56	89	39
Eastwood Hanley	42	10	6	26	45	76	36
Penrith	42	9	9	24	44	88	36

Congleton Town 3 points deducted. Droylsden 7 points deducted.

1990-91

Premier Division

Witton Albion	40	28	9	3	81	31	93
Stalybridge Celtic	40	22	11	7	44	26	77
Morecambe	40	19	16	5	72	44	73
Fleetwood Town	40	20	9	11	69	44	69
Southport	40	18	14	8	66	48	68
Marine	40	18	11	11	56	39	65
Bishop Auckland	40	17	10	13	62	56	61
Buxton	40	17	11	12	66	61	59
Leek Town	40	15	11	14	48	44	56
Frickley Athletic	40	16	6	18	64	62	54
Hyde United	40	14	11	15	73	63	53
Goole Town	40	14	10	16	68	74	52
Droylsden	40	12	11	17	67	70	47
Chorley	40	12	10	18	55	55	46
Mossley	40	13	10	17	55	68	45
Horwich	40	13	6	21	62	81	45
Matlock Town	40	12	7	21	52	70	43
Bangor City	40	9	12	19	52	70	39
South Liverpool	40	10	9	21	58	92	39
Gainsborough Trinity	40	9	11	20	57	84	38
Shepshed Charterhouse	40	6	7	27	38	83	25

First Division

Whitley Bay	42	25	10	7	95	38	85
Emley	42	24	12	6	78	37	84
Worksop Town	42	25	7	10	85	56	82
Accrington Stanley	42	21	13	8	83	57	76
Rhyl	42	21	7	14	62	63	70
Eastwood Town	42	17	11	14	70	60	62
Warrington Town	42	17	10	15	68	52	61
Lancaster City	42	19	8	15	58	56	61
Bridlington Town	42	15	15	12	72	52	60
Curzon Ashton	42	14	14	14	49	57	56
Congleton Town	42	14	12	16	57	71	54
Netherfield	42	14	11	17	67	66	53
Newtown	42	13	12	17	68	75	51
Caernarfon Town	42	13	10	19	51	64	49
Rossendale United	42	12	13	17	66	67	48
Radcliffe Borough	42	12	12	18	50	69	48
Irlam Town	42	12	11	19	55	76	47
Winsford United	42	11	13	18	51	66	46
Harrogate Town	42	11	13	18	55	73	46
Workington	42	11	11	20	54	67	41
Farsley Celtic	42	11	9	22	49	78	39
Alfreton Town	42	7	12	23	41	84	33

1991-92

Premier Division

Stalybridge Celtic	42	26	14	2	84	33	92
Marine	42	23	9	10	64	32	78
Morecambe	42	21	13	8	70	44	76
Leek Town	42	21	10	11	62	49	73
Buxton	42	21	9	12	65	47	72
Emley	42	18	11	13	69	47	65
Southport	42	16	17	9	57	48	65
Accrington Stanley	42	17	12	13	78	62	63
Hyde United	42	17	9	16	69	67	60
Fleetwood United	42	17	8	17	67	64	59
Bishop Auckland	42	16	9	17	48	58	57
Goole Town	42	15	9	18	60	72	54
Horwich	42	13	14	15	44	52	53
Frickley Athletic	42	12	16	14	61	57	52
Droylsden	42	12	14	16	62	72	50
Mossley	42	15	4	23	51	73	49
Whitley Bay	42	13	9	20	53	79	48
Gainsborough Trinity	42	11	13	18	48	63	46
Matlock Town	42	12	9	21	59	87	45
Bangor City	42	11	10	21	46	57	43
Chorley	42	11	9	22	61	82	42
Shepshed Albion	42	6	8	28	46	79	26

First Division

Colwyn Bay	42	30	4	8	99	49	94
Winsford United	42	29	6	7	96	41	93
Worksop Town	42	25	5	12	101	54	80
Guiseley	42	22	12	8	93	56	78
Caernarfon Town	42	23	9	10	78	47	78
Bridlington Town	42	22	9	11	86	46	75
Warrington Town	42	20	8	14	79	64	68
Knowsley United	42	18	10	14	69	52	64
Netherfield	42	18	7	17	54	61	61
Harrogate Town	42	14	16	12	73	69	58
Curzon Ashton	42	15	9	18	71	83	54
Farsley Celtic	42	15	9	18	79	101	53
Radcliffe Borough	42	15	9	18	67	72	51
Newtown	42	15	6	21	60	95	51
Eastwood Town	42	13	11	18	59	70	50
Lancaster City	42	10	19	13	55	62	49
Congleton Town	42	14	5	23	59	81	47
Rhyl	42	11	10	21	59	69	43
Rossendale United	42	9	11	22	61	90	38
Alfreton Town	42	12	2	28	63	98	38
Irlam Town	42	9	7	26	45	95	33
Workington	42	7	8	27	45	99	28

Farsley Celtic 1 point deducted. Radcliffe Borough 3 points deducted.

1992-93

Premier Division

Southport	42	29	9	4	103	31	96
Winsford United	42	27	9	6	91	43	90
Morecambe	42	25	11	6	93	51	86
Marine	42	26	8	8	83	47	86
Leek Town	42	21	11	10	86	51	74
Accrington Stanley	42	20	13	9	79	45	73
Frickley Athletic	42	21	6	15	62	52	69
Barrow	42	18	11	13	71	55	65
Hyde United	42	17	13	12	87	71	64
Bishop Auckland	42	17	11	14	63	52	62
Gainsborough Trinity	42	17	8	17	63	66	59
Colwyn Bay	42	16	6	20	80	79	54
Horwich	42	14	10	18	72	79	52
Buxton	42	13	10	19	60	75	49
Matlock Town	42	13	11	18	56	79	47
Emley	42	13	6	23	62	91	45
Whitley Bay	42	11	8	23	57	96	41
Chorley	42	10	10	22	52	93	40
Fleetwood Town	42	10	7	25	50	77	37
Droylsden	42	10	7	25	47	84	37
Mossley	42	7	8	27	53	95	29
Goole Town	42	6	9	27	47	105	27

Matlock Town had 3 points deducted

First Division

Bridlington Town	40	25	11	4	84	35	86
Knowsley United	40	23	7	10	86	48	76
Ashton United	40	22	8	10	81	54	74
Guiseley	40	20	10	10	90	64	70
Warrington Town	40	19	10	11	85	57	67
Gretna	40	17	12	11	64	47	63
Curzon Ashton	40	16	15	9	69	63	63
Great Harwood Town	40	17	9	14	66	57	60
Alfreton Town	40	15	9	16	80	80	54
Harrogate Town	40	14	12	14	77	81	54
Worksop Town	40	15	9	16	66	70	54
Radcliffe Borough	40	13	14	13	66	69	53
Workington	40	13	13	14	51	61	52
Eastwood Town	40	13	11	16	49	52	50
Netherfield	40	11	14	15	68	63	47
Caernarfon Town	40	13	8	19	66	74	47
Farsley Celtic	40	12	8	20	64	77	44
Lancaster City	40	10	12	18	49	76	42
Shepshed Albion	40	9	12	19	46	66	39
Congleton Town	40	10	7	23	58	95	37
Rossendale United	40	5	5	30	50	126	20

1993-94

Premier Division

Marine	42	27	9	6	106	62	90
Leek Town	42	27	8	7	79	50	89
Boston United	42	23	9	10	90	43	78
Bishop Auckland	42	23	9	10	73	58	78
Frickley Athletic	42	21	12	9	90	51	75
Colwyn Bay	42	18	14	10	74	51	68
Morecambe	42	20	7	15	90	56	67
Barrow	42	18	10	14	59	51	64
Hyde United	42	17	10	15	80	71	61
Chorley	42	17	10	15	70	67	61
Whitley Bay	42	17	9	16	61	72	60
Gainsborough Trinity	42	15	11	16	64	66	56
Emley	42	12	16	14	63	71	52
Matlock Town	42	13	12	17	71	76	51
Buxton	42	13	10	19	67	73	49
Accrington Stanley	42	14	7	21	63	85	49
Droylsden	42	11	14	17	57	82	47
Knowsley United	42	11	11	20	52	66	44
Winsford United	42	9	11	22	50	74	38
Horwich RMI	42	8	12	22	50	75	35
Bridlington Town	42	7	10	25	41	91	28
Fleetwood Town	42	7	7	28	55	114	28

Horwich RMI 1 point deducted. Bridlington Town 3 points deducted

First Division

Guiseley	40	29	6	5	87	37	93
Spennymoor United	40	25	6	9	95	50	81
Ashton United	40	24	7	9	85	41	79
Lancaster City	40	20	10	10	74	46	70
Netherfield	40	20	6	14	68	60	66
Alfreton Town	40	18	10	12	83	70	64
Warrington Town	40	17	11	12	52	48	62
Goole Town	40	16	11	13	72	58	59
Great Harwood Town	40	15	14	11	56	60	59
Gretna	40	16	7	17	64	65	55
Workington	40	14	10	16	70	74	52
Worksop Town	40	14	9	17	79	87	51
Bamber Bridge	40	13	11	16	62	59	50
Curzon Ashton	40	13	8	19	62	71	47
Congleton Town	40	12	9	19	53	68	45
Radcliffe Borough	40	10	14	16	62	75	44
Mossley	40	10	12	18	44	68	39
Caernarfon Town	40	9	11	20	54	88	38
Farsley Celtic	40	6	16	18	42	77	34
Harrogate Town	40	8	9	23	40	86	33
Eastwood Town	40	7	11	22	47	63	32

Mossley had 3 points deducted

1994-95

Premier Division

Marine	42	29	11	2	83	27	98
Morecambe	42	28	10	4	99	34	94
Guiseley	42	28	9	5	96	50	93
Hyde United	42	22	10	10	89	59	76
Boston United	42	20	11	11	80	43	71
Spennymoor United	42	20	11	11	66	52	71
Buxton	42	18	9	15	65	62	63
Gainsborough Trinity	42	16	13	13	69	61	61
Bishop Auckland	42	16	12	14	68	55	57
Witton Albion	42	14	14	14	54	56	56
Barrow	42	17	5	20	68	71	56
Colwyn Bay	42	16	8	18	71	80	56
Emley	42	14	13	15	62	68	55
Matlock Town	42	15	5	22	62	72	50
Accrington Stanley	42	12	13	17	55	77	49
Knowsley United	42	11	14	17	64	83	47
Winsford United	42	10	11	21	56	75	41
Chorley	42	11	7	24	64	87	40
Frickley Athletic	42	10	10	22	53	79	40
Droylsden	42	10	8	24	56	93	38
Whitley Bay	42	8	8	26	46	97	32
Horwich RMI	42	9	4	29	49	94	31

Bishop Auckland had 3 points deducted

First Division

Blyth Spartans	42	26	9	7	95	55	87
Bamber Bridge	42	25	10	7	101	51	85
Warrington Town	42	25	9	8	74	40	84
Alfreton Town	42	25	7	10	94	49	82
Lancaster City	42	23	10	9	81	44	79
Worksop Town	42	19	14	9	95	68	71
Radcliffe Borough	42	18	10	14	76	70	64
Ashton United	42	18	8	16	80	70	62
Netherfield	42	17	7	118	54	56	58
Eastwood Town	42	14	13	15	67	61	55
Gretna	42	14	13	15	64	66	55
Atherton Laburnum Rovers	42	14	8	20	60	67	50
Harrogate Town	42	14	8	20	57	78	50
Caernarfon Town	42	13	10	19	59	62	49
Curzon Ashton	42	10	16	16	64	80	46
Great Harwood Town	42	11	13	18	66	87	46
Congleton Town	42	11	13	18	52	75	46
Fleetwood	42	12	11	19	51	74	44
Farsley Celtic	42	12	7	23	66	100	43
Workington	42	12	6	24	61	91	42
Goole Town	42	11	7	24	46	81	40
Mossley	42	11	5	26	52	90	37

Mossley had 1 point deducted. Fleetwood had 3 points deducted

1995-96

Premier Division

Bamber Bridge	42	20	16	6	81	49	76
Boston United	42	23	6	13	86	59	75
Hyde United	42	21	11	10	86	51	74
Barrow	42	20	13	9	69	42	73
Gainsborough Trinity	42	20	13	9	60	41	73
Blyth Spartans	42	17	13	12	75	61	64
Accrington Stanley	42	17	14	11	62	54	62
Emley	42	17	10	15	57	53	61
Spennymoor United	42	14	18	10	67	61	60
Guiseley	42	15	14	13	62	57	59
Bishop Auckland	42	16	11	15	60	55	59
Marine	42	15	14	13	59	54	59
Witton Albion	42	17	8	17	60	62	59
Chorley	42	14	9	19	67	74	48
Knowsley United	42	14	6	22	61	89	48
Winsford United	42	10	16	16	56	79	46
Leek Town	42	10	15	17	52	55	45
Colwyn Bay	42	8	21	13	43	57	45
Frickley Athletic	42	11	14	17	63	87	44
Buxton	42	9	11	22	43	72	38
Droylsden	42	10	8	24	58	100	38
Matlock Town	42	8	11	23	71	86	35

Accrington Stanley, Chorley & Frickley Town all had 3 points deducted

First Division

Lancaster City	40	24	11	5	79	38	83
Alfreton Town	40	23	9	8	79	47	78
Lincoln United	40	22	7	11	80	56	73
Curzon Ashton	40	20	7	13	73	53	67
Farsley Celtic	40	19	9	12	66	61	66
Radcliffe Borough	40	17	13	10	70	48	64
Eastwood Town	40	18	9	13	60	47	63
Whitley Bay	40	18	8	14	72	62	62
Ashton United	40	19	7	14	73	65	60
Atherton Laburnum Rovers	40	15	12	13	60	61	57
Worksop Town	40	16	8	16	84	90	56
Gretna	40	13	13	14	75	65	52
Warrington Town	40	13	10	17	75	72	49
Leigh	40	14	7	19	53	59	49
Netherfield	40	13	10	17	64	73	49
Workington	40	11	12	17	50	62	45
Bradford Park Avenue	40	9	14	17	57	72	41
Congleton Town	40	11	11	18	36	59	41
Great Harwood Town	40	9	7	24	44	78	33
Fleetwood	40	7	10	23	41	81	31
Harrogate Town	40	7	10	23	54	96	31

Great Harwood Town had 1 point deducted, Congleton Town had 3 points deducted and Ashton United had 4 points deducted

1996-97

Premier Division

Leek Town	44	28	9	7	71	35	93
Bishop Auckland	44	23	14	7	88	43	83
Hyde United	44	22	16	6	93	46	82
Emley	44	23	12	9	89	54	81
Barrow	44	23	11	10	71	45	80
Boston United	44	22	13	9	74	47	79
Blyth Spartans	44	22	11	11	74	49	77
Marine	44	20	15	9	53	37	75
Guiseley	44	20	11	13	63	54	71
Gainsborough Trinity	44	18	12	14	65	46	66
Accrington Stanley	44	18	12	14	77	70	66
Runcorn	44	15	15	14	63	62	60
Chorley	44	16	9	19	69	66	57
Winsford United	44	13	14	17	50	56	53
Knowsley United	44	12	14	18	58	79	49
Colwyn Bay	44	11	13	20	60	76	46
Lancaster City	44	12	9	23	48	75	45
Frickley Athletic	44	12	8	24	62	91	44
Spennymoor United	44	10	10	24	52	68	40
Bamber Bridge	44	11	7	26	59	99	40
Alfreton Town	44	8	13	23	45	83	37
Witton Albion	44	5	14	25	41	91	39
Buxton	44	5	12	27	33	86	27

Knowsley United had 1 point deducted

First Division

Radcliffe Borough	42	26	7	9	77	33	85
Leigh	42	24	11	7	65	33	83
Lincoln United	42	25	8	9	78	4/	83
Farsley Celtic	42	23	8	11	75	48	77
Worksop Town	42	20	12	10	68	38	69
Stocksbridge Park Steels	42	19	11	12	66	54	68
Bradford Park Avenue	42	20	8	14	58	50	68
Ashton United	42	17	14	11	73	52	65
Great Harwood Town	42	16	12	14	56	46	60
Droylsden	42	15	14	13	69	67	59
Matlock Town	42	16	10	16	61	69	58
Whitley Bay	42	14	12	16	47	54	54
Flixton	42	15	7	20	57	72	52
Netherfield	42	12	14	16	54	56	50
Eastwood Town	42	12	14	16	42	50	50
Gretna	42	10	18	14	55	68	48
Harrogate Town	42	13	8	21	55	76	47
Congleton Town	42	12	9	21	47	64	45
Workington	42	10	12	20	45	63	42
Curzon Ashton	42	8	10	24	48	79	34
Warrington Town	42	5	18	19	42	79	33
Atherton Laburnum Rovers	42	7	9	26	45	85	30

Worksop Town had 3 points deducted

1997-98

Premier Division

Barrow	42	25	8	9	61	29	83
Boston United	42	22	12	8	55	40	78
Leigh RMI	42	21	13	8	63	41	76
Runcorn	42	22	9	11	80	50	75
Gainsborough Trinity	42	22	9	11	60	39	75
Emley	42	22	8	12	81	61	74
Winsford United	42	19	12	11	54	43	69
Altrincham	42	18	11	13	76	44	65
Guiseley	42	16	16	10	61	53	64
Bishop Auckland	42	17	12	13	78	60	63
Marine	42	15	11	16	56	59	56
Hyde United	42	13	16	13	60	55	55
Colwyn Bay	42	15	9	18	53	57	54
Spennymoor United	42	14	11	17	58	72	52
Chorley	42	14	7	21	51	70	49
Frickley Athletic	42	12	12	18	45	62	48
Lancaster City	42	13	8	21	55	74	47
Blyth Spartans	42	12	13	17	52	63	39
Bamber Bridge	42	9	12	21	51	74	39
Accrington Stanley	42	8	14	20	49	68	38
Radcliffe Borough	42	6	12	24	39	70	30
Alfreton Town	42	3	13	26	32	86	22

Spennymoor United had 1 point deducted
Blyth Spartans had 10 points deducted

First Division

Whitby Town	42	30	8	4	99	48	98
Worksop Town	42	28	7	7	93	44	91
Ashton Town	42	26	9	7	93	43	87
Droylsden	42	24	8	10	70	49	80
Lincoln United	42	20	11	11	76	62	71
Farsley Celtic	42	20	10	12	72	66	70
Witton Albion	42	19	9	14	77	55	66
Eastwood Town	42	18	12	12	68	51	66
Bradford Park Avenue	42	18	11	13	62	46	65
Belper Town	42	18	7	17	68	66	61
Stocksbridge Park Steels	42	17	9	16	68	63	60
Trafford	42	16	6	20	59	61	54
Whitley Bay	42	14	12	16	60	63	54
Matlock Town	42	14	11	17	68	65	53
Gretna	42	13	9	20	58	64	48
Netherfield	42	12	11	19	55	75	47
Flixton	42	10	12	20	45	73	42
Congleton Town	42	11	8	23	65	101	41
Harrogate Town	42	8	14	20	57	80	38
Great Harwood Town	42	8	12	22	42	88	36
Workington	42	8	7	27	38	84	31
Buxton	42	7	3	32	41	87	24

1998-99

Premier Division

Altrıncham	42	23	11	8	67	33	80
Worksop Town	42	22	10	10	66	48	76
Guiseley	42	21	9	12	64	47	72
Bamber Bridge	42	18	15	9	63	48	69
Gateshead	42	18	11	13	69	58	65
Gainsborough Trinity	42	19	8	15	65	59	65
Whitby Town	42	17	13	12	77	62	64
Leigh	42	16	15	11	63	54	63
Hyde United	42	16	11	15	61	48	59
Stalybridge Celtic	42	16	11	15	71	63	59
Winsford United	42	14	15	13	56	52	57
Runcorn	42	12	19	11	46	49	55
Emley	42	12	17	13	47	49	53
Blyth Spartans	42	14	9	19	56	64	51
Colwyn Bay	42	12	13	17	60	71	49
Frickley Athletic	42	11	15	16	55	71	48
Marine	42	10	17	15	61	69	47
Spennymoor United	42	12	11	19	52	71	47
Lancaster City	42	11	13	18	50	62	46
Bishop Auckland	42	10	15	17	49	67	45
Chorley	42	8	15	19	45	68	39
Accrington Stanley	42	9	9	24	47	77	36

First Division

Droylsden	42	26	8	8	97	55	86
Hucknall Town	42	26	11	5	80	38	86
Ashton United	42	22	12	8	79	46	78
Lincoln United	42	20	12	10	94	65	72
Eastwood Town	42	20	8	14	65	69	68
Radcliffe Borough	42	19	8	15	78	62	65
Burscough	42	19	8	15	67	61	65
Witton Albion	42	18	9	15	70	63	63
Bradford Park Avenue	42	17	11	14	64	55	62
Stocksbridge Park Steels	42	16	13	13	64	60	61
Harrogate Town	42	17	7	18	75	77	58
Gretna	42	16	10	16	73	80	58
Belper Town	42	15	11	16	58	57	56
Trafford	42	14	11	17	50	58	53
Netherfield Kendal	42	13	10	19	51	64	49
Flixton	42	12	12	18	50	64	48
Matlock Town	42	14	6	22	53	72	48
Farsley Celtic	42	11	13	18	56	73	46
Whitley Bay	42	10	9	23	53	77	39
Congleton Town	42	8	15	19	65	91	39
Great Harwood Town	42	10	8	24	51	73	38
Alfreton Town	42	9	8	25	53	86	35

Hucknall Town had 3 points deducted

1999-2000

Premier Division

Leigh	44	28	8	8	91	45	92
Hyde United	44	24	13	7	77	44	85
Gateshead	44	23	13	8	79	41	82
Marine	44	21	16	7	78	46	79
Emley	44	20	12	12	54	41	72
Lancaster City	44	20	11	13	65	55	71
Stalybridge Celtic	44	18	12	14	64	54	66
Bishop Auckland	44	18	11	15	63	61	65
Runcorn	44	18	10	16	64	55	64
Worksop Town	44	19	6	19	78	65	63
Gainsborough Trinity	44	16	15	13	59	49	63
Whitby Town	44	15	13	16	66	66	58
Barrow	44	14	15	15	65	59	57
Blyth Spartans	44	15	9	20	62	67	54
Droylsden	44	14	12	18	53	60	54
Frickley Athletic	44	15	9	20	64	85	54
Bamber Bridge	44	14	11	19	70	67	53
Hucknall Town	44	14	11	19	55	61	53
Leek Town	44	14	10	20	58	79	52
Colwyn Bay	44	12	12	20	46	85	48
Spennymoor United	44	10	13	21	41	71	42
Guiseley	44	8	17	19	52	72	41
Winsford United	44	3	7	34	40	116	16

Spennymoor United had 1 point deducted

First Division

	P	W	D	L	F	A	Pts
Accrington Stanley	42	25	9	8	96	43	84
Burscough	42	22	18	2	81	35	84
Witton Albion	42	23	15	4	88	46	84
Bradford Park Avenue	42	23	9	10	77	48	78
Radcliffe Borough	42	22	12	8	71	48	78
Farsley Celtic	42	19	11	12	66	52	68
Matlock Town	42	17	16	9	72	55	67
Ossett Town	42	17	8	17	77	55	59
Stocksbridge Park Steels	42	16	8	18	55	70	56
Eastwood Town	42	15	11	16	64	65	55
Harrogate Town	42	14	12	16	65	67	54
Congleton Town	42	14	12	16	63	73	54
Chorley	42	13	15	14	53	64	54
Ashton United	42	12	16	14	65	67	52
Workington	42	13	13	16	49	55	52
Lincoln United	42	13	12	17	52	80	51
Belper Town	42	13	11	18	59	72	50
Trafford	42	11	12	19	55	63	45
Gretna	42	11	7	24	48	78	40
Netherfield Kendal	42	8	9	25	46	82	33
Flixton	42	7	9	26	47	85	30
Whitley Bay	42	7	9	26	41	87	30

Eastwood Town had 1 point deducted

2000-2001

Premier Division

	P	W	D	L	F	A	Pts
Stalybridge Celtic	44	31	9	4	96	32	102
Emley	44	31	8	5	86	42	101
Bishop Auckland	44	26	7	11	89	53	85
Lancaster City	44	24	9	11	84	60	81
Worksop Town	44	20	13	11	102	60	73
Barrow	44	21	9	14	83	53	72
Altrincham	44	20	10	14	80	59	70
Gainsborough Trinity	44	17	14	13	59	56	65
Accrington Stanley	44	18	10	16	72	65	64
Hucknall Town	44	17	12	15	57	63	63
Gateshead	44	16	12	16	67	61	60
Bamber Bridge	44	17	8	19	63	65	59
Runcorn	44	15	10	19	56	71	55
Blyth Spartans	44	15	9	20	61	64	54
Burscough	44	14	10	20	59	68	52
Hyde United	44	13	12	19	72	79	51
Whitby Town	44	13	11	20	60	76	50
Marine	44	12	13	19	62	78	49
Colwyn Bay	44	12	10	22	68	102	46
Frickley Athletic	44	10	15	19	50	79	45
Droylsden	44	13	6	25	50	80	45
Leek Town	44	12	8	24	45	70	44
Spennymoor United	44	4	5	35	32	108	17

First Division

	P	W	D	L	F	A	Pts
Bradford Park Avenue	42	28	5	9	83	40	89
Vauxhall Motors	42	23	10	9	95	50	79
Ashton United	42	23	9	10	91	49	78
Stocksbridge Park Steels	42	19	13	10	80	60	70
Trafford	42	20	9	13	70	62	68
Belper Town	42	18	11	13	71	62	65
Witton Albion	42	15	16	11	51	50	61
Ossett Town	42	16	12	14	66	58	60
Radcliffe Borough	42	17	8	17	72	71	59
Chorley	42	15	14	13	71	70	59
Harrogate Town	42	15	10	17	60	70	55
Matlock Town	42	14	10	18	70	74	52
North Ferriby United	42	14	10	18	64	73	52
Workington	42	13	12	17	53	60	51
Lincoln United	42	13	12	17	60	75	51
Gretna	42	12	12	18	72	82	48
Guiseley	42	11	15	16	37	50	48
Kendal Town	42	12	12	18	60	69	47
Farsley Celtic	42	12	11	19	53	71	47
Eastwood Town	42	12	8	21	40	63	47
Winsford United	42	13	11	18	61	70	44
Congleton Town	42	13	6	28	43	94	30

Trafford and Kendal Town both had 1 point deducted
Winsford United had 6 points deducted

2001-2002

Premier Division

	P	W	D	L	F	A	Pts
Burton Albion	44	31	11	2	106	30	104
Vauxhall Motors	44	27	8	9	86	55	89
Lancaster City	44	23	9	12	80	57	78
Worksop Town	44	23	9	12	74	51	78
Emley	44	22	9	13	69	55	75
Accrington Stanley	44	21	9	14	89	64	72
Runcorn FC Halton	44	21	8	15	76	53	71
Barrow	44	19	10	15	75	59	67
Altrincham	44	19	9	16	66	58	66
Bradford Park Avenue	44	18	5	21	77	76	59
Droylsden	44	17	8	19	65	78	59
Blyth Spartans	44	14	16	14	59	62	58
Frickley Athletic	44	16	11	17	63	69	58
Gateshead	44	14	14	16	58	71	56
Whitby Town	44	15	8	21	61	76	53
Hucknall Town	44	14	9	21	50	68	51
Marine	44	11	17	16	62	71	50
Burscough	44	15	5	24	69	86	50
Gainsborough Trinity	44	13	10	21	61	76	49
Colwyn Bay	44	12	11	21	49	82	47
Bishop Auckland	44	12	8	24	46	68	44
Hyde United	44	10	10	24	61	87	40
Bamber Bridge	44	7	10	27	38	88	30

First Division

	P	W	D	L	F	A	Pts
Harrogate Town	42	25	11	6	80	35	86
Ossett Town	42	21	13	8	73	44	76
Ashton United	42	21	12	9	90	63	75
Spennymoor United	42	22	6	14	75	73	72
Radcliffe Borough	42	20	8	14	73	51	68
Leek Town	42	20	8	14	67	51	68
Gretna	42	19	7	16	66	66	63
Eastwood Town	42	17	11	14	61	59	62
Rossendale United	42	17	10	15	69	58	61
Witton Albion	42	17	10	15	72	68	61
Guiseley	42	18	7	17	60	67	61
North Ferriby United	42	14	16	12	71	60	58
Chorley	42	16	9	17	59	57	57
Matlock Town	42	15	9	18	49	48	54
Trafford	42	14	9	19	64	80	51
Workington	42	12	12	18	51	57	48
Farsley Celtic	42	12	11	19	64	78	47
Belper Town	42	12	11	19	49	66	47
Lincoln United	42	11	14	17	62	80	47
Stocksbridge Park Steels	42	12	9	21	55	76	45
Kendal Town	42	9	9	24	52	76	36
Ossett Albion	42	8	8	26	43	92	32

2002-2003

Premier Division

	P	W	D	L	F	A	Pts
Accrington Stanley	44	30	10	4	97	44	100
Barrow	44	24	12	8	84	52	84
Vauxhall Motors	44	22	10	12	81	46	76
Stalybridge Celtic	44	21	13	10	77	51	76
Worksop Town	44	21	9	14	82	67	72
Harrogate Town	44	21	8	15	75	63	71
Bradford Park Avenue	44	20	10	14	73	70	70
Hucknall Town	44	17	15	12	72	62	66
Droylsden	44	18	10	16	62	52	64
Whitby Town	44	17	12	15	80	69	63
Marine	44	17	10	17	63	60	61
Wakefield & Emley	44	14	18	12	46	49	60
Runcorn FC Halton	44	15	15	14	69	74	60
Altrincham	44	17	9	18	58	63	60
Gainsborough Trinity	44	16	11	17	67	66	59
Ashton United	44	15	13	16	71	79	58
Lancaster City	44	16	9	19	71	75	57
Burscough	44	14	9	21	44	51	51
Blyth Spartans	44	14	9	21	67	87	51
Frickley Athletic	44	13	8	23	45	78	47
Gateshead	44	10	11	23	60	81	41
Colwyn Bay	44	5	9	30	52	99	24
Hyde United	44	5	8	31	40	98	23

Division One

Alfreton Town	42	26	9	7	106	59	87
Spennymoor United	42	27	6	9	81	42	87
Radcliffe Borough	42	25	10	7	90	46	85
North Ferriby United	42	23	9	10	78	45	78
Chorley	42	21	10	11	80	51	73
Belper Town	42	20	13	9	53	42	73
Witton Albion	42	19	15	8	67	50	72
Matlock Town	42	20	10	12	67	48	70
Leek Town	42	20	9	13	63	46	69
Workington	42	19	10	13	73	60	67
Farsley Celtic	42	17	11	14	66	67	62
Kendal Town	42	18	7	17	68	58	61
Bamber Bridge	42	15	9	18	55	59	54
Guiseley	42	14	11	17	68	63	53
Bishop Auckland	42	13	10	19	58	83	49
Lincoln United	42	12	9	21	67	77	45
Stocksbridge PS	42	11	9	22	54	81	42
Rossendale United	42	12	5	25	58	88	41
Kidsgrove Athletic	42	9	11	22	49	71	38
Ossett Town	42	8	9	25	39	80	33
Eastwood Town	42	5	8	29	33	92	23
Trafford	42	5	6	31	34	99	21

2003-2004

Premier Division

Hucknall Town	44	29	8	7	83	38	95
Droylsden	44	26	8	10	96	64	86
Barrow	44	22	14	8	82	52	80
Alfreton Town	44	23	9	12	73	43	78
Harrogate Town	44	24	5	15	79	63	77
Southport	44	20	10	14	71	52	70
Worksop Town	44	19	13	12	69	50	70
Lancaster City	44	20	9	15	62	49	69
Vauxhall Motors	44	19	10	15	78	75	67
Gainsborough Trinity	44	17	13	14	70	52	64
Stalybridge Celtic	44	18	10	16	72	66	64
Altrincham	44	16	15	13	66	51	63
Runcorn FC Halton	44	16	13	15	67	63	61
Ashton United	44	17	8	19	59	79	59
Whitby Town	44	14	11	19	55	70	53
Marine	44	13	12	19	62	74	51
Bradford Park Avenue	44	12	14	18	48	62	50
Spennymoor United	44	14	6	24	55	93	48
Burscough	44	10	15	19	47	67	45
Radcliffe Borough	44	12	6	26	74	99	42
Blyth Spartans	44	10	10	24	54	74	40
Frickley Athletic	44	11	7	26	51	83	40
Wakefield & Emley	44	8	6	30	45	99	30

Division One

Hyde United	42	24	8	10	79	49	80
Matlock Town	42	23	7	12	78	51	76
Farsley Celtic	42	20	14	8	78	56	74
Lincoln United	42	20	11	11	73	53	71
Witton Albion	42	17	12	13	61	56	63
Gateshead	42	21	4	17	65	68	63
Workington	42	17	11	14	70	58	62
Leek Town	42	16	13	13	56	47	61
Guiseley	42	16	12	14	66	54	60
Bamber Bridge	42	16	12	14	64	53	60
Bridlington Town	42	16	10	16	70	68	58
Prescot Cables	42	16	10	16	63	65	58
Bishop Auckland	42	14	13	15	61	64	55
Ossett Town	42	15	10	17	62	73	52
Rossendale United	42	13	12	17	53	62	51
Colwyn Bay	42	14	9	19	56	82	51
North Ferriby United	42	13	11	18	64	70	50
Chorley	42	13	10	19	54	70	49
Stocksbridge Park Steels	42	12	12	18	57	69	48
Belper Town	42	9	15	18	44	58	42
Kendal Town	42	11	7	24	53	79	40
Kidsgrove Athletic	42	10	9	23	45	67	39

2004-2005

Premier Division

Hyde United	42	25	13	4	80	43	88
Workington	42	26	7	9	73	30	85
Farsley Celtic	42	25	8	9	81	41	83
Whitby Town	42	23	11	8	65	49	80
Prescot Cables	42	21	8	13	63	54	71
Burscough	42	21	7	14	93	74	70
Leek Town	42	16	15	11	63	52	63
Witton Albion	42	15	17	10	56	44	62
Radcliffe Borough	42	16	14	12	60	60	62
Guiseley	42	16	13	13	70	64	61
Matlock Town	42	14	13	15	59	67	55
Blyth Spartans	42	13	13	16	53	55	52
Wakefield & Emley	42	14	10	18	60	67	52
Lincoln United	42	15	4	23	53	66	49
Marine	42	10	18	14	53	60	48
Ossett Town	42	11	13	18	53	62	46
Gateshead	42	11	12	19	61	84	45
Frickley Athletic	42	10	14	18	44	57	44
Bishop Auckland	42	11	7	24	51	74	40
Bridlington Town	42	7	14	21	43	66	35
Bamber Bridge	42	9	7	26	48	92	34
Spennymoor United	42	9	10	23	44	65	25

Spennymoor United had 12 points deducted.

Division One

North Ferriby United	42	25	8	9	83	49	83
Ilkeston Town	42	24	9	9	64	40	81
AFC Telford United	42	23	11	8	78	44	80
Willenhall Town	42	22	12	8	71	46	78
Kendal Town	42	21	8	13	89	69	71
Eastwood Town	42	20	9	13	73	54	69
Mossley	42	20	6	16	81	56	66
Brigg Town	42	15	19	8	59	46	64
Gresley Rovers	42	17	12	13	57	53	63
Kidsgrove Athletic	42	15	15	12	60	55	60
Woodley Sports	42	16	11	15	68	74	59
Ossett Albion	42	15	13	14	83	74	58
Colwyn Bay	42	14	13	15	54	62	55
Stocksbridge PS	42	15	9	18	58	58	51
Shepshed Dynamo	42	13	11	18	53	75	50
Chorley	42	13	9	20	62	69	48
Belper Town	42	13	8	21	57	66	47
Spalding United	42	13	8	21	57	69	47
Clitheroe	42	12	10	20	47	57	46
Warrington Town	42	11	13	18	45	59	46
Rossendale United	42	10	10	22	64	87	40
Rocester	42	0	6	36	31	132	6

Stocksbridge Park Steels had 3 points deducted.

2005-2006

Premier Division

Blyth Spartans	42	26	11	5	79	32	89
Frickley Athletic	42	26	8	8	72	36	86
Marine	42	23	12	7	61	25	81
Farsley Celtic	42	23	10	9	84	34	79
North Ferriby United	42	21	10	11	77	54	73
Whitby Town	42	18	10	14	60	59	64
Burscough	42	19	6	17	64	64	63
Witton Albion	42	17	9	16	68	55	60
Matlock Town	42	16	11	15	60	55	59
AFC Telford United	42	14	17	11	54	52	59
Ossett Town	42	17	7	18	57	61	58
Leek Town	42	14	14	14	50	53	56
Prescot Cables	42	15	8	19	49	60	53
Guiseley	42	14	9	19	45	58	51
Ashton United	42	13	10	19	62	63	49
Ilkeston Town	42	12	13	17	48	51	49
Gateshead	42	12	10	20	52	77	46
Radcliffe Borough	42	12	8	22	54	62	44
Lincoln United	42	10	14	18	44	64	44
Wakefield Emley	42	11	9	22	38	69	42
Bradford Park Avenue	42	10	9	23	64	86	39
Runcorn FC Halton	42	6	11	25	36	108	29

Division One

Mossley	42	23	9	10	83	55	78
Fleetwood Town	42	22	10	10	72	48	76
Kendal Town	42	22	10	10	81	58	76
Woodley Sports	42	22	8	12	85	53	74
Gresley Rovers	42	20	10	12	79	64	70
Stocksbridge PS	42	17	16	9	66	43	67
Eastwood Town	42	16	14	12	66	58	62
Brigg Town	42	16	14	12	70	64	62
Belper Town	42	17	8	17	53	56	59
Shepshed Dynamo	42	15	13	14	57	56	58
Bridlington Town	42	16	10	16	61	68	58
Colwyn Bay	42	15	11	16	56	53	56
Bamber Bridge	42	13	15	14	65	59	54
Ossett Albion	42	15	9	18	54	64	54
Rossendale United	42	12	17	13	58	61	53
Clitheroe	42	15	8	19	54	73	53
Kidsgrove Athletic	42	14	9	19	66	69	51
Chorley	42	14	8	20	58	59	50
Warrington Town	42	11	15	16	62	74	48
Spalding United	42	10	15	17	49	70	45
Goole	42	11	11	20	55	85	43
Bishop Auckland	42	3	6	33	39	99	15

Goole had 1 point deducted.

WESTERN LEAGUE

The Western League was formed in 1892 as the Bristol & District League, becoming the Western League in 1895. For many of its nine founder members, it was their first taste of league football although Wells City had already twice been champions of the Somerset Senior League.

Several of the published tables contained errors, principally in the goals scored record. Additional research has succeeded in correcting many of these, totals that still do not balance are shown below the relevant columns in italics.

Bristol & District League

1892-93

Warmley	16	11	3	2	72	19	25
Trowbridge Town	16	10	4	2	66	17	24
St. George	16	9	5	2	36	22	23
Bedminster	16	6	5	5	30	34	17
Clevedon	16	6	4	6	25	36	16
Eastville Rovers	16	6	3	7	36	40	15
Clifton	16	4	2	10	27	61	10
Mangotsfield	16	3	2	11	19	45	8
Wells City	16	1	4	11	14	51	6

Wells City left and returned to the Somerset Senior League while Gloucester and Staple Hill joined, making a 10-club First Division. A 10-club Second Division was formed by the Reserves of Bedminster, Clifton, Eastville Rovers, Mangotsfield, St. George, Trowbridge Town and Warmley plus the first XI's of Barton Hill, St. Paul's, and Waverley.

1893-94

Division One

Warmley	18	12	5	1	32	13	27
St. George	18	10	6	2	39	23	26
Trowbridge Town	18	9	4	5	54	33	22
Bedminster	18	9	2	7	41	36	20
Clevedon	18	7	5	6	34	40	19
Clifton	18	6	4	8	37	30	16
Staple Hill	18	5	5	8	23	33	15
Gloucester	18	6	1	11	32	45	13
Eastville Rovers	18	5	2	11	30	39	12
Mangotsfield	18	2	4	12	19	48	8
					341	*340*	

Warmley had 2 points deducted for fielding an alleged professional player.
Hereford Thistle and Swindon Wanderers joined, increasing Division One to 12 clubs.

Division Two

Warmley Reserves	18	16	1	1	66	12	33
St. George Reserves	18	15	0	3	50	22	30
Trowbridge Town Reserves	18	11	1	6	47	22	23
St. Paul's	18	9	3	6	44	51	21
Barton Hill	18	7	4	7	40	32	18
Bedminster Reserves	18	6	3	9	35	42	15
Mangotsfield Reserves	18	6	1	11	26	41	13
Clifton Reserves	18	5	2	11	29	59	12
Eastville Rovers Reserves	18	4	2	12	23	45	10
Waverley	18	2	4	12	22	53	8
			81	21	78	*382*	*379*	*183*

Trowbridge Town Reserves left the League but Willsbridge joined from the South Bristol & District League and Staple Hill Reserves also joined, increasing Division Two to 11 clubs.

1894-95

Division One

Hereford Thistle	22	18	3	1	93	21	39
St. George	22	18	3	1	76	21	39
Warmley	22	14	2	6	74	30	30
Staple Hill	22	11	4	7	56	38	26
Gloucester	22	10	4	8	64	54	24
Eastville Rovers	22	10	4	8	46	40	24
Trowbridge Town	22	9	4	9	68	48	22
Clifton	22	8	2	12	47	55	18
Bedminster	22	7	0	15	39	73	14
Swindon Wanderers	22	5	3	14	40	63	13
Mangotsfield	22	5	2	15	22	68	12
Clevedon	22	1	1	20	23	136	3
					648	*647*	

Hereford Thistle left and joined the Birmingham League and Clevedon also left. They were replaced by Cardiff, and St. Paul's who were promoted from Division Two.

Division Two

Warmley Reserves	20	17	0	3	75	20	34
St. Paul's	20	16	0	4	79	31	32
Willsbridge	20	15	1	4	48	21	31
St. George Reserves	20	14	1	5	69	33	29
Barton Hill	20	11	1	8	57	31	23
Bedminster Reserves	20	8	1	11	36	30	17
Eastville Rovers Reserves	20	8	0	12	45	45	16
Clifton Reserves	20	7	0	13	40	68	14
Mangotsfield Reserves	20	4	2	14	30	84	10
Staple Hill Reserves	20	4	1	15	32	79	9
Waverley	20	2	1	17	15	74	5
					526	*516*	

St. Paul's were promoted in place of Warmley Reserves. Mangotsfield Reserves, Waverley and Willsbridge left the League. Cumberland, Eastville Wanderers, Fishponds and Frenchay joined the League.

1895-96

Division One

Warmley	20	16	3	1	65	13	35
Eastville Rovers	20	14	1	5	57	22	29
Staple Hill	20	13	3	4	48	19	29
Trowbridge Town	20	13	1	6	50	31	27
St. George	20	10	4	6	47	38	24
Clifton	20	8	3	9	44	50	17
Gloucester	20	6	4	10	29	42	16
Bedminster	20	6	2	12	36	41	14
Swindon Wanderers	20	4	4	12	22	57	12
Mangotsfield	20	3	3	14	17	54	9
St. Paul's	20	2	2	16	12	60	6

Clifton had 2 points deducted for a breach of the rules. Cardiff were expelled in January 1896 for non-payment of fines and their record was expunged.
Eastville Rovers and Staple Hill were declared joint runners-up, both clubs receiving silver medals.
Gloucester and Swindon Wanderers left and Mangotsfield were relegated to Division Two. Bristol South End joined. Division One was reduced to 9 clubs.

Division Two

Barton Hill	18	15	2	1	45	16	32
Fishponds	18	11	4	3	33	14	26
St. George Reserves	18	11	3	4	52	22	25
Eastville Wanderers	18	10	2	6	34	23	22
Eastville Rovers Reserves	18	8	4	6	43	31	20
Cumberland	18	7	3	8	47	35	17
Staple Hill Reserves	18	7	2	9	34	58	16
Bedminster Reserves	18	6	1	11	35	38	13
Warmley Reserves	18	4	1	13	23	29	9
Clifton Reserves	18	0	0	18	10	84	0
					356	*350*	

Frenchay resigned during the season and their record was expunged. Cumberland, Clifton Reserves, St. George Reserves and Warmley Reserves all left. Division Two was reduced to 7 clubs.

1896-97

Division One

Warmley	16	13	2	1	42	9	28
South End	16	11	0	5	28	22	22
Bedminster	16	8	2	6	32	16	18
St. George	16	8	1	7	27	23	17
Eastville Rovers	16	7	2	7	25	23	14
Trowbridge Town	16	5	3	8	21	30	13
St. Paul's	16	3	5	8	29	31	11
Staple Hill	16	5	0	11	18	39	10
Clifton	16	4	1	11	19	48	9

Eastville Rovers had 2 points deducted for fielding an ineligible player.

Division Two

Eastville Wanderers	12	7	4	1	25	9	18
Barton Hill	12	7	3	2	28	7	17
Mangotsfield	12	6	3	3	23	14	15
Fishponds	12	4	5	3	17	16	13
Bedminster Reserves	12	6	1	5	19	20	13
Eastville Rovers Reserves	12	1	3	8	7	33	5
Staple Hill Reserves	12	1	1	10	8	34	3
					127	133	

A new 8-club Professional Section was formed. Eastville Rovers, South End (having changed their name to Bristol City), St. George (as Bristol St. George), Trowbridge Town and Warmley moved from Division One to this new section and were joined by three new members, Eastleigh, Reading and Swindon Town. Reading and Swindon Town also continued to play in the Southern League.
The original Division One and Two continued as the amateur section. Midsomer Norton and Radstock joined Division One while continuing to play in the Somerset Senior League and the amateur division was made up to 10 clubs by the promotion of Eastville Wanderers, Barton Hill, Mangotsfield and Fishponds from Division Two.
Eastville Rovers Reserves and Staple Hill Reserves left Division Two but Barton Hill Reserves, Cotham, Eastville Wanderers Reserves, Fishponds Reserves, Hanham, Royal Artillery (Horfield) and St. Paul's Reserves joined, increasing the division to 8 clubs.

1897-98

Professional Section

Bristol City	14	11	1	2	51	16	23
Swindon Town	14	9	1	4	32	15	19
Reading	14	7	2	5	29	25	16
Bristol St. George	14	6	3	5	25	27	15
Eastville Rovers	14	6	2	6	38	25	14
Warmley	14	5	3	6	36	27	13
Eastleigh	14	3	2	9	22	55	8
Trowbridge Town	14	2	0	12	15	58	4

Eastleigh left and joined the Southern League and Bristol City and Reading also left to concentrate solely on the Southern League. Southampton joined while continuing to play in the Southern League and Bedminster moved from Division One of the Amateur section. The Professional Section was reduced to 7 clubs and changed its title to Division One. Eastville Rovers changed their name to Bristol Eastville Rovers.

Amateur – Division One

Bedminster	16	15	0	1	65	11	30
Staple Hill	16	11	1	4	38	15	23
Fishponds	16	8	2	6	26	30	18
Midsomer Norton	16	7	2	7	23	33	16
Barton Hill	16	6	2	8	25	25	14
Radstock	16	5	4	7	17	28	14
St. Paul's	16	4	3	9	15	28	11
Eastville Wanderers	14	4	1	11	15	16	9
Mangotsfield	16	1	7	8	5	29	9
					229	215	

Clifton resigned early in the season and their record was expunged.

Amateur – Division Two

Hanham	10	9	1	0	32	8	19
Cotham	10	8	0	2	32	16	16
Barton Hill Reserves	10	4	2	4	20	14	10
St. Paul's Reserves	10	2	2	6	19	26	6
Fishponds Reserves	10	1	1	8	10	25	3
Bedminster Reserves	10	1	0	9	10	34	2
		25	6	29			56

Fishponds Reserves had 2 points deducted for fielding an ineligible player.
Royal Artillery (Horfield) and Eastville Wanderers Reserves resigned during the season and their records were expunged. At the end of the season, the two amateur divisions were combined into one which was renamed Division Two. Radstock left to concentrate solely on the Somerset Senior League and Barton Hill Reserves, Bedminster Reserves, Eastville Wanderers, Fishponds Reserves, Mangotsfield, St. Paul's and St. Paul's Reserves also left. Bristol Amateurs and Mount Hill joined making a new Division Two of 8 clubs.

1898-99

Division One

Swindon Town	8	5	1	2	16	10	11
Bristol St. George	8	4	1	3	18	15	9
Southampton	8	4	0	4	18	15	8
Bristol Eastville Rovers	8	2	2	4	14	18	6
Bedminster	8	2	2	4	9	16	6
					75	74	

Trowbridge Town (October 1898) and Warmley (January 1899) both disbanded during the season and their records were expunged. Their records at the time were:

Warmley	5	2	0	3	6	15	4
Trowbridge Town	5	0	0	5	4	18	0

Bristol St. George disbanded and Southampton left to concentrate on the Southern League. Bristol City joined while continuing to play in the Southern League. The Division was reduced to 4 clubs. Bristol Eastville Rovers changed their name to Bristol Rovers.

Amateur Section – Division Two

Staple Hill	14	11	1	2	55	15	23
Fishponds	14	10	2	2	42	15	22
Mount Hill	14	5	3	6	31	28	13
Midsomer Norton	14	6	3	5	20	32	13
Bristol Amateurs	14	5	2	7	31	32	12
Hanham	14	4	3	7	16	28	11
Barton Hill	14	4	1	9	14	31	9
Cotham	14	2	3	9	22	41	7
					231	222	

Midsomer Norton 2 points deducted for fielding an ineligible player. Midsomer Norton left to concentrate on the Somerset Senior League and Barton Hill, Bristol Amateurs, Hanham and Mount Hill also left. Bristol East and Weston (Bath) joined. Division was reduced to 5 clubs.

1899-1900

Division One

Bristol Rovers	6	3	1	2	8	6	7
Bedminster	6	3	1	2	10	12	7
Swindon Town	6	3	0	3	7	7	6
Bristol City	6	2	0	4	12	12	4

Bedminster amalgamated with Bristol City but Millwall, Portsmouth, Queen's Park Rangers, Reading, Southampton and Tottenham Hotspur all joined, increasing the division to 9 clubs, all of whom also played in the Southern League.

Division Two

Bristol East	8	6	2	0	31	3	14
Staple Hill	8	4	4	0	22	3	12
Fishponds	8	3	1	4	16	29	7
Weston (Bath)	8	1	1	6	7	19	3
Cotham	8	1	0	7	8	26	2
		15	8	17	84	80	38

Paulton Rovers joined and also continued to play in the Somerset Senior League. Weston Super Mare and Bedminster St. Francis also joined. Division increased to 8 clubs.

1900-01

Division One

Portsmouth	16	11	2	3	36	23	24
Millwall	16	9	5	2	33	14	23
Tottenham Hotspur	16	8	5	3	37	19	21
Queen's Park Rangers	16	7	4	5	39	24	18
Bristol City	16	6	4	6	27	24	16
Reading	16	5	5	6	23	31	15
Southampton	16	5	2	9	19	29	12
Bristol Rovers	16	4	1	11	18	42	9
Swindon Town	16	2	2	12	9	35	6

West Ham United replaced Bristol City.

Division Two

Bristol East	12	11	0	1	41	8	22
Paulton Rovers	9	6	2	1	32	12	14
Staple Hill	10	6	1	3	34	17	13
Cotham	11	3	2	6	20	49	8
Bedminster St. Francis	6	3	1	2	16	13	7
Weston Super Mare	10	2	0	8	18	22	4
Fishponds	12	1	0	11	6	40	0
					167	161	

Fishponds had 2 points deducted for fielding an ineligible player. The unplayed games were ignored. Weston (Bath) resigned during the season before playing a game.
Bedminster St. Francis and Fishponds left and Bristol Rovers Reserves, St. George, Swindon Town Reserves and Trowbridge Town joined. Division increased to 9 clubs. Cotham changed their name to Cotham Amateurs.

1901-02

Division One

Portsmouth	16	13	1	2	53	16	27
Tottenham Hotspur	16	11	3	2	42	17	25
Reading	16	7	3	6	29	22	17
Millwall	16	8	1	7	25	29	17
Bristol Rovers	16	8	0	8	25	31	16
Southampton	16	7	1	8	30	28	15
West Ham United	16	6	2	8	30	20	14
Queen's Park Rangers	16	5	1	10	17	43	11
Swindon Town	16	0	2	14	8	53	2

Brentford replaced Swindon Town.

Division Two

Bristol East	16	13	1	2	55	11	27
Bristol Rovers Reserves	16	10	3	3	54	18	23
Paulton Rovers	16	9	3	4	51	29	21
Staple Hill	16	9	3	4	30	24	21
Swindon Town Reserves	16	7	2	7	44	35	16
Trowbridge Town	16	6	3	7	30	43	15
St. George	16	6	2	8	29	36	14
Weston Super Mare	16	1	2	13	19	68	4
Cotham Amateurs	16	1	1	14	23	71	3

Weston Super Mare left. Division reduced to 8 clubs.

1902-03

Division One

Portsmouth	16	10	4	2	34	14	24
Bristol Rovers	16	9	2	5	36	22	20
Southampton	16	7	6	3	32	20	20
Tottenham Hotspur	16	6	7	3	20	14	19
Millwall	16	6	3	7	23	29	15
Reading	16	7	0	9	20	21	14
Queen's Park Rangers	16	6	2	8	18	31	14
Brentford	16	3	4	9	16	34	10
West Ham United	16	2	4	10	15	29	8

Plymouth Argyle replaced Millwall.

Division Two

Bristol Rovers Reserves	14	10	2	2	45	10	22
St. George	14	9	1	4	37	25	19
Swindon Town Reserves	14	8	0	6	59	24	16
Bristol East	14	6	3	5	23	27	15
Staple Hill	14	5	3	6	27	20	13
Paulton Rovers	14	6	1	7	27	27	13
Trowbridge Town	14	5	1	8	20	48	11
Cotham Amateurs	14	1	1	12	14	71	3

St. George and Cotham Amateurs left. Welton Rovers joined from the Somerset Senior League and Bristol City Reserves, Radstock Town and Warmley also joined. Division increased to 10 clubs.

1903-04

Division One

Tottenham Hotspur	16	11	3	2	32	12	25
Southampton	16	9	3	4	30	18	21
Plymouth Argyle	16	8	4	4	23	19	20
Portsmouth	16	7	2	7	24	22	16
Brentford	16	6	4	6	19	23	16
Queen's Park Rangers	16	5	5	6	15	21	15
Reading	16	4	4	8	16	26	12
Bristol Rovers	16	4	3	9	29	29	11
West Ham United	16	2	4	10	13	31	8

Fulham and Millwall joined. Division increased to 11 clubs.

Division Two

Bristol City Reserves	18	15	2	1	64	17	32
Staple Hill	18	13	1	4	53	19	27
Swindon Town Reserves	18	10	3	5	50	30	23
Bristol Rovers Reserves	18	9	2	7	50	30	20
Bristol East	18	9	1	8	30	27	19
Paulton Rovers	18	9	1	8	37	46	19
Trowbridge Town	18	6	2	10	22	57	14
Warmley	18	3	3	12	32	52	9
Welton Rovers	18	3	3	12	32	67	9
Radstock Town	18	3	2	13	26	54	8
					396	399	

Paulton Rovers moved to the Somerset Senior League. Chippenham Town joined.

1904-05

Division One

Plymouth Argyle	20	13	4	3	52	18	30
Brentford	20	11	6	3	30	22	28
Southampton	20	11	2	7	45	22	24
Portsmouth	20	10	3	7	29	30	23
West Ham United	20	8	4	8	37	42	20
Fulham	20	7	3	10	29	32	17
Millwall	20	7	3	10	32	40	17
Tottenham Hotspur	20	5	6	9	20	28	16
Reading	20	6	3	11	27	37	15
Bristol Rovers	20	7	1	12	32	44	15
Queen's Park Rangers	20	6	3	11	27	45	15

Division Two

Bristol Rovers Reserves	16	13	3	0	76	5	29
Bristol City Reserves	16	14	1	1	46	8	29
Swindon Town Reserves	16	11	2	3	53	21	24
Staple Hill	16	7	3	6	27	23	17
Bristol East	16	7	1	8	38	27	15
Welton Rovers	16	5	1	10	27	58	11
Radstock Town	14	4	1	11	21	57	9
Trowbridge Town	16	2	2	12	25	64	6
Chippenham Town	16	2	0	14	24	74	4

Warmley disbanded after playing 10 games and their record was expunged.
Swindon Town Reserves left but Paulton Rovers from the Somerset Senior League and Salisbury City from the Hampshire League both joined.

1905-06

Division One

Queen's Park Rangers	20	11	4	5	33	27	26
Southampton	20	10	5	5	41	35	25
Plymouth Argyle	20	8	8	4	34	23	24
Tottenham Hotspur	20	7	7	6	28	17	21
Bristol Rovers	20	8	3	9	34	34	19
Millwall	20	7	5	8	28	29	19
Portsmouth	20	6	7	7	26	29	19
West Ham United	20	7	5	8	32	35	19
Reading	20	6	6	8	28	35	18
Fulham	20	5	5	10	23	32	15
Brentford	20	6	3	11	25	36	15

Chelsea joined and the division split into two sections of 6 clubs each.

Division Two

Bristol Rovers Reserves	18	16	1	1	90	19	33
Bristol City Reserves	18	14	2	2	79	13	30
Welton Rovers	18	10	1	7	40	45	21
Radstock Town	18	8	2	8	37	31	18
Salisbury City	18	8	2	8	29	34	18
Staple Hill	18	8	1	9	32	38	17
Paulton Rovers	18	7	2	9	26	41	16
Chippenham Town	18	5	2	11	23	47	12
Bristol East	17	3	1	13	14	41	7
Trowbridge Town	17	2	2	13	13	73	6
					383	382	

Bristol East did not travel to play Trowbridge on 17th March. Salisbury City moved to the Southern League and Bristol East and Chippenham Town also left. Newport and Treharris joined from the South Wales League and 121st R.F.A. also joined.

1906-07

Division One – Section A

Fulham	10	7	1	2	16	9	15
Queen's Park Rangers	10	5	1	4	17	11	11
Brentford	10	5	1	4	19	19	11
Reading	10	4	1	5	12	18	9
Bristol Rovers	10	3	1	6	17	17	7
Chelsea	10	2	3	5	7	14	7

Division One – Section B

West Ham United	10	7	1	2	25	14	15
Plymouth Argyle	10	5	3	2	16	10	13
Portsmouth	10	4	2	4	16	19	10
Tottenham Hotspur	10	3	3	4	13	15	9
Southampton	10	4	0	6	14	16	8
Millwall	10	1	3	6	5	15	5

Championship decider: West Ham United 1 Fulham 0 (played at Stamford Bridge on 15th April 1907).
Chelsea and Fulham left and Brighton & Hove Albion, Crystal Palace, Leyton and Luton Town joined. Sections reorganised.

Division Two

Staple Hill	18	12	2	4	44	28	26
Newport	18	11	3	4	52	38	25
Bristol City Reserves	18	11	2	5	54	19	24
Treharris	18	12	0	6	62	24	24
Bristol Rovers Reserves	18	11	1	6	60	27	23
Radstock Town	18	7	3	8	37	41	17
Welton Rovers	18	7	1	10	33	54	15
Paulton Rovers	18	4	4	10	36	53	12
121st R.F.A.	18	5	2	11	27	53	12
Trowbridge Town	18	1	0	17	18	86	2

Newport disbanded, Trowbridge Town left to join the Wiltshire County League and 121st R.F.A. also left. Kingswood Rovers and Weymouth joined. Division reduced to 9 clubs.

1907-08

Division One – Section A

Southampton	12	8	1	3	30	12	17
Portsmouth	12	7	1	4	25	18	15
Brighton & Hove Albion	12	6	2	4	19	19	14
Plymouth Argyle	12	5	2	5	14	12	12
Queen's Park Rangers	12	5	1	6	20	23	11
Brentford	12	2	5	5	13	21	9
Leyton	12	2	2	8	11	27	6

Division One – Section B

Millwall	12	9	2	1	31	13	20
Tottenham Hotspur	12	7	0	5	26	15	14
Bristol Rovers	12	6	2	4	22	29	14
Luton Town	12	4	4	4	16	21	12
Reading	12	4	3	5	20	25	11
Crystal Palace	12	3	4	5	16	17	10
West Ham United	12	1	1	10	16	27	3

Championship decider: Millwall 1 Southampton 0 (played at Tottenham on 13th April 1908).
Croydon Common replaced Tottenham Hotspur. Sections reorganised.

Division Two

Bristol City Reserves	16	12	1	3	55	13	25
Bristol Rovers Reserves	16	11	3	2	44	15	25
Treharris	16	11	1	4	53	19	23
Kingswood Rovers	16	7	1	8	27	33	15
Paulton Rovers	16	7	1	8	34	46	15
Welton Rovers	16	4	4	8	23	46	12
Weymouth	16	5	2	9	25	23	12
Radstock Town	16	4	3	9	25	39	11
Staple Hill	16	3	0	13	18	40	6
					304	274	

Barry District joined from the South Wales League and Aberdare and Bath City also joined. Division increased to 12 clubs.

1908-09

Division One – Section A

Brighton & Hove Albion	12	7	2	3	23	13	16
Queen's Park Rangers	12	6	1	5	28	24	13
Crystal Palace	12	5	2	5	23	22	12
Luton Town	12	5	2	5	24	24	12
Croydon Common	12	5	2	5	16	24	12
Reading	12	4	2	6	19	21	10
Leyton	12	4	1	7	16	21	9

Division One – Section B

Millwall	12	8	2	2	24	11	18
Southampton	12	7	0	5	20	20	14
Plymouth Argyle	12	6	1	5	12	13	13
Portsmouth	12	5	2	5	21	21	12
West Ham United	12	5	0	7	21	23	10
Bristol Rovers	12	4	1	7	16	23	9
Brentford	12	3	2	7	10	13	8

Championship decider: Millwall 2 Brighton 1 (this match was a replay after a 1-1 draw, both games were played at West Ham).
All 14 clubs resigned. Division One was scrapped.

Division Two

Bristol City Reserves	22	15	4	3	59	16	34
Bristol Rovers Reserves	22	16	0	6	81	29	32
Aberdare	22	12	5	5	56	30	29
Treharris	22	12	2	8	57	45	26
Staple Hill	22	9	4	9	41	60	22
Radstock Town	22	8	5	9	37	60	21
Weymouth	22	8	4	10	47	64	20
Bath City	22	6	7	9	39	45	19
Barry District	22	8	3	11	42	50	19
Welton Rovers	22	7	3	12	41	54	17
Kingswood Rovers	22	5	3	14	24	55	13
Paulton Rovers	22	5	2	15	39	55	12

Staple Hill disbanded. Merthyr Town and Ton Pentre joined. Aberdare changed their name to Aberdare Town. The League became a single division of 13 clubs.

1909-10

Treharris	24	20	2	2	84	21	42
Bristol City Reserves	24	18	3	3	86	23	39
Bristol Rovers Reserves	24	15	3	6	79	25	33
Ton Pentre	24	14	4	6	68	26	32
Merthyr Town	24	14	3	7	57	24	31
Welton Rovers	24	13	5	6	51	46	31
Aberdare Town	23	13	2	8	57	30	28
Barry District	23	11	1	11	57	57	23
Bath City	24	5	6	13	31	66	15
Kingswood Rovers	23	4	2	17	28	80	10
Radstock Town	24	4	1	19	24	88	9
Weymouth	23	3	2	18	25	93	8
Paulton Rovers	24	2	2	20	28	96	6

Bath City had 1 point deducted for a breach of the rules.
Aberdare did not travel to Weymouth on 26th April and Kingswood Rovers did not travel to Barry on 27th April. Aberdare Town, Kingswood Rovers, Merthyr Town, Radstock Town, Ton Pentre and Treharris left. Camerton, Clevedon and Weston-super-Mare joined and the League was reduced to 10 clubs.

1910-11

Bristol City Reserves	18	15	3	0	58	14	33
Bristol Rovers Reserves	18	9	6	3	45	26	24
Bath City	18	9	4	5	38	30	22
Barry District	18	8	4	6	49	37	20
Welton Rovers	18	7	3	8	34	35	17
Weymouth	18	7	1	10	42	45	15
Weston super Mare	18	5	5	8	32	36	15
Camerton	18	3	7	8	31	42	13
Clevedon	18	4	3	11	22	54	11
Paulton Rovers	18	4	2	12	20	52	10

Bristol City Reserves left and Peasedown St. John and Street joined. League increased to 11 clubs.

1911-12

Welton Rovers	20	15	2	3	52	19	32
Barry District	20	13	2	5	56	28	28
Weymouth	20	12	3	5	58	29	27
Bristol Rovers Reserves	20	12	1	7	53	39	25
Bath City	20	10	2	8	31	27	22
Camerton	20	8	1	11	30	35	17
Weston super Mare	20	7	3	10	24	30	17
Street	20	7	1	12	32	42	15
Peasedown St. John	20	6	2	12	22	37	14
Paulton Rovers	20	5	2	13	28	70	12
Clevedon	20	5	1	14	21	46	11
					407	402	

Cardiff City Reserves joined. League increased to 12 clubs.

1912-13

Bristol Rovers Reserves	22	17	3	2	85	23	37
Cardiff City Reserves	22	17	1	4	72	24	35
Welton Rovers	22	14	5	3	56	16	33
Bath City	22	13	1	8	52	35	27
Barry District	22	10	4	8	48	40	24
Peasedown St. John	22	9	3	10	33	35	21
Street	22	10	1	11	44	58	21
Weymouth	22	6	4	12	35	55	16
Weston super Mare	22	6	3	13	37	55	15
Camerton	22	6	3	13	27	48	15
Paulton Rovers	22	4	2	16	29	79	10
Clevedon	22	2	6	14	15	68	10
					533	536	

Trowbridge Town replaced Barry District who left and joined the Southern League.

1913-14

Cardiff City Reserves	22	18	3	1	88	10	39
Bath City	22	17	2	3	67	34	36
Bristol Rovers Reserves	22	16	3	3	72	18	35
Weymouth	22	13	2	7	51	35	28
Peasedown St. John	22	12	4	6	33	35	28
Welton Rovers	22	12	2	8	55	33	26
Street	22	7	6	9	37	48	20
Trowbridge Town	22	7	2	13	33	43	16
Camerton	22	5	2	15	33	72	12
Paulton Rovers	22	4	2	16	24	73	10
Clevedon	22	3	3	16	19	60	9
Weston super Mare	22	2	1	19	21	72	5

1914-1919

No competition was held between these years.
When the league resumed after the war, Camerton, Cardiff City Reserves, Clevedon, Weston super Mare and Weymouth did not rejoin. There were however 11 new members and the league was split into two divisions.

Douglas and Horfield United and the reserves of Barry, Bristol City, Newport County, Swansea Town and Swindon Town joined pre-war members Bath City, Bristol Rovers Reserves and Welton Rovers in a 10-club Division One. Frome Town, Glastonbury, Timsbury Athletic and Yeovil & Petters United joined pre-war members Paulton Rovers, Peasedown St. John, Street and Trowbridge Town in an 8-club Division Two.

1919-20

Division One

Douglas	18	12	4	2	58	18	28
Swansea Town Reserves	18	13	2	3	39	15	28
Bristol City Reserves	18	12	1	5	41	17	25
Swindon Town Reserves	18	11	3	4	30	21	25
Bath City	18	8	2	8	48	29	18
Welton Rovers	18	6	1	11	39	47	13
Barry Reserves	18	6	0	12	27	37	12
Bristol Rovers Reserves	18	4	4	10	28	51	12
Newport County Reserves	18	5	1	12	25	57	11
Horfield United	18	1	4	13	21	54	6

Horfield United and Newport County Reserves left. Abertillery Town joined while continuing in the Southern League and Mid-Rhondda, Pontypridd and Ton Pentre joined from the Welsh League (South). Cardiff City Reserves, Cardiff Corinthians and Exeter City Reserves also joined. Division One increased to 16 clubs.

Division Two

Frome Town	14	10	2	2	33	20	22
Trowbridge Town	14	8	2	4	36	18	18
Peasedown St. John	14	8	2	4	22	14	18
Paulton Rovers	14	6	4	4	26	21	16
Yeovil & Petters United	14	7	2	5	41	34	16
Timsbury Athletic	14	4	1	9	19	32	9
Street	14	2	3	9	18	29	7
Glastonbury	14	2	2	10	8	35	6

Yeovil & Petters United were the promoted club this season.
Clandown, Radstock Town and Welton Amateurs joined, increasing Division Two to 10 clubs.

1920-21

Division One

Bristol City Reserves	30	18	5	7	58	27	41
Cardiff City Reserves	30	20	1	9	64	42	41
Abertillery Town	30	16	7	7	61	35	39
Swansea Town Reserves	30	15	8	7	60	29	38
Douglas	30	15	8	7	52	32	38
Pontypridd	30	15	6	9	60	40	36
Yeovil & Petters United	30	13	6	11	52	46	32
Bath City	30	12	7	11	45	45	31
Swindon Town Reserves	30	12	6	12	62	50	30
Exeter City Reserves	30	10	9	11	48	53	29
Bristol Rovers Reserves	30	10	5	15	46	53	25
Ton Pentre	30	10	5	15	43	60	25
Welton Rovers	30	9	6	15	39	67	24
Mid Rhondda	30	8	6	16	23	57	22
Barry Reserves	30	6	5	19	33	72	17
Cardiff Corinthians	30	4	4	22	24	62	12

Bath City moved to the Southern League and Mid Rhondda moved to the Welsh League (South). Abertillery Town, Douglas, Pontypridd and Ton Pentre and the reserves of Barry, Bristol City, Bristol Rovers, Cardiff City, Exeter City, Swansea Town and Swindon Town also left. Torquay United joined from the Plymouth & District League, Weymouth joined from the Dorset League and Horfield United also joined. Division reduced to 8 clubs.

Division Two

Peasedown St. John	18	13	3	2	34	12	29
Radstock Town	18	10	4	4	31	23	24
Trowbridge Town	18	10	3	5	36	18	23
Paulton Rovers	18	9	4	5	33	26	22
Timsbury Athletic	18	6	4	8	22	27	16
Street	18	7	2	9	21	35	16
Frome Town	18	5	3	10	26	30	13
Glastonbury	18	5	3	10	17	28	13
Clandown	18	5	3	10	13	24	13
Welton Amateurs	18	2	7	9	20	30	11

Peasedown St. John and Trowbridge Town were the two clubs promoted. Coleford Athletic joined. Division reduced to 9 clubs.

1921-22

Division One

Yeovil & Petters United	14	10	2	2	26	9	22
Trowbridge Town	14	8	1	5	18	15	17
Welton Rovers	14	7	2	5	31	27	16
Cardiff Corinthians	14	7	1	6	30	22	15
Torquay United	14	6	2	6	25	17	14
Peasedown St. John	14	5	3	6	21	19	13
Weymouth	14	5	1	8	15	25	11
Horfield United	14	1	2	11	10	42	4

Division Two

Clandown	16	10	5	1	22	5	25
Coleford Athletic	16	11	1	4	35	19	23
Radstock Town	16	7	4	5	23	14	18
Timsbury Athletic	16	7	2	7	23	22	16
Welton Amateurs	16	8	0	8	22	22	16
Glastonbury	16	6	2	8	21	36	14
Paulton Rovers	16	4	5	7	26	22	13
Frome Town	16	5	2	9	21	29	12
Street	16	2	3	11	25	49	7

Torquay United moved to the Southern League and Clandown, Coleford Athletic, Frome Town, Glastonbury, Horfield United, Paulton Rovers, Street, Timsbury Athletic and Welton Amateurs also left. Bath City and Hanham Athletic joined. League reverted to a single division of 9 clubs.

1922-23

Weymouth	16	10	2	4	35	14	22
Welton Rovers	16	9	2	5	27	14	20
Yeovil & Petters United	16	7	5	4	28	19	19
Trowbridge Town	16	6	6	4	14	22	18
Peasedown St. John	16	5	5	6	20	22	15
Radstock Town	16	4	7	5	14	19	15
Hanham Athletic	16	5	3	8	18	31	13
Bath City	16	4	3	9	15	19	11
Cardiff Corinthians	16	3	5	8	14	25	11

Welton Rovers moved to the Somerset Senior League and Hanham Athletic also left. Poole joined from the Hampshire League and Lovells Athletic, Minehead and Paulton Rovers also joined. League increased to 11 clubs.

1923-24

Lovells Athletic	20	16	3	1	43	10	35
Radstock Town	20	13	3	4	43	12	29
Weymouth	20	10	5	5	38	24	25
Cardiff Corinthians	20	11	3	6	32	26	25
Poole	20	8	6	6	37	35	22
Yeovil & Petters United	20	9	2	9	35	42	20
Trowbridge Town	20	6	2	12	29	42	14
Peasedown St. John	20	6	2	12	23	42	14
Minehead	20	5	3	12	32	44	13
Bath City	20	5	2	13	21	38	12
Paulton Rovers	20	3	5	12	20	38	11

Cardiff Corinthians left and joined the Welsh League (South). Welton Rovers joined from the Somerset Senior League and Frome Town and Swindon Victoria also joined. League increased to 13 clubs.

1924-25

Yeovil & Petters United	24	19	3	2	65	20	41
Weymouth	24	18	3	3	74	17	39
Swindon Victoria	24	14	3	7	51	48	31
Welton Rovers	24	9	10	5	50	28	28
Poole	24	11	6	7	50	38	28
Radstock Town	24	9	9	6	35	31	27
Frome Town	24	10	6	8	50	44	26
Trowbridge Town	24	9	6	9	46	37	24
Paulton Rovers	24	6	7	11	39	54	19
Minehead	24	7	1	16	47	74	15
Bath City	24	4	5	15	26	58	13
Peasedown St. John	24	4	5	15	19	65	13
Lovells Athletic	24	1	6	17	25	63	8

Peasedown St. John left but 10 additional clubs joined the league which was split into two divisions. Taunton United and Torquay United and the reserves of Bristol City, Bristol Rovers, Exeter City, Plymouth Argyle, Swindon Town joined Bath City, Weymouth and Yeovil & Petters United in a 10-club Division One. Portland United and the reserves of Bath City, Weymouth and Yeovil & Petters United joined the nine other existing members in a 13-club Division Two.

1925-26

Division One

Bristol City Reserves	18	10	7	1	58	19	27
Bristol Rovers Reserves	18	11	2	5	53	36	24
Torquay United	18	9	4	5	28	22	22
Yeovil & Petters United	18	7	7	4	33	27	21
Swindon Town Reserves	18	6	8	4	32	33	20
Weymouth	18	7	4	7	37	45	18
Plymouth Argyle Reserves	18	6	5	7	31	25	17
Exeter City Reserves	18	6	4	8	33	41	16
Taunton United	18	3	3	12	18	45	9
Bath City	18	1	4	13	20	50	6

Division increased to 12 clubs.

Division Two

Poole	24	17	3	4	76	30	37
Welton Rovers	24	16	4	4	62	37	36
Weymouth Reserves	24	12	4	8	69	47	28
Lovells Athletic	24	8	8	8	52	46	24
Radstock Town	24	9	6	9	31	28	24
Minehead	24	10	4	10	42	53	24
Portland United	24	8	7	9	49	56	23
Trowbridge Town	24	8	6	10	56	68	22
Swindon Victoria	24	9	3	12	55	71	21
Paulton Rovers	24	7	6	11	48	68	20
Bath City Reserves	24	7	5	12	50	53	19
Yeovil & Petters United Res.	24	7	4	13	48	57	18
Frome Town	24	5	6	13	40	64	16

Poole and Lovells Athletic were the two clubs promoted this season. Bath City Reserves, Paulton Rovers and Swindon Victoria left and Lovells Athletic Reserves and Poole Reserves joined. Division reduced to 10 clubs.

1926-27

Division One

Bristol City Reserves	22	16	2	4	59	32	34
Torquay United	22	14	4	4	47	27	32
Plymouth Argyle Reserves	22	13	1	8	63	37	27
Lovells Athletic	22	11	5	6	47	36	27
Bristol Rovers Reserves	22	12	3	7	49	41	27
Exeter City Reserves	22	10	3	9	61	53	23
Yeovil & Petters United	22	10	1	11	48	44	21
Swindon Town Reserves	22	9	2	11	41	47	20
Bath City	22	8	3	11	35	50	19
Poole	22	6	2	14	40	69	14
Taunton United	22	4	3	15	28	55	11
Weymouth	22	3	3	16	30	57	9

Poole left and continued in the Southern League and Swindon Town Reserves also left. Salisbury City joined from the Hampshire League and Torquay United were replaced by their reserves. Division reduced to 11 clubs. Taunton United changed their name to Taunton Town.

Division Two

Poole Reserves	18	14	2	2	68	19	30
Radstock Town	18	12	1	5	43	29	25
Portland United	18	12	0	6	62	31	24
Welton Rovers	18	9	2	7	61	39	20
Yeovil & Petters United Reserves	18	8	3	7	44	40	19
Lovells Athletic Reserves	18	8	0	10	48	48	16
Trowbridge Town	18	5	2	11	44	52	12
Frome Town	18	5	2	11	28	62	12
Weymouth Reserves	18	4	4	10	25	60	12
Minehead	18	5	0	13	24	67	10

Frome Town left and joined the Somerset Senior League and Lovells Athletic Reserves also left. Division reduced to 8 clubs.

1927-28

Division One

Plymouth Argyle Reserves	20	13	5	2	76	32	31
Exeter City Reserves	20	13	4	3	50	24	30
Yeovil & Petters United	20	12	2	6	56	44	26
Bristol City Reserves	20	10	4	6	71	40	24
Bristol Rovers Reserves	20	11	2	7	61	39	24
Taunton Town	20	9	5	6	36	33	23
Lovells Athletic	20	7	2	11	40	49	16
Torquay United Reserves	20	5	6	9	34	52	16
Bath City	20	5	3	12	36	54	13
Weymouth	20	3	3	14	16	60	9
Salisbury City	20	3	2	15	23	72	8

Lovells Athletic left and joined the Southern League. Salisbury City and Weymouth relegated. Division reduced to 8 clubs.

Division Two

Trowbridge Town	14	12	0	2	43	16	24
Yeovil & Petters United Reserves	14	10	2	2	56	21	22
Portland United	14	7	1	6	35	30	15
Welton Rovers	14	7	0	7	44	26	14
Radstock Town	14	6	1	7	48	41	13
Weymouth Reserves	14	4	1	9	22	52	9
Poole Reserves	14	4	1	9	25	54	9
Minehead	14	3	0	11	17	50	6

Minehead, Poole Reserves and Weymouth Reserves left and Bristol St. George and Bath City Reserves joined. Division increased to 9 clubs.

1928-29

Division One

Bristol Rovers Reserves	14	10	0	4	39	21	20
Plymouth Argyle Reserves	14	6	4	4	31	19	16
Bath City	14	6	4	4	33	30	16
Taunton Town	14	7	2	5	32	30	16
Bristol City Reserves	14	7	1	6	34	31	15
Exeter City Reserves	14	4	4	6	36	42	12
Torquay United Reserves	14	3	3	8	21	30	9
Yeovil & Petters United	14	2	4	8	19	42	8

Division Two

Bath City Reserves	16	12	0	4	44	28	24
Portland United	16	10	3	3	44	26	23
Trowbridge Town	16	8	3	5	31	33	19
Yeovil & Petters United Reserves	16	8	1	7	51	33	17
Welton Rovers	16	5	5	6	30	32	15
Weymouth	16	4	6	6	35	41	14
Salisbury City	16	5	3	8	28	36	13
Bristol St. George	16	4	3	9	41	56	11
Radstock Town	16	3	2	11	27	46	8

Salisbury City left and joined the Hampshire League and Yeovil & Petters United Reserves also left. Wells City joined from the Somerset Senior League and Bristol City "A" and Paulton Rovers also joined. Division increased to 10 clubs.

1929-30

Division One

Yeovil & Petters United	14	10	2	2	32	13	22
Exeter City Reserves	14	5	5	4	26	17	15
Bristol City Reserves	14	5	5	4	28	27	15
Plymouth Argyle Reserves	14	6	2	6	23	20	14
Taunton Town	14	6	2	6	17	30	14
Bath City	14	4	5	5	35	33	13
Torquay United Reserves	14	4	3	7	27	32	11
Bristol Rovers Reserves	14	3	2	9	18	34	8

Bath City left and continued in the Southern League. Division reduced to 7 clubs.

Division Two

Trowbridge Town	18	12	2	4	50	28	26
Portland United	18	11	3	4	50	27	25
Wells City	18	10	3	5	52	31	23
Bristol City "A"	18	9	3	6	54	41	21
Welton Rovers	18	9	3	6	50	48	21
Bath City Reserves	18	6	6	6	43	39	18
Paulton Rovers	18	4	5	9	26	50	13
Bristol St. George	18	5	1	12	41	51	11
Radstock Town	18	5	1	12	32	57	11
Weymouth	18	4	3	11	26	52	11

Poole Town joined from the Southern League, Salisbury City joined from the Hampshire League and Chippenham Town, Coleford Athletic, Petters Westland, Street and Warminster Town also joined. Division increased to 17 clubs.

1930-31

Division One

Exeter City Reserves	12	9	1	2	34	24	19
Yeovil & Petters United	12	7	2	3	43	27	16
Bristol Rovers Reserves	12	6	3	3	28	19	15
Bristol City Reserves	12	4	2	6	34	28	10
Taunton Town	12	5	0	7	20	34	10
Plymouth Argyle Reserves	12	3	1	8	23	33	7
Torquay United Reserves	12	1	5	6	18	35	7

Lovells Athletic joined from the London Combination. Division increased to 8 clubs.

Division Two

Portland United	32	24	3	5	111	47	51
Salisbury City	32	22	4	6	93	50	48
Welton Rovers	32	20	6	6	106	64	46
Wells City	32	21	2	9	92	61	44
Bristol City "A"	32	19	5	8	111	72	43
Bath City Reserves	32	18	3	11	102	56	39
Warminster Town	32	15	5	12	94	77	35
Radstock Town	32	15	5	12	63	85	35
Poole Town	32	14	4	14	76	72	32
Chippenham Town	32	10	8	14	82	68	28
Trowbridge Town	32	9	9	14	58	60	27
Paulton Rovers	32	8	10	14	45	67	26
Petters Westland	32	10	2	20	76	101	22
Bristol St. George	32	10	1	21	80	135	21
Weymouth	32	9	1	22	81	128	19
Street	32	6	4	22	52	96	16
Coleford Athletic	32	6	0	26	60	143	12

Petters Westland left and Frome Town and Glastonbury joined. Division increased to 18 clubs.

1931-32

Division One

Plymouth Argyle Reserves	14	10	1	3	41	15	21
Yeovil & Petters United	14	8	3	3	42	26	19
Lovells Athletic	14	7	3	4	33	25	17
Bristol Rovers Reserves	14	8	0	6	32	28	16
Torquay United Reserves	14	5	4	5	29	35	14
Bristol City Reserves	14	4	3	7	26	37	11
Exeter City Reserves	14	4	1	9	23	37	9
Taunton Town	14	2	1	11	18	41	5

Plymouth Argyle Reserves left and Bath City and Cardiff City Reserves joined. Division increased to 9 clubs.

Division Two

Portland United	34	27	1	6	122	55	55
Salisbury City	34	23	5	6	122	50	51
Bath City Reserves	34	23	4	7	104	53	50
Trowbridge Town	34	19	5	10	103	68	43
Bristol City "A"	34	19	2	13	124	89	40
Street	34	17	4	13	100	84	38
Paulton Rovers	34	17	3	14	78	59	37
Frome Town	34	18	1	15	86	105	37
Poole Town	34	16	4	14	81	82	36
Wells City	34	15	5	14	119	89	35
Weymouth	34	13	4	17	86	103	30
Chippenham Town	34	11	6	17	99	105	28
Bristol St. George	34	12	4	18	74	110	28
Welton Rovers	34	10	7	17	72	90	27
Glastonbury	34	12	2	20	86	113	26
Radstock Town	34	9	5	20	64	101	23
Warminster Town	34	8	6	20	68	119	22
Coleford Athletic	34	1	4	29	43	156	6

Swindon Town Reserves replaced Coleford Athletic.

1932-33

Division One

Exeter City Reserves	16	11	2	3	59	29	24
Torquay United Reserves	16	11	1	4	55	29	23
Yeovil & Petters United	16	10	0	6	51	31	20
Bath City	16	8	1	7	39	39	17
Bristol City Reserves	16	6	4	6	54	42	16
Bristol Rovers Reserves	16	7	2	7	34	34	16
Lovells Athletic	16	6	3	7	36	35	15
Cardiff City Reserves	16	3	1	12	31	66	7
Taunton Town	16	2	2	12	13	67	6

Bristol City Reserves and Cardiff City Reserves left. Division reduced to 7 clubs.

Division Two

Swindon Town Reserves	34	28	1	5	124	51	57
Street	34	20	9	5	105	60	49
Bristol City "A"	34	18	6	10	91	64	42
Bath City Reserves	34	16	6	12	100	68	38
Bristol St. George	34	17	4	13	92	86	38
Salisbury City	34	16	4	14	92	70	36
Portland United	34	15	5	14	95	72	35
Radstock Town	34	15	5	14	71	65	35
Frome Town	34	16	2	16	92	112	34
Weymouth	34	15	3	16	109	92	33
Wells City	34	11	8	15	82	83	30
Glastonbury	34	13	4	17	67	92	30
Welton Rovers	34	13	3	18	72	91	29
Poole Town	34	13	3	18	75	97	29
Trowbridge Town	34	11	5	18	66	106	27
Warminster Town	34	10	4	20	68	125	24
Chippenham Town	34	9	5	20	71	99	23
Paulton Rovers	34	9	5	20	50	89	23

1933-34

Division One

Bath City	12	8	2	2	33	14	18
Torquay United Reserves	12	6	3	3	31	17	15
Bristol Rovers Reserves	12	7	1	4	40	22	15
Yeovil & Petters United	12	5	3	4	22	21	13
Lovells Athletic	12	5	2	5	21	20	12
Exeter City Reserves	12	5	1	6	25	31	11
Taunton Town	12	0	0	12	10	57	0

Taunton Town disbanded and were replaced by Cardiff City Reserves.

Division Two

Weymouth	34	20	7	7	101	54	47
Bath City Reserves	34	20	7	7	101	53	47
Swindon Town Reserves	34	20	6	8	99	61	46
Salisbury City	34	18	7	9	71	37	43
Portland United	34	17	6	11	99	73	40
Glastonbury	34	17	5	12	99	70	39
Street	34	16	5	13	98	89	37
Poole Town	34	14	8	12	83	66	36
Welton Rovers	34	15	5	14	77	82	35
Paulton Rovers	34	14	5	15	73	75	33
Radstock Town	34	13	6	15	67	70	32
Trowbridge Town	34	12	8	14	62	86	32
Wells City	34	11	9	14	69	85	31
Bristol City "A"	34	10	8	16	60	79	28
Frome Town	34	10	8	16	74	96	28
Chippenham Town	34	11	3	20	73	95	25
Warminster Town	34	6	5	23	43	95	17
Bristol St. George	34	7	2	25	62	145	16

Weymouth beat Bath City Reserves in a championship decider. Bristol Rovers "A" replaced Poole Town who left and joined the Hampshire League.

1934-35

Division One

Yeovil & Petters United	12	9	1	2	38	21	19
Bath City	12	7	2	3	32	16	16
Bristol Rovers Reserves	12	6	3	3	34	21	15
Torquay United Reserves	12	4	2	6	25	25	10
Cardiff City Reserves	12	3	3	6	19	30	9
Exeter City Reserves	12	2	4	6	18	26	8
Lovells Athletic	12	3	1	8	15	42	7

Exeter City Reserves left. Division reduced to 6 clubs.

Division Two

Swindon Town Reserves	34	25	5	4	108	33	55
Salisbury City	34	21	6	7	86	41	48
Portland United	34	22	3	9	105	65	47
Weymouth	34	19	8	7	107	39	46
Frome Town	34	19	7	8	113	67	45
Bath City Reserves	34	18	5	11	85	52	41
Glastonbury	34	15	9	10	96	64	39
Street	34	14	8	12	83	65	36
Trowbridge Town	34	14	7	13	79	84	35
Bristol City "A"	34	15	4	15	87	69	34
Paulton Rovers	34	13	7	14	60	70	33
Bristol Rovers "A"	34	15	0	19	68	88	30
Welton Rovers	34	10	8	16	71	84	28
Warminster Town	34	11	4	19	63	112	26
Wells City	34	10	5	19	70	83	25
Radstock Town	34	6	7	21	48	101	19
Chippenham Town	34	7	3	24	53	126	17
Bristol St. George	34	2	4	28	43	173	8

Bristol St. George left and were replaced by Poole Town from the Hampshire League.

1935-36

Division One

Bristol Rovers Reserves	10	5	4	1	29	22	14
Lovells Athletic	10	4	4	2	17	18	12
Torquay United Reserves	10	4	3	3	28	20	11
Bath City	10	3	3	4	15	16	9
Cardiff City Reserves	10	3	3	4	13	18	9
Yeovil & Petters United	10	1	3	6	22	30	5

Bath City left and continued in the Southern League and Cardiff City Reserves also left. Bristol City Reserves joined. Division reduced to five clubs.

Division Two

Swindon Town Reserves	34	28	4	2	140	40	60
Weymouth	34	22	4	8	116	54	48
Street	34	21	5	8	106	54	47
Frome Town	34	17	5	12	92	86	39
Bath City Reserves	34	14	10	10	93	78	38
Portland United	34	16	6	12	95	82	38
Glastonbury	34	15	7	12	97	72	37
Poole Town	34	16	5	13	77	89	37
Paulton Rovers	34	14	8	12	69	77	36
Radstock Town	34	15	5	14	77	80	35
Salisbury City	34	13	8	13	60	65	34
Bristol City "A"	34	14	3	17	71	76	31
Wells City	34	12	7	15	61	72	31
Trowbridge Town	34	12	6	16	87	91	30
Warminster Town	34	9	4	21	58	103	22
Bristol Rovers "A"	34	8	5	21	57	78	21
Welton Rovers	34	5	5	24	49	125	15
Chippenham Town	34	6	1	27	64	147	13

Yeovil & Petters United Reserves replaced Bath City Reserves.

1936-37

Division One

Bristol Rovers Reserves	8	6	0	2	26	15	12
Yeovil & Petters United	8	5	1	2	23	12	11
Bristol City Reserves	8	4	2	2	18	15	10
Torquay United Reserves	8	2	0	6	13	24	4
Lovells Athletic	8	1	1	6	11	25	3

Division Two

Weymouth	34	27	4	3	144	38	58
Swindon Town Reserves	34	27	4	3	139	49	58
Salisbury City	34	20	9	5	97	45	49
Trowbridge Town	34	22	3	9	89	62	47
Portland United	34	21	3	10	115	60	45
Street	34	18	4	12	90	73	40
Wells City	34	14	9	11	65	60	37
Radstock Town	34	15	7	12	91	92	37
Warminster Town	34	14	7	13	64	69	35
Glastonbury	34	14	3	17	92	98	31
Frome Town	34	9	7	18	68	94	25
Chippenham Town	34	11	3	20	71	98	25
Bristol City "A"	34	11	2	21	62	90	24
Bristol Rovers "A"	34	8	7	19	84	112	23
Yeovil & Petters United Reserves	34	9	5	20	80	131	23
Welton Rovers	34	11	0	23	60	116	22
Poole Town	34	8	3	23	51	95	19
Paulton Rovers	34	5	4	25	46	126	14

Bath City Reserves replaced Swindon Town Reserves.

1937-38

Division One

Bristol City Reserves	8	6	1	1	21	7	13
Yeovil & Petters United	8	5	1	2	20	16	11
Bristol Rovers Reserves	8	4	0	4	15	14	8
Torquay United Reserves	8	3	1	4	12	15	7
Lovells Athletic	8	0	1	7	9	25	1

Bath City joined while continuing in the Southern League.

Division Two

Weymouth	34	27	4	3	121	34	58
Street	34	21	4	9	113	53	46
Portland United	34	17	6	11	109	57	40
Yeovil & Petters United Reserves	34	15	10	9	99	61	40
Salisbury City	34	18	4	12	94	76	40
Chippenham Town	34	18	4	12	91	90	40
Radstock Town	34	18	4	12	79	80	40
Trowbridge Town	34	16	7	11	102	76	39
Glastonbury	34	18	2	14	85	67	38
Poole Town	34	14	7	13	79	67	35
Wells City	34	13	8	13	75	87	34
Bristol City "A"	34	15	1	18	86	100	31
Warminster Town	34	10	9	15	66	92	29
Frome Town	34	9	7	18	66	94	25
Bristol Rovers "A"	34	9	6	19	63	89	24
Paulton Rovers	34	9	6	19	61	124	24
Welton Rovers	34	5	7	22	52	142	17
Bath City Reserves	34	3	6	25	51	103	12

1938-39

Division One

Lovells Athletic	10	7	2	1	27	14	16
Yeovil & Petters United	10	6	2	2	32	20	14
Bristol City Reserves	10	4	1	5	24	24	9
Bath City	10	2	5	3	16	22	9
Torquay United Reserves	10	2	4	4	14	17	8
Bristol Rovers Reserves	10	1	2	7	9	25	4

Division abandoned upon the outbreak of war but Bristol City Reserves joined Division Two.

Division Two

Trowbridge Town	34	27	3	4	166	49	57
Yeovil & Petters United Reserves	34	22	4	8	112	66	48
Street	34	21	5	8	93	57	47
Poole Town	34	21	4	9	106	67	46
Weymouth	34	19	5	10	105	51	43
Radstock Town	34	19	5	10	97	64	43
Portland United	34	18	4	12	107	64	40
Bristol City "A"	34	17	6	11	87	58	40
Welton Rovers	34	14	4	16	64	118	32
Glastonbury	34	13	5	16	76	89	31
Frome Town	34	11	9	14	76	104	31
Bath City Reserves	34	8	8	18	64	100	24
Wells City	34	10	3	21	63	104	23
Warminster Town	34	8	7	19	49	105	23
Bristol Rovers "A"	34	9	4	21	58	92	22
Paulton Rovers	34	8	6	20	57	117	22
Salisbury City	34	7	7	20	50	93	21
Chippenham Town	34	8	3	23	56	87	19
					1486	1485	

Bristol City "A", Bristol Rovers "A", Frome Town, Poole Town, Portland United, Salisbury City, Street, Warminster Town, Weymouth and Yeovil & Petters United Reserves withdrew.
Bristol Aeroplane Company and Peasedown Miners Welfare joined to make a single division of 11 clubs.

1939-40

Trowbridge Town	20	18	0	2	87	31	36
Bristol Aeroplane Company	20	13	4	3	78	33	30
Radstock Town	20	12	1	7	68	54	25
Peasedown Miners Welfare	20	9	5	6	45	36	23
Glastonbury	20	9	5	6	49	43	23
Bristol City Reserves	20	9	2	9	54	43	20
Chippenham Town	20	7	2	11	51	78	16
Welton Rovers	20	6	1	13	44	65	13
Wells City	20	6	1	13	37	66	13
Bath City Reserves	20	4	3	13	35	69	11
Paulton Rovers	20	3	4	13	34	64	10

1940-45

No competition. The league restarted in 1945 with a single division of 14 clubs: Bristol Aeroplane Company, Bristol City Reserves, Bristol Rovers Reserves, Chippenham Town, Clandown, Clevedon, Douglas, Paulton Rovers, Peasedown Miners Welfare, Radstock Town, Soundwell, Trowbridge Town, Welton Rovers, Yeovil Town Reserves.

1945-46

Bristol Rovers Reserves	26	17	6	3	120	46	40
Chippenham Town	26	15	4	7	84	41	34
Trowbridge Town	26	16	2	8	114	62	34
Peasedown Miners Welfare	26	13	8	5	75	44	34
Yeovil Town Reserves	26	12	5	9	66	58	29
Douglas	26	12	3	11	82	84	27
Bristol City Reserves	26	10	6	10	90	68	26
Clevedon	26	11	2	13	80	102	24
Bristol Aeroplane Company	26	10	4	12	62	81	24
Paulton Rovers	26	10	3	13	67	93	23
Clandown	26	10	2	14	58	66	22
Radstock Town	26	9	2	15	65	82	20
Soundwell	26	6	3	17	67	132	15
Welton Rovers	26	4	4	18	44	115	12

17 extra clubs joined the league which was split into two divisions. Clandown, Douglas and Soundwell were placed in a 13-club Division Two, the other 11 existing members were placed in an 18-club Division One. Of the 17 additional clubs, Bath City Reserves, Frome Town, Glastonbury, Poole Town, Portland United, Street and Wells City joined Division One and B.A.C. Reserves, Chippenham Town Reserves, Cinderford Town (from the Gloucestershire Northern Senior League), Hoffman Athletic, RAF Colerne, RAF Locking, RAF Melksham, Swindon Town Reserves, Thorney Pitts (from the Bath & District League) and Trowbridge Town Reserves joined Division Two.

1946-47

Automatic promotion and relegation introduced. Due to the severe winter, fixtures were not completed and the season was abandoned on 5th June.

Division One

Trowbridge Town	31	27	1	3	123	43	55
Poole Town	29	20	5	4	86	26	45
Bristol Rovers Reserves	31	19	4	8	96	53	42
Chippenham Town	31	20	2	9	115	68	42
Yeovil Town Reserves	30	16	4	10	85	56	36
Clevedon	30	15	5	10	87	62	35
Portland United	31	14	4	13	92	69	32
Street	32	13	5	14	75	80	31
Paulton Rovers	31	13	3	15	79	110	29
Glastonbury	29	12	3	14	56	68	27
Bristol Aeroplane Company	29	12	3	14	72	87	27
Wells City	31	8	9	14	52	78	25
Radstock Town	29	9	3	17	66	92	21
Peasedown Miners Welfare	21	7	6	8	43	49	20
Bristol City Reserves	24	7	1	16	50	92	15
Bath City Reserves	26	5	4	17	34	72	14
Frome Town	29	4	3	22	45	129	11
Welton Rovers	20	2	3	15	40	72	7
					1296	1306	

Division Two

Clandown	23	20	2	1	130	33	42
Soundwell	24	17	3	4	111	44	37
Douglas	23	14	2	7	107	77	30
Trowbridge Town Reserves	22	13	3	6	82	50	29
Swindon Town Reserves	24	11	3	10	91	77	25
Hoffman Athletic	20	11	2	7	62	37	24
RAF Locking	21	11	1	9	83	69	23
RAF Melksham	23	7	4	12	56	83	18
Cinderford Town	21	7	3	11	58	60	17
B.A.C. Reserves	23	6	3	14	50	76	15
Chippenham Town Reserves	20	4	3	13	47	86	11
RAF Colerne	20	2	5	13	48	99	9
Thorney Pitts	18	1	0	17	24	158	2

Thorney Pitts disbanded but Cheltenham Town Reserves, Dorchester Town (from the Dorset Combination), National Smelting Company, Salisbury (a new club), Stonehouse and Weymouth joined. Division increased to 18 clubs.

1947-48

Division One

Trowbridge Town	34	29	3	2	131	33	61
Glastonbury	34	26	3	5	119	40	55
Street	34	23	7	4	98	40	53
Bristol Rovers Reserves	34	21	6	7	121	60	48
Clevedon	34	20	4	10	117	66	44
Clandown	34	16	5	13	84	80	37
Poole Town	33	14	6	13	73	72	34
Yeovil Town Reserves	34	14	4	16	70	79	32
Paulton Rovers	34	13	5	16	78	93	31
Portland United	34	11	7	16	64	72	29
Bristol City Reserves	34	11	7	16	69	104	29
Bath City Reserves	34	10	8	16	56	82	28
Wells City	34	11	5	18	58	71	27
Peasedown Miners Welfare	34	11	5	18	74	96	27
Soundwell	32	8	7	17	64	103	23
Chippenham Town	33	8	6	19	65	97	22
Radstock Town	34	8	3	23	64	108	19
Bristol Aeroplane Company	34	4	1	29	56	165	9

Division Two

Salisbury	34	29	1	4	145	33	59
Weymouth	34	26	4	4	148	37	56
Cheltenham Town Reserves	34	25	3	6	142	42	53
Welton Rovers	34	21	3	10	85	49	45
Frome Town	33	22	0	11	114	76	44
Hoffman Athletic	34	19	5	10	79	50	43
Trowbridge Town Reserves	33	17	5	11	92	59	39
Swindon Town Reserves	34	17	4	13	95	76	38
Douglas	34	18	2	14	104	88	38
Dorchester Town	34	13	6	15	64	79	32
Cinderford Town	34	12	7	15	87	103	31
National Smelting Company	34	13	5	16	80	102	31
Stonehouse	34	7	7	20	64	113	21
Chippenham Town Reserves	34	8	4	22	63	117	20
RAF Locking	33	9	1	23	52	126	19
RAF Melksham	34	7	4	23	63	136	18
RAF Colerne	33	6	4	23	64	146	16
B.A.C. Reserves	34	2	1	31	48	157	5

The 2 unplayed games in each division were ignored.
Bristol City's and Bristol Rovers' Reserve sides were both replaced by their Colts.
BAC Reserves, RAF Colerne and RAF Locking left and were replaced by Barnstaple Town, Chippenham United (a new club) and Weston-super-Mare.

1948-49

Division One

Glastonbury	34	24	6	4	93	50	54
Trowbridge Town	34	22	6	6	109	44	50
Weymouth	34	22	4	8	100	44	48
Chippenham Town	34	19	5	10	94	50	43
Street	34	18	4	12	90	58	40
Salisbury	34	17	5	12	78	51	39
Bristol Rovers Colts	34	12	12	10	65	63	36
Paulton Rovers	34	13	6	15	57	64	32
Wells City	34	14	4	16	51	67	32
Bath City Reserves	34	14	4	16	63	92	32
Poole Town	34	13	5	16	59	65	31
Soundwell	34	13	5	16	76	100	31
Peasedown Miners Welfare	34	12	3	19	54	81	27
Clandown	34	12	3	19	55	102	27
Portland United	34	11	4	19	51	70	26
Yeovil Town Reserves	34	7	12	15	61	81	26
Clevedon	34	5	10	19	48	74	20
Bristol City Colts	34	7	4	23	57	105	18

Division Two

Chippenham United	34	29	3	2	145	35	61
Cheltenham Town Reserves	34	26	3	5	133	48	55
Welton Rovers	34	23	4	7	139	68	50
Radstock Town	34	21	5	8	107	64	47
Weston-super-Mare	34	21	5	8	101	63	47
Hoffman Athletic	34	20	2	12	88	41	42
Trowbridge Town Reserves	34	17	5	12	124	75	39
Frome Town	34	16	4	14	85	73	36
Cinderford Town	34	13	6	15	82	103	32
Dorchester Town	34	13	5	16	78	96	31
Barnstaple Town	34	13	3	18	94	88	29
Douglas	34	14	1	19	77	112	29
Chippenham Town Reserves	34	11	4	19	81	89	26
Swindon Town Reserves	34	10	6	18	78	107	26
Stonehouse	34	11	2	21	71	102	24
Bristol Aeroplane Company	34	9	5	20	74	109	23
RAF Melksham	34	5	0	29	50	167	10
National Smelting Company	34	2	1	31	42	209	5

Weymouth joined the Southern League and were replaced by their Reserves and Swindon Town replaced their Reserves with their Colts. RAF Melksham left and Bridgwater Town replaced them in Division Two.
An 11-club Third Division was formed by the reserves of Barnstaple Town, Bridgwater Town, Chippenham United, Clevedon, Stonehouse, Welton Rovers and Weston-super-Mare, plus Bristol Rovers "A" and the first XI's of Bideford Town, Ilfracombe Town (from the Exeter & District League) and Minehead.

1949-50

Division One

Wells City	34	22	7	5	87	43	51
Poole Town	34	22	7	5	88	45	51
Glastonbury	34	23	4	7	78	38	50
Trowbridge Town	34	22	5	7	104	40	49
Cheltenham Town Reserves	34	21	4	9	91	58	46
Chippenham United	34	16	8	10	57	49	40
Bristol Rovers Colts	34	15	7	12	54	50	37
Chippenham Town	34	13	7	14	77	70	33
Street	34	12	9	13	71	75	33
Weymouth Reserves	34	13	5	16	67	49	31
Salisbury	34	14	3	17	64	66	31
Yeovil Town Reserves	34	13	5	16	55	102	31
Paulton Rovers	34	12	3	19	60	76	27
Peasedown Miners Welfare	34	8	9	17	56	82	25
Portland United	34	8	6	20	44	74	22
Clandown	34	8	5	21	46	80	21
Soundwell	34	6	6	22	61	116	18
Bath City Reserves	34	5	6	23	45	103	16
					1205	*1216*	

Division Two

Barnstaple Town	34	23	7	4	102	41	53
Dorchester Town	34	21	8	5	96	51	50
Welton Rovers	34	20	7	7	87	63	47
Stonehouse	34	19	6	9	83	63	44
Bridgwater Town	34	17	8	9	86	49	42
Trowbridge Town Reserves	34	17	8	9	81	53	42
Clevedon	34	18	6	10	92	61	42
Weston-super-Mare	34	16	9	9	86	73	41
Bristol City Colts	34	14	8	12	89	60	36
Cinderford Town	34	13	9	12	82	80	35
Chippenham Town Reserves	34	14	4	16	74	73	32
Frome Town	34	12	7	15	72	74	31
Radstock Town	34	10	7	17	72	98	27
National Smelting Company	34	8	9	17	69	99	25
Swindon Town Colts	34	9	3	22	58	89	21
Hoffman Athletic	34	4	13	17	33	69	21
Bristol Aeroplane Company	34	3	6	25	43	138	12
Douglas	34	3	5	26	49	114	11
					1354	*1348*	

Division Three

Bideford Town	20	19	1	0	103	20	39
Ilfracombe Town	20	16	0	4	74	37	32
Minehead	20	11	5	4	49	30	27
Clevedon Reserves	20	9	7	4	50	41	25
Chippenham United Reserves	20	8	2	10	45	48	18
Weston-super-Mare Reserves	20	7	3	10	44	64	17
Bristol Rovers "A"	20	5	6	9	36	43	16
Barnstaple Town Reserves	20	5	5	10	31	45	15
Welton Rovers Reserves	20	5	2	13	36	64	12
Bridgwater Town Reserves	20	5	1	14	38	62	11
Stonehouse Reserves	20	2	4	14	19	69	8
					525	*523*	

Division Three was disbanded and those clubs who had not been promoted left the league. Bristol Aeroplane Company and Douglas also left. Chipping Sodbury joined, increasing Division Two to 20 clubs.

1950-51

Division One

Glastonbury	34	26	6	2	102	27	58
Wells City	34	22	9	3	83	39	53
Chippenham Town	34	18	8	8	86	48	44
Chippenham United	34	18	6	10	72	44	42
Trowbridge Town	34	17	7	10	83	49	41
Barnstaple Town	34	18	4	12	71	62	40
Poole Town	34	18	3	13	71	71	39
Salisbury	34	14	7	13	65	55	35
Dorchester Town	34	13	8	13	64	58	34
Street	34	13	8	13	74	69	34
Weymouth Reserves	34	13	6	15	54	56	32
Cheltenham Town Reserves	34	12	7	15	56	46	31
Bristol Rovers Colts	34	11	8	15	60	85	30
Clandown	34	10	9	15	49	58	29
Paulton Rovers	34	9	9	16	62	75	27
Portland United	34	6	7	21	56	112	19
Yeovil Town Reserves	34	8	3	23	38	79	19
Peasedown Miners Welfare	34	1	3	30	25	123	5
					1171	*1156*	

Division Two

Stonehouse	38	29	7	2	133	36	65
Bath City Reserves	38	28	5	5	114	44	61
Bideford Town	38	27	6	5	158	54	60
Cinderford Town	38	21	12	5	112	51	54
Bridgwater Town	38	24	5	9	124	50	53
Ilfracombe Town	38	23	5	10	105	68	51
Clevedon	38	18	6	14	95	81	42
Welton Rovers	38	18	5	15	103	95	41
Minehead	38	16	8	14	73	74	40
Hoffman Athletic	38	16	4	18	74	66	36
Frome Town	38	12	10	16	81	102	34
Bristol City Colts	38	14	5	19	75	84	33
Radstock Town	38	11	9	18	85	112	31
Chippenham Town Reserves	38	12	6	20	83	115	30
Swindon Town Colts	38	10	9	19	88	95	29
Trowbridge Town Reserves	38	11	6	21	69	100	28
Chipping Sodbury	38	10	3	25	75	113	23
Weston-super-Mare	38	8	7	23	46	100	23
Soundwell	38	6	3	29	46	164	15
National Smelting Company	38	3	2	33	50	184	8
	760	317	123	320	*1789*	*1788*	*757*

National Smelting Company and Soundwell left. Gloucester City Reserves joined. Division reduced to 19 clubs.

1951-52

Division One

Chippenham Town	34	23	4	7	103	41	50
Glastonbury	34	20	6	8	87	64	46
Barnstaple Town	34	18	6	10	87	62	42
Weymouth Reserves	34	18	5	11	84	54	41
Trowbridge Town	34	19	3	12	85	58	41
Stonehouse	34	15	7	12	82	61	37
Wells City	34	12	13	9	65	60	37
Bath City Reserves	34	14	8	12	53	51	36
Cheltenham Town Reserves	34	13	8	13	58	55	34
Street	34	14	6	14	65	71	34
Clandown	34	11	10	13	63	75	32
Salisbury	34	10	9	15	62	68	29
Dorchester Town	34	11	7	16	61	81	29
Chippenham United	34	10	8	16	59	70	28
Portland United	34	9	8	17	49	73	26
Paulton Rovers	34	10	5	19	64	96	25
Bristol Rovers Colts	34	6	11	17	46	75	23
Poole Town	34	8	6	20	50	106	22
					1223	*1221*	

Division Two

Bideford Town	36	29	3	4	179	55	61
Bridgwater Town	36	28	1	7	126	38	57
Ilfracombe Town	36	25	4	7	106	50	54
Minehead	36	24	2	10	80	60	50
Gloucester City Reserves	36	19	5	12	107	73	43
Cinderford Town	36	18	6	12	95	69	42
Peasedown Miners Welfare	36	17	8	11	80	72	42
Bristol City Colts	36	17	7	12	87	58	41
Yeovil Town Reserves	36	18	4	14	94	102	40
Frome Town	36	15	7	14	89	76	37
Clevedon	36	16	5	15	98	89	37
Radstock Town	36	17	2	17	108	103	36
Chippenham Town Reserves	36	12	5	19	63	89	29
Hoffman Athletic	36	13	3	20	66	101	29
Welton Rovers	36	11	2	23	73	116	24
Weston-super-Mare	36	7	5	24	42	115	19
Swindon Town Colts	36	7	4	25	54	120	18
Trowbridge Town Reserves	36	5	4	27	56	117	14
Chipping Sodbury	36	3	5	28	43	143	11

Cheltenham Town Reserves, Chipping Sodbury and Swindon Town Colts left. Stonehouse Reserves joined. Division One reduced to 17 clubs and Division Two to 18 clubs.

1952-53

Division One

Barnstaple Town	32	18	8	6	77	37	44
Street	32	19	6	7	89	43	44
Trowbridge Town	32	17	7	8	76	48	41
Bideford Town	32	13	13	6	79	52	39
Chippenham Town	32	17	3	12	84	58	37
Weymouth Reserves	32	16	5	11	75	58	37
Chippenham United	32	15	5	12	62	62	35
Salisbury	32	11	10	11	60	65	32
Glastonbury	32	15	1	16	61	49	31
Bath City Reserves	32	10	11	11	64	63	31
Stonehouse	32	11	8	13	57	58	30
Portland United	32	11	8	13	66	77	30
Bridgwater Town	32	12	4	16	58	73	28
Wells City	32	9	6	17	52	71	24
Clandown	32	7	9	16	40	74	23
Dorchester Town	32	8	5	19	46	74	21
Paulton Rovers	32	6	5	21	42	125	17
					1088	*1087*	

Division Two

Chippenham Town Reserves	34	24	4	6	99	51	52
Ilfracombe Town	34	20	11	3	67	28	51
Poole Town	34	21	7	6	97	42	49
Peasedown Miners Welfare	34	19	3	12	76	63	41
Minehead	34	15	8	11	81	53	38
Clevedon	34	17	3	14	82	92	37
Cinderford Town	34	15	6	13	77	50	36
Bristol City Colts	34	14	6	14	75	56	34
Bristol Rovers Colts	34	12	9	13	74	54	33
Frome Town	34	13	6	15	66	66	32
Yeovil Town Reserves	34	13	5	16	83	78	31
Gloucester City Reserves	34	11	6	17	81	97	28
Radstock Town	34	11	6	17	74	102	28
Trowbridge Town Reserves	34	11	4	19	70	89	26
Stonehouse Reserves	34	10	6	18	68	107	26
Welton Rovers	34	10	6	18	53	98	26
Weston-super-Mare	34	10	4	20	66	113	24
Hoffman Athletic	34	8	4	22	60	109	20
					1349	*1348*	

Chippenham Town Reserves could not be promoted to join their first XI in Division One and so Poole Town were promoted in their place and Poole Town Reserves joined Division Two.
Division One increased to 18 clubs.

1953-54

Division One

Weymouth Reserves	34	21	4	9	102	53	46
Poole Town	34	18	8	8	73	49	44
Trowbridge Town	34	19	5	10	78	62	43
Barnstaple Town	34	17	7	10	74	42	41
Chippenham Town	34	18	5	11	79	49	41
Salisbury	34	17	6	11	74	60	40
Portland United	34	18	3	13	71	63	39
Wells City	34	15	7	12	63	68	37
Bridgwater Town	34	15	6	13	72	76	36
Bideford Town	34	13	8	13	70	66	34
Dorchester Town	34	14	5	15	79	69	33
Chippenham United	34	13	6	15	60	63	32
Glastonbury	34	12	8	14	59	70	32
Street	34	12	8	14	55	69	32
Bath City Reserves	34	10	6	18	40	66	26
Ilfracombe Town	34	9	5	20	40	77	23
Stonehouse	34	7	6	21	51	80	20
Clandown	34	4	5	25	29	87	13

Division Two

Bristol Rovers Colts	34	24	6	4	89	43	54
Bristol City Colts	34	22	6	6	87	39	50
Frome Town	34	21	7	6	99	50	49
Chippenham Town Reserves	34	18	9	7	87	58	45
Welton Rovers	34	16	6	12	54	53	38
Cinderford Town	34	15	7	12	82	72	37
Poole Town Reserves	34	15	5	14	79	61	35
Weston-super-Mare	34	14	7	13	89	70	35
Trowbridge Town Reserves	34	12	9	13	90	88	33
Gloucester City Reserves	34	13	7	14	89	96	33
Hoffman Athletic	34	13	5	16	74	61	31
Yeovil Town Reserves	34	12	7	15	90	89	31
Paulton Rovers	34	12	7	15	69	84	31
Minehead	34	11	6	17	62	78	28
Clevedon	34	11	4	19	77	101	26
Radstock Town	34	10	4	20	71	107	24
Peasedown Miners Welfare	34	8	5	21	56	133	21
Stonehouse Reserves	34	4	3	27	45	102	11
					1389	*1385*	

Taunton Town (from the Somerset Senior League) replaced Stonehouse Reserves.

1954-55

Division One

Dorchester Town	34	23	5	6	103	46	51
Chippenham Town	34	21	7	6	83	39	49
Bath City Reserves	34	22	4	8	87	52	48
Salisbury	34	17	8	9	71	50	42
Portland United	34	18	6	10	89	70	42
Bideford Town	34	18	6	10	69	56	42
Bridgwater Town	34	18	5	11	91	69	41
Poole Town	34	13	12	9	80	62	38
Bristol Rovers Colts	34	16	5	13	73	55	37
Barnstaple Town	34	13	8	13	69	66	34
Trowbridge Town	34	14	5	15	65	55	33
Bristol City Colts	34	11	4	19	53	62	26
Weymouth Reserves	34	10	6	18	49	67	26
Chippenham United	34	10	5	19	57	97	25
Glastonbury	34	8	9	17	51	89	25
Wells City	34	5	9	20	49	90	19
Street	34	7	4	23	51	100	18
Ilfracombe Town	34	5	6	23	35	100	16

Division Two

Yeovil Town Reserves	34	23	5	6	115	49	51
Frome Town	34	24	3	7	106	49	51
Weston-super-Mare	34	22	4	8	122	58	48
Chippenham Town Reserves	34	18	8	8	102	60	44
Taunton Town	34	20	3	11	95	57	43
Gloucester City Reserves	34	16	8	10	80	61	40
Minehead	34	15	6	13	104	65	36
Cinderford Town	34	12	12	10	85	79	36
Stonehouse	34	15	5	14	87	83	35
Poole Town Reserves	34	15	4	15	82	71	34
Welton Rovers	34	13	6	15	70	77	32
Peasedown Miners Welfare	34	12	6	16	79	102	30
Clandown	34	12	6	16	45	75	30
Clevedon	34	12	4	18	82	90	28
Hoffman Athletic	34	11	3	20	53	97	25
Trowbridge Town Reserves	34	10	3	21	43	86	23
Radstock Town	34	5	6	23	54	135	16
Paulton Rovers	34	5	0	29	47	157	10

Bath City Reserves left Division One which was reduced to 17 clubs while Frome Town Reserves and Torquay United Reserves joined Division Two which increased to 20 clubs.

1955-56

Division One

Trowbridge Town	32	24	2	6	100	36	50
Poole Town	32	20	7	5	79	33	47
Dorchester Town	32	21	4	7	106	57	46
Chippenham Town	32	20	4	8	70	50	44
Salisbury	32	17	7	8	64	31	41
Bideford Town	32	14	10	8	58	50	38
Portland United	32	16	3	13	87	76	35
Barnstaple Town	32	15	4	13	61	66	34
Weymouth Reserves	32	10	12	10	63	70	32
Frome Town	32	10	7	15	69	64	27
Yeovil Town Reserves	32	11	5	16	57	86	27
Bristol Rovers Colts	32	10	4	18	49	65	24
Bristol City Colts	32	8	7	17	43	63	23
Wells City	32	8	7	17	53	92	23
Bridgwater Town	32	7	5	20	59	98	19
Chippenham United	32	7	5	20	54	90	19
Glastonbury	32	3	9	20	47	92	15

Division Two

Torquay United Reserves	38	27	6	5	135	38	60
Taunton Town	38	26	3	9	115	46	55
Gloucester City Reserves	38	24	5	9	104	56	53
Weston-super-Mare	38	21	9	8	126	59	51
Stonehouse	38	21	7	10	92	55	49
Trowbridge Town Reserves	38	20	7	11	98	74	47
Minehead	38	20	6	12	104	69	46
Clevedon	38	19	8	11	99	71	46
Frome Town Reserves	38	20	6	12	101	96	46
Ilfracombe Town	38	18	5	15	82	70	41
Poole Town Reserves	38	14	8	16	86	71	36
Chippenham Town Reserves	38	13	7	18	80	97	33
Clandown	38	13	6	19	87	105	32
Cinderford Town	38	13	5	20	85	82	31
Welton Rovers	38	12	6	20	73	95	30
Street	38	11	4	23	70	112	26
Peasedown Miners Welfare	38	8	9	21	57	141	25
Hoffman Athletic	38	7	6	25	46	109	20
Radstock Town	38	7	3	28	52	165	17
Paulton Rovers	38	6	4	28	56	157	16

Chippenham Town Reserves and Frome Town Reserves left Division Two and were replaced by Bath City Reserves and Dorchester Town Reserves. As no clubs were relegated, Division One was increased to 19 clubs and Division Two reduced to 18 clubs.

1956-57

Division One

Poole Town	36	26	4	6	115	48	56
Trowbridge Town	36	21	5	10	83	55	47
Salisbury	36	20	5	11	98	60	45
Torquay United Reserves	36	18	8	10	91	55	44
Portland United	36	18	8	10	84	64	44
Bridgwater Town	36	17	7	12	58	54	41
Dorchester Town	36	16	7	13	83	70	39
Chippenham Town	36	16	7	13	77	67	39
Yeovil Town Reserves	36	18	2	16	79	73	38
Glastonbury	36	16	3	17	82	102	35
Bristol Rovers Colts	36	14	6	16	67	90	34
Weymouth Reserves	36	16	1	19	87	94	33
Barnstaple Town	36	14	4	18	76	70	32
Bideford Town	36	12	8	16	70	71	32
Taunton Town	36	11	9	16	59	71	31
Chippenham United	36	12	6	18	80	97	30
Bristol City Colts	36	13	4	19	58	74	30
Frome Town	36	10	2	24	46	91	22
Wells City	36	4	4	28	46	133	12

Division Two

Cinderford Town	34	28	2	4	114	31	58
Trowbridge Town Reserves	34	25	4	5	112	35	54
Poole Town Reserves	34	23	6	5	87	39	52
Minehead	34	20	5	9	83	52	45
Dorchester Town Reserves	34	18	6	10	113	69	42
Gloucester City Reserves	34	17	7	10	81	50	41
Welton Rovers	34	18	3	13	87	74	39
Stonehouse	34	14	10	10	98	70	38
Bath City Reserves	34	16	6	12	91	82	38
Weston-super-Mare	34	11	7	16	68	80	29
Peasedown Miners Welfare	34	10	6	18	69	99	26
Hoffman Athletic	34	8	10	16	52	92	26
Street	34	9	7	18	48	68	25
Clevedon	34	10	4	20	64	85	24
Ilfracombe Town	34	7	8	19	43	82	22
Radstock Town	34	9	3	22	65	141	21
Paulton Rovers	34	7	3	24	50	111	17
Clandown	34	6	3	25	49	114	15

Cinderford Town and Minehead were the two clubs promoted this season. Poole Town left and joined the Southern League and Taunton Town Reserves joined.

1957-58

Division One

Salisbury	36	18	11	7	55	30	47
Bridgwater Town	36	20	5	11	78	53	45
Dorchester Town	36	19	9	11	87	57	44
Barnstaple Town	36	17	7	12	83	48	41
Trowbridge Town	36	15	11	10	80	61	41
Bristol Rovers Colts	36	16	8	12	80	74	40
Torquay United Reserves	36	15	9	12	70	56	39
Bristol City Colts	36	16	7	13	70	59	39
Minehead	36	16	5	15	68	76	37
Frome Town	36	16	5	15	66	77	37
Cinderford Town	36	17	2	17	72	70	36
Taunton Town	36	11	13	12	48	55	35
Bideford Town	36	14	5	17	62	55	33
Weymouth Reserves	36	13	7	16	89	85	33
Chippenham Town	36	13	7	16	71	74	33
Glastonbury	36	12	7	17	50	79	31
Yeovil Town Reserves	36	13	4	19	66	92	30
Portland United	36	12	3	21	58	80	27
Chippenham United	36	5	6	25	51	123	16

Division Two

Poole Town Reserves	34	26	3	5	141	48	55
Gloucester City Reserves	34	24	5	5	109	40	53
Weston-super-Mare	34	22	9	3	102	46	53
Dorchester Town Reserves	34	19	6	9	73	41	44
Welton Rovers	34	18	6	10	87	64	42
Trowbridge Town Reserves	34	19	3	12	88	69	41
Wells City	34	16	6	12	82	68	38
Street	34	13	7	14	60	73	33
Bath City Reserves	34	12	8	14	76	64	32
Peasedown Miners Welfare	34	13	6	15	75	98	32
Ilfracombe Town	34	13	3	18	84	99	29
Radstock Town	34	11	5	18	78	114	27
Clandown	34	10	7	17	52	78	27
Hoffman Athletic	34	9	5	20	55	85	23
Taunton Town Reserves	34	9	4	21	51	89	22
Paulton Rovers	34	7	7	20	59	98	21
Clevedon	34	9	2	23	67	112	20
Stonehouse	34	8	4	22	62	115	20

Trowbridge Town left and joined the Southern League. Clevedon also left and Bridgwater Town Reserves joined. Division Two reduced to 17 clubs.

1958-59

Division One

Yeovil Town Reserves	36	26	3	7	115	54	55
Salisbury	36	24	3	9	91	53	51
Dorchester Town	36	23	2	11	110	61	48
Bridgwater Town	36	21	6	9	81	57	48
Barnstaple Town	36	20	5	11	85	68	45
Chippenham Town	36	20	3	13	104	66	43
Bideford Town	36	15	11	10	83	60	41
Torquay United Reserves	36	18	3	15	70	70	39
Weymouth Reserves	36	18	2	16	84	63	38
Cinderford Town	36	15	4	17	60	63	34
Bristol Rovers Colts	36	14	6	16	73	77	34
Glastonbury	36	15	3	18	63	81	33
Taunton Town	36	15	2	19	53	68	32
Bristol City Colts	36	12	7	17	75	88	31
Portland United	36	13	5	18	68	82	31
Poole Town Reserves	36	10	7	19	63	91	27
Gloucester City Reserves	36	9	5	22	64	91	23
Minehead	36	6	7	23	50	111	19
Frome Town	36	4	4	28	52	140	12

Division Two

Bath City Reserves	32	20	7	5	95	39	47
Trowbridge Town Reserves	32	20	5	7	88	56	45
Street	32	18	5	9	73	56	41
Bridgwater Town Reserves	32	16	8	8	81	55	40
Welton Rovers	32	18	3	11	80	53	39
Dorchester Town Reserves	32	16	6	10	73	52	38
Weston-super-Mare	32	16	5	11	80	59	37
Paulton Rovers	32	16	5	11	87	71	37
Stonehouse	32	16	4	12	85	47	36
Chippenham United	32	14	7	11	65	54	35
Taunton Town Reserves	32	11	6	15	58	81	28
Peasedown Miners Welfare	32	9	9	14	64	89	27
Clandown	32	10	6	16	58	74	26
Radstock Town	32	10	5	17	61	76	25
Ilfracombe Town	32	7	5	20	48	108	19
Hoffman Athletic	32	4	4	24	49	107	12
Wells City	32	5	2	25	44	112	12

Cinderford Town, Hoffman Athletic and Ilfracombe Town left. Division Two reduced to 14 clubs.

1959-60

Division One

Torquay United Reserves	36	29	5	2	132	40	63
Salisbury	36	20	7	9	85	43	47
Chippenham Town	36	18	6	12	70	56	42
Bridgwater Town	36	18	5	13	79	62	41
Weymouth Reserves	36	18	4	14	72	58	40
Portland United	36	17	6	13	61	68	40
Bideford Town	36	15	8	13	61	62	38
Bath City Reserves	36	15	7	14	63	61	37
Yeovil Town Reserves	36	17	3	16	74	77	37
Poole Town Reserves	36	15	6	15	73	66	36
Dorchester Town	36	17	2	17	87	88	36
Minehead	36	12	11	13	68	72	35
Bristol Rovers Colts	36	13	8	15	79	80	34
Glastonbury	36	11	10	15	66	78	32
Barnstaple Town	36	13	5	18	50	65	31
Taunton Town	36	11	7	18	67	96	29
Bristol City Colts	36	12	4	20	65	82	28
Gloucester City Reserves	36	9	4	23	49	92	22
Trowbridge Town Reserves	36	5	6	25	36	91	16

Division Two

Welton Rovers	26	20	2	4	95	40	42
Stonehouse	26	17	4	5	78	43	38
Weston-super-Mare	26	15	6	5	100	42	36
Frome Town	26	14	5	7	63	38	33
Chippenham United	26	14	2	10	64	52	30
Clandown	26	9	9	8	48	43	27
Paulton Rovers	26	11	5	10	58	64	27
Radstock Town	26	12	3	11	48	62	27
Street	26	10	5	11	48	53	25
Wells City	26	8	5	13	46	73	21
Bridgwater Town Reserves	26	8	4	14	58	64	20
Taunton Town Reserves	26	5	7	14	43	59	17
Dorchester Town Reserves	26	5	5	16	43	82	15
Peasedown Miners Welfare	26	1	4	21	38	114	6
					830	*829*	

Welton Rovers and Weston-super-Mare were the two clubs promoted. Chippenham United disbanded and Frome Town and Clandown left to join the Wiltshire Premier League. Bridgwater Town Reserves, Dorchester Town Reserves, Gloucester City Reserves, Paulton Rovers, Peasedown Miners Welfare, Radstock Town, Stonehouse, Street, Taunton Town Reserves and Wells City also all left. Exeter City Reserves joined from the South-Western League and Welton Rovers and Weston-super-Mare were promoted to form a single division of 21 clubs.

1960-61

Salisbury	40	31	4	5	135	42	66
Dorchester Town	40	26	6	8	115	63	58
Minehead	40	24	8	8	100	62	56
Torquay United Reserves	40	23	6	11	122	70	52
Bridgwater Town	40	18	12	10	88	71	48
Exeter City Reserves	40	21	5	14	99	68	47
Weymouth Reserves	40	19	9	12	91	79	47
Bristol City Colts	40	18	10	12	94	70	46
Welton Rovers	40	20	5	15	119	110	45
Portland United	40	16	10	14	93	87	42
Yeovil Town Reserves	40	18	5	17	73	73	41
Chippenham Town	40	18	5	17	79	81	41
Bristol Rovers Colts	40	12	12	16	80	74	36
Bath City Reserves	40	11	11	18	75	79	33
Weston-super-Mare	40	13	7	20	76	98	33
Bideford Town	40	12	9	19	76	99	33
Glastonbury	40	13	4	23	66	114	30
Poole Town Reserves	40	8	9	23	57	87	25
Trowbridge Town Reserves	40	9	7	24	62	122	25
Barnstaple Town	40	8	4	28	55	111	20
Taunton Town	40	5	6	29	59	153	16
					1814	*1813*	

Exeter City Reserves and Trowbridge Town Reserves left and Bristol City Colts were replaced by Bristol City Reserves. Bridport joined. League reduced to 20 clubs.

1961-62

Bristol City Reserves	38	28	7	3	132	36	63
Salisbury	38	27	2	9	105	41	56
Bideford Town	38	21	11	6	84	49	53
Torquay United Reserves	38	20	5	13	95	78	45
Poole Town Reserves	38	19	5	14	115	85	43
Dorchester Town	38	19	5	14	102	85	43
Bridgwater Town	38	17	8	13	89	69	42
Minehead	38	17	8	13	80	68	42
Chippenham Town	38	17	6	15	79	71	40
Portland United	38	16	8	14	92	85	40
Weston-super-Mare	38	14	11	13	63	68	39
Weymouth Reserves	38	16	6	16	85	71	38
Bath City Reserves	38	13	9	16	74	80	35
Bridport	38	11	8	19	72	93	30
Yeovil Town Reserves	38	13	3	22	74	99	29
Welton Rovers	38	11	7	20	61	104	29
Taunton Town	38	11	4	23	59	114	26
Bristol Rovers Colts	38	6	13	19	59	93	25
Barnstaple Town	38	8	7	23	52	120	23
Glastonbury	38	7	5	26	44	107	19

Andover (from the Hampshire League) and Exeter City Reserves joined. League increased to 22 clubs.

1962-63

Bristol City Reserves	42	31	5	6	120	56	67
Bideford Town	42	29	7	6	115	51	65
Minehead	42	25	6	11	102	62	56
Andover	42	25	5	12	106	59	55
Bridgwater Town	42	23	8	11	77	48	54
Salisbury	42	21	9	12	89	56	51
Portland United	42	23	5	14	80	66	51
Weymouth Reserves	42	20	5	17	104	78	45
Yeovil Town Reserves	42	18	9	15	67	72	45
Barnstaple Town	42	19	6	17	81	75	44
Dorchester Town	42	17	9	16	92	79	43
Chippenham Town	42	15	12	15	92	60	42
Poole Town Reserves	42	17	7	18	82	77	41
Exeter City Reserves	42	15	10	17	55	74	40
Bath City Reserves	42	14	6	22	82	96	34
Weston-super-Mare	42	11	9	22	72	108	31
Welton Rovers	42	11	8	23	71	107	30
Glastonbury	42	13	4	25	56	114	30
Torquay United Reserves	42	10	8	24	48	78	28
Bridport	42	9	8	25	66	111	26
Taunton Town	42	11	4	27	56	112	26
Bristol Rovers Colts	42	6	8	28	56	120	20
					1769	1759	

Bristol Rovers Colts left and were replaced by Frome Town.

1963-64

Bideford	42	30	6	6	113	36	66
Bristol City Reserves	42	24	15	3	122	43	63
Bridgwater Town	42	25	10	7	82	32	60
Welton Rovers	42	24	6	12	84	54	54
Dorchester Town	42	19	14	9	94	56	52
Salisbury	42	21	8	13	80	61	50
Barnstaple Town	42	20	9	13	92	69	49
Minehead	42	20	8	14	96	85	48
Weymouth Reserves	42	16	12	14	94	74	44
Andover	42	17	10	15	89	78	44
Torquay United Reserves	42	18	7	17	81	73	43
Yeovil Town Reserves	42	17	9	16	73	99	43
Chippenham Town	42	15	8	19	75	62	38
Bath City Reserves	42	12	12	18	77	92	36
Frome Town	42	11	11	20	69	97	33
Weston-super-Mare	42	11	11	20	58	86	33
Glastonbury	42	11	9	22	70	91	31
Exeter City Reserves	42	8	15	19	73	100	31
Poole Town Reserves	42	11	6	25	56	98	28
Bridport	42	7	14	21	40	100	28
Portland United	42	10	5	27	63	127	25
Taunton Town	42	8	9	25	37	105	25

1964-65

Welton Rovers	42	35	3	4	148	36	73
Bideford	42	32	6	4	120	29	70
Minehead	42	27	7	8	88	42	61
Dorchester Town	42	26	4	12	89	53	56
Weston-super-Mare	42	22	9	11	89	58	53
Weymouth Reserves	42	24	4	14	96	46	52
Bridgwater Town	42	20	9	13	74	59	49
Torquay United Reserves	42	21	5	16	74	59	47
Bristol City Reserves	42	21	4	17	96	82	46
Salisbury	42	17	9	16	60	67	43
Frome Town	42	17	8	17	66	71	42
Exeter City Reserves	42	18	5	19	92	84	41
Chippenham Town	42	16	8	18	75	82	40
Glastonbury	42	15	6	21	69	109	36
Yeovil Town Reserves	42	15	5	22	65	99	35
Andover	42	13	8	21	74	66	34
Bath City Reserves	42	12	6	24	54	98	30
Bridport	42	11	7	24	60	99	29
Taunton Town	42	10	8	24	54	104	28
Barnstaple Town	42	11	5	26	51	89	27
Portland United	42	6	8	28	40	122	20
Poole Town Reserves	42	5	2	35	49	149	12

Bath City Reserves, Chippenham Town, Poole Town Reserves and Yeovil Town Reserves left. Bristol City Colts replaced Bristol City Reserves. League reduced to 18 clubs.

1965-66

Welton Rovers	34	25	9	0	105	28	59
Portland United	34	23	2	9	75	50	48
Bideford	34	19	8	7	90	49	46
Andover	34	16	8	10	74	57	40
Minehead	34	13	12	9	46	44	38
Frome Town	34	14	9	11	53	53	37
Glastonbury	34	12	11	11	61	46	35
Taunton Town	34	15	5	14	73	69	35
Bridgwater Town	34	12	10	12	63	62	34
Salisbury	34	12	8	14	62	57	32
Torquay United Reserves	34	11	10	13	56	56	32
Exeter City Reserves	34	13	4	17	63	70	30
Weymouth Reserves	34	11	8	15	65	76	30
Weston-super-Mare	34	12	5	17	48	61	29
Bridport	34	12	5	17	57	90	29
Dorchester Town	34	9	5	20	41	79	23
Barnstaple Town	34	7	8	19	35	59	22
Bristol City Colts	34	4	5	25	33	94	13

Plymouth Argyle Colts, St. Luke's College (from the South-Western League) and Yeovil Town Reserves joined. League increased to 21 clubs.

1966-67

Welton Rovers	40	29	7	4	102	37	65
Minehead	40	25	10	5	98	42	60
Bridgwater Town	40	25	7	8	93	47	57
Salisbury	40	22	9	9	83	54	53
Dorchester Town	40	22	8	10	89	48	52
Bideford	40	23	6	11	76	47	52
Glastonbury	40	20	9	11	71	54	49
Exeter City Reserves	40	17	7	16	54	63	41
Torquay United Reserves	40	15	9	16	66	56	39
Andover	40	13	13	14	69	60	39
Portland United	40	15	7	18	61	76	37
Frome Town	40	17	1	22	60	82	35
Bristol City Colts	40	13	8	19	63	64	34
Weston-super-Mare	40	12	9	19	52	69	33
Taunton Town	40	11	10	19	67	77	32
Plymouth Argyle Colts	40	12	8	20	66	97	32
Bridport	40	11	8	21	50	80	30
Weymouth Reserves	40	12	4	24	39	75	28
St. Luke's College	40	10	7	23	61	90	27
Barnstaple Town	40	8	8	24	50	92	24
Yeovil Town Reserves	40	8	5	27	52	111	21
					1422	1421	

Exeter City Reserves and Weymouth Reserves left and were replaced by Bath City Reserves and Devizes Town.

1967-68

Bridgwater Town	40	27	8	5	92	41	62
Salisbury	40	28	3	9	105	35	59
Glastonbury	40	24	7	9	103	64	55
Bath City Reserves	40	21	9	10	81	63	51
Frome Town	40	22	6	12	98	72	50
Minehead	40	18	13	9	72	49	49
Dorchester Town	40	17	14	9	81	50	48
Welton Rovers	40	20	6	14	74	55	46
Plymouth Argyle Colts	40	18	7	15	76	72	43
Bridport	40	18	5	17	68	58	41
Torquay United Reserves	40	17	7	16	58	55	41
Andover	40	17	5	18	61	66	39
Taunton Town	40	11	15	14	76	68	37
Bideford	40	13	9	18	52	63	35
St. Luke's College	40	12	9	19	60	78	33
Portland United	40	10	12	18	39	80	32
Bristol City Colts	40	9	10	21	33	59	28
Weston-super-Mare	40	9	10	21	40	79	28
Barnstaple Town	40	8	6	26	48	91	22
Devizes Town	40	7	7	26	56	113	21
Yeovil Town Reserves	40	5	10	25	36	98	20

Salisbury left and joined the Southern League and Plymouth Argyle Colts also left. League reduced to 19 clubs.

1968-69

Taunton Town	36	24	5	7	96	53	53
Bideford	36	21	7	8	77	44	49
Bridgwater Town	36	18	12	6	72	30	48
Glastonbury	36	22	4	10	85	49	48
Frome Town	36	18	11	7	57	38	47
Andover	36	16	9	11	63	43	41
Minehead	36	16	9	11	57	43	41
Welton Rovers	36	14	9	13	51	51	37
Dorchester Town	36	15	6	15	63	53	36
Bath City Reserves	36	15	6	15	58	49	36
Barnstaple Town	36	14	7	15	58	67	35
Devizes Town	36	14	7	15	56	77	35
Torquay United Reserves	36	15	3	18	51	60	33
Bristol City Colts	36	13	6	17	64	68	32
Bridport	36	8	11	17	34	54	27
Weston-super-Mare	36	7	11	18	29	54	25
St. Luke's College	36	9	5	22	44	74	23
Portland United	36	7	8	21	36	80	22
Yeovil Town Reserves	36	4	8	24	41	105	16

Weymouth Reserves joined. League increased to 20 clubs.

1969-70

Glastonbury	38	29	5	4	100	37	63
Andover	38	26	6	6	76	20	58
Bridgwater Town	38	23	7	8	97	41	53
Minehead	38	21	10	7	70	37	52
Taunton Town	38	21	8	9	84	56	50
Bideford	38	20	7	11	84	58	47
Dorchester Town	38	18	8	12	78	69	44
Torquay United Reserves	38	15	10	13	70	54	40
Bath City Reserves	38	16	7	15	71	67	39
Welton Rovers	38	17	3	18	72	62	37
Weston-super-Mare	38	14	8	16	53	72	36
Frome Town	38	12	10	16	62	73	34
Portland United	38	14	6	18	63	94	34
Bristol City Colts	38	13	7	18	58	76	33
Devizes Town	38	10	9	19	44	70	29
Barnstaple Town	38	11	6	21	58	73	28
Yeovil Town Reserves	38	9	6	23	38	78	24
Weymouth Reserves	38	10	4	24	34	74	24
Bridport	38	6	9	23	43	86	21
St. Luke's College	38	4	6	28	35	93	14

Portland United, Weymouth Reserves and Yeovil Town Reserves left. Plymouth City joined. League reduced to 18 clubs.

1970-71

Bideford	34	26	4	4	96	39	56
Andover	34	21	8	5	65	24	50
Bridgwater Town	34	20	9	5	63	38	49
Glastonbury	34	18	8	8	78	52	44
Minehead	34	18	5	11	66	40	41
Taunton Town	34	17	7	10	66	42	41
Plymouth City	34	17	6	11	67	41	40
Welton Rovers	34	17	6	11	60	56	40
Dorchester Town	34	16	6	12	58	50	38
Devizes Town	34	12	11	11	53	50	35
Barnstaple Town	34	13	7	14	60	61	33
Bridport	34	11	8	15	43	49	30
Weston-super-Mare	34	9	6	19	36	73	24
Torquay United Reserves	34	8	6	20	43	54	22
Bristol City Colts	34	7	8	19	40	78	22
Frome Town	34	8	3	23	50	91	19
Bath City Reserves	34	7	5	22	33	77	19
St. Luke's College	34	2	5	27	21	83	9

Andover left and joined the Southern League and Bath City Reserves, Bristol City Colts and Plymouth City also left. League reduced to 14 clubs.

1971-72

Bideford	26	19	4	3	63	21	42
Minehead	26	18	5	3	59	22	41
Glastonbury	26	16	5	5	58	26	37
Devizes Town	26	11	9	6	44	33	31
Welton Rovers	26	10	7	9	38	37	27
Frome Town	26	9	7	10	33	45	25
Dorchester Town	26	9	6	11	39	38	24
Weston-super-Mare	26	9	5	12	39	45	23
Bridport	26	9	5	12	32	47	23
Bridgwater Town	26	7	9	10	28	42	23
Taunton Town	26	7	7	12	50	54	21
Torquay United Reserves	26	5	9	12	29	55	19
Barnstaple Town	26	6	6	14	40	46	18
St. Luke's College	26	3	4	19	25	66	10

Bideford, Dorchester Town and Minehead all left and joined the Southern League. Avon (Bradford), Ashtonians United, Bristol City Colts, Exeter City Reserves and Mangotsfield United (from the Avon Premier Combination) joined. League increased to 16 clubs.

1972-73

Devizes Town	30	21	5	4	68	27	47
Taunton Town	30	19	7	4	69	26	45
Mangotsfield United	30	21	3	6	69	35	45
Bridgwater Town	30	17	7	6	65	24	41
Weston-super-Mare	30	13	9	8	42	36	35
Glastonbury	30	14	6	10	45	44	34
Barnstaple Town	30	13	7	10	57	52	33
Bridport	30	10	10	10	40	30	30
Torquay United Reserves	30	11	6	13	53	47	28
Frome Town	30	9	9	12	30	44	27
Welton Rovers	30	9	8	13	35	41	26
Exeter City Reserves	30	7	11	12	39	47	25
St. Luke's College	30	9	3	18	33	73	21
Avon (Bradford)	30	6	3	21	27	68	15
Bristol City Colts	30	5	4	21	35	76	14
Ashtonians United	30	4	6	20	26	63	14

Bristol City Colts and Torquay United Reserves left. Dawlish, Exmouth Town and Tiverton Town joined from the Devon & Exeter League, Chippenham Town joined from the Hellenic League and Keynsham Town also joined. League increased to 19 clubs.

1973-74

Welton Rovers	36	27	5	4	80	32	59
Taunton Town	36	25	8	3	86	19	58
Bridgwater Town	36	23	6	7	71	34	52
Exeter City Reserves	36	21	7	8	61	33	49
Devizes Town	36	18	9	9	73	44	45
Glastonbury	36	18	7	11	69	46	43
Frome Town	36	16	9	11	64	43	41
Barnstaple Town	36	17	7	12	76	60	41
Mangotsfield United	36	17	7	12	57	52	41
Dawlish	36	17	6	13	53	67	40
St. Luke's College	36	14	5	17	48	48	33
Weston-super-Mare	36	13	7	16	44	50	33
Keynsham Town	36	11	5	20	39	65	27
Tiverton Town	36	7	11	18	42	67	25
Bridport	36	10	5	21	41	67	25
Exmouth Town	36	6	11	19	31	70	23
Ashtonians United	36	8	5	23	43	75	21
Avon (Bradford)	36	5	6	25	36	85	16
Chippenham Town	36	3	6	27	25	82	12

Ashtonians United merged with Clevedon who took over Ashtonians' place in the league. Avon (Bradford) left and joined the Wiltshire County League and Exeter City Reserves also left. Falmouth Town joined from the South-Western League, Paulton Rovers joined from the Somerset Senior League and Melksham Town and Westland Yeovil also joined. League increased to 21 clubs.

1974-75   (Three points for a win from this season)

Falmouth Town	40	31	9	0	122	26	102
Taunton Town	40	30	9	1	136	24	99
Bridgwater Town	40	27	8	5	92	38	89
Mangotsfield United	40	24	6	10	88	44	78
Barnstaple Town	40	17	11	12	79	66	62
Frome Town	40	17	10	13	65	59	61
Glastonbury	40	17	10	13	62	57	61
Westland Yeovil	40	17	7	16	66	60	58
Welton Rovers	40	15	11	14	63	59	56
Dawlish	40	16	7	17	69	72	55
Keynsham Town	40	15	10	15	63	67	55
Paulton Rovers	40	13	11	16	63	59	50
Devizes Town	40	11	11	18	39	59	44
Weston-super-Mare	40	11	10	19	39	52	43
Chippenham Town	40	10	12	18	55	85	42
St. Luke's College	40	11	7	22	44	83	40
Tiverton Town	40	9	12	19	45	79	39
Bridport	40	9	7	24	71	110	34
Melksham Town	40	7	12	21	39	82	33
Clevedon	40	8	8	24	52	94	32
Exmouth Town	40	8	6	26	39	96	30
					1391	1371	

Bideford joined from the Southern League and Exeter City Reserves also joined. League increased to 23 clubs.

1975-76

Falmouth Town	44	35	5	4	134	43	110
Taunton Town	44	27	8	9	86	43	89
Clevedon	44	27	6	11	77	51	87
Bridgwater Town	44	25	10	9	81	44	85
Glastonbury	44	23	10	11	84	49	79
Barnstaple Town	44	21	9	14	95	66	72
Tiverton Town	44	20	12	12	73	70	72
Paulton Rovers	44	19	12	13	60	58	69
Mangotsfield United	44	18	10	16	63	63	64
Bideford	44	17	12	15	60	56	63
Frome Town	44	17	10	17	76	61	61
Exeter City Reserves	44	16	10	18	64	69	57
St. Luke's College	44	16	7	21	60	70	55
Weston-super-Mare	44	13	15	16	52	57	54
Westland Yeovil	44	14	11	19	66	82	53
Welton Rovers	44	14	9	21	57	71	51
Bridport	44	13	11	20	49	72	50
Dawlish	44	13	10	21	51	69	49
Devizes Town	44	10	15	19	45	59	45
Chippenham Town	44	12	7	25	66	94	43
Melksham Town	44	12	7	25	66	106	43
Keynsham Town	44	8	6	30	50	86	30
Exmouth Town	44	5	10	29	38	114	25

Exeter City Reserves had 1 point deducted for fielding an ineligible player. The League split into two divisions. The top 18 clubs formed the new Premier Division while the bottom 5 plus Brixham United (from the Plymouth & District League), Chard Town and Shepton Mallet Town (both from the Somerset Senior League), Clandown, Heavitree United, Ilminster Town, Larkhall Athletic, Ottery St. Mary and Saltash United (both from the South-Western League), Portway-Bristol, Swanage Town & Herston, Torquay United Reserves and Yeovil Town Reserves formed the new 18-club First Division.

1976-77

Premier Division

Falmouth Town	34	26	2	6	69	24	80
Weston-super-Mare	34	18	12	4	57	31	66
Clevedon	34	18	10	6	58	31	64
Bridgwater Town	34	17	10	7	51	36	61
Barnstaple Town	34	16	9	9	64	48	57
Bideford	34	15	11	8	70	38	56
Bridport	34	16	8	10	53	35	56
Paulton Rovers	34	13	10	11	52	46	49
Taunton Town	34	14	6	14	49	46	48
Dawlish	34	11	10	13	36	41	43
Glastonbury	34	11	8	15	56	58	41
Frome Town	34	10	11	13	45	52	41
Tiverton Town	34	11	7	16	35	61	40
Welton Rovers	34	9	9	16	35	46	36
Mangotsfield United	34	10	4	20	36	66	34
St. Luke's College	34	7	6	21	32	61	27
Exeter City Reserves	34	7	3	24	36	76	23
Westland Yeovil	34	4	10	20	31	69	22

Exeter City Reserves had 1 point deducted for fielding ineligible player.

First Division

Saltash United	34	24	6	4	81	29	78
Shepton Mallet Town	34	23	7	4	84	39	76
Keynsham Town	34	23	2	9	87	38	71
Melksham Town	34	20	7	7	69	36	67
Chippenham Town	34	17	6	11	53	43	57
Devizes Town	34	15	8	11	58	44	52
Torquay United Reserves	34	15	3	16	61	59	48
Portway-Bristol	34	13	9	12	57	58	48
Larkhall Athletic	34	13	7	14	59	69	46
Clandown	34	10	12	12	54	58	42
Yeovil Town Reserves	34	11	7	16	52	55	40
Brixham United	34	9	8	17	45	77	35
Ottery St. Mary	34	8	10	16	41	61	34
Exmouth Town	34	9	7	18	40	68	34
Chard Town	34	8	9	17	43	63	33
Swanage Town & Herston	34	8	9	17	48	72	33
Ilminster Town	34	8	9	17	39	69	33
Heavitree United	34	4	10	20	23	56	22

Devizes Town had 1 point deducted for fielding an ineligible player. Taunton Town moved to the Southern League. Bristol Manor Farm (from the Somerset Senior League) and Odd Down joined Division One which increased to 19 clubs. Clevedon changed their name to Clevedon Town.

1977-78

(Goal difference replaced goal average to decide places for teams with an equal number of points)

Premier Division

Falmouth Town	34	26	5	3	98	30	83
Bideford	34	25	8	1	86	25	83
Barnstaple Town	34	18	10	6	75	37	64
Saltash United	34	17	7	10	66	53	58
Bridport	34	14	13	7	44	21	55
Clevedon Town	34	16	9	9	62	41	55
Frome Town	34	14	8	12	43	39	50
Paulton Rovers	34	15	5	14	55	52	50
Weston-super-Mare	34	14	8	12	44	48	50
Exeter City Reserves	34	11	13	10	48	41	46
Bridgwater Town	34	12	9	13	52	56	45
Tiverton Town	34	8	10	16	47	61	34
Shepton Mallet Town	34	9	6	19	52	93	33
Glastonbury	34	9	5	20	46	77	32
Mangotsfield United	34	7	10	17	50	75	31
Welton Rovers	34	8	6	20	34	68	30
Dawlish	34	6	10	18	39	67	28
St. Luke's College	34	1	10	23	20	78	13
					961	962	

Clevedon Town had 2 points deducted for fielding an ineligible player.

First Division

Keynsham Town	36	23	10	3	77	22	79
Clandown	36	22	4	10	77	36	70
Ilminster Town	36	21	6	9	69	47	69
Bristol Manor Farm	36	20	5	11	67	38	65
Devizes Town	36	20	5	11	73	52	65
Torquay United Reserves	36	18	5	13	69	53	59
Portway-Bristol	36	17	8	11	57	42	59
Melksham Town	36	17	7	12	76	60	58
Ottery St. Mary	36	16	7	13	55	55	55
Larkhall Athletic	36	15	8	13	58	66	53
Exmouth Town	36	13	7	16	41	55	46
Brixham United	36	11	9	16	61	79	41
Chard Town	36	12	5	19	56	81	41
Westland Yeovil	36	8	12	16	40	52	36
Odd Down	36	9	9	18	52	75	36
Yeovil Town Reserves	36	9	8	19	52	65	35
Heavitree United	36	9	5	22	32	64	32
Swanage Town & Herston	36	6	11	19	48	85	29
Chippenham Town	36	8	4	24	40	74	28
		274	135	275	1100	1101	956

Brixham United had 1 point deducted for fielding an ineligible player. St. Luke's College disbanded. AFC Bournemouth Reserves, Elmore (from the South-Western League) and Wellington joined. Premier Division increased to 20 clubs.

1978-79

Premier Division

Frome Town	38	21	12	5	60	29	75
Bideford	38	22	8	8	76	39	74
Saltash United	38	19	10	9	65	39	67
Barnstaple Town	38	18	10	10	65	35	64
Tiverton Town	38	17	9	12	71	60	60
Clandown	38	16	11	11	58	49	59
Weston-super-Mare	38	14	15	9	65	48	57
Falmouth Town	38	15	9	14	51	47	54
Paulton Rovers	38	15	9	14	40	48	54
Bridport	38	13	13	12	54	50	52
Bridgwater Town	38	14	9	15	57	53	51
Keynsham Town	38	13	12	13	47	57	51
Mangotsfield United	38	15	2	21	53	64	47
Ilminster Town	38	11	12	15	45	55	45
Welton Rovers	38	11	8	19	44	59	41
Exeter City Reserves	38	12	5	21	48	75	41
Clevedon Town	38	11	7	20	50	64	40
Dawlish	38	10	10	18	43	61	40
Shepton Mallet Town	38	10	10	18	48	74	40
Glastonbury	38	8	9	21	42	76	33

First Division

AFC Bournemouth Reserves	36	25	6	5	101	41	81
Portway-Bristol	36	23	5	8	81	43	74
Bristol Manor Farm	36	20	5	11	59	47	65
Chippenham Town	36	19	7	10	56	43	64
Torquay United Reserves	36	20	4	12	82	47	62
Melksham Town	36	18	4	14	58	57	58
Devizes Town	36	16	9	11	71	54	57
Wellington	36	18	3	15	48	46	57
Chard Town	36	15	6	15	57	58	51
Brixham United	36	15	5	16	55	61	50
Elmore	36	15	3	18	48	65	48
Ottery St. Mary	36	13	5	18	51	60	43
Larkhall Athletic	36	12	6	18	52	56	42
Westland Yeovil	36	11	9	16	43	53	42
Heavitree United	36	12	5	19	39	61	41
Swanage Town & Herston	36	11	6	19	51	60	39
Odd Down	36	10	5	21	38	71	35
Exmouth Town	36	8	9	19	41	72	33
Yeovil Town Reserves	36	5	10	21	30	65	24
					1061	1060	

Torquay United Reserves had 2 points deducted for fielding ineligible players. Ottery St. Mary and Yeovil Town Reserves had 1 point deducted for fielding ineligible players. Bath City Reserves, Liskeard Athletic (from the South-Western League) and Radstock Town (from the Somerset Senior League) joined. Division One increased to 22 clubs.

1979-80 (Two points for a win from this season)

Premier Division

Barnstaple Town	38	23	10	5	67	31	56
AFC Bournemouth Reserves	38	24	7	7	100	26	55
Weston-super-Mare	38	22	11	5	81	45	55
Frome Town	38	19	10	9	57	38	48
Bridgwater Town	38	17	12	9	64	43	46
Exeter City Reserves	38	16	11	11	71	59	43
Clevedon Town	38	16	10	12	74	58	42
Portway-Bristol	38	16	10	12	66	53	42
Saltash United	38	14	14	10	64	51	42
Bideford	38	16	10	12	61	51	42
Keynsham Town	38	16	10	12	56	53	42
Falmouth Town	38	14	10	14	58	53	38
Dawlish	38	10	11	17	39	67	31
Clandown	38	12	6	20	53	76	30
Tiverton Town	38	8	14	16	36	65	30
Welton Rovers	38	10	9	19	59	84	29
Paulton Rovers	38	11	6	21	50	68	28
Mangotsfield United	38	7	10	21	37	80	24
Bridport	38	4	14	20	31	67	21
Ilminster Town	38	2	11	25	31	87	15

Bridport had 1 point deducted for fielding an ineligible player.

First Division

Melksham Town	42	27	8	7	78	27	62
Devizes Town	42	25	9	8	91	42	59
Liskeard Athletic	42	23	10	9	70	31	56
Bath City Reserves	42	22	8	12	89	62	52
Exmouth Town	42	22	8	12	67	43	52
Torquay United Reserves	42	21	10	11	84	61	52
Elmore	42	20	9	13	63	45	49
Bristol Manor Farm	42	20	9	13	70	58	49
Ottery St. Mary	42	16	12	14	64	52	44
Glastonbury	42	16	11	15	60	68	43
Chippenham Town	42	16	10	16	58	62	42
Radstock Town	42	15	10	17	63	75	40
Shepton Mallet Town	42	15	9	18	75	78	39
Chard Town	42	14	11	17	51	59	39
Yeovil Town Reserves	42	14	10	18	71	85	38
Brixham United	42	14	9	19	60	70	37
Heavitree United	42	11	14	17	57	69	36
Larkhall Athletic	42	11	10	21	48	85	32
Odd Down	42	9	12	21	46	76	30
Wellington	42	8	13	21	38	59	29
Swanage Town & Herston	42	6	13	23	45	91	24
Westland Yeovil	42	5	9	28	31	81	19

Swanage Town & Herston had 1 point deducted for fielding an ineligible player. Westland Yeovil left and joined the Dorset Combination and AFC Bournemouth Reserves and Exeter City Reserves also left. First Division reduced to 19 clubs.

1980-81

Premier Division

Bridgwater Town	38	25	6	7	54	25	56
Barnstaple Town	38	22	6	10	58	40	50
Frome Town	38	21	6	11	74	51	48
Falmouth Town	38	18	9	11	71	53	45
Bideford	38	18	8	12	58	42	44
Saltash United	38	17	9	12	73	47	43
Portway-Bristol	38	16	11	11	55	45	43
Clevedon Town	38	15	11	12	65	52	41
Clandown	38	16	9	13	60	53	41
Devizes Town	38	14	13	11	61	56	41
Bridport	38	12	15	11	56	52	39
Keynsham Town	38	12	15	11	33	34	39
Melksham Town	38	13	11	14	45	49	37
Liskeard Athletic	38	11	11	16	58	70	33
Mangotsfield United	38	8	15	15	43	66	31
Dawlish Town	38	7	16	15	40	50	30
Welton Rovers	38	9	11	18	50	69	29
Weston-super-Mare	38	11	7	20	42	61	29
Paulton Rovers	38	9	11	18	45	72	29
Tiverton Town	38	1	10	27	23	77	12

First Division

Chippenham Town	36	25	8	3	76	24	58
Wellington	36	22	8	6	80	36	52
Exmouth Town	36	22	7	7	74	37	51
Bath City Reserves	36	19	11	6	79	44	49
Odd Down	36	20	8	8	59	41	47
Yeovil Town Reserves	36	18	9	9	58	38	45
Torquay United Reserves	36	16	11	9	60	35	43
Swanage Town & Herston	36	13	11	12	58	55	37
Chard Town	36	11	14	11	42	38	36
Bristol Manor Farm	36	14	8	14	53	57	36
Shepton Mallet Town	36	13	8	15	68	75	34
Elmore	36	12	10	14	44	53	34
Glastonbury	36	9	10	17	44	60	28
Brixham United	36	11	5	20	50	70	27
Larkhall Athletic	36	5	12	19	44	76	22
Ottery St. Mary	36	7	8	21	37	77	22
Heavitree United	36	7	8	21	40	86	22
Ilminster Town	36	7	6	23	39	70	20
Radstock Town	36	8	4	24	47	80	20

Odd Down had 1 point deducted for fielding an ineligible player.
Brixham United moved to the South Devon League and were replaced by Wimborne Town from the Dorset County League.

1981-82

Premier Division

Bideford	38	26	10	2	88	20	62
Barnstaple Town	38	26	8	4	78	31	59
Bridgwater Town	38	16	16	6	70	46	48
Clandown	38	17	12	9	49	37	46
Melksham Town	38	17	11	10	58	50	45
Frome Town	38	16	9	13	67	58	41
Weston-super-Mare	38	15	11	12	47	42	41
Saltash United	38	15	7	16	47	53	37
Devizes Town	38	14	7	17	53	60	35
Dawlish Town	38	11	13	14	45	53	35
Liskeard Athletic	38	11	12	15	39	48	34
Bridport	38	12	10	16	43	54	34
Clevedon Town	38	11	12	15	58	60	33
Chippenham Town	38	12	9	17	33	39	33
Falmouth Town	38	12	9	17	46	55	33
Portway-Bristol	38	9	13	16	40	47	31
Wellington	38	10	11	17	50	62	31
Keynsham Town	38	9	13	16	39	55	31
Mangotsfield United	38	11	6	21	30	59	28
Welton Rovers	38	7	7	24	37	88	21

Barnstaple Town and Clevedon Town both had 1 point deducted for fielding ineligible players.

First Division

Shepton Mallet Town	36	25	8	3	88	30	58
Exmouth Town	36	24	8	4	74	31	56
Swanage Town & Herston	36	21	5	10	90	47	47
Wimborne Town	36	19	9	8	67	35	47
Bath City Reserves	36	19	6	11	72	46	44
Elmore	36	19	6	11	58	45	44
Paulton Rovers	36	17	6	13	54	48	40
Bristol Manor Farm	36	15	9	12	58	50	39
Torquay United Reserves	36	15	9	12	50	44	39
Tiverton Town	36	13	8	15	62	63	34
Chard Town	36	12	10	14	43	55	34
Odd Down	36	14	5	17	51	57	33
Radstock Town	36	10	11	15	44	67	31
Glastonbury	36	12	6	18	63	69	30
Heavitree United	36	11	7	18	39	69	29
Yeovil Town Reserves	36	10	8	18	40	53	28
Larkhall Athletic	36	10	5	21	42	85	25
Ottery St. Mary	36	6	3	27	28	79	15
Ilminster Town	36	3	5	28	20	70	11

Bridgwater Town left and joined the Southern League and were replaced in the Premier Division by Plymouth Argyle Reserves from the Football Combination.
Ilminster Town left and joined the Somerset Senior League and Torquay United Reserves also left. They were replaced by Bristol City Reserves and Weymouth Reserves.

1982-83

Premier Division

Bideford	38	26	9	3	67	32	61
Frome Town	38	23	10	5	75	34	56
Dawlish Town	38	20	8	10	68	47	48
Clandown	38	19	9	10	54	39	46
Saltash United	38	14	18	6	50	39	46
Falmouth Town	38	16	13	9	63	57	45
Plymouth Argyle Reserves	38	15	14	9	67	41	44
Barnstaple Town	38	18	6	14	67	57	42
Liskeard Athletic	38	16	9	13	69	47	41
Weston-super-Mare	38	15	11	12	57	46	41
Shepton Mallet Town	38	15	4	19	50	55	34
Devizes Town	38	12	9	17	50	58	33
Chippenham Town	38	12	8	18	40	54	32
Clevedon Town	38	9	12	17	36	56	30
Bridport	38	8	13	17	49	60	29
Exmouth Town	38	10	9	19	40	59	29
Melksham Town	38	8	13	17	43	63	29
Wellington	38	8	12	18	46	74	28
Keynsham Town	38	7	11	20	32	68	25
Portway-Bristol	38	8	4	26	35	72	20

First Division

Bristol Manor Farm	36	26	7	3	85	31	59
Mangotsfield United	36	24	8	4	75	32	56
Paulton Rovers	36	20	12	4	75	37	52
Odd Down	36	19	9	8	56	41	47
Glastonbury	36	15	15	6	69	47	45
Swanage Town & Herston	36	21	1	14	83	54	43
Wimborne Town	36	17	9	10	74	51	43
Bath City Reserves	36	14	9	13	64	49	37
Chard Town	36	15	5	16	54	50	35
Weymouth Reserves	36	12	8	16	43	56	32
Welton Rovers	36	12	8	16	46	61	32
Yeovil Town Reserves	36	14	3	19	49	55	31
Bristol City Reserves	36	9	11	16	57	77	29
Elmore	36	12	4	20	48	65	28
Heavitree United	36	11	5	20	40	66	27
Larkhall Athletic	36	9	8	19	40	64	26
Radstock Town	36	9	6	21	50	79	24
Tiverton Town	36	8	5	23	42	85	21
Ottery St. Mary	36	8	1	27	35	85	17

Bridport left and joined the Dorset Combination and Falmouth Town left and joined the Cornwall Combination. They were replaced in the Premier Division by Minehead and Taunton Town, both from the Southern League. Backwell United (from the Somerset Senior League) and Warminster Town (from the Wiltshire County League) joined the First Division which increased to 21 clubs.

1983-84

Premier Division

Exmouth Town	38	21	11	6	59	35	53
Saltash United	38	22	7	9	72	39	51
Barnstaple Town	38	21	9	8	68	40	51
Frome Town	38	20	10	8	78	35	50
Liskeard Athletic	38	18	9	11	64	38	45
Bideford	38	16	10	12	71	49	42
Clevedon Town	38	16	8	14	55	56	40
Bristol Manor Farm	38	14	11	13	54	42	39
Plymouth Argyle Reserves	38	16	8	14	68	58	38
Minehead	38	15	7	16	55	68	37
Shepton Mallet Town	38	14	9	15	55	74	37
Taunton Town	38	10	15	13	46	52	35
Mangotsfield United	38	12	10	16	47	48	34
Dawlish Town	38	13	8	17	38	43	34
Weston-super-Mare	38	13	8	17	46	54	34
Chippenham Town	38	13	8	17	44	56	34
Clandown	38	12	10	16	34	51	34
Melksham Town	38	9	11	18	49	66	29
Devizes Town	38	7	11	20	41	74	25
Wellington	38	4	8	26	29	95	16

Plymouth Argyle Reserves had 2 points deducted for fielding ineligible players.

First Division

Bristol City Reserves	40	26	8	6	96	36	60
Chard Town	40	22	8	10	82	44	52
Paulton Rovers	40	20	12	8	74	46	52
Swanage Town & Herston	40	19	12	9	89	61	50
Keynsham Town	40	19	11	10	50	36	49
Backwell United	40	18	13	9	47	42	49
Glastonbury	40	15	9	16	68	61	39
Welton Rovers	40	13	13	14	49	56	39
Portway-Bristol	40	13	12	15	57	49	38
Wimborne Town	40	14	10	16	51	60	38
Bath City Reserves	40	13	11	16	61	57	37
Warminster Town	40	15	7	18	61	67	37
Odd Down	40	12	13	15	60	66	37
Larkhall Athletic	40	12	12	16	50	55	36
Radstock Town	40	13	10	17	51	63	36
Heavitree United	40	14	8	18	66	80	36
Yeovil Town Reserves	40	11	13	16	65	72	35
Ottery St. Mary	40	14	7	19	42	58	35
Elmore	40	11	12	17	47	78	34
Weymouth Reserves	40	12	7	21	43	64	31
Tiverton Town	40	5	10	25	37	95	20

Ilfracombe Town (from the North Devon League), Torrington (South-Western League) and Westbury United (Wiltshire County League) joined. Both divisions increased to 22 clubs.

1984-85

Premier Division

Saltash United	42	26	12	4	88	43	64
Bideford	42	26	8	8	78	29	60
Bristol City Reserves	42	21	14	7	69	49	56
Exmouth Town	42	22	8	12	83	51	52
Paulton Rovers	42	20	11	11	61	45	51
Bristol Manor Farm	42	21	7	14	70	55	49
Chippenham Town	42	16	14	12	62	49	46
Mangotsfield United	42	17	11	14	63	56	45
Melksham Town	42	17	11	14	57	59	45
Liskeard Athletic	42	17	10	15	69	54	44
Chard Town	42	15	13	14	58	57	43
Minehead	42	16	9	17	55	54	41
Barnstaple Town	42	18	5	19	65	65	41
Clandown	42	14	12	16	51	52	40
Plymouth Argyle Reserves	42	12	14	16	58	62	38
Dawlish Town	42	12	13	17	44	54	37
Clevedon Town	42	12	12	18	45	56	35
Frome Town	42	10	14	18	56	63	34
Weston-super-Mare	42	11	11	20	58	78	33
Taunton Town	42	11	11	20	53	74	33
Shepton Mallet Town	42	4	15	23	35	86	22
Devizes Town	42	2	9	31	34	121	13

Clevedon Town and Shepton Mallet Town both had 1 point deducted for fielding ineligible players.

First Division

Portway-Bristol	42	30	3	9	97	42	63
Torrington	42	27	8	7	83	35	62
Wimborne Town	42	26	7	9	81	37	59
Swanage Town & Herston	42	23	13	6	86	50	59
Wellington	42	20	12	10	78	57	52
Radstock Town	42	23	5	14	79	47	51
Backwell United	42	21	9	12	59	42	51
Keynsham Town	42	20	9	13	70	54	49
Ottery St. Mary	42	17	14	11	58	51	48
Larkhall Athletic	42	18	7	17	51	46	43
Heavitree United	42	14	11	17	81	84	39
Glastonbury	42	14	11	17	55	63	39
Bath City Reserves	42	16	7	19	60	69	39
Elmore	42	16	6	20	69	95	38
Yeovil Town Reserves	42	14	10	18	53	63	37
Welton Rovers	42	14	9	19	61	72	37
Tiverton Town	42	11	12	19	61	66	34
Weymouth Reserves	42	14	3	25	67	96	31
Warminster Town	42	8	13	21	54	93	29
Westbury United	42	10	7	25	57	99	27
Ilfracombe Town	42	6	7	29	47	101	19
Odd Down	42	5	7	30	38	83	17

Yeovil Town reserved had 1 point deducted for an fielding ineligible player. Torrington were the club promoted this season.

1985-86

Premier Division

Exmouth Town	42	30	9	3	95	31	69
Liskeard Athletic	42	31	6	5	103	34	68
Bideford	42	27	8	7	97	27	62
Saltash United	42	21	13	8	78	46	55
Chippenham Town	42	21	10	11	60	45	52
Mangotsfield United	42	18	13	11	87	58	49
Taunton Town	42	19	9	14	59	54	47
Dawlish Town	42	19	8	15	53	49	45
Bristol City Reserves	42	18	6	18	74	61	42
Clevedon Town	42	12	18	12	55	47	42
Bristol Manor Farm	42	16	9	17	71	73	41
Minehead	42	16	9	17	55	70	41
Frome Town	42	14	12	16	49	62	39
Clandown	42	15	8	19	46	57	38
Torrington	42	13	11	18	51	62	37
Melksham Town	42	11	13	18	50	77	35
Barnstaple Town	42	13	7	22	46	68	33
Weston-super-Mare	42	12	8	22	69	90	32
Paulton Rovers	42	9	12	21	50	82	30
Plymouth Argyle Reserves	42	9	11	22	60	67	29
Chard Town	42	8	4	30	35	109	20
Shepton Mallet Town	42	4	8	30	36	110	15

Dawlish Town, Frome Town and Shepton Mallet Town all had 1 point deducted for fielding ineligible players.

First Division

Portway-Bristol	42	27	9	6	100	42	63
Radstock Town	42	26	9	7	116	54	61
Yeovil Town Reserves	42	25	7	10	79	36	56
Wimborne Town	42	18	13	11	77	51	49
Larkhall Athletic	42	18	11	13	72	56	47
Backwell United	42	19	9	14	63	47	47
Ottery St. Mary	42	18	11	13	61	60	47
Swanage Town & Herston	42	18	9	15	91	79	45
Weymouth Reserves	42	18	8	16	84	78	44
Heavitree United	42	17	10	15	60	69	44
Bath City Reserves	42	16	10	16	74	69	42
Wellington	42	14	12	16	70	70	40
Tiverton Town	42	16	7	19	68	74	39
Devizes Town	42	10	18	14	43	58	38
Elmore	42	12	13	17	56	78	37
Keynsham Town	42	9	18	15	37	53	36
Welton Rovers	42	13	9	20	61	84	35
Glastonbury	42	12	11	19	52	79	35
Ilfracombe Town	42	10	14	18	55	69	34
Westbury United	42	10	10	22	55	82	30
Odd Down	42	9	12	21	57	90	30
Warminster Town	42	9	6	27	40	93	24

Yeovil Town Reserves had 1 point deducted for fielding an ineligible player.   Radstock Town were the promoted club this season.
Shepton Mallet Town moved to the Somerset Premier League. Calne Town joined from the Wiltshire County League.

1986-87

Premier Division

Saltash United	42	31	8	3	101	40	70
Exmouth Town	42	22	10	10	82	62	54
Bristol City Reserves	42	23	5	14	94	57	51
Liskeard Athletic	42	20	9	13	69	45	49
Bristol Manor Farm	42	19	10	13	58	46	48
Bideford	42	21	4	17	58	57	46
Plymouth Argyle Reserves	42	21	4	17	92	55	45
Taunton Town	42	17	9	16	61	64	43
Chippenham Town	42	14	14	14	53	50	42
Mangotsfield United	42	17	8	17	69	71	42
Barnstaple Town	42	15	12	15	55	66	42
Clevedon Town	42	14	13	15	58	60	41
Weston-super-Mare	42	13	13	16	66	70	39
Dawlish Town	42	14	10	18	63	62	38
Torrington	42	14	10	18	61	71	38
Paulton Rovers	42	14	8	20	55	72	36
Radstock Town	42	11	13	18	55	73	35
Melksham Town	42	10	15	17	39	64	35
Frome Town	42	12	10	20	50	65	34
Clandown	42	12	10	20	40	59	34
Minehead	42	10	12	20	53	86	32
Chard Town	42	11	7	24	52	89	29

Plymouth Argyle Reserves had 1 point deducted for fielding an ineligible player.

First Division

Swanage Town & Herston	42	25	12	5	93	52	62
Portway-Bristol	42	25	8	9	103	51	58
Bath City Reserves	42	25	6	11	85	58	56
Yeovil Town Reserves	42	21	10	11	85	53	52
Wimborne Town	42	23	6	13	96	58	51
Devizes Town	42	21	10	11	62	43	51
Larkhall Athletic	42	21	8	13	71	53	50
Welton Rovers	42	20	6	16	66	53	46
Backwell United	42	15	15	12	55	53	45
Warminster Town	42	18	10	14	72	71	45
Ottery St. Mary	42	17	6	19	66	68	40
Odd Down	42	13	13	16	57	65	39
Keynsham Town	42	16	7	19	57	69	39
Elmore	42	14	10	18	60	69	38
Tiverton Town	42	12	12	18	66	79	36
Weymouth Reserves	42	12	12	18	75	87	35
Wellington	42	14	7	21	55	67	35
Westbury United	42	10	12	20	78	87	34
Calne Town	42	11	12	19	54	73	34
Ilfracombe Town	42	11	8	23	40	68	30
Heavitree United	42	9	9	24	48	96	26
Glastonbury	42	5	7	30	38	109	17

Wimborne Town, Devizes Town, Warminster Town, Weymouth Reserves and Heavitree United had 1 point deducted for fielding ineligible players. Portway-Bristol disbanded, Wimborne Town left and joined the Wessex League and Weymouth Reserves also left.

1987-88

Premier Division

Liskeard Athletic	42	29	10	3	98	33	68
Saltash United	42	27	6	9	116	41	60
Mangotsfield United	42	25	10	7	99	38	60
Plymouth Argyle Reserves	42	26	8	8	105	46	60
Weston-super-Mare	42	21	8	13	81	62	50
Exmouth Town	42	19	10	13	61	55	48
Bristol City Reserves	42	16	15	11	76	53	47
Bristol Manor Farm	42	17	14	11	66	52	47
Taunton Town	42	15	15	12	49	48	45
Bideford	42	17	9	16	60	61	43
Swanage Town & Herston	42	16	10	16	73	63	42
Barnstaple Town	42	17	6	19	62	72	40
Clevedon Town	42	13	12	17	42	56	38
Paulton Rovers	42	13	10	19	46	72	36
Dawlish Town	42	14	6	22	49	77	34
Radstock Town	42	13	9	20	44	57	33
Torrington	42	12	7	23	49	83	31
Frome Town	42	9	13	20	36	69	30
Minehead	42	10	10	22	47	87	30
Chippenham Town	42	10	8	24	35	62	28
Melksham Town	42	7	14	21	45	84	28
Clandown	42	5	12	25	33	102	22
					1372	1373	

Bristol Manor Farm and Frome Town both had 1 point deducted and Radstock Town had 2 points deducted for fielding ineligible players.

First Division

Welton Rovers	36	21	12	3	74	36	54
Chard Town	36	21	11	4	75	41	53
Tiverton Town	36	21	7	8	82	46	49
Bath City Reserves	36	18	11	7	61	46	47
Larkhall Athletic	36	17	8	11	72	49	42
Devizes Town	36	15	9	12	44	38	39
Keynsham Town	36	16	7	13	53	54	39
Westbury United	36	15	7	14	61	56	37
Ottery St. Mary	36	16	5	15	43	41	37
Backwell United	36	11	13	12	49	52	35
Warminster Town	36	15	5	16	46	55	35
Wellington	36	14	6	16	60	67	34
Calne Town	36	11	10	15	45	59	32
Odd Down	36	10	11	15	51	62	31
Ilfracombe Town	36	11	7	18	45	59	29
Heavitree United	36	11	6	19	49	62	28
Yeovil Town Reserves	36	7	11	18	39	57	25
Elmore	36	7	6	23	46	81	20
Glastonbury	36	5	8	23	39	73	18

Bristol City Reserves left. Bridport joined from the Dorset Combination. Premier Division reduced to 21 clubs and First Division increased to 20 clubs.

1988-89

Premier Division

Saltash United	40	26	10	4	90	35	62
Exmouth Town	40	29	4	7	79	43	62
Taunton Town	40	23	10	7	95	41	56
Liskeard Athletic	40	20	12	8	46	25	52
Plymouth Argyle Reserves	40	19	13	8	84	39	51
Bristol Manor Farm	40	20	7	13	72	49	47
Weston-super-Mare	40	17	8	15	73	52	42
Paulton Rovers	40	14	14	12	60	53	42
Barnstaple Town	40	17	7	16	61	54	41
Swanage Town & Herston	40	15	10	15	71	73	40
Clevedon Town	40	16	7	17	63	70	39
Chippenham Town	40	11	14	15	48	52	36
Welton Rovers	40	13	10	17	50	57	36
Radstock Town	40	9	18	13	38	65	36
Chard Town	40	12	11	17	49	78	35
Bideford	40	12	9	19	49	72	33
Frome Town	40	11	10	19	54	80	32
Mangotsfield United	40	10	9	21	53	74	29
Dawlish Town	40	11	7	22	48	69	29
Torrington	40	7	12	21	46	84	26
Minehead	40	5	4	31	30	94	14

First Division

Larkhall Athletic	38	25	11	2	88	40	61
Tiverton Town	38	27	6	5	108	33	60
Bridport	38	24	7	7	90	35	55
Calne Town	38	17	14	7	58	34	48
Devizes Town	38	19	9	10	55	39	47
Odd Down	38	17	12	9	57	45	46
Wellington	38	17	11	10	72	56	45
Ilfracombe Town	38	16	13	9	59	47	45
Backwell United	38	15	8	15	49	46	38
Keynsham Town	38	11	13	14	55	55	35
Heavitree United	38	13	9	16	54	58	35
Melksham Town	38	11	13	14	43	49	35
Ottery St. Mary	38	12	8	18	46	71	32
Clandown	38	10	11	17	47	63	31
Bath City Reserves	38	11	7	20	60	67	29
Westbury United	38	10	9	19	59	66	29
Yeovil Town Reserves	38	10	9	19	42	49	29
Warminster Town	38	5	11	22	34	84	21
Glastonbury	38	6	9	23	38	97	21
Elmore	38	8	2	28	38	118	18

Tiverton Town were the club promoted this season.

1989-90 (Three points for a win from this season)

Premier Division

Taunton Town	40	28	8	4	80	41	92
Liskeard Athletic	40	28	7	5	91	30	91
Mangotsfield United	40	27	7	6	96	42	88
Tiverton Town	40	26	6	8	92	51	84
Exmouth Town	40	24	5	11	74	37	77
Weston-super-Mare	40	20	8	12	86	56	68
Plymouth Argyle Reserves	40	19	10	11	75	47	67
Saltash United	40	19	9	12	62	41	66
Swanage Town & Herston	40	18	7	15	77	67	61
Clevedon Town	40	16	8	16	58	60	56
Paulton Rovers	40	16	7	17	51	52	55
Bristol Manor Farm	40	13	12	15	49	59	51
Chippenham Town	40	14	7	19	36	46	49
Dawlish Town	40	12	7	21	55	78	43
Chard Town	40	8	14	18	50	74	38
Bideford	40	8	14	18	37	76	38
Torrington	40	8	11	21	48	74	35
Barnstaple Town	40	8	10	22	38	75	34
Radstock Town	40	7	12	21	43	82	33
Frome Town	40	4	14	22	43	77	26
Welton Rovers	40	3	5	32	30	106	14

First Division

Ottery St. Mary	38	27	4	7	72	36	85
Backwell United	38	21	10	7	63	32	73
Ilfracombe Town	38	20	11	7	67	38	71
Bridport	38	20	8	10	69	46	68
Odd Down	38	20	6	12	53	44	66
Larkhall Athletic	38	19	8	11	73	57	65
Westbury United	38	17	8	13	66	55	59
Keynsham Town	38	15	11	12	57	46	56
Melksham Town	38	16	7	15	46	41	55
Devizes Town	38	14	12	12	38	44	54
Heavitree United	38	15	8	15	53	44	53
Calne Town	38	14	11	13	52	45	53
Clandown	38	14	8	16	45	45	50
Elmore	38	14	5	19	46	60	47
Warminster Town	38	10	12	16	43	54	42
Yeovil Town Reserves	38	9	9	20	46	67	36
Wellington	38	7	13	18	40	60	34
Bath City Reserves	38	9	4	25	37	82	31
Glastonbury	38	7	7	24	35	72	28
Minehead	38	5	12	21	29	62	27

Swanage Town & Herston left and joined the Wessex League. Crediton United joined from the Devon & Exeter League and Torquay United Reserves also joined. First Division increased to 21 clubs.

1990-91

Premier Division

Mangotsfield United	40	28	8	4	113	39	92
Torrington	40	25	7	8	91	41	82
Plymouth Argyle Reserves	40	25	8	7	100	28	81
Tiverton Town	40	22	11	7	85	45	77
Weston-super-Mare	40	20	10	10	74	57	70
Saltash United	40	20	6	14	67	46	66
Taunton Town	40	18	9	13	62	49	63
Liskeard Athletic	40	18	7	15	85	69	61
Dawlish Town	40	15	16	9	58	49	61
Paulton Rovers	40	16	11	13	74	60	59
Clevedon Town	40	16	10	14	52	55	58
Bideford	40	13	10	17	61	76	49
Frome Town	40	14	6	20	56	78	48
Bristol Manor Farm	40	12	9	19	52	66	45
Welton Rovers	40	11	11	18	40	61	44
Chard Town	40	11	10	19	48	86	43
Chippenham Town	40	10	12	18	42	64	42
Ottery St. Mary	40	11	4	25	43	88	37
Exmouth Town	40	9	8	23	59	93	35
Barnstaple Town	40	8	10	22	44	86	34
Radstock Town	40	4	5	31	46	116	17

Plymouth Argyle Reserves had 2 points deducted for fielding ineligible players.

First Division

Minehead	40	28	9	3	102	42	93
Elmore	40	24	6	10	89	47	78
Calne Town	40	25	2	13	85	55	77
Odd Down	40	22	10	8	59	36	76
Westbury United	40	21	9	10	60	44	72
Bridport	40	18	11	11	65	48	65
Torquay United Reserves	40	17	10	13	62	52	61
Devizes Town	40	17	10	13	68	66	61
Ilfracombe Town	40	15	12	13	62	54	57
Crediton United	40	14	13	13	55	48	55
Wellington	40	15	10	15	58	55	55
Bath City Reserves	40	14	11	15	67	64	53
Keynsham Town	40	14	9	17	59	58	51
Clandown	40	14	8	18	43	71	50
Melksham Town	40	13	10	17	54	60	49
Backwell United	40	11	9	20	56	70	42
Yeovil Town Reserves	40	10	6	24	59	91	36
Warminster Town	40	9	9	22	39	74	36
Larkhall Athletic	40	9	8	23	38	70	35
Heavitree United	40	6	12	22	32	81	30
Glastonbury	40	5	14	21	39	65	29

Yeovil Town Reserves left. Bishop Sutton and Brislington both joined from the Somerset Senior League. First Division increased to 22 clubs.

1991-92

Premier Division

Weston-super-Mare	40	32	2	6	110	44	98
Clevedon Town	40	28	5	7	90	28	89
Tiverton Town	40	27	5	8	106	47	85
Bideford	40	25	9	6	102	49	84
Saltash United	40	24	5	11	89	51	77
Plymouth Argyle Reserves	40	24	4	12	89	52	76
Taunton Town	40	17	11	12	88	56	62
Mangotsfield United	40	16	13	11	53	39	61
Elmore	40	17	10	13	76	72	61
Paulton Rovers	40	16	11	13	71	60	59
Minehead	40	16	10	14	65	74	58
Liskeard Athletic	40	14	10	16	68	69	52
Dawlish Town	40	15	5	20	77	76	50
Chippenham Town	40	13	7	20	58	95	46
Torrington	40	11	10	19	48	62	43
Bristol Manor Farm	40	10	10	20	42	66	40
Exmouth Town	40	10	8	22	56	97	38
Chard Town	40	8	8	24	48	76	32
Frome Town	40	9	5	26	44	91	32
Welton Rovers	40	8	6	26	32	78	30
Ottery St. Mary	40	2	2	36	26	156	8

Tiverton Town had 1 point deducted for fielding an ineligible player.

First Division

Westbury United	42	27	10	5	80	39	91
Torquay United Reserves	42	26	11	5	96	32	89
Crediton United	42	20	12	10	57	32	72
Bath City Reserves	42	22	6	14	91	68	72
Warminster Town	42	19	13	10	80	49	70
Keynsham Town	42	19	13	10	80	69	70
Calne Town	42	20	9	13	73	49	69
Brislington	42	21	6	15	70	51	69
Bridport	42	17	16	9	61	50	67
Ilfracombe Town	42	17	14	11	76	44	65
Odd Down	42	20	5	17	58	46	65
Backwell United	42	17	10	15	64	49	61
Bishop Sutton	42	17	10	15	58	50	61
Glastonbury	42	14	8	20	52	61	50
Larkhall Athletic	42	12	12	18	58	65	48
Radstock Town	42	11	14	17	65	68	47
Barnstaple Town	42	12	8	22	42	55	44
Clandown	42	10	13	19	56	72	43
Wellington	42	9	11	22	42	70	38
Devizes Town	42	8	13	21	57	84	37
Melksham Town	42	8	12	22	44	77	36
Heavitree United	42	2	2	38	26	206	8

Weston-super-Mare left and joined the Southern League, Clandown left and joined the Somerset Senior League and Bath City Reserves also left. Clyst Rovers joined from the South-Western League. Premier Division reduced to 20 clubs, First Division reduced to 21 clubs.

1992-93

Premier Division

Clevedon Town	38	34	4	0	137	23	106
Tiverton Town	38	28	8	2	134	30	92
Saltash United	38	22	8	8	98	51	74
Taunton Town	38	22	8	8	62	37	74
Mangotsfield United	38	20	8	10	89	47	68
Torrington	38	17	10	11	69	44	61
Westbury United	38	18	7	13	50	45	61
Paulton Rovers	38	15	10	13	76	51	55
Torquay United Reserves	38	16	7	15	58	62	55
Plymouth Argyle Reserves	38	15	9	14	72	64	54
Exmouth Town	38	14	9	15	47	59	51
Elmore	38	14	5	19	54	71	47
Bristol Manor Farm	38	10	13	15	49	59	43
Bideford	38	11	8	19	59	66	41
Frome Town	38	9	12	17	57	75	39
Chippenham Town	38	8	14	16	65	86	38
Minehead	38	10	8	20	59	88	38
Liskeard Athletic	38	8	9	21	61	87	33
Chard Town	38	6	3	29	37	119	21
Dawlish Town	38	2	2	34	17	186	8

First Division

Odd Down	40	27	10	3	87	26	91
Calne Town	40	23	12	5	97	47	81
Crediton United	40	23	11	6	79	43	80
Brislington	40	22	8	10	77	41	74
Warminster Town	40	22	7	11	70	50	73
Clyst Rovers	40	18	13	9	75	48	67
Keynsham Town	40	19	10	11	66	50	67
Backwell United	40	16	14	10	68	52	62
Barnstaple Town	40	15	10	15	62	58	55
Bridport	40	14	13	13	67	66	55
Heavitree United	40	14	9	17	64	69	51
Devizes Town	40	15	6	19	61	84	51
Bishop Sutton	40	14	8	18	55	55	50
Welton Rovers	40	12	11	17	69	65	47
Wellington	40	11	14	15	53	65	47
Glastonbury	40	13	5	22	52	70	44
Larkhall Athletic	40	11	5	24	59	81	38
Ilfracombe Town	40	8	9	23	47	94	33
Ottery St. Mary	40	9	5	26	53	116	32
Radstock Town	40	7	10	23	38	60	31
Melksham Town	40	6	12	22	39	98	30

Clevedon Town left and joined the Southern League, Melksham Town left and joined the Wiltshire County League and Plymouth Argyle Reserves and Torquay United Reserves also left. Pewsey Vale joined from the Wiltshire County League. Premier Division reduced to 18 clubs, First Division reduced to 20 clubs.

1993-94

Premier Division

Tiverton Town	34	31	3	0	125	22	96
Taunton Town	34	26	2	6	98	38	80
Mangotsfield United	34	19	6	9	75	40	63
Paulton Rovers	34	18	7	9	55	42	61
Saltash United	34	18	6	10	67	36	60
Torrington	34	16	10	8	66	46	58
Liskeard Athletic	34	16	5	13	66	50	53
Chippenham Town	34	14	7	13	58	51	49
Bideford	34	13	8	13	58	69	44
Odd Down Athletic	34	10	12	12	59	58	42
Crediton United	34	10	8	16	42	65	38
Westbury United	34	9	9	16	40	61	36
Bristol Manor Farm	34	11	3	20	51	71	36
Calne Town	34	8	9	17	50	76	33
Frome Town	34	9	6	19	33	61	33
Elmore	34	8	8	18	51	83	32
Exmouth Town	34	6	4	24	35	93	22
Minehead	34	6	3	25	38	105	15

Bideford had 3 points deducted and Minehead had 6 points deducted for fielding ineligible players.

First Division

Barnstaple Town	38	27	8	3	107	39	89
Bridport	38	24	7	7	90	46	79
Brislington	38	23	8	7	73	35	77
Pewsey Vale	38	20	11	7	84	47	71
Keynsham Town	38	21	7	10	80	50	70
Clyst Rovers	38	16	15	7	68	50	63
Backwell United	38	18	8	12	64	45	62
Welton Rovers	38	16	10	12	73	53	58
Devizes Town	38	16	10	12	64	61	58
Chard Town	38	16	9	13	48	51	57
Ilfracombe Town	38	16	8	14	70	42	56
Bishop Sutton	38	12	14	12	58	48	50
Glastonbury	38	14	8	16	68	66	50
Larkhall Athletic	38	12	7	19	52	69	43
Warminster Town	38	8	11	19	47	57	35
Wellington	38	9	6	23	51	92	33
Dawlish Town	38	9	5	24	46	125	32
Heavitree United	38	8	7	23	47	90	31
Radstock Town	38	8	6	24	44	73	30
Ottery St. Mary	38	2	5	31	37	132	11

Ottery St. Mary left and joined the Devon County League and Radstock Town left and joined the Somerset Senior League. Amesbury Town and Melksham Town joined from the Wiltshire League and Bridgwater Town joined from the Somerset Senior League. First Division increased to 21 clubs.

1994-95

Premier Division

Tiverton Town	34	28	3	3	128	23	87
Elmore	34	27	5	2	94	39	86
Taunton Town	34	15	12	7	59	28	57
Barnstaple Town	34	16	8	10	58	48	56
Westbury United	34	16	6	12	71	53	54
Mangotsfield United	34	16	6	12	51	50	54
Paulton Rovers	34	15	7	12	62	71	52
Chippenham Town	34	14	9	11	54	54	51
Bristol Manor Farm	34	14	6	14	51	48	48
Liskeard Athletic	34	12	9	13	59	55	45
Saltash United	34	12	9	13	38	43	45
Odd Down Athletic	34	11	9	14	47	53	42
Bridport	34	11	6	17	44	59	39
Calne Town	34	11	3	20	36	68	36
Bideford	34	10	5	19	48	69	35
Crediton United	34	8	6	20	43	77	30
Torrington	34	6	10	18	49	89	28
Frome Town	34	3	3	28	36	101	12

First Division

Brislington	40	30	7	3	113	25	97
Glastonbury	40	26	8	6	91	35	86
Backwell United	40	26	8	6	75	33	86
Warminster Town	40	26	7	7	93	42	85
Chard Town	40	25	10	5	74	35	85
Bridgwater Town	40	18	13	9	62	47	67
Keynsham Town	40	17	11	12	73	62	62
Bishop Sutton	40	17	7	16	61	61	58
Exmouth Town	40	16	6	18	55	63	54
Melksham Town	40	14	10	16	62	61	52
Clyst Rovers	40	15	5	20	60	84	50
Amesbury Town	40	14	7	19	67	61	49
Wellington	40	14	7	19	55	59	49
Ilfracombe Town	40	13	8	19	64	58	47
Heavitree United	40	12	7	21	52	94	43
Welton Rovers	40	11	9	20	50	62	42
Devizes Town	40	11	7	22	57	82	40
Pewsey Vale	40	10	8	22	52	77	38
Larkhall Athletic	40	8	8	24	39	89	32
Dawlish Town	40	8	8	24	41	92	32
Minehead	40	5	7	28	24	98	22

Brislington and Backwell United were the two clubs promoted from the First Division. Liskeard Athletic and Saltash United left and joined the South-Western League. First Division reduced to 19 clubs.

1995-96

Premier Division

Taunton Town	34	25	7	2	84	20	82
Tiverton Town	34	25	4	5	101	34	79
Mangotsfield United	34	22	7	5	88	23	73
Torrington	34	23	4	7	64	37	73
Brislington	34	16	6	12	60	41	54
Bideford	34	16	7	11	63	47	55
Backwell United	34	15	7	12	54	46	52
Paulton Rovers	34	14	10	10	59	53	52
Calne Town	34	14	9	11	41	40	51
Chippenham Town	34	11	12	11	53	41	45
Bridport	34	13	5	16	51	60	44
Bristol Manor Farm	34	11	6	17	55	69	39
Westbury United	34	9	9	16	39	53	36
Barnstaple Town	34	10	6	18	61	78	36
Odd Down Athletic	34	6	6	22	39	77	24
Elmore	34	6	6	22	30	91	24
Frome Town	34	5	7	22	30	84	22
Crediton United	34	3	6	25	18	96	15

First Division

Bridgwater Town	36	29	3	4	93	29	90
Chard Town	36	28	6	2	65	17	90
Keynsham Town	36	22	7	7	69	35	73
Bishop Sutton	36	18	9	9	48	36	63
Clyst Rovers	36	18	7	11	74	52	61
Welton Rovers	36	15	11	10	52	43	56
Devizes Town	36	15	10	11	61	50	55
Dawlish Town	36	14	9	13	56	53	51
Melksham Town	36	13	11	12	59	54	50
Warminster Town	36	14	6	16	51	57	48
Glastonbury	36	12	10	14	45	54	46
Wellington	36	12	8	16	47	52	44
Pewsey Vale	36	10	6	20	34	71	36
Heavitree United	36	9	8	19	64	81	35
Larkhall Athletic	36	10	4	22	50	78	34
Amesbury Town	36	7	10	19	37	67	31
Minehead	36	8	7	21	41	73	31
Exmouth Town	36	9	3	24	44	67	30
Ilfracombe Town	36	6	11	19	43	64	29

Yeovil Town Reserves joined. First Division increased to 20 clubs.

1996-97

Premier Division

Tiverton Town	34	31	1	2	103	20	94
Taunton Town	34	24	6	4	99	28	78
Mangotsfield United	34	19	8	7	75	44	65
Paulton Rovers	34	17	10	7	86	42	61
Chippenham Town	34	12	12	10	58	52	48
Brislington	34	12	9	13	53	48	45
Calne Town	34	13	6	15	55	52	45
Torrington	34	11	11	12	54	54	44
Bridgwater Town	34	12	8	14	53	55	44
Bridport	34	11	10	13	41	50	43
Odd Down	34	11	15	8	42	46	39
Bideford	34	11	6	17	51	84	39
Barnstaple Town	34	10	8	16	54	62	38
Bristol Manor Farm	34	9	10	15	40	60	37
Backwell United	34	9	9	16	42	55	36
Chard Town	34	9	7	18	45	67	34
Westbury United	34	8	6	20	40	70	30
Elmore	34	4	4	26	30	132	16

Odd Down had 9 points for fielding ineligible players.

First Division

Melksham Town	38	27	8	3	82	20	89
Keynsham Town	38	27	7	4	77	21	88
Exmouth Town	38	23	7	8	77	42	76
Clyst Rovers	38	23	6	9	92	48	75
Bishop Sutton	38	21	7	10	96	52	70
Wellington	38	21	5	12	82	62	68
Devizes Town	38	18	11	9	75	39	65
Dawlish Town	38	18	9	11	66	36	63
Ilfracombe Town	38	15	12	11	62	44	57
Welton Rovers	38	15	7	16	68	59	52
Minehead	38	16	4	18	61	56	52
Frome Town	38	12	11	15	45	60	47
Yeovil Town Reserves	38	12	8	18	66	77	44
Glastonbury	38	12	7	19	54	72	43
Crediton United	38	12	4	22	58	91	40
Warminster Town	38	9	8	21	44	75	35
Larkhall Athletic	38	7	13	18	51	92	34
Heavitree United	38	7	11	20	44	95	32
Pewsey Vale	38	5	4	29	26	105	19
Amesbury Town	38	1	9	28	27	107	12

Amesbury Town left but Bitton joined from the Gloucestershire County League and Street joined from the Somerset Senior League. Premier Division increased to 20 clubs and First Division reduced to 19 clubs.

1997-98

Premier Division

Tiverton Town	38	36	2	0	154	20	110
Taunton Town	38	31	3	4	107	28	96
Melksham Town	38	22	7	9	75	37	73
Bridgwater Town	38	22	6	10	73	43	72
Paulton Rovers	38	19	6	13	76	69	63
Mangotsfield United	38	18	8	12	76	50	62
Barnstaple Town	38	18	5	15	79	64	59
Brislington	38	17	8	13	62	55	59
Calne Town	38	16	9	13	68	67	57
Backwell United	38	15	7	16	70	68	52
Bridport	38	16	4	18	62	72	52
Chippenham Town	38	13	11	14	53	57	50
Bideford	38	14	6	18	68	90	48
Elmore	38	10	8	20	54	100	38
Westbury United	38	9	8	21	39	65	35
Bristol Manor Farm	38	8	10	20	37	73	34
Keynsham Town	38	10	4	24	46	94	34
Odd Down	38	9	6	23	33	80	33
Chard Town	38	8	8	22	44	77	32
Torrington	38	2	8	28	21	88	14

First Division

Bishop Sutton	36	26	8	2	86	25	86
Yeovil Town Reserves	36	24	6	6	95	47	78
Devizes Town	36	22	7	7	83	38	73
Street	36	21	7	8	61	32	70
Clyst Rovers	36	20	10	6	89	39	67
Minehead	36	16	14	6	60	39	62
Dawlish Town	36	17	10	9	78	48	58
Crediton United	36	15	8	13	65	67	53
Exmouth Town	36	15	6	15	68	60	51
Bitton	36	14	8	14	55	53	50
Wellington	36	13	10	13	72	54	49
Ilfracombe Town	36	14	7	15	75	67	49
Larkhall Athletic	36	12	7	17	45	58	43
Welton Rovers	36	9	6	21	51	78	33
Warminster Town	36	9	5	22	40	83	32
Glastonbury	36	9	4	23	41	86	31
Frome Town	36	8	6	22	47	74	30
Heavitree United	36	3	7	26	34	135	16
Pewsey Vale	36	3	8	25	40	102	14

Clyst Rovers, Dawlish Town and Pewsey Vale all had 3 points deducted. Crediton United left and joined the Devon County League. They were replaced by Corsham Town from the Wiltshire League.

1998-99

Premier Division

Taunton Town	38	33	3	2	134	33	102
Tiverton Town	38	29	4	5	118	27	91
Chippenham Town	38	25	7	6	93	41	82
Melksham Town	38	20	10	8	73	44	70
Paulton Rovers	38	18	12	8	70	42	66
Brislington	38	18	10	10	74	44	64
Yeovil Town Reserves	38	18	4	16	70	66	58
Bridport	38	16	7	15	61	68	55
Bridgwater Town	38	15	9	14	68	51	54
Backwell United	38	15	7	16	56	48	52
Mangotsfield United	38	14	9	15	60	58	51
Barnstaple Town	38	14	8	16	72	55	50
Bristol Manor Farm	38	15	4	19	61	57	49
Elmore	38	14	6	18	68	82	48
Bishop Sutton	38	12	7	19	65	81	43
Westbury United	38	9	8	21	42	103	35
Bideford	38	10	1	27	40	108	31
Odd Down	38	5	15	18	44	86	30
Keynsham Town	38	6	7	25	33	99	25
Calne Town	38	3	4	31	34	143	13

First Division

Minehead	36	31	4	1	124	25	97
Dawlish Town	36	27	6	3	83	28	87
Street	36	27	4	5	85	36	85
Devizes Town	36	20	7	9	79	43	67
Clyst Rovers	36	21	4	11	76	51	67
Wellington	36	20	6	10	71	42	66
Exmouth Town	36	20	4	12	80	49	64
Pewsey Vale	36	18	4	14	72	46	58
Corsham	36	15	10	11	47	58	55
Welton Rovers	36	13	7	16	61	58	46
Bitton	36	12	9	15	67	59	45
Larkhall Athletic	36	13	5	18	51	65	44
Ilfracombe Town	36	12	7	17	61	71	43
Torrington	36	13	0	23	56	79	39
Warminster Town	36	9	3	24	40	79	30
Chard Town	36	9	2	25	49	102	29
Frome Town	36	7	5	24	44	102	26
Glastonbury	36	3	6	27	47	111	15
Heavitree United	36	4	3	29	31	120	15

Tiverton Town moved up to the Southern League, Glastonbury moved down to the Somerset Senior League and Heavitree United moved down to the Devon County League. Premier Division reduced to 19 clubs and First Division reduced to 17 clubs.

1999-2000

Premier Division

Taunton Town	36	30	4	2	116	37	94
Mangotsfield United	36	23	9	4	95	31	78
Brislington	36	20	5	11	64	43	65
Chippenham Town	36	18	9	9	69	41	63
Paulton Rovers	36	16	11	9	53	34	59
Melksham Town	36	15	11	10	50	46	56
Backwell United	36	15	9	12	50	44	54
Bridport	36	12	13	11	56	56	49
Dawlish Town	36	12	11	13	51	45	47
Yeovil Town Reserves	36	11	14	11	64	63	47
Elmore	36	13	8	15	51	63	47
Bishop Sutton	36	13	4	19	51	73	43
Bideford	36	10	10	16	46	68	40
Bridgwater Town	36	10	8	18	42	53	38
Barnstaple Town	36	9	7	20	35	51	34
Westbury United	36	9	7	20	39	67	34
Bristol Manor Farm	36	8	9	19	48	78	33
Odd Down	36	9	6	21	36	82	33
Minehead	36	9	5	22	60	101	32

First Division

Devizes Town	32	23	9	0	88	30	78
Welton Rovers	32	22	4	6	74	19	70
Clyst Rovers	32	19	5	8	83	39	62
Exmouth Town	32	16	9	7	67	43	57
Keynsham Town	32	16	9	7	48	34	57
Bitton	32	16	6	10	60	47	54
Torrington	32	16	6	10	62	50	54
Street	32	13	10	9	56	40	49
Larkhall Athletic	32	11	8	13	45	55	41
Wellington	32	11	7	14	46	44	40
Ilfracombe Town	32	12	2	18	59	65	38
Warminster Town	32	10	6	16	40	77	36
Calne Town	32	10	5	17	48	71	35
Pewsey Vale	32	10	2	20	51	88	32
Chard Town	32	8	7	17	31	52	31
Corsham Town	32	5	5	22	36	86	20
Frome Town	32	3	2	27	30	84	11

Mangotsfield United moved up to the Southern League. Cadbury Heath joined from the Gloucestershire County League, Hallen joined from the Hellenic League and Worle St. Johns (an amalgamation of Worle from the Somerset Senior League and Weston St. Johns), Team Bath and Bath City Reserves (both newly formed) also joined. Both divisions increased to 20 clubs.

2000-01

Premier Division

Taunton Town	38	31	4	3	133	41	97
Chippenham Town	38	30	5	3	109	27	95
Paulton Rovers	38	23	10	5	92	44	79
Yeovil Town Reserves	38	21	8	9	84	46	71
Bideford	38	19	10	9	71	45	67
Backwell United	38	19	7	12	59	37	64
Devizes Town	38	19	5	14	88	62	62
Brislington	38	17	10	11	67	48	61
Melksham Town	38	17	6	15	58	54	57
Welton Rovers	38	15	8	15	63	53	53
Dawlish Town	38	14	6	18	50	68	48
Elmore	38	14	4	20	67	80	46
Bridport	38	10	13	15	51	63	43
Barnstaple Town	38	12	7	19	45	79	43
Bridgwater Town	38	11	11	16	45	58	41
Odd Down	38	10	8	20	34	57	38
Bishop Sutton	38	9	11	18	57	86	38
Bristol Manor Farm	38	8	8	22	37	66	32
Westbury United	38	3	5	30	27	101	14
Minehead	38	5	0	33	34	156	15

Bridgwater Town had 3 points deducted.

First Division

Team Bath	36	26	6	4	108	22	84
Keynsham Town	36	25	7	4	79	35	82
Frome Town	36	21	4	11	77	45	67
Hallen	36	20	6	10	81	52	66
Bitton	36	19	7	10	66	49	64
Bath City Reserves	36	17	6	13	74	70	57
Exmouth Town	36	15	7	14	76	54	52
Warminster Town	36	14	10	12	48	53	52
Corsham Town	36	14	4	16	60	67	52
Torrington	36	14	8	14	69	72	50
Chard Town	36	11	9	16	52	75	42
Pewsey Vale	36	12	6	18	48	79	42
Street	36	10	9	17	40	63	39
Wellington	36	11	5	20	40	63	38
Larkhall Athletic	36	11	5	20	46	73	38
Ilfracombe Town	36	9	10	17	48	64	37
Cadbury Heath	36	10	5	21	48	68	35
Worle St. Johns	36	10	5	21	64	87	35
Calne Town	36	8	7	21	35	68	31

Clyst Rovers failed to complete the season due to the outbreak of Foot and Mouth Disease. Their record was expunged but they rejoined for 2001-02.
Chippenham Town moved to the Southern League, Pewsey Vale moved to the Hellenic League. Shepton Mallet Town joined from Somerset Senior League and Willand Rovers joined from the Devon County League. Worle St. Johns changed their name to Weston St. Johns.

2001-02

Premier Division

Bideford	38	28	7	3	105	37	91
Taunton Town	38	26	5	7	104	43	83
Brislington	38	24	11	3	72	32	83
Team Bath	38	22	7	9	74	36	73
Devizes Town	38	22	4	12	72	51	70
Dawlish Town	38	21	6	11	86	56	69
Paulton Rovers	38	18	11	9	77	54	65
Bridgwater Town	38	17	9	12	53	45	60
Backwell United	38	16	9	13	56	41	57
Melksham Town	38	15	9	14	47	46	54
Odd Down	38	13	11	14	49	45	50
Barnstaple Town	38	12	8	18	57	66	44
Keynsham Town	38	11	9	18	47	71	42
Elmore	38	10	7	21	47	96	37
Bishop Sutton	38	9	8	21	53	89	35
Yeovil Town Reserves	38	10	4	24	57	86	34
Bridport	38	9	6	23	51	86	33
Welton Rovers	38	7	9	22	46	67	30
Bristol Manor Farm	38	7	8	23	30	80	29
Westbury United	38	7	4	27	35	91	25

First Division

Frome Town	38	29	5	4	104	22	92
Bath City Reserves	38	24	12	2	79	22	81
Exmouth Town	38	23	11	4	84	39	80
Torrington	38	23	5	10	87	49	74
Clyst Rovers	38	18	11	9	73	53	65
Bitton	38	18	9	11	66	55	63
Shepton Mallet Town	38	18	8	12	59	47	62
Street	38	17	10	11	76	58	61
Corsham Town	38	14	13	11	55	48	55
Hallen	38	16	6	16	69	60	54
Chard Town	38	14	8	16	66	59	50
Larkhall Athletic	38	13	8	17	55	71	47
Weston St. Johns	38	13	7	18	71	78	46
Ilfracombe Town	38	14	4	20	59	84	46
Willand Rovers	38	9	15	14	59	58	42
Cadbury Heath	38	10	7	21	55	84	37
Wellington	38	9	8	21	48	89	35
Minehead Town	38	9	5	24	52	90	32
Calne Town	38	6	7	25	40	86	25
Warminster Town	38	2	3	33	35	140	9

Bath City Reserves had 3 points deducted. Taunton Town moved up to the Southern League and Yeovil Town Reserves also left. Warminster Town moved down to the Wiltshire League. Premier Division reduced to 18 clubs, First Division reduced to 19 clubs.

2002-03

Premier Division

Team Bath	34	27	3	4	109	28	84
Brislington	34	22	7	5	71	28	73
Bideford	34	21	7	6	105	35	70
Backwell United	34	21	4	9	70	33	67
Paulton Rovers	34	18	9	7	68	35	63
Bridgwater Town	34	17	8	9	71	43	59
Bath City Reserves	34	14	5	15	66	57	47
Melksham Town	34	12	7	15	65	68	43
Odd Down	34	12	6	16	49	67	42
Keynsham Town	34	11	7	16	55	65	40
Frome Town	34	11	7	16	49	62	40
Bishop Sutton	34	11	5	18	57	83	38
Dawlish Town	34	11	5	18	47	107	38
Bridport	34	9	8	17	40	54	35
Barnstaple Town	34	8	8	18	41	68	32
Welton Rovers	34	9	5	20	40	99	32
Elmore	34	8	7	19	45	81	31
Devizes Town	34	6	8	20	40	75	26

First Division

Torrington	36	27	5	4	113	47	86
Exmouth Town	36	26	7	3	83	29	85
Westbury United	36	20	8	8	92	65	68
Hallen	36	19	6	11	70	56	63
Calne Town	36	16	9	11	62	43	57
Clyst Rovers	36	17	5	14	67	55	56
Willand Rovers	36	16	6	14	63	53	54
Bitton	36	13	10	13	50	48	49
Shepton Mallet Town	36	13	10	13	53	55	49
Chard Town	36	12	10	14	59	60	46
Bristol Manor Farm	36	14	4	18	56	71	46
Wellington	36	12	8	16	49	57	44
Larkhall Athletic	36	13	4	19	48	73	43
Cadbury Heath	36	10	11	15	49	61	41
Street	36	13	7	16	59	81	40
Corsham Town	36	8	12	16	44	51	36
Weston St. Johns	36	9	4	23	54	76	31
Ilfracombe Town	36	7	9	20	47	85	30
Minehead Town	36	7	5	24	34	86	26

Street had 6 points deducted.
Team Bath left and joined the Southern League and Bath City Reserves left and joined the Severnside Reserve League. Clevedon United joined from the Somerset County League and Shrewton United joined from the Wiltshire League.

2003-04

Premier Division

Bideford	34	25	7	2	110	30	82
Paulton Rovers	34	25	2	7	85	28	77
Frome Town	34	21	5	8	84	43	68
Backwell United	34	20	5	9	67	35	65
Exmouth Town	34	19	7	8	70	34	64
Bridgwater Town	34	19	3	12	67	47	60
Brislington	34	18	4	12	57	40	58
Welton Rovers	34	14	7	13	62	54	49
Odd Down	34	13	10	11	48	44	49
Barnstaple Town	34	12	11	11	47	42	47
Torrington	34	12	10	12	69	74	46
Bridport	34	12	6	16	52	52	42
Devizes Town	34	11	2	21	55	69	35
Melksham Town	34	9	6	19	38	61	33
Keynsham Town	34	8	5	21	45	84	29
Bishop Sutton	34	8	4	22	42	77	28
Dawlish Town	34	6	5	23	30	103	23
Elmore	34	4	1	29	26	137	13

First Division

Hallen	36	24	7	5	75	26	79
Bitton	36	23	7	6	84	37	76
Bristol Manor Farm	36	20	14	2	74	38	74
Clyst Rovers	36	21	9	6	74	41	72
Corsham Town	36	19	9	8	70	41	66
Willand Rovers	36	17	8	11	72	50	59
Shrewton United	36	17	4	15	86	70	55
Larkhall Athletic	36	15	10	11	65	54	55
Calne Town	36	13	10	13	49	45	49
Wellington	36	14	7	15	54	55	49
Westbury United	36	14	6	16	52	56	48
Street	36	11	10	15	54	51	43
Clevedon United	36	11	9	16	60	75	42
Weston St. Johns	36	11	9	16	72	95	42
Cadbury Heath	36	9	10	17	50	64	37
Ilfracombe Town	36	7	6	23	43	106	27
Chard Town	36	7	5	24	48	87	26
Shepton Mallet Town	36	5	9	22	49	82	24
Minehead Town	36	5	9	22	35	93	24

Paulton Rovers left and joined the Southern League. Almondsbury (from the Gloucestershire County League), Biddestone (from the Wiltshire League), Radstock Town (from the Somerset County League) and Saltash United (South-Western League) all joined. Both divisions increased to 20 clubs.

2004-05

Premier Division

Bideford	38	28	4	6	105	26	88
Corsham Town	38	25	8	5	79	33	83
Frome Town	38	23	7	8	78	35	76
Hallen	38	23	6	9	81	38	75
Exmouth Town	38	21	8	9	64	39	71
Bridgwater Town	38	22	4	12	66	46	70
Bristol Manor Farm	38	17	7	14	56	59	58
Bitton	38	15	12	11	64	66	57
Backwell United	38	14	13	11	58	46	55
Brislington	38	14	8	16	50	51	50
Keynsham Town	38	14	7	17	39	62	49
Barnstaple Town	38	15	3	20	51	68	48
Odd Down	38	12	9	17	47	57	45
Melksham Town	38	10	9	19	57	70	39
Devizes Town	38	10	8	20	37	63	38
Torrington	38	11	5	22	50	83	38
Welton Rovers	38	8	12	18	59	80	36
Bishop Sutton	38	9	9	20	44	71	36
Bridport	38	10	4	24	52	75	34
Clyst Rovers	38	3	9	26	44	113	18

First Division

Willand Rovers	38	27	7	4	88	31	88
Calne Town	38	23	10	5	91	30	79
Radstock Town	38	24	7	7	67	38	79
Dawlish Town	38	20	12	6	81	42	72
Larkhall Athletic	38	21	8	9	65	35	71
Shrewton United	38	22	3	13	83	56	69
Street	38	17	12	9	68	46	63
Ilfracombe Town	38	16	11	11	72	76	59
Clevedon United	38	15	7	16	61	64	52
Elmore	38	14	7	17	59	67	49
Weston St. Johns	38	14	7	17	62	88	49
Almondsbury	38	11	10	17	55	79	43
Cadbury Heath	38	10	12	16	46	58	42
Wellington	38	11	9	18	58	76	42
Chard Town	38	11	8	19	43	63	41
Westbury United	38	8	14	16	57	75	38
Saltash United	38	8	11	19	61	77	35
Minehead Town	38	8	10	20	41	64	34
Biddestone	38	3	14	21	40	81	23
Shepton Mallet Town	38	3	9	26	38	90	18

Bradford Town (from the Wiltshire League), Portishead (from the Somerset County League) and Longwell Green Sports (from the Gloucestershire County League) joined. Premier Division increased to 21 clubs and First Division to 22 clubs.

First Division

Dawlish Town	42	33	6	3	115	33	105
Chard Town	42	29	10	3	87	27	97
Street	42	24	11	7	80	39	83
Ilfracombe Town	42	23	9	10	82	50	78
Westbury United	42	22	10	10	95	50	76
Bridport	42	22	6	14	81	60	72
Larkhall Athletic	42	19	11	12	93	56	68
Portishead	42	18	12	12	59	49	66
Shrewton United	42	18	7	17	88	79	61
Bradford Town	42	15	13	14	71	81	58
Clevedon United	42	15	12	15	62	67	57
Longwell Green Sports	42	15	9	18	49	52	51
Weston St. Johns	42	18	3	21	63	81	57
Cadbury Heath	42	15	8	19	70	62	53
Saltash United	42	15	7	20	71	84	52
Biddestone	42	13	11	18	54	59	50
Wellington	42	14	8	20	69	81	50
Almondsbury	42	10	11	21	46	70	41
Minehead Town	42	9	9	24	47	100	36
Shepton Mallet Town	42	10	4	28	34	85	34
Clyst Rovers	42	7	7	28	47	92	28
Elmore	42	4	4	34	42	148	16

Weston St. Johns had 3 points deducted.

2005-06

Premier Division

Bideford	38	29	7	2	93	25	94
Corsham Town	38	24	10	4	78	30	82
Bristol Manor Farm	38	24	4	10	86	43	76
Welton Rovers	38	19	12	7	61	39	69
Calne Town	38	19	10	9	70	41	67
Willand Rovers	38	18	11	9	63	42	65
Frome Town	38	18	10	10	61	45	64
Bitton	38	18	9	11	63	41	63
Hallen	38	15	12	11	71	54	57
Brislington	38	15	8	15	55	53	53
Bridgwater Town	38	15	7	16	66	54	52
Radstock Town	38	14	5	19	62	73	47
Barnstaple Town	38	12	9	17	54	62	45
Melksham Town	38	12	8	18	43	68	44
Odd Down	38	11	10	17	34	44	43
Bishop Sutton	38	7	13	18	36	52	34
Keynsham Town	38	5	11	22	34	78	26
Devizes Town	38	7	5	26	27	94	26
Torrington	38	6	7	25	33	89	25
Backwell United	38	3	10	25	30	93	19

Exmouth Town resigned in January 2006 and their record was expunged.

SOUTH-WESTERN LEAGUE

The South-Western League was formed in 1951 to accommodate clubs from Cornwall and Devon. Several of its founder members came from the Cornwall Senior League while others came from Devon-based leagues such as the Plymouth & District League although Torquay United Reserves moved from the Southern League.

Abbreviation: ECPL = East Cornwall Premier League.

Several of the published tables contained errors in the goals scored record. Additional research has succeeded in correcting many of these, totals that still do not balance are shown below the relevant columns in italics.

1951-52

Torquay United Reserves	22	16	4	2	77	22	36
St. Blazey	22	12	2	8	77	56	26
St. Austell	22	11	3	8	49	43	25
Barnstaple Town Reserves	22	11	2	9	62	55	24
Newquay	22	9	5	8	67	69	23
Plymouth Argyle "A"	22	7	7	8	45	41	21
Saltash United	22	10	1	11	47	53	21
Penzance	22	7	6	9	48	51	20
Falmouth Town	22	6	7	9	37	53	19
Newton Abbot	22	6	6	10	46	49	18
Truro City	22	6	6	10	45	59	18
Bideford Reserves	22	5	3	14	36	85	13

Tavistock joined from the Plymouth & District League and Wadebridge Town also joined, extending the league to 14 clubs.

1952-53

Torquay United Reserves	26	21	1	4	100	32	43
Saltash United	26	16	4	6	78	55	36
Wadebridge Town	26	12	8	6	76	62	32
Bideford Reserves	26	14	2	10	73	54	30
Newton Abbot	26	13	4	9	63	52	30
Penzance	26	11	4	11	62	64	26
Plymouth Argyle "A"	26	11	3	12	72	65	25
St. Austell	26	9	7	10	48	59	25
Newquay	26	10	4	12	66	68	24
St. Blazey	26	8	5	13	72	69	21
Barnstaple Town Reserves	26	8	5	13	60	62	21
Tavistock	26	8	5	13	51	76	21
Truro City	26	7	2	17	48	95	16
Falmouth Town	26	6	2	18	45	95	14
					914	*908*	

Newton Abbot left. Bodmin Town, Helston Athletic, Ilfracombe Town Reserves and United Services joined, extending the league to 17 clubs.

1953-54

Saltash United	32	21	3	8	93	68	45
Plymouth Argyle "A"	32	20	3	9	98	48	43
St. Austell	32	18	6	8	92	58	42
Tavistock	32	18	5	9	76	53	41
Wadebridge Town	32	16	7	9	86	76	39
St. Blazey	32	16	6	10	95	72	38
Torquay United Reserves	32	13	8	11	62	55	34
Newquay	32	15	4	13	86	80	34
Truro City	32	12	9	11	63	68	33
Helston Athletic	32	13	5	14	81	80	31
Penzance	32	11	7	14	56	73	29
United Services	32	10	8	14	69	79	28
Barnstaple Town Reserves	32	10	7	15	67	71	27
Bideford Reserves	32	11	2	19	65	88	24
Bodmin Town	32	10	2	20	50	74	22
Falmouth Town	32	5	8	19	37	81	18
Ilfracombe Town Reserves	32	6	4	22	50	110	16
					1226	*1234*	

Ilfracombe Town Reserves and United Services left, reducing the league to 15 clubs.

1954-55

St. Blazey	28	21	3	4	102	46	45
Truro City	28	18	5	5	70	41	41
Torquay United Reserves	28	17	5	6	73	36	39
Penzance	28	13	8	7	71	53	34
Tavistock	28	14	3	11	89	71	31
Bodmin Town	28	11	8	9	58	51	30
Newquay	28	11	4	13	69	76	26
Saltash United	28	10	6	12	84	93	26
Wadebridge Town	28	11	4	13	64	83	26
St. Austell	28	9	6	13	46	68	24
Helston Athletic	28	9	6	13	46	48	24
Barnstaple Town Reserves	28	9	5	14	59	69	23
Plymouth Argyle "A"	28	7	5	16	55	77	19
Bideford Reserves	28	8	3	17	58	88	19
Falmouth Town	28	4	5	19	47	92	13
					991	*992*	

Torquay United Reserves left and joined the Western League and Barnstaple Town Reserves also left. They were replaced by Camelford and Bugle.

1955-56

Penzance	28	20	4	4	103	50	44
St. Blazey	28	16	5	7	84	60	37
Plymouth Argyle "A"	28	17	2	9	84	49	36
Newquay	28	16	4	8	87	59	36
Bodmin Town	28	14	4	10	83	69	32
Tavistock	28	13	6	9	83	76	32
Wadebridge Town	28	14	4	10	67	63	32
Truro City	28	13	4	11	66	63	30
Falmouth Town	28	12	4	12	84	84	28
Saltash United	28	10	5	13	70	89	25
St. Austell	28	8	6	14	51	61	22
Camelford	28	9	4	15	54	73	22
Helston Athletic	28	7	5	16	36	70	19
Bideford Reserves	28	6	4	18	61	92	16
Bugle	28	3	3	22	46	101	9

1956-57

Penzance	28	17	5	6	110	43	39
St. Blazey	28	16	5	7	107	73	37
Falmouth Town	28	16	4	8	78	46	36
Plymouth Argyle "A"	28	14	4	10	59	58	32
Newquay	28	14	3	11	89	55	31
Tavistock	28	14	3	11	80	70	31
Truro City	28	14	3	11	78	79	31
St. Austell	28	12	5	11	67	60	29
Saltash United	28	12	4	12	92	78	28
Helston Athletic	28	11	3	14	43	69	25
Bugle	28	10	5	13	67	97	25
Bodmin Town	28	11	3	14	80	70	23
Bideford Reserves	28	9	4	15	54	80	22
Wadebridge Town	28	8	5	15	62	99	21
Camelford	28	2	4	22	40	129	8

Bodmin Town had 2 points deducted.
Bideford Reserves left, reducing the league to 14 clubs.

1957-58

St. Blazey	26	20	2	4	106	49	42
Newquay	26	18	3	5	88	34	39
Penzance	26	15	5	6	67	38	35
Truro City	26	15	5	6	61	36	35
Plymouth Argyle "A"	26	15	4	7	111	46	34
Bodmin Town	26	15	4	7	64	42	34
St. Austell	26	11	4	11	59	59	26
Falmouth Town	26	10	6	10	57	58	26
Saltash United	26	11	3	12	66	81	25
Wadebridge Town	26	6	6	14	42	60	18
Camelford	26	8	2	16	48	108	18
Bugle	26	6	1	19	46	94	13
Helston Athletic	26	3	4	19	36	79	10
Tavistock	26	3	3	20	38	105	9

Launceston and Exeter City Reserves joined, extending the league to 16 clubs.

1958-59

Newquay	30	23	3	4	123	45	49
Falmouth Town	30	22	3	5	121	42	47
Truro City	30	21	5	4	98	53	47
Bodmin Town	30	18	1	11	73	67	37
Plymouth Argyle "A"	30	16	4	10	88	50	36
St. Austell	30	18	0	12	81	68	36
Penzance	30	15	3	12	89	65	33
Launceston	30	13	7	10	77	70	33
St. Blazey	30	13	3	14	80	101	29
Exeter City Reserves	30	10	6	14	56	75	26
Wadebridge Town	30	10	3	17	77	80	23
Helston Athletic	30	8	4	18	58	86	20
Camelford	30	7	5	18	51	88	19
Saltash United	30	8	2	20	52	113	18
Bugle	30	8	0	22	53	86	16
Tavistock	30	4	3	23	47	130	11
					1224	1219	

Saltash United left and joined the ECPL. Newton Abbott Spurs joined.

1959-60

Newquay	30	19	7	4	92	46	45
Plymouth Argyle "A"	30	21	4	5	91	28	44
St. Blazey	30	19	1	10	113	69	39
Truro City	30	17	5	8	100	63	39
Falmouth Town	30	15	6	9	73	43	36
Exeter City Reserves	30	15	6	9	75	48	36
Launceston	30	14	5	11	81	62	33
Camelford	30	13	4	13	61	73	30
Penzance	30	12	4	14	73	65	28
Wadebridge Town	30	11	6	13	79	87	28
Bodmin Town	30	13	2	15	62	87	28
St. Austell	30	11	2	17	64	81	24
Helston Athletic	30	10	4	16	65	84	24
Newton Abbott Spurs	30	6	4	20	43	92	16
Tavistock	30	6	4	20	48	103	16
Bugle	30	5	2	23	42	131	12

Plymouth Argyle "A" 2 points deducted for fielding an ineligible player. Exeter City Reserves left and joined the Western League, league reduced to 15 clubs.

1960-61

Truro City	28	19	6	3	110	36	44
Plymouth Argyle "A"	28	18	3	7	97	54	39
St. Blazey	28	16	4	8	97	43	36
Falmouth Town	28	15	5	8	87	37	35
Bugle	28	13	9	6	79	55	35
Newquay	28	13	6	9	89	59	32
Helston Athletic	28	15	2	11	63	55	32
St. Austell	28	13	4	11	62	67	30
Penzance	28	12	5	11	68	69	29
Wadebridge Town	28	12	3	13	58	64	27
Camelford	28	9	5	14	47	67	23
Launceston	28	9	5	14	68	86	23
Newton Abbott Spurs	28	9	3	16	48	71	21
Bodmin Town	28	2	3	23	41	142	7
Tavistock	28	2	3	23	31	135	7
					1045	1040	

Nanpean Rovers joined but Launceston and Tavistock left, league reduced to 14 clubs.

1961-62

Falmouth Town	26	20	3	3	97	31	43
St. Blazey	26	19	1	6	89	45	39
Truro City	26	17	3	6	77	51	37
Newquay	26	16	3	7	86	47	35
Bugle	26	14	3	9	81	57	31
Nanpean Rovers	26	12	6	8	75	52	30
St. Austell	26	14	1	11	79	61	29
Penzance	26	9	6	11	62	65	24
Wadebridge Town	26	11	1	14	62	70	23
Newton Abbott Spurs	26	8	4	14	45	72	20
Bodmin Town	26	8	2	16	50	98	18
Plymouth Argyle "A"	26	6	5	15	61	83	17
Helston Athletic	26	7	1	18	48	94	15
Camelford	26	1	1	24	21	107	3

Bodmin Town left but Saltash United joined from the ECPL and Launceston and Torpoint Athletic also joined, league increased to 16 clubs.

1962-63

St. Blazey	30	20	6	4	115	51	46
Truro City	30	22	1	7	98	54	45
Falmouth Town	30	20	4	6	119	50	44
Torpoint Athletic	30	19	3	8	92	59	41
Penzance	30	16	4	10	98	63	36
St. Austell	30	12	8	10	89	84	32
Plymouth Argyle "A"	30	13	5	12	77	89	31
Newton Abbott Spurs	30	14	3	13	61	78	31
Helston Athletic	30	12	5	13	76	79	29
Launceston	30	12	4	14	72	71	28
Saltash United	30	11	5	14	89	99	27
Newquay	30	12	3	15	77	89	27
Bugle	30	11	2	17	71	85	24
Nanpean Rovers	30	9	2	19	81	106	20
Wadebridge Town	30	4	5	21	52	103	13
Camelford	30	1	4	25	38	145	6

Camelford left and were replaced by St. Luke's College.

1963-64

St. Blazey	30	22	5	3	119	39	49
St. Austell	30	19	5	6	108	58	43
Newquay	30	19	1	10	88	58	39
Falmouth Town	30	16	5	9	83	51	37
Penzance	30	17	3	10	83	64	37
Torpoint Athletic	30	15	5	10	83	78	35
Plymouth Argyle "A"	30	16	2	12	93	64	34
St. Luke's College	30	13	4	13	80	74	30
Newton Abbott Spurs	30	13	3	14	59	69	29
Nanpean Rovers	30	12	4	14	85	88	28
Truro City	30	11	4	15	76	82	26
Wadebridge Town	30	7	9	14	64	79	23
Saltash United	30	8	5	17	63	119	21
Helston Athletic	30	8	3	19	42	81	19
Launceston	30	6	6	18	57	115	18
Bugle	30	2	8	20	57	121	12

1964-65

Torpoint Athletic	30	23	5	2	117	41	51
Falmouth Town	30	24	4	2	130	38	50
Helston Athletic	30	19	6	5	88	50	44
St. Blazey	30	19	3	8	87	55	41
St. Austell	30	18	4	8	118	73	40
Wadebridge Town	30	16	4	10	84	71	36
St. Luke's College	30	15	5	10	95	56	35
Plymouth Argyle "A"	30	13	2	15	89	86	28
Penzance	30	12	4	14	60	73	28
Truro City	30	12	2	16	64	77	26
Newton Abbott Spurs	30	8	7	15	44	69	23
Newquay	30	9	3	18	60	75	21
Saltash United	30	9	2	19	64	102	20
Launceston	30	6	2	22	45	114	14
Nanpean Rovers	30	5	2	23	53	120	12
Bugle	30	4	1	25	31	139	9

Falmouth Town had 2 points deducted for fielding an unregistered player.
Plymouth Argyle "A" left and joined the Western League, league reduced to 15 clubs.

1965-66

Falmouth Town	28	25	0	3	117	36	50
St. Austell	28	20	2	6	103	51	42
Truro City	28	19	3	6	93	51	41
Torpoint Athletic	28	17	3	8	102	66	37
Helston Athletic	28	14	4	10	69	56	32
St. Blazey	28	14	2	12	95	63	30
St. Luke's College	28	15	0	13	82	66	30
Wadebridge Town	28	13	3	12	75	63	29
Saltash United	28	10	3	15	53	97	23
Penzance	28	9	4	15	52	72	22
Nanpean Rovers	28	8	5	15	69	96	21
Newton Abbott Spurs	28	8	3	17	44	86	19
Newquay	28	6	6	16	36	78	18
Bugle	28	7	2	19	58	100	16
Launceston	28	4	2	22	39	106	10

St. Luke's College left and joined the Western League and Launceston left and joined the ECPL. Liskeard Athletic joined from the Plymouth & District League, league reduced to 14 clubs.

1966-67

Torpoint Athletic	26	19	5	2	104	48	43
Truro City	26	20	2	4	88	31	42
St. Blazey	26	17	6	3	87	35	40
Falmouth Town	26	17	3	6	88	36	37
St. Austell	26	16	2	8	69	55	34
Newquay	26	12	5	9	49	48	29
Penzance	26	11	3	12	57	57	25
Helston Athletic	26	10	4	12	56	52	24
Wadebridge Town	26	10	3	13	50	64	23
Liskeard Athletic	26	9	5	12	55	74	23
Bugle	26	8	4	14	47	77	20
Newton Abbott Spurs	26	4	4	18	35	67	12
Saltash United	26	3	1	22	46	95	7
Nanpean Rovers	26	2	1	23	32	124	5

Porthleven joined from the Cornwall Combination, league increased to 15 clubs.

1967-68

Falmouth Town	28	22	3	3	79	29	47
Truro City	28	20	5	3	111	33	45
Torpoint Athletic	28	18	4	6	87	40	40
St. Austell	28	17	5	6	85	41	39
Porthleven	28	17	4	7	71	40	38
Wadebridge Town	28	16	3	9	84	49	35
Penzance	28	16	1	11	77	60	33
St. Blazey	28	14	4	10	64	57	32
Newton Abbott Spurs	28	9	4	15	30	71	22
Liskeard Athletic	28	9	3	16	54	73	21
Nanpean Rovers	28	9	2	17	54	74	20
Helston Athletic	28	5	5	18	41	72	15
Newquay	28	4	6	18	54	88	14
Bugle	28	4	4	20	42	127	12
Saltash United	28	2	3	23	38	117	7

Tavistock and St. Luke's College Reserves joined, league increased to 17 clubs.

1968-69

St. Austell	32	24	4	4	132	35	52
Wadebridge Town	32	21	6	5	99	52	48
Falmouth Town	32	21	5	6	93	45	47
Truro City	32	21	3	8	100	37	45
Saltash United	32	20	3	9	97	56	43
Newquay	32	16	5	11	88	61	37
Torpoint Athletic	32	15	6	11	86	53	36
Tavistock	32	15	6	11	83	73	36
St. Blazey	32	14	7	11	86	62	35
Penzance	32	13	6	13	61	66	32
Porthleven	32	14	3	15	69	66	31
Nanpean Rovers	32	11	4	17	68	77	26
Liskeard Athletic	32	12	1	19	83	97	25
St. Luke's College Reserves	32	8	4	20	57	94	20
Helston Athletic	32	4	4	24	33	181	12
Newton Abbott Spurs	32	4	3	25	29	125	11
Bugle	32	2	4	26	38	120	8

Bodmin Town joined from the ECPL, league increased to 18 clubs.

1969-70

Truro City	34	26	4	4	122	35	56
Falmouth Town	34	25	4	5	119	39	54
Wadebridge Town	34	18	5	11	89	57	41
Liskeard Athletic	34	17	7	10	88	59	41
St. Austell	34	18	4	12	82	53	40
Newquay	34	17	6	11	91	67	40
St. Blazey	34	15	10	9	73	56	40
Torpoint Athletic	34	14	11	9	79	72	39
Saltash United	34	17	4	13	76	67	38
Bugle	34	14	6	14	84	69	34
Nanpean Rovers	34	12	7	15	68	88	31
Tavistock	34	12	4	18	59	85	28
Helston Athletic	34	10	7	17	53	93	27
Bodmin Town	34	11	5	18	72	119	27
Porthleven	34	9	8	17	50	72	26
Penzance	34	7	5	22	58	93	19
St. Luke's College Reserves	34	7	5	22	49	90	19
Newton Abbott Spurs	34	4	4	26	33	136	12
					1345	1350	

1970-71

Falmouth Town	34	31	3	0	130	21	65
Truro City	34	25	4	5	104	52	54
St. Austell	34	19	7	8	88	53	45
Newquay	34	17	7	10	82	54	41
Bodmin Town	34	18	5	11	98	70	41
St. Blazey	34	18	5	11	99	78	41
Tavistock	34	17	5	12	71	66	39
Porthleven	34	15	8	11	90	60	38
Wadebridge Town	34	15	6	13	85	75	36
Liskeard Athletic	34	13	9	12	73	61	35
Saltash United	34	14	5	15	66	70	33
Penzance	34	12	6	16	71	77	30
St. Luke's College Reserves	34	11	5	18	51	70	27
Bugle	34	8	6	20	52	98	22
Torpoint Athletic	34	7	4	23	59	95	18
Newton Abbott Spurs	34	6	6	22	60	129	18
Nanpean Rovers	34	6	4	24	46	119	16
Helston Athletic	34	4	5	25	48	125	13

Newton Abbott Spurs left and were replaced by Holsworthy.

1971-72

Falmouth Town	34	29	3	2	144	31	61
St. Austell	34	25	5	4	96	25	55
Bodmin Town	34	24	6	4	107	38	54
Wadebridge Town	34	23	7	4	93	39	53
Holsworthy	34	23	4	7	76	33	50
Newquay	34	16	8	10	64	46	40
Penzance	34	14	7	13	67	56	35
Liskeard Athletic	34	13	7	14	67	50	33
Saltash United	34	13	6	15	59	74	32
Truro City	34	10	10	14	64	64	30
Porthleven	34	11	6	17	71	79	28
Bugle	34	11	6	17	64	78	28
Tavistock	34	10	8	16	54	77	28
Torpoint Athletic	34	8	8	18	50	82	24
St. Blazey	34	7	7	20	35	74	21
St. Luke's College Reserves	34	5	8	21	30	97	18
Helston Athletic	34	7	2	25	42	103	16
Nanpean Rovers	34	2	2	30	23	155	6

Helston Athletic left and joined the Cornwall Combination, league reduced to 17 clubs.

1972-73

Falmouth Town	32	30	1	1	136	20	61
St. Austell	32	24	2	6	94	33	50
Penzance	32	24	2	6	95	44	50
Holsworthy	32	19	5	8	67	34	43
Bodmin Town	32	17	7	8	68	49	41
Truro City	32	16	7	9	62	54	39
Wadebridge Town	32	16	5	11	70	49	37
Porthleven	32	13	4	15	64	73	30
Liskeard Athletic	32	11	6	15	56	52	28
Saltash United	32	11	6	15	65	70	28
Newquay	32	12	2	18	58	77	26
Tavistock	32	10	6	16	53	74	26
St. Blazey	32	11	3	18	63	80	25
Torpoint Athletic	32	8	7	17	76	97	23
St. Luke's College Reserves	32	7	3	22	53	99	17
Nanpean Rovers	32	4	4	24	31	122	12
Bugle	32	3	2	27	30	114	6

Bugle had 2 points deducted. Nanpean Rovers left, league reduced to 16 clubs.

1973-74

Falmouth Town	30	26	2	2	143	29	54
Saltash United	30	18	7	5	100	40	43
Wadebridge Town	30	18	5	7	73	47	41
St. Blazey	30	17	4	9	69	55	38
Newquay	30	15	8	7	57	46	38
Porthleven	30	12	12	6	60	43	36
Bodmin Town	30	14	6	10	56	46	34
Penzance	30	13	8	9	54(57)	50	32
Holsworthy	30	10	12	8	61	62	32
Liskeard Athletic	30	9	11	10	55	63	29
St. Austell	30	10	5	15	48	62	25
Truro City	30	8	6	16	56	76	22
Tavistock	30	6	6	18	30	72	18
Torpoint Athletic	30	5	4	21	45	93	14
Bugle	30	6	2	22	37	107	14
St. Luke's College Reserves	30	2	4	24	32	88	8

Penzance had 3 goals and 2 points deducted from their totals. Falmouth Town left and joined the Western League. Elmore and Ottery St. Mary joined from the Devon & Exeter League, Exeter City Reserves joined from the Western League and Illogan RBL also joined. League increased to 19 clubs.

1974-75

Penzance	36	24	11	1	113	35	59
Saltash United	36	27	4	5	127	37	58
Wadebridge Town	36	26	5	5	111	55	57
Liskeard Athletic	36	21	6	9	72	44	48
Exeter City Reserves	36	20	6	10	61	38	46
Ottery St. Mary	36	20	4	12	92	67	44
Tavistock	36	15	10	11	63	53	40
Newquay	36	16	6	14	68	49	38
Elmore	36	16	6	14	66	55	38
Porthleven	36	15	8	13	80	73	38
Holsworthy	36	13	8	15	69	63	34
Torpoint Athletic	36	12	8	16	63	81	32
St. Austell	36	11	10	15	45	58	32
Bodmin Town	36	11	10	15	45	64	32
Illogan RBL	36	11	6	19	65	94	28
Truro City	36	8	4	24	51	110	20
St. Luke's College Reserves	36	5	8	23	38	94	18
St. Blazey	36	5	3	28	47	112	13
Bugle	36	2	5	29	35	129	9

Exeter City Reserves left and joined the Western League and Truro City left and joined the Cornwall Combination. They were replaced by Plymouth Argyle "A" from the Plymouth & District League and Louis International.

1975-76

Saltash United	36	30	4	2	119	25	64
Liskeard Athletic	36	22	10	4	90	35	54
Bodmin Town	36	21	8	7	79	33	50
Elmore	36	21	8	7	71	56	50
Wadebridge Town	36	22	3	11	96	50	47
Louis International	35	16	13	6	67	37	47
Holsworthy	36	19	6	11	70	44	44
Penzance	36	15	8	13	66	60	38
Tavistock	36	15	7	14	58	60	37
Ottery St. Mary	36	14	8	14	60	54	35
Newquay	36	15	4	17	64	54	34
Illogan RBL	36	12	8	16	61	66	32
Plymouth Argyle "A"	36	12	10	14	50	51	30
Porthleven	35	12	5	18	52	92	29
St. Luke's College Reserves	36	9	2	25	45	78	20
St. Blazey	36	7	5	24	48	103	19
Torpoint Athletic	36	7	5	24	48	104	19
St. Austell	36	5	5	26	47	100	15
Bugle	36	5	5	26	33	126	15
					1224	1228	

Ottery St. Mary had 1 point deducted and Plymouth Argyle "A" had 4 points deducted for fielding ineligible players. Louis International were awarded two points after Porthleven failed to appear for a game. Ottery St. Mary and Saltash United left and joined the Western League and Plymouth Command joined from the Plymouth & District League. League reduced to 18 clubs.

1976-77

Liskeard Athletic	34	24	8	2	82	34	56
Bodmin Town	34	19	10	5	75	40	48
Tavistock	34	18	9	7	65	37	45
Holsworthy	34	20	5	9	58	37	45
Newquay	34	20	5	9	87	45	43
Elmore	34	18	7	9	76	51	43
Wadebridge Town	34	17	8	9	77	45	42
Plymouth Command	34	16	4	14	59	48	36
Penzance	34	12	11	11	56	43	35
Torpoint Athletic	34	13	9	12	51	55	35
Illogan RBL	34	11	9	14	59	68	30
Louis International	34	11	8	15	45	59	30
Plymouth Argyle "A"	34	11	7	16	40	54	29
Bugle	34	11	6	17	49	66	28
St. Blazey	34	8	6	20	48	86	22
Porthleven	34	5	6	23	28	75	16
St. Luke's College Reserves	34	4	7	23	35	77	15
St. Austell	34	4	3	27	43	113	11

Newquay had 2 points deducted and Illogan RBL had 1 point deducted for fielding ineligible players.
Porthleven left and joined the Cornwall Combination and St. Luke's College Reserves also left. Newton Abbot Dynamoes joined from the South Devon League, league reduced to 17 clubs.

1977-78

Newquay	32	24	5	3	88	33	53
Liskeard Athletic	32	19	9	4	73	32	47
Wadebridge Town	32	20	6	6	79	40	46
Torpoint Athletic	32	17	7	8	59	40	41
Bodmin Town	32	17	5	10	67	43	39
St. Blazey	32	14	5	13	62	67	33
St. Austell	32	13	6	13	64	44	32
Elmore	32	10	12	10	53	53	32
Illogan RBL	32	12	7	13	59	72	31
Bugle	32	13	5	14	47	64	31
Holsworthy	32	10	10	12	50	49	30
Penzance	32	13	4	15	56	62	30
Louis International	32	12	5	15	50	59	29
Tavistock	32	8	5	19	38	68	21
Plymouth Command	32	6	5	21	48	78	17
Newton Abbot Dynamoes	32	5	6	21	34	61	16
Plymouth Argyle "A"	32	6	4	22	33	95	16

Elmore left and joined the Western League and Plymouth Argyle "A" also left. Torrington joined from the Devon & Exeter League and Plymouth Civil Service, Appledore and Truro City also joined. League increased to 19 clubs.

1978-79

Liskeard Athletic	36	26	5	5	98	42	57
Wadebridge Town	36	23	7	6	91	36	53
Newquay	36	22	9	5	74	33	53
Plymouth Civil Service	36	20	7	9	71	45	47
St. Blazey	36	17	7	12	60	49	41
Torpoint Athletic	36	16	9	11	73	69	41
Louis International	36	15	10	11	57	52	40
Truro City	36	15	9	12	69	57	39
Holsworthy	36	15	8	13	66	59	38
St. Austell	36	15	7	14	57	59	37
Tavistock	36	11	14	11	61	64	33
Penzance	36	11	10	15	63	65	32
Bugle	36	11	7	18	43	71	29
Appledore	36	10	8	18	47	58	28
Bodmin Town	36	9	7	20	43	81	25
Illogan RBL	36	6	12	18	58	88	24
Torrington	36	8	9	19	50	80	23
Newton Abbot Dynamoes	36	8	6	22	33	59	22
Plymouth Command	36	6	8	22	34	82	20
					1148	1149	

Torrington had 2 points deducted. Liskeard Athletic left and joined the Western League and were replaced by Launceston.

1979-80

Newquay	36	24	9	3	110	34	57
Wadebridge Town	36	23	10	3	95	29	56
Penzance	36	21	7	8	80	47	49
Plymouth Civil Service	36	19	8	9	83	43	46
St. Blazey	36	19	6	11	77	65	44
Tavistock	36	15	12	9	60	47	42
Appledore	36	16	9	11	56	41	41
Louis International	36	15	11	10	57	55	41
Newton Abbot Dynamoes	36	13	12	11	54	48	38
Torpoint Athletic	36	15	8	13	69	73	38
St. Austell	36	14	8	14	55	63	36
Truro City	36	14	6	16	65	59	34
Launceston	36	13	4	19	57	71	30
Holsworthy	36	10	8	18	43	60	28
Torrington	36	8	11	17	50	67	27
Bodmin Town	36	10	5	21	57	82	25
Plymouth Command	36	6	6	24	37	81	18
Illogan RBL	36	7	4	25	40	106	18
Bugle	36	5	6	25	30	104	16

Louis International left but Millbrook and Plymouth Argyle "A" joined. League increased to 20 clubs.

1980-81

St. Blazey	38	26	8	4	71	24	60
Torrington	38	23	7	8	74	43	53
Newquay	38	20	10	8	67	38	50
Wadebridge Town	38	21	8	9	73	44	50
Plymouth Civil Service	38	17	12	9	69	44	46
Appledore	38	16	11	11	63	45	43
Torpoint Athletic	38	17	7	14	64	63	41
Penzance	38	16	7	15	77	62	39
Holsworthy	38	12	14	12	49	49	38
Millbrook	38	12	13	13	56	54	37
Bugle	38	14	9	15	58	58	37
Plymouth Argyle "A"	38	16	4	18	68	63	36
Truro City	38	14	9	15	55	68	36
Newton Abbot Dynamoes	38	13	8	17	42	53	34
Launceston	38	12	7	19	60	65	31
Tavistock	38	10	10	18	40	63	30
Plymouth Command	38	11	8	19	60	79	28
St. Austell	38	7	10	21	49	90	24
Bodmin Town	38	6	10	22	41	77	22
Illogan RBL	38	6	10	22	36	90	22

Truro City had 1 point deducted and Plymouth Command had 2 points deducted. Illogan RBL left and were replaced by Clyst Rovers who moved from Sunday football. Newton Abbot Dynamoes changed their name to Newton Abbot.

1981-82

Newquay	36	24	5	7	89	43	53
Millbrook	36	23	6	7	75	38	52
Torpoint Athletic	36	22	7	7	106	66	51
St. Blazey	36	23	4	9	81	44	50
Torrington	36	21	6	9	74	38	48
Wadebridge Town	36	18	10	8	77	39	46
Plymouth Civil Service	36	21	3	12	53	40	45
Penzance	36	19	5	12	63	48	43
Bugle	36	14	10	12	78	70	38
Launceston	36	14	8	14	75	65	36
St. Austell	36	10	10	16	47	70	30
Plymouth Argyle "A"	36	12	5	19	69	76	29
Tavistock	36	10	9	17	51	72	29
Newton Abbot	36	10	8	18	38	51	28
Appledore	36	10	8	18	49	72	28
Clyst Rovers	36	7	10	19	41	78	24
Bodmin Town	36	8	7	21	54	85	23
Truro City	36	5	7	24	40	89	17
Holsworthy	36	1	12	23	32	108	14

Plymouth Command withdrew on 6th April 1982 due to the Falkland Islands conflict and their results were deleted from the table. They rejoined for 1982-83. Plymouth Argyle "A" left and were replaced by Teignmouth from the South Devon League.

1982-83

St. Blazey	38	28	6	4	114	33	62
Torrington	38	24	5	9	105	53	53
Wadebridge Town	38	21	9	8	85	41	51
Millbrook	38	21	7	10	87	49	49
Bugle	38	22	5	11	77	53	49
Launceston	38	19	8	11	69	37	46
Newton Abbot	38	15	13	10	69	58	43
Plymouth Civil Service	38	17	9	12	65	56	43
Teignmouth	38	18	5	15	59	49	41
St. Austell	38	15	11	12	63	55	41
Penzance	38	18	5	15	62	65	41
Torpoint Athletic	38	15	8	15	69	72	38
Newquay	38	15	8	15	61	64	38
Appledore	38	14	8	16	66	76	36
Bodmin Town	38	8	10	20	56	97	26
Tavistock	38	8	10	20	43	86	26
Holsworthy	38	7	11	20	43	80	25
Plymouth Command	38	6	9	23	53	112	21
Clyst Rovers	38	6	8	24	56	106	20
Truro City	38	3	5	30	36	110	11

1983-84

(Goal difference replaced goal average to decide places for teams with equal points)

Newquay	38	26	8	4	87	26	60
Launceston	38	24	6	8	99	54	54
Millbrook	38	22	8	8	79	37	52
Bugle	38	24	9	5	68	33	52
St. Austell	38	22	6	10	85	49	50
Newton Abbot	38	21	6	11	83	51	48
St. Blazey	38	17	13	8	88	64	47
Appledore	38	20	6	12	76	54	46
Wadebridge Town	38	18	8	12	74	56	44
Torpoint Athletic	38	16	10	12	66	65	42
Plymouth Civil Service	38	17	5	16	78	58	39
Torrington	38	13	9	16	57	56	35
Truro City	38	14	9	15	63	75	34
Tavistock	38	13	4	21	52	69	30
Holsworthy	38	11	6	21	51	65	28
Clyst Rovers	38	10	8	20	60	75	28
Teignmouth	38	9	7	22	50	89	25
Penzance	38	5	7	26	43	94	17
Plymouth Command	38	3	5	30	40	130	11
Bodmin Town	38	3	4	31	45	145	10
					1345	1347	

Bugle had 5 points deducted and Truro City had 3 points deducted. Torrington left and joined the Western League and Plymouth Command also left.
Falmouth Town joined from the Cornwall Combination. League reduced to 19 clubs.

1984-85

	P	W	D	L	F	A	Pts
Bugle	36	28	4	4	102	32	60
St. Blazey	36	23	9	4	91	36	55
Newquay	36	20	10	6	86	38	50
Wadebridge Town	36	20	8	8	65	37	48
Millbrook	36	19	8	9	63	36	46
Falmouth Town	36	17	8	11	91	59	42
Appledore	36	18	6	12	63	43	42
Truro City	36	17	6	13	60	51	41
Torpoint Athletic	36	12	16	8	53	47	40
Newton Abbot	36	17	5	14	67	47	39
Clyst Rovers	36	12	10	14	56	65	34
Tavistock	36	13	8	15	39	70	34
Plymouth Civil Service	36	11	9	16	47	64	31
Teignmouth	36	12	5	19	58	74	29
Launceston	36	11	7	18	57	73	28
St. Austell	36	10	8	18	52	75	28
Penzance	36	6	8	22	36	75	20
Bodmin Town	36	3	3	30	33	120	9
Holsworthy	36	1	6	29	30	108	8
					1149	1150	

Launceston had 1 point deducted, Truro City had an additional point awarded.
Plymouth Civil Service left but Penryn Athletic joined from the Cornwall Combination and Torquay United Reserves also joined.
League increased to 20 clubs. Appledore became Appledore-Bideford AAC.

1985-86

	P	W	D	L	F	A	Pts
Falmouth Town	38	27	6	5	113	42	60
Newquay	38	24	7	7	94	55	55
Millbrook	38	23	7	8	88	41	53
Bodmin Town	38	25	3	10	84	44	53
Bugle	38	19	11	8	71	40	49
Truro City	38	21	5	12	85	64	47
Wadebridge Town	38	19	7	12	77	47	45
St. Austell	38	19	7	12	74	63	45
St. Blazey	38	14	13	11	77	47	41
Newton Abbot	38	14	13	11	58	54	41
Clyst Rovers	38	14	8	16	74	89	36
Torpoint Athletic	38	12	11	15	71	93	35
Torquay United Reserves	38	12	7	19	69	80	31
Appledore-Bideford AAC	38	11	8	19	52	71	30
Penryn Athletic	38	11	6	21	66	97	28
Tavistock	38	12	3	23	54	91	27
Penzance	38	8	9	21	51	96	25
Teignmouth	38	9	6	23	46	67	24
Launceston	38	7	10	21	49	85	24
Holsworthy	38	4	3	31	41	128	11

Penryn Athletic left and joined the Cornwall Combination. League reduced to 19 clubs.

1986-87

	P	W	D	L	F	A	Pts
Falmouth Town	36	28	6	2	112	26	62
St. Blazey	36	27	6	3	93	26	60
Millbrook	36	25	7	4	84	29	57
Wadebridge Town	36	19	12	5	60	34	50
Bodmin Town	36	20	9	7	75	38	49
St. Austell	36	19	7	10	73	41	45
Torquay United Reserves	36	15	10	11	62	56	40
Newquay	36	14	10	12	60	52	38
Newton Abbot	36	13	11	12	51	56	37
Clyst Rovers	36	13	8	15	56	69	34
Truro City	36	9	14	13	53	55	32
Bugle	36	9	7	20	46	88	25
Teignmouth	36	9	7	20	39	83	25
Appledore-Bideford AAC	36	10	4	22	47	62	24
Torpoint Athletic	36	8	7	21	48	80	23
Tavistock	36	6	10	20	34	64	22
Launceston	36	7	8	21	49	81	22
Holsworthy	36	7	8	21	44	97	22
Penzance	36	4	9	23	41	96	17
					1127	1133	

Bodmin Town had 2 points deducted. Oak Villa joined, increasing league to 20 clubs.

1987-88

	P	W	D	L	F	A	Pts
Newquay	38	28	9	1	97	18	65
Falmouth Town	38	27	8	3	106	42	62
St. Blazey	38	24	8	6	94	49	56
Bodmin Town	38	21	8	9	77	46	50
Millbrook	38	20	9	9	86	57	49
St. Austell	38	18	10	10	83	49	46
Wadebridge Town	38	20	4	14	69	41	44
Truro City	38	15	12	11	51	47	42
Torquay United Reserves	38	16	8	14	62	49	40
Teignmouth	38	14	10	14	51	46	38
Newton Abbot	38	14	10	14	58	55	38
Appledore-Bideford AAC	38	14	9	15	43	55	37
Launceston	38	13	10	15	55	59	36
Torpoint Athletic	38	10	19	9	59	74	28
Penzance	38	9	7	22	49	84	25
Oak Villa	38	7	10	21	57	84	24
Holsworthy	38	8	7	23	40	103	23
Tavistock	38	8	4	26	36	92	20
Clyst Rovers	38	5	10	23	46	111	20
Bugle	38	5	7	26	49	107	17

Torquay United Reserves left and joined the Capital Finance League and Teignmouth left and joined the South Devon League. League reduced to 18 clubs.

1988-89

	P	W	D	L	F	A	Pts
Falmouth Town	34	24	7	3	95	27	55
St. Blazey	34	23	7	4	73	29	53
Bodmin Town	34	22	9	3	69	29	53
Newquay	34	22	8	4	68	24	52
Launceston	34	14	15	5	45	26	43
Truro City	34	16	8	10	60	51	40
Wadebridge Town	34	14	12	8	57	48	40
Torpoint Athletic	34	12	10	12	52	72	34
Tavistock	34	10	10	14	48	57	30
Millbrook	34	12	5	17	48	57	29
Oak Villa	34	10	9	15	42	61	29
St. Austell	34	8	9	17	32	52	25
Newton Abbot	34	10	5	19	41	63	25
Clyst Rovers	34	7	10	17	40	66	24
Bugle	34	7	9	18	34	50	23
Penzance	34	7	8	19	45	72	22
Holsworthy	34	5	10	19	33	66	20
Appledore-Bideford AAC	34	5	5	24	44	76	15

Oak Villa left and joined the Plymouth & District League and Newton Abbot left and joined the South Devon League. Porthleven joined from the Cornwall Combination. League reduced to 17 clubs.

1989-90

	P	W	D	L	F	A	Pts
Falmouth Town	32	26	2	4	99	29	54
St. Blazey	32	21	8	3	84	40	50
Bodmin Town	32	18	8	6	73	28	44
Newquay	32	17	10	5	66	32	44
Bugle	32	16	7	9	55	44	39
Millbrook	32	16	4	12	61	42	36
Launceston	32	14	7	11	55	45	35
Clyst Rovers	32	14	5	13	42	56	33
Tavistock	32	14	4	14	53	57	32
Truro City	32	11	9	12	55	52	31
Appledore-Bideford AAC	32	13	4	15	43	53	30
Wadebridge Town	32	10	9	13	49	53	29
St. Austell	32	8	6	18	39	71	22
Torpoint Athletic	32	6	7	19	35	69	19
Penzance	32	5	8	19	37	79	18
Porthleven	32	5	7	20	53	91	17
Holsworthy	32	4	3	25	27	85	11

1990-91

Bodmin Town	32	25	5	2	87	31	55
St. Blazey	32	22	8	2	105	29	52
Falmouth Town	32	18	9	5	82	39	45
Newquay	32	20	5	7	73	40	45
St. Austell	32	17	7	8	83	46	41
Torpoint Athletic	32	16	8	8	66	37	40
Truro City	32	16	6	10	67	44	38
Bugle	32	16	6	10	57	37	38
Appledore-Bideford AAC	32	13	5	14	66	59	31
Wadebridge Town	32	10	8	14	47	52	28
Millbrook	32	12	3	17	70	79	27
Tavistock	32	8	9	15	46	67	25
Porthleven	32	11	2	19	52	72	24
Clyst Rovers	32	10	1	21	43	100	21
Launceston	32	6	8	18	46	75	20
Holsworthy	32	3	4	25	32	110	10
Penzance	32	1	2	29	31	136	4

Devon & Cornwall Police joined, increasing league to 18 clubs.

1991-92

Falmouth Town	34	26	5	3	91	20	57
Newquay	34	23	5	6	88	31	51
Bugle	34	16	9	9	65	46	41
Truro City	34	14	11	9	74	49	39
Bodmin Town	34	15	9	10	53	51	39
Clyst Rovers	34	15	8	11	59	60	38
Appledore-Bideford AAC	34	16	5	13	78	56	37
Porthleven	34	14	8	12	77	69	36
St. Blazey	34	15	6	13	72	67	36
Torpoint Athletic	34	14	7	13	49	50	35
Holsworthy	34	9	16	9	37	46	34
Wadebridge Town	34	12	7	15	45	52	31
St. Austell	34	10	8	16	45	63	28
Millbrook	34	9	9	16	45	70	27
Launceston	34	8	6	20	45	73	22
Devon & Cornwall Police	34	7	8	19	43	78	22
Tavistock	34	8	5	21	53	79	21
Penzance	34	7	4	23	35	94	18

Bugle left and joined the ECPL and Clyst Rovers left and joined the Western League. Mullion joined from the Cornwall Combination. League reduced to 17 clubs.

1992-93

Truro City	32	23	3	6	72	28	49
Bodmin Town	32	20	6	6	84	46	46
Newquay	32	20	5	7	75	39	45
Launceston	32	17	10	5	81	41	44
St. Blazey	32	14	9	9	71	65	37
Falmouth Town	32	15	6	11	77	51	36
Holsworthy	32	12	8	12	49	54	32
Tavistock	32	11	7	14	53	77	29
Mullion	32	9	10	13	51	61	28
Appledore-Bideford AAC	32	10	8	14	56	73	28
Penzance	32	10	6	16	65	69	26
Devon & Cornwall Police	32	12	5	15	61	69	26
Porthleven	32	9	7	16	69	82	25
Wadebridge Town	32	8	9	15	49	87	25
Millbrook	32	8	8	16	50	69	24
Torpoint Athletic	32	8	7	17	44	68	23
St. Austell	32	7	4	21	61	89	18

Devon & Cornwall Police had 3 Points deducted. Okehampton Argyle joined from the Devon & Exeter League. League increased to 18 clubs.

1993-94 (Three points for a win from this season)

Bodmin Town	34	26	2	6	103	27	80
Newquay	34	24	8	2	92	33	80
Truro City	34	25	4	5	98	31	79
Falmouth Town	34	20	10	4	75	43	70
Launceston	34	19	7	8	86	43	64
Porthleven	34	16	6	12	71	66	54
Torpoint Athletic	34	14	10	10	67	59	52
St. Austell	34	14	6	14	71	57	48
Holsworthy	34	13	9	12	44	50	48
Tavistock	34	13	7	14	70	69	46
St. Blazey	34	12	9	13	76	59	45
Mullion	34	11	6	17	56	77	39
Devon & Cornwall Police	34	8	10	16	54	70	34
Appledore-Bideford AAC	34	8	8	18	44	75	32
Millbrook	34	6	7	21	48	86	25
Wadebridge Town	34	6	5	23	34	94	23
Penzance	34	5	6	23	54	107	21
Okehampton Argyle	34	3	6	25	19	116	15

1994-95

Launceston	34	26	6	2	115	24	84
Bodmin Town	34	25	4	5	89	36	79
Truro City	34	23	4	7	93	45	73
Falmouth Town	34	22	5	7	106	45	71
Torpoint Athletic	34	21	5	8	78	40	68
Porthleven	34	16	9	9	84	54	57
Millbrook	34	14	11	9	68	58	53
Holsworthy	34	14	9	11	44	44	51
Wadebridge Town	34	14	7	13	66	75	49
Tavistock	34	12	8	14	46	71	43
Appledore-Bideford AAC	34	10	4	20	55	79	34
Mullion	34	8	10	16	46	77	34
Newquay	34	9	6	19	66	86	33
St. Blazey	34	9	6	19	56	74	33
Okehampton Argyle	34	8	4	22	49	100	28
Devon & Cornwall Police	34	8	3	23	52	95	27
Penzance	34	6	7	21	35	79	25
St. Austell	34	4	6	24	31	97	18

Tavistock had 1 point deducted. Mullion left and joined the Cornwall Combination and Devon & Cornwall Police also left. They were replaced by Liskeard Athletic and Saltash United, both from the Western League.

1995-96

Truro City	34	26	4	4	99	27	82
Torpoint Athletic	34	23	8	3	81	32	77
Falmouth Town	34	22	4	8	87	37	70
Launceston	34	20	9	5	95	29	69
Bodmin Town	34	18	10	6	91	36	64
Penzance	34	18	5	11	64	43	59
Newquay	34	18	4	12	73	54	58
Holsworthy	34	17	5	12	58	43	56
Wadebridge Town	34	16	5	13	65	55	53
Saltash United	34	14	8	12	66	67	50
Porthleven	34	13	5	16	61	66	44
St. Austell	34	10	5	19	57	79	35
Millbrook	34	9	7	18	40	59	34
Liskeard Athletic	34	9	6	19	58	96	33
Appledore-Bideford AAC	34	7	7	20	43	80	28
Tavistock	34	6	6	22	55	99	24
St. Blazey	34	4	4	26	38	106	16
Okehampton Argyle	34	4	2	28	24	143	14
					1155	1151	

Okehampton Argyle left and joined the Devon & Exeter League and Appledore-Bideford AAC left and joined the Devon County League. League reduced to 16 clubs.

1996-97

Falmouth Town	30	24	0	6	90	27	72
Truro City	30	22	6	2	68	25	72
Porthleven	30	20	6	4	70	28	66
Bodmin Town	30	16	6	8	60	34	54
Saltash United	30	15	8	7	63	42	53
Penzance	30	14	7	9	62	37	49
Liskeard Athletic	30	13	7	10	39	31	46
Torpoint Athletic	30	11	9	10	52	49	42
Tavistock	30	11	4	15	48	71	37
Newquay	30	10	6	14	44	63	36
Holsworthy	30	8	8	14	28	43	32
St. Blazey	30	9	5	16	51	70	32
St. Austell	30	8	4	18	38	59	28
Millbrook	30	5	7	18	32	70	22
Wadebridge Town	30	4	6	20	21	49	18
Launceston	30	4	3	23	26	94	15

1997-98

Truro City	30	23	3	4	76	15	72
Falmouth Town	30	22	5	3	76	33	71
Porthleven	30	20	6	4	88	24	66
St. Blazey	30	16	3	11	60	39	51
Torpoint Athletic	30	15	4	11	71	56	49
Millbrook	30	14	7	9	52	42	49
Bodmin Town	30	15	4	11	51	48	49
Penzance	30	13	8	9	54	46	47
Saltash United	30	14	3	13	63	60	45
Holsworthy	30	13	5	12	61	67	44
Wadebridge Town	30	11	2	17	40	53	35
Liskeard Athletic	30	7	6	17	45	64	27
Newquay	30	8	3	19	37	73	27
St. Austell	30	5	8	17	33	82	23
Tavistock	30	3	6	21	38	87	15
Launceston	30	3	3	24	27	83	12

Plymouth Parkway joined from the Devon County League.

1998-99

St. Blazey	32	23	5	4	69	25	74
Porthleven	32	22	7	3	102	36	73
Truro City	32	18	8	6	65	37	62
Falmouth Town	32	17	8	7	57	35	59
Wadebridge Town	32	17	6	9	64	34	57
Millbrook	32	17	5	10	55	32	56
Saltash United	32	15	7	10	56	45	52
Bodmin Town	32	15	5	12	65	57	50
Penzance	32	12	7	13	58	62	43
Holsworthy	32	11	8	13	50	56	41
Plymouth Parkway	32	10	6	16	50	74	36
Liskeard Athletic	32	8	9	15	47	62	33
Tavistock	32	8	8	16	32	47	32
Newquay	32	10	2	20	40	64	32
St. Austell	32	7	5	20	29	67	26
Torpoint Athletic	32	5	5	22	39	73	20
Launceston	32	4	5	23	33	105	17

Callington Town joined from the ECPL. League increased to 18 clubs.

1999-2000

Falmouth Town	34	24	8	2	88	25	80
St. Blazey	34	25	5	4	97	36	80
Porthleven	34	23	9	2	91	41	78
Liskeard Athletic	34	18	7	9	80	40	61
Millbrook	34	17	9	8	68	47	60
Saltash United	34	18	3	13	61	50	57
Wadebridge Town	34	17	4	13	66	59	55
Tavistock	34	14	9	11	51	46	51
Plymouth Parkway	34	15	6	13	57	73	51
Newquay	34	14	5	15	67	76	47
Bodmin Town	34	14	4	16	60	64	46
Truro City	34	10	5	19	55	71	35
Penzance	34	10	4	20	51	76	34
Torpoint Athletic	34	9	6	19	53	74	33
Holsworthy	34	7	10	17	51	63	31
Callington Town	34	7	6	21	41	85	27
Launceston	34	5	5	24	35	95	20
St. Austell	34	4	5	25	31	82	17

Penryn Athletic joined from the Cornwall Combination.

2000-01

St. Blazey	36	27	6	3	124	33	87
Porthleven	36	25	8	3	90	26	83
Liskeard Athletic	36	24	7	5	97	55	79
Holsworthy	36	24	3	9	84	44	75
Millbrook	36	22	6	8	94	45	72
Saltash United	36	21	8	7	85	43	71
Falmouth Town	36	18	10	8	72	46	64
Penzance	36	16	9	11	65	59	57
Tavistock	36	14	8	14	50	52	50
Torpoint Athletic	36	14	7	15	56	60	49
Plymouth Parkway	36	12	4	20	53	77	40
Callington Town	36	11	6	19	63	93	39
Newquay	36	10	8	18	58	81	38
Truro City	36	11	4	21	58	81	37
Penryn Athletic	36	10	5	21	49	80	35
St. Austell	36	7	6	23	41	76	27
Launceston	36	8	3	25	39	92	27
Wadebridge Town	36	6	4	26	51	115	22
Bodmin Town	36	5	2	29	39	110	17

2001-02

St. Blazey	36	33	3	0	120	25	102
Porthleven	36	27	4	5	105	32	85
Liskeard Athletic	36	25	4	7	121	53	79
Holsworthy	36	24	5	7	94	47	77
Plymouth Parkway	36	21	6	9	88	50	69
Penzance	36	16	8	12	79	62	56
Falmouth Town	36	16	6	14	82	86	54
Tavistock	36	15	7	14	61	53	52
Saltash United	36	15	5	16	62	76	50
Newquay	36	14	7	15	76	68	49
Bodmin Town	36	13	9	14	66	81	48
Torpoint Athletic	36	13	6	17	67	74	45
Wadebridge Town	36	13	6	17	58	70	45
Launceston	36	12	2	22	65	91	38
Millbrook	36	8	7	21	44	93	31
Callington Town	36	8	5	23	57	112	29
Truro City	36	6	10	20	57	82	28
Penryn Athletic	36	8	3	25	42	84	27
St. Austell	36	2	3	31	20	125	9

2002-03

St. Blazey	36	30	5	1	126	23	95
Tavistock	36	24	5	7	87	41	77
Porthleven	36	23	5	8	95	48	74
Plymouth Parkway	36	23	4	9	83	55	73
Liskeard Athletic	36	21	4	11	95	59	67
Wadebridge Town	36	17	9	10	61	46	60
Launceston	36	18	6	12	79	78	60
Holsworthy	36	17	7	12	59	48	58
Saltash United	36	17	3	16	79	68	54
Falmouth Town	36	16	5	15	60	61	53
Newquay	36	13	4	19	64	77	43
Penzance	36	12	5	19	53	55	41
Torpoint Athletic	36	11	8	17	48	69	41
Millbrook	36	12	4	20	56	80	40
Callington Town	36	11	6	19	64	80	39
Truro City	36	9	6	21	44	74	33
Penryn Athletic	36	7	7	22	51	84	28
St. Austell	36	7	6	23	45	108	27
Bodmin Town	36	3	3	30	30	125	12

Holsworthy left and joined the Devon County League. League reduced to 18 clubs.

2003-04

St. Blazey	34	27	5	2	90	26	86
Bodmin Town	34	26	4	4	88	29	82
Porthleven	34	19	5	10	68	46	62
Millbrook	34	14	14	6	75	42	56
Saltash United	34	16	8	10	62	58	56
St. Austell	34	16	6	12	58	45	54
Wadebridge Town	34	14	11	9	57	39	53
Penzance	34	14	8	12	50	46	50
Plymouth Parkway	34	12	9	13	51	60	45
Tavistock	34	12	7	15	52	71	43
Launceston	34	11	8	15	52	67	41
Liskeard Athletic	34	11	6	17	43	50	39
Falmouth Town	34	11	5	18	52	72	38
Torpoint Athletic	34	10	6	18	53	72	36
Truro City	34	7	10	17	47	69	31
Penryn Athletic	34	9	4	21	67	90	31
Newquay	34	7	5	22	41	81	26
Callington Town	34	7	5	22	50	93	26

Saltash United left and joined the Western League. League reduced to 17 clubs.

2004-05

St. Blazey	32	26	3	3	109	25	81
Bodmin Town	32	24	2	6	102	23	74
Millbrook	32	21	7	4	77	39	70
Falmouth Town	32	20	6	6	76	30	66
Liskeard Athletic	32	20	6	6	80	39	66
Truro City	32	17	4	11	66	49	55
Wadebridge Town	32	15	8	9	56	44	53
Plymouth Parkway	32	14	6	12	65	54	48
St. Austell	32	14	3	15	69	73	45
Launceston	32	12	6	14	59	62	42
Newquay	32	10	6	16	48	64	36
Torpoint Athletic	32	9	5	18	47	81	32
Penryn Athletic	32	8	6	18	45	85	30
Penzance	32	6	8	18	48	78	26
Tavistock	32	4	8	20	48	88	20
Callington Town	32	5	2	25	37	120	17
Porthleven	32	3	2	27	30	108	11

Goonhavern joined from the Cornwall Combination. League increased to 18 clubs.

2005-06

Bodmin Town	34	25	6	3	89	31	81
Truro City	34	22	7	5	78	29	70
Falmouth Town	34	22	5	7	88	42	70
Liskeard Athletic	34	20	9	5	93	34	69
St. Blazey	34	19	12	3	92	44	69
Penryn Athletic	34	21	3	10	98	47	66
Plymouth Parkway	34	19	8	7	78	54	65
Wadebridge Town	34	17	5	12	47	46	56
Tavistock	34	15	6	13	67	59	51
Porthleven	34	12	5	17	50	62	41
Launceston	34	11	7	16	51	66	40
Millbrook	34	10	9	15	37	54	39
Penzance	34	10	4	20	52	74	34
Newquay	34	7	9	18	44	76	30
Goonhavern	34	6	6	22	31	80	24
Callington Town	34	5	3	26	31	88	18
Torpoint Athletic	34	4	6	24	23	85	18
St. Austell	34	5	2	27	39	117	17

Truro City had 3 points deducted and Falmouth Town had 1 point deducted. Truro City left and joined the Western League.

GLOUCESTERSHIRE COUNTY LEAGUE

Until the Gloucestershire County League was formed in 1968, clubs in the north and south of the county had their own competitions. The Avon Premier Combination was the principal competition for those in the Bristol area while the Gloucestershire Northern Senior League catered for those in the north. The new Gloucestershire County League combined many of the top clubs from these two competitions.

Abbreviations:

APC = Avon Premier Combination

GNSL = Gloucestershire Northern Senior League.

Several of the published tables contained errors in the goals scored record. Additional research has succeeded in correcting many of these, totals that still do not balance are shown below the relevant columns in italics.

1968-69

Stonehouse	30	26	4	0	102	27	56
Bristol St. George	30	20	6	4	91	34	46
Hanham Athletic	30	16	7	7	85	48	39
Yate Y.M.C.A.	30	16	6	8	74	45	38
Cirencester Town	30	15	4	11	70	52	34
Forest Green Rovers	30	13	8	9	43	44	34
Old Patchwegians	30	11	7	12	49	64	29
Sharpness	30	11	6	13	58	58	28
Cinderford Town Reserves	30	12	4	14	56	59	28
Cadbury Heath	30	10	8	12	37	52	28
Charlton Kings	30	10	7	13	51	63	27
Gloucester City Reserves	30	10	6	14	51	72	26
Matson Athletic	30	9	2	19	44	71	20
Thornbury	30	5	8	17	45	71	18
Bristol Rovers "A"	30	6	6	18	41	79	18
Brimscombe	30	3	5	22	27	85	11

Cinderford Town joined from the West Midlands League, replacing their reserves. Cirencester Town left and joined the Hellenic League and were replaced by Old Georgians. Yate Y.M.C.A. changed their name to Yate Town.

1969-70

Bristol St. George	30	23	7	0	97	32	53
Cinderford Town	30	20	8	2	76	22	48
Forest Green Rovers	30	18	7	5	84	48	43
Sharpness	30	18	5	7	71	53	41
Old Georgians	30	13	6	11	57	47	32
Yate Town	30	12	6	12	48	54	30
Stonehouse	30	9	11	10	62	62	29
Cadbury Heath	30	11	6	13	43	50	28
Hanham Athletic	30	8	10	12	45	55	26
Bristol Rovers "A"	30	8	10	12	62	92	26
Matson Athletic	30	9	6	15	45	60	24
Old Patchwegians	30	8	8	14	30	45	24
Gloucester City Reserves	30	9	4	17	52	64	22
Thornbury	30	8	5	17	49	68	21
Brimscombe	30	5	8	17	30	67	18
Charlton Kings	30	6	3	21	35	76	15
					886	*895*	

Gloucester City Reserves left but Lydbrook Athletic joined from the Midland Combination and Clifton St. Vincent and Worrall Hill also joined, increasing the league to 18 clubs.

1970-71

Cadbury Heath	34	25	6	3	89	24	56
Sharpness	34	24	7	3	80	33	55
Forest Green Rovers	34	25	3	6	96	45	53
Cinderford Town	34	23	5	6	85	30	51
Worrall Hill	34	14	14	6	46	24	42
Old Georgians	34	18	5	11	77	49	41
Stonehouse	34	17	5	12	73	51	39
Old Patchwegians	34	12	8	14	52	63	32
Clifton St. Vincent	34	10	9	15	50	68	29
Bristol St. George	34	11	6	17	55	62	28
Matson Athletic	34	9	9	16	41	53	27
Yate Town	34	9	9	16	44	61	27
Hanham Athletic	34	11	4	19	41	68	26
Brimscombe	34	9	6	19	32	63	24
Bristol Rovers "A"	34	8	7	19	44	68	23
Charlton Kings	34	8	6	20	44	77	22
Thornbury	34	7	8	19	34	79	22
Lydbrook Athletic	34	5	5	24	25	90	15

1971-72

Cadbury Heath	34	25	7	2	94	26	57
Cinderford Town	34	20	12	2	77	30	52
Bristol St. George	34	20	6	8	86	38	46
Forest Green Rovers	34	18	6	10	62	48	42
Old Georgians	34	16	7	11	60	50	39
Stonehouse	34	15	9	10	68	59	39
Worrall Hill	34	14	7	13	58	53	35
Bristol Rovers "A"	34	13	8	13	63	57	34
Sharpness	34	11	12	11	56	54	34
Matson Athletic	34	15	4	15	54	59	34
Charlton Kings	34	14	6	14	55	67	34
Old Patchwegians	34	9	11	14	42	53	29
Brimscombe	34	11	6	17	52	71	28
Clifton St. Vincent	34	9	7	18	49	68	25
Yate Town	34	9	7	18	36	56	25
Lydbrook Athletic	34	9	5	20	33	60	23
Thornbury	34	3	14	17	37	74	20
Hanham Athletic	34	5	6	23	42	101	16

1972-73

Cadbury Heath	34	27	4	3	102	28	58
Bristol St. George	34	24	5	5	89	44	53
Cinderford Town	34	18	10	6	76	34	46
Old Georgians	34	19	8	7	84	51	46
Charlton Kings	34	19	6	9	66	43	44
Thornbury	34	13	13	8	59	52	39
Sharpness	34	14	8	12	58	55	36
Stonehouse	34	12	12	10	61	71	36
Forest Green Rovers	34	11	12	11	60	57	34
Matson Athletic	34	12	9	13	59	53	33
Worrall Hill	34	10	11	13	49	48	31
Bristol Rovers "A"	34	11	8	15	48	57	30
Old Patchwegians	34	12	5	17	41	55	29
Yate Town	34	10	6	18	53	54	26
Lydbrook Athletic	34	8	5	21	51	96	21
Hanham Athletic	34	7	7	20	54	98	19
Clifton St. Vincent	34	4	8	22	41	87	16
Brimscombe	34	5	3	26	46	115	13
					1097	*1098*	

Hanham Athletic had 2 points deducted for fielding an ineligible player.
Brimscombe left and joined the GNSL and were replaced by Wilton Rovers.
Old Patchwegians changed their name to Patchway.

1973-74

Cadbury Heath	34	26	6	2	87	28	58
Cinderford Town	34	26	4	4	89	25	56
Matson Athletic	34	21	7	6	79	48	49
Bristol Rovers "A"	34	18	7	9	79	56	43
Worrall Hill	34	16	8	10	59	46	40
Old Georgians	34	16	7	11	64	56	39
Sharpness	34	14	9	11	63	60	37
Yate Town	34	16	4	14	56	48	36
Hanham Athletic	34	14	9	11	62	49	35
Forest Green Rovers	34	14	5	15	49	55	33
Patchway	34	9	13	12	48	52	31
Charlton Kings	34	13	5	16	46	51	31
Bristol St. George	34	11	6	17	47	58	28
Thornbury	34	8	9	17	42	57	25
Stonehouse	34	7	8	19	47	75	22
Lydbrook Athletic	34	6	8	20	48	87	20
Clifton St. Vincent	34	8	4	22	37	69	20
Wilton Rovers	34	2	3	29	19	101	7

Hanham Athletic had 2 points deducted for fielding an ineligible player. Cinderford Town left and joined the Midland Combination and were replaced by Oldland (Decora).

1974-75

Matson Athletic	34	25	4	5	91	36	54
Cadbury Heath	34	24	5	5	95	25	53
Yate Town	34	20	6	8	57	36	46
Lydbrook Athletic	34	16	12	6	78	47	44
Worrall Hill	34	16	8	10	42	32	40
Forest Green Rovers	34	16	7	11	72	62	39
Oldland (Decora)	34	14	10	10	53	48	38
Clifton St. Vincent	34	13	8	13	52	56	34
Patchway	34	12	8	14	36	41	32
Sharpness	34	14	3	17	74	79	31
Old Georgians	34	12	6	16	57	68	30
Bristol St. George	34	11	8	15	42	54	30
Charlton Kings	34	11	6	17	48	58	28
Stonehouse	34	11	6	17	52	63	28
Thornbury Town	34	9	8	17	43	65	26
Hanham Athletic	34	9	5	20	41	66	23
Bristol Rovers "A"	34	8	5	21	41	82	21
Wilton Rovers	34	2	11	21	35	85	15
					1009	1003	

Forest Green Rovers left and joined the Hellenic League and Cadbury Heath left and joined the Midland Combination. They were replaced by Almondsbury Greenway from the APC and Shortwood United from the GNSL.

1975-76

Matson Athletic	34	29	2	3	102	20	60
Almondsbury Greenway	34	23	6	5	84	35	52
Oldland (Decora)	34	21	7	6	68	36	49
Bristol St. George	34	17	9	8	70	44	43
Yate Town	34	17	8	9	78	47	42
Worrall Hill	34	15	7	12	66	53	37
Patchway	34	13	11	10	45	45	37
Thornbury Town	34	16	4	14	75	41	36
Old Georgians	34	12	8	14	45	44	32
Lydbrook Athletic	34	12	6	16	41	58	30
Wilton Rovers	34	9	12	13	37	51	30
Clifton St. Vincent	34	10	5	19	42	74	25
Bristol Rovers "A"	34	9	7	18	48	81	25
Charlton Kings	34	7	10	17	40	58	24
Hanham Athletic	34	7	10	17	48	87	24
Shortwood United	34	8	8	18	50	90	24
Sharpness	34	7	9	18	35	65	23
Stonehouse	34	5	9	20	40	85	19

Bristol Rovers "A" left, reducing the league to 17 clubs.

1976-77

Almondsbury Greenway	32	26	4	2	90	22	56
Matson Athletic	32	21	5	6	78	25	47
Old Georgians	32	20	7	5	54	27	47
Oldland (Decora)	32	20	4	8	67	41	44
Yate Town	32	18	6	8	71	37	42
Worrall Hill	32	16	7	9	60	43	39
Sharpness	32	12	10	10	52	43	34
Shortwood United	32	11	9	12	52	54	31
Hanham Athletic	32	12	6	14	40	41	30
Bristol St. George	32	12	4	16	42	50	28
Clifton St. Vincent	32	12	4	16	48	65	28
Charlton Kings	32	8	7	17	42	69	23
Patchway	32	9	5	18	41	68	23
Wilton Rovers	32	7	9	16	36	62	23
Lydbrook Athletic	32	6	7	19	38	68	19
Thornbury Town	32	3	10	19	41	86	14
Stonehouse	32	5	4	23	32	83	14

Thornbury Town had 2 points deducted for fielding an ineligible player. Thornbury Town left but Gloucester City Reserves and Hambrook joined, increasing the league to 18 clubs.

1977-78

Almondsbury Greenway	34	28	2	4	112	28	58
Hambrook	34	22	6	6	55	26	50
Matson Athletic	34	21	4	9	83	43	46
Old Georgians	34	20	6	8	62	36	46
Yate Town	34	20	4	10	77	46	44
Worrall Hill	34	17	8	9	60	39	42
Shortwood United	34	14	9	11	63	57	37
Oldland (Decora)	34	13	9	12	59	61	35
Patchway	34	10	12	12	56	66	32
Bristol St. George	34	11	8	15	61	61	30
Gloucester City Reserves	34	12	6	16	49	65	30
Stonehouse	34	10	9	15	50	72	29
Hanham Athletic	34	11	6	17	46	68	28
Wilton Rovers	34	9	9	16	48	48	27
Sharpness	34	10	7	17	52	60	27
Charlton Kings	34	8	5	21	32	76	21
Lydbrook Athletic	34	6	8	20	53	87	20
Clifton St. Vincent	34	4	2	28	24	91	10
					1042	1030	

Port of Bristol joined from the Bristol & Suburban League but Charlton Kings and Clifton St. Vincent left, reducing the league to 17 clubs.

1978-79

Almondsbury Greenway	32	23	3	6	112	36	49
Hambrook	32	22	4	6	73	44	48
Worrall Hill	32	18	7	7	64	45	43
Port of Bristol	32	16	10	6	72	45	42
Matson Athletic	32	16	9	7	67	44	41
Sharpness	32	16	3	13	64	48	35
Yate Town	32	13	9	10	58	44	35
Hanham Athletic	32	15	5	12	55	44	35
Old Georgians	32	13	9	10	53	48	35
Stonehouse	32	12	10	10	47	55	34
Bristol St. George	32	10	5	17	45	54	25
Lydbrook Athletic	32	8	9	15	42	69	25
Patchway	32	7	9	16	39	75	23
Wilton Rovers	32	9	4	19	33	68	22
Oldland (Decora)	32	6	9	17	33	61	21
Shortwood United	32	3	10	19	43	88	16
Gloucester City Reserves	32	3	9	20	33	65	15

Worrall Hill left and joined the Hellenic League but Frampton United and Newent Town joined, increasing the league to 18 clubs.

1979-80

Almondsbury Greenway	34	24	5	5	123	44	53
Shortwood United	34	19	8	7	89	60	46
Sharpness	34	13	15	6	53	42	41
Matson Athletic	34	14	12	8	67	54	40
Yate Town	34	15	10	9	66	57	40
Port of Bristol	34	15	8	11	78	52	38
Hambrook	34	12	12	10	52	42	36
Bristol St. George	34	11	14	9	51	42	36
Oldland (Decora)	34	12	11	11	58	59	35
Frampton United	34	13	8	13	59	72	34
Newent Town	34	11	9	14	53	57	31
Hanham Athletic	34	8	14	12	50	61	30
Lydbrook Athletic	34	10	10	14	47	59	30
Old Georgians	34	10	9	15	43	65	29
Stonehouse	34	11	4	19	46	80	26
Gloucester City Reserves	34	9	7	18	45	74	25
Wilton Rovers	34	3	18	13	25	42	24
Patchway	34	4	10	20	43	86	18

Patchway left and were replaced by Cadbury Heath from the APC.
Bristol St. George became Immediate Bristol St. George.

1980-81

Almondsbury Greenway	34	27	4	3	108	45	58
Shortwood United	34	23	3	8	73	37	49
Wilton Rovers	34	22	4	8	72	43	48
Port of Bristol	34	17	9	8	65	45	43
Matson Athletic	34	18	5	11	85	54	41
Sharpness	34	13	11	10	49	39	37
Immediate Bristol St. George	34	14	9	11	51	44	37
Lydbrook Athletic	34	12	12	10	55	53	36
Gloucester City Reserves	34	16	4	14	63	71	36
Frampton United	34	15	5	14	59	56	35
Yate Town	34	15	4	15	62	55	34
Hambrook	34	15	4	15	52	51	34
Newent Town	34	11	9	14	49	57	31
Oldland (Decora)	34	8	12	14	39	57	28
Hanham Athletic	34	9	2	23	47	79	20
Old Georgians	34	5	7	22	26	64	17
Cadbury Heath	34	5	7	22	27	68	17
Stonehouse	34	3	5	26	43	107	11

Gloucester City Reserves left, reducing the league to 17 clubs.

1981-82

(Goal difference replaced goal average to decide places for teams with equal points)

Shortwood United	32	22	6	4	92	49	50
Almondsbury Greenway	32	21	7	4	88	32	49
Lydbrook Athletic	32	17	11	4	69	36	45
Wilton Rovers	32	18	6	8	66	44	42
Immediate Bristol St. George	32	19	5	8	75	42	41
Port of Bristol	32	16	6	10	70	53	38
Old Georgians	32	16	6	10	56	39	38
Hambrook	32	13	8	11	54	57	34
Sharpness	32	11	10	11	60	49	32
Oldland (Decora)	32	10	9	13	44	57	29
Hanham Athletic	32	6	15	11	41	50	27
Yate Town	32	8	8	16	53	81	24
Newent Town	32	7	9	16	29	54	23
Matson Athletic	32	8	6	18	43	72	22
Frampton United	32	6	8	18	41	60	20
Cadbury Heath	32	4	8	20	27	74	16
Stonehouse	32	3	6	23	34	93	12

Immediate Bristol St. George had 2 points deducted for fielding an ineligible player.
Almondsbury Greenway and Shortwood United left and joined the Hellenic League and Matson Athletic also left. They were replaced by Avon St. Philips from the APC, Harrow Hill from the GNSL and Lawrence Weston Hallen.

1982-83

Old Georgians	32	26	3	3	73	23	55
Port of Bristol	32	20	7	5	64	33	47
Lawrence Weston Hallen	32	18	6	8	52	29	42
Hanham Athletic	32	16	10	6	49	28	42
Sharpness	32	14	8	10	51	48	36
Wilton Rovers	32	13	7	12	51	44	33
Hambrook	32	12	8	12	49	38	32
Avon St. Philips	32	11	10	11	53	50	32
Immediate Bristol St. George	32	11	9	12	57	48	31
Harrow Hill	32	13	3	16	55	63	29
Lydbrook Athletic	32	11	7	14	45	55	29
Frampton United	32	9	10	13	44	49	28
Yate Town	32	10	7	15	44	60	27
Oldland (Decora)	32	10	6	16	41	50	26
Cadbury Heath	32	7	8	17	52	72	22
Newent Town	32	6	10	16	41	65	22
Stonehouse	32	3	5	24	28	94	11

Yate Town left and joined the Hellenic League but Frampton Athletic from the APC and Wotton Rovers from the GNSL both joined, increasing the league to 18 clubs. Immediate Bristol St. George became Bristol St. George and Hanham Athletic became Mount Hill Hanham Athletic.

1983-84

Sharpness	34	29	4	1	116	26	62
Old Georgians	34	24	7	3	76	29	55
Bristol St. George	34	17	9	8	61	40	43
Port of Bristol	34	14	11	9	50	41	39
Avon St. Philips	34	15	5	11	65	59	38
Lawrence Weston Hallen	34	16	4	14	54	51	36
Hambrook	34	14	6	14	43	46	34
Frampton Athletic	34	15	3	16	61	60	33
Oldland (Decora)	34	12	9	13	59	61	33
Hanham Mount Hill Athletic	34	12	9	13	47	50	33
Harrow Hill	34	11	9	14	40	48	31
Wotton Rovers	34	10	10	14	43	51	30
Wilton Rovers	34	10	9	15	41	61	29
Frampton United	34	9	9	16	43	58	27
Newent Town	34	10	7	17	48	65	27
Lydbrook Athletic	34	10	6	18	57	63	26
Cadbury Heath	34	6	10	18	35	64	22
Stonehouse	34	4	6	24	38	104	14

Sharpness left and joined the Hellenic League. Ellwood from the GNSL and Cinderford Town from the Midland Combination joined, increasing the league to 19 clubs. Hanham Mount Hill Athletic reverted to Hanham Athletic and Cadbury Heath became Cadbury Heath St. Josephs.

1984-85

Old Georgians	36	23	10	3	109	46	56
Port of Bristol	36	20	10	6	78	42	50
Hanham Athletic	36	18	10	8	62	36	46
Lydbrook Athletic	36	19	7	10	80	51	45
Lawrence Weston Hallen	36	16	12	8	64	49	44
Ellwood	36	18	7	11	70	56	43
Cinderford Town	36	16	11	9	44	32	43
Harrow Hill	36	16	8	12	74	58	40
Hambrook	36	16	8	12	56	56	40
Avon St. Philips	36	11	11	14	54	54	33
Frampton United	36	10	13	13	43	55	33
Wotton Rovers	36	8	15	13	47	60	31
Cadbury Heath St. Josephs	36	10	9	17	52	67	29
Stonehouse	36	10	9	17	49	71	29
Newent Town	36	10	9	17	38	67	29
Oldland (Decora)	36	9	8	19	38	63	26
Bristol St. George	36	7	11	18	57	76	25
Wilton Rovers	36	6	9	21	52	72	24
Frampton Athletic	36	6	6	24	44	100	18

Frampton Athletic left and joined the APC and Wilton Rovers left and joined the GNSL. They were replaced by Brimscombe & Thrupp from the GNSL and Patchway from the APC.

1985-86

Patchway	36	27	5	4	80	20	59
Old Georgians	36	22	9	5	80	25	53
Ellwood	36	21	8	7	78	45	50
Brimscombe & Thrupp	36	19	9	8	54	45	47
Wotton Rovers	36	17	11	8	53	42	45
Cinderford Town	36	16	10	10	52	37	42
Lydbrook Athletic	36	17	7	12	66	47	41
Port of Bristol	36	14	12	10	59	46	40
Bristol St. George	36	17	4	15	57	52	38
Harrow Hill	36	14	10	12	66	64	38
Hanham Athletic	36	11	10	15	49	61	32
Avon St. Philips	36	11	8	17	54	66	30
Cadbury Heath St. Josephs	36	12	5	19	54	69	29
Lawrence Weston Hallen	36	8	9	19	44	62	25
Hambrook	36	8	9	19	31	58	25
Stonehouse	36	8	9	19	41	69	25
Frampton United	36	8	8	20	38	59	24
Newent Town	36	7	10	19	39	71	24
Oldland (Decora)	36	3	11	22	42	99	17

Newent Town and Oldland (Decora) left and were replaced by Henbury Old Boys from the APC and Gala Wilton.

1986-87

Old Georgians	36	28	5	3	95	21	61
Ellwood	36	24	6	6	86	43	54
Patchway	36	22	6	8	86	49	50
Bristol St. George	36	15	16	5	67	42	46
Harrow Hill	36	20	5	11	64	43	45
Henbury Old Boys	36	17	8	11	64	42	42
Hanham Athletic	36	16	7	13	53	51	39
Wotton Rovers	36	16	7	13	61	47	39
Lawrence Weston Hallen	36	13	12	11	55	50	38
Cinderford Town	36	15	7	14	60	61	37
Cadbury Heath St. Josephs	36	12	10	14	64	71	34
Port of Bristol	36	12	8	16	47	53	32
Frampton United	36	11	9	16	51	55	31
Brimscombe & Thrupp	36	10	9	17	51	53	29
Gala Wilton	36	11	7	18	43	68	29
Hambrook	36	11	4	21	35	67	26
Stonehouse	36	10	7	19	62	95	24
Lydbrook Athletic	36	4	10	22	35	86	18
Avon St. Philips	36	1	5	30	28	110	7

Stonehouse had 3 points deducted. Bymacks and D.R.G. (FP) joined but Avon St. Philips, Bristol St. George and Lydbrook Athletic left, reducing the league to 18 clubs. Cadbury Heath St. Josephs reverted to Cadbury Heath.

1987-88

Old Georgians	34	26	4	4	108	45	56
Lawrence Weston Hallen	34	23	9	2	78	29	55
Ellwood	34	22	5	7	77	37	49
Henbury Old Boys	34	21	6	7	83	36	48
Patchway	34	17	8	9	65	42	42
Harrow Hill	34	15	8	11	55	49	38
Hambrook	34	15	6	13	49	47	36
D.R.G. (FP)	34	12	9	13	63	51	33
Port of Bristol	34	11	8	15	55	55	30
Wotton Rovers	34	9	12	13	48	64	30
Brimscombe & Thrupp	34	10	9	15	40	51	29
Frampton United	34	9	10	15	30	51	28
Cadbury Heath	34	10	8	16	39	61	28
Bymacks	34	9	10	15	28	50	28
Cinderford Town	34	11	4	19	49	59	26
Hanham Athletic	34	6	13	15	35	56	25
Gala Wilton	34	8	7	19	39	74	23
Stonehouse	34	1	6	27	33	117	4

Stonehouse had 4 Points deducted. Bymacks disbanded and Gala Wilton and Stonehouse were relegated to the GNSL. They were replaced by Campden Town from the Worcestershire Senior League, Pucklechurch Sports from the APC and Tuffley Rovers from the GNSL.

1988-89 (Three points for a win from this season)

Lawrence Weston Hallen	34	24	5	5	86	28	77
Henbury Old Boys	34	23	7	4	87	33	76
Ellwood	34	24	3	7	76	37	75
Old Georgians	34	18	6	10	77	44	60
Pucklechurch Sports	34	18	6	10	78	53	60
Patchway	34	15	14	5	55	39	59
Harrow Hill	34	12	11	11	43	41	47
Campden Town	34	13	7	14	49	50	46
Port of Bristol	34	12	8	14	45	51	44
Hambrook	34	12	7	15	47	55	43
Tuffley Rovers	34	11	8	15	54	60	39
Cinderford Town	34	10	8	16	57	74	38
D.R.G. (FP)	34	8	13	13	47	62	37
Cadbury Heath	34	9	7	18	44	61	34
Wotton Rovers	34	8	8	18	43	77	32
Frampton United	34	6	13	15	37	51	31
Hanham Athletic	34	7	10	17	40	67	31
Brimscombe & Thrupp	34	1	9	24	22	104	12

Tuffley Rovers had 2 points deducted. Brimscombe & Thrupp left and joined the GNSL and Hanham Athletic left and joined the APC. St. Philips Marsh Adult School from the APC and Berkeley Town both joined.

1989-90

Ellwood	34	27	3	4	84	32	84
Old Georgians	34	22	6	6	82	39	72
Henbury Old Boys	34	19	6	9	84	48	63
Lawrence Weston Hallen	34	17	9	8	69	57	60
Cadbury Heath	34	18	5	11	69	45	59
Harrow Hill	34	16	8	10	66	40	56
St. Philips Marsh Adult School	34	16	7	11	65	58	55
D.R.G. (FP)	34	14	10	10	66	57	52
Patchway	34	11	8	15	57	68	41
Wotton Rovers	34	12	4	18	45	66	40
Cinderford Town	34	10	9	15	52	60	39
Port of Bristol	34	10	9	15	51	65	39
Hambrook	34	9	10	15	45	56	37
Pucklechurch Sports	34	8	12	14	44	57	36
Tuffley Rovers	34	9	8	17	47	61	35
Berkeley Town	34	8	11	15	32	46	35
Campden Town	34	8	6	20	36	84	30
Frampton United	34	4	5	25	29	84	17

Cinderford Town left and joined the Hellenic League and Frampton United left and joined the GNSL. They were replaced by Stapleton from the APC and St. Marks C.A. Lawrence Weston Hallen changed their name to Hallen.

1990-91

Tuffley Rovers	34	23	2	9	87	34	71
Cadbury Heath	34	21	6	7	80	42	69
Ellwood	34	20	7	7	84	46	67
Henbury Old Boys	34	18	11	5	51	32	65
Hallen	34	20	4	10	85	56	64
Patchway	34	18	3	13	71	55	55
St. Philips Marsh Adult School	34	14	10	10	77	55	52
Old Georgians	34	14	7	13	48	64	49
D.R.G. (FP)	34	11	10	13	45	59	43
Hambrook	34	12	6	16	55	58	42
St. Marks C.A.	34	12	5	17	52	63	41
Harrow Hill	34	10	9	15	41	49	39
Port of Bristol	34	8	11	15	54	70	35
Stapleton	34	10	5	19	36	64	35
Wotton Rovers	34	8	9	17	54	73	33
Pucklechurch Sports	34	7	12	15	40	70	33
Campden Town	34	8	5	21	51	80	29
Berkeley Town	34	5	12	17	52	93	27

Dowty Dynamos joined from the GNSL. Berkeley Town left and joined the GNSL and Tuffley Rovers left and joined the Hellenic League. League reduced to 17 clubs.

1991-92

Patchway Town	32	24	5	3	87	29	77
Cadbury Heath	32	19	11	2	85	27	68
Hallen	32	19	8	5	83	46	65
D.R.G. (FP)	32	18	9	5	56	37	63
Ellwood	32	17	5	10	60	47	56
St. Philips Marsh Adult School	32	14	10	8	70	48	52
Pucklechurch Sports	32	11	11	10	43	49	44
Wotton Rovers	32	12	7	13	59	41	43
Henbury Old Boys	32	12	4	16	53	53	40
Campden Town	32	11	5	16	39	55	38
Stapleton	32	9	7	16	42	66	34
Old Georgians	32	9	7	16	24	50	34
Harrow Hill	32	8	9	15	41	53	33
Hambrook	32	9	6	17	43	56	33
St. Marks C.A.	32	8	8	16	34	59	32
Dowty Dynamos	32	8	6	18	39	71	30
Port of Bristol	32	4	2	26	33	104	14

Port of Bristol left and joined the Bristol & Suburban League. Smiths Athletic joined from the GNSL and Winterbourne United joined from the APC. League increased to 18 clubs.

1992-93

Hallen	34	26	2	6	91	35	80
Old Georgians	34	24	5	5	77	37	77
Ellwood	34	21	4	9	93	50	67
D.R.G. (FP)	34	20	3	11	74	42	63
Wotton Rovers	34	16	9	9	61	56	57
Harrow Hill	34	16	6	12	67	54	54
Patchway Town	34	14	11	9	59	43	53
Cadbury Heath	34	15	6	13	52	51	51
Henbury Old Boys	34	13	11	10	52	49	50
Pucklechurch Sports	34	14	4	16	46	56	46
St. Philips Marsh Adult School	34	12	7	15	53	51	43
St. Marks C.A.	34	12	6	16	43	52	42
Campden Town	34	10	10	14	39	55	40
Winterbourne United	34	10	7	17	47	70	37
Dowty Dynamos	34	8	8	18	49	63	32
Smiths Athletic	34	8	8	18	42	62	32
Stapleton	34	6	5	23	42	87	23
Hambrook	34	2	6	26	19	93	12

Hallen left and joined the Hellenic League and Hambrook left and joined the APC. They were replaced by Endsleigh from the GNSL and Totterdown Athletic from the Bristol & Suburban League. D.R.G. (FP) changed their name to D.R.G.

1993-94

Cadbury Heath	34	24	5	5	68	28	77
Endsleigh	34	23	5	6	78	27	74
St. Philips Marsh Adult School	34	23	4	7	66	22	73
Ellwood	34	18	9	7	67	34	63
Henbury Old Boys	34	18	8	8	67	41	62
Patchway Town	34	16	11	7	67	35	59
Harrow Hill	34	16	5	13	73	42	53
Totterdown Athletic	34	15	7	12	63	56	52
D.R.G.	34	15	5	14	54	50	50
Old Georgians	34	14	6	14	46	53	48
Pucklechurch Sports	34	13	8	13	41	51	47
St. Marks C.A.	34	13	7	14	50	47	46
Wotton Rovers	34	13	3	18	56	56	42
Smiths Athletic	34	11	9	14	50	56	42
Stapleton	33	8	5	20	34	69	29
Winterbourne United	34	7	6	21	42	70	27
Campden Town	33	2	4	27	27	116	10
Dowty Dynamos	34	1	3	30	30	126	6

Stapleton vs Campden Town was not played as Campden Town could not raise a side.
Dowty Dynamos left and joined the GNSL, Endsleigh left and joined the Hellenic League and Campden Town also left. Broadwell Amateurs joined from the GNSL and Oldland joined from the APC. League reduced to 17 clubs. Totterdown Athletic merged with Port of Bristol and became Totterdown Port of Bristol.

1994-95

Henbury Old Boys	32	19	10	3	62	29	67
Harrow Hill	32	17	10	5	52	32	61
Pucklechurch Sports	32	17	4	11	49	43	55
Ellwood	32	15	9	8	66	45	54
D.R.G.	32	14	7	11	51	50	49
Old Georgians	32	13	8	11	52	48	47
Cadbury Heath	32	13	8	11	57	54	47
Stapleton	32	13	8	11	45	45	47
Totterdown Port of Bristol	32	12	6	14	48	42	42
St. Marks C.A.	32	10	9	13	41	50	39
Wotton Rovers	32	9	11	12	40	48	38
Broadwell Amateurs	32	10	7	15	40	42	37
Winterbourne United	32	11	3	18	59	66	36
Patchway Town	32	7	11	14	42	52	32
Smiths Athletic	32	8	8	16	37	58	32
Oldland	32	5	15	12	40	58	30
St. Philips Marsh Adult School	32	9	6	17	47	65	33
					828	827	

St. Philips Marsh Adult School had 3 points deducted. Harrow Hill left and joined the Hellenic League, St. Philips Marsh Adult School left and joined the Bristol Premier Combination and Oldland also left. Broad Plain House Old Boys joined from the Bristol & Suburban League, Bitton and Frampton Athletic both joined from the Bristol Premier Combination and Brockworth joined from the GNSL. League increased to 18 clubs.

1995-96

D.R.G.	34	23	7	4	74	30	76
Cadbury Heath	34	19	6	9	70	36	63
Broad Plain House Old Boys	34	18	9	7	68	46	63
Brockworth	34	19	5	10	62	42	62
Bitton	34	15	11	8	63	37	56
Frampton Athletic	34	14	9	11	53	49	51
Wotton Rovers	34	14	7	13	54	53	49
Patchway Town	34	13	6	15	51	62	45
Old Georgians	34	11	12	11	49	60	45
Henbury Old Boys	34	11	10	13	49	55	43
St. Marks C.A.	34	11	10	13	68	76	43
Totterdown Port of Bristol	34	11	8	15	58	62	41
Ellwood	34	9	12	13	35	49	39
Broadwell Amateurs	34	9	9	16	38	60	36
Pucklechurch Sports	34	8	11	15	39	63	35
Stapleton	34	8	10	16	38	52	34
Smiths Athletic	34	8	5	21	45	62	29
Winterbourne United	34	6	11	17	43	63	29

Smiths Athletic left and joined the GNSL and Winterbourne United also left. They were replaced by Dursley Town from the GNSL and Oldland.

1996-97

Old Georgians	34	19	13	2	58	27	70
Bitton	34	19	10	5	68	38	67
Frampton Athletic	34	17	10	7	80	54	61
Henbury Old Boys	34	16	10	8	66	44	58
Cadbury Heath	34	16	9	9	64	44	57
Dursley Town	34	15	11	8	44	33	56
Brockworth	34	15	4	15	47	46	49
D.R.G.	34	12	11	11	63	47	47
Broad Plain House Old Boys	34	13	8	13	52	57	47
Oldland	34	12	7	15	51	73	43
Patchway Town	34	10	11	13	41	51	41
Pucklechurch Sports	34	11	7	16	45	52	40
Stapleton	34	10	9	15	46	59	39
Broadwell Amateurs	34	8	11	15	54	61	35
Wotton Rovers	34	9	8	17	40	63	35
Totterdown Port of Bristol	34	9	6	19	36	57	33
Ellwood	34	8	7	19	39	57	31
St. Marks C.A.	34	9	4	21	40	71	31

Bitton left and joined the Western League and St. Marks C.A. left and joined the GNSL. They were replaced by Viney St. Swithins and Winterbourne United.

1997-98

Cadbury Heath	34	24	5	5	81	27	77
Henbury Old Boys	34	19	8	7	55	31	65
Pucklechurch Sports	34	18	9	7	52	31	63
Dursley Town	34	16	12	6	40	23	60
Patchway Town	34	15	11	8	51	36	56
D.R.G.	34	15	10	9	78	56	55
Wotton Rovers	34	14	8	12	53	58	50
Broadwell Amateurs	34	13	9	12	54	48	48
Viney St. Swithins	34	13	8	13	56	47	47
Frampton Athletic	34	12	11	11	43	46	47
Winterbourne United	34	11	12	11	68	59	45
Totterdown Port of Bristol	34	12	6	16	41	55	42
Old Georgians	34	11	6	17	46	60	39
Brockworth	34	9	10	15	36	58	37
Ellwood	34	9	7	18	38	54	34
Broad Plain House Old Boys	34	8	7	19	39	58	31
Oldland	34	5	8	21	46	82	23
Stapleton	34	6	5	23	31	77	23
					908	906	

Stapleton left and joined the Bristol Premier Combination and Oldland also left. They were replaced by Highridge United from the Bristol Premier Combination and Tytherington Rocks from the Bristol Suburban League.

1998-99

Cadbury Heath	34	27	4	3	89	32	85
Highridge United	34	21	8	5	79	32	71
Winterbourne United	34	20	7	7	69	35	67
Patchway Town	34	19	10	5	57	37	67
Dursley Town	34	17	7	10	46	31	58
D.R.G.	34	15	8	11	59	48	53
Frampton Athletic	34	14	10	10	57	38	52
Old Georgians	34	16	4	14	51	56	52
Broad Plain House Old Boys	34	14	7	13	57	47	49
Henbury Old Boys	34	13	10	11	51	43	49
Ellwood	34	10	12	12	28	41	42
Broadwell Amateurs	34	11	8	15	32	47	41
Pucklechurch Sports	34	10	7	17	41	55	37
Brockworth	34	9	8	17	31	51	35
Viney St. Swithins	34	8	8	18	33	61	32
Tytherington Rocks	34	7	10	17	47	63	31
Totterdown Port of Bristol	34	4	7	23	33	66	19
Wotton Rovers	34	2	3	29	26	103	9

Wotton Rovers left and joined the GNSL and Totterdown Port of Bristol also left. They were replaced by Hardwicke from the GNSL and Roman Glass St. George from the Bristol Premier Combination.

1999-2000

Highridge United	34	26	5	3	68	29	83
Cadbury Heath	34	22	6	6	81	42	72
Patchway Town	34	19	6	9	70	33	63
Hardwicke	34	18	5	11	62	47	59
D.R.G.	34	16	10	8	63	35	58
Henbury Old Boys	34	17	6	11	51	41	57
Ellwood	34	16	8	10	54	37	56
Tytherington Rocks	34	17	3	14	67	60	54
Winterbourne United	34	13	7	14	73	67	46
Old Georgians	34	13	7	14	47	62	46
Frampton Athletic	34	13	5	16	50	49	44
Roman Glass St. George	34	12	5	17	57	74	41
Viney St. Swithins	34	10	10	14	43	48	40
Broad Plain House Old Boys	34	10	9	15	35	51	39
Pucklechurch Sports	34	11	5	18	47	70	38
Brockworth	34	7	9	18	40	61	30
Broadwell Amateurs	34	6	3	25	38	93	21
Dursley Town	34	4	3	27	29	76	15

Broadwell Amateurs and Dursley Town both left and joined the GNSL and Cadbury Heath left and joined the Western League. Whitminster from the GNSL, AXA from the Bristol Premier Combination and Totterdown Port of Bristol all joined.
D.R.G. merged with Stapleton and became D.R.G. Stapleton.
Frampton Athletic became Frampton Athletic Rangers.

2000-01

Winterbourne United	34	24	4	6	89	48	76
Highridge United	34	22	4	8	71	28	70
Patchway Town	34	20	9	5	66	31	69
Tytherington Rocks	34	17	7	10	75	48	58
Whitminster	34	15	9	10	59	44	54
Brockworth	34	15	9	10	59	52	54
Roman Glass St. George	34	16	6	12	52	49	54
D.R.G. Stapleton	34	12	11	11	59	52	47
Pucklechurch Sports	34	14	5	15	50	47	47
Totterdown Port of Bristol	34	13	7	14	56	63	46
AXA	34	13	5	16	62	72	44
Hardwicke	34	11	7	16	61	70	40
Viney St. Swithins	34	10	10	14	51	63	40
Ellwood	34	10	6	18	46	66	36
Henbury Old Boys	34	10	5	19	46	64	35
Broad Plain House Old Boys	34	9	7	18	43	65	34
Old Georgians	34	9	6	19	45	75	33
Frampton Athletic Rangers	34	7	1	26	40	93	22

Winterbourne United left and joined the Hellenic League, Brockworth left and joined the GNSL and Frampton Athletic Rangers also left. Almondsbury joined from the Bristol & Suburban League and Slimbridge Town joined from the GNSL. League reduced to 17 clubs.

2001-02

Roman Glass St. George	32	22	3	7	83	40	69
Slimbridge Town	32	21	5	6	81	33	68
Highridge United	32	20	8	4	68	33	68
Ellwood	32	19	5	8	57	36	62
Patchway Town	32	15	11	6	55	27	56
Almondsbury	32	17	5	10	65	38	56
D.R.G. Stapleton	32	13	10	9	51	41	49
Henbury Old Boys	32	11	12	9	50	46	45
Tytherington Rocks	32	10	8	14	35	49	38
Viney St. Swithins	32	11	5	16	43	68	38
AXA	32	10	7	15	47	60	37
Whitminster	32	10	7	15	38	61	37
Hardwicke	32	9	5	18	44	56	32
Pucklechurch Sports	32	7	10	15	31	43	31
Old Georgians	32	8	5	19	31	62	29
Totterdown Port of Bristol	32	5	9	18	39	69	24
Broad Plain House Old Boys	32	3	7	22	41	97	16

Broad Plain House Old Boys left and joined the Bristol & Suburban League and Slimbridge Town left and joined the Hellenic League. Wotton Rovers and Taverners both joined from the GNSL and Thornbury Town joined from the Bristol Premier Combination. League increased to 18 clubs.

2002-03

Patchway Town	34	23	7	4	69	18	76
Henbury Old Boys	34	21	6	7	73	36	69
Wotton Rovers	34	18	11	5	70	39	65
Almondsbury	34	19	5	10	76	49	62
Tytherington Rocks	34	18	3	13	72	57	57
Highridge United	34	17	5	12	54	49	56
Thornbury Town	34	16	7	11	65	48	55
D.R.G. Stapleton	34	13	7	14	62	52	46
AXA	34	13	6	15	59	64	45
Roman Glass St. George	34	12	7	15	53	60	43
Taverners	34	12	6	16	40	46	42
Old Georgians	34	12	5	17	55	70	41
Hardwicke	34	12	5	17	57	84	41
Ellwood	34	9	9	16	36	48	36
Pucklechurch Sports	34	10	4	20	55	88	34
Totterdown Port of Bristol	34	8	9	17	39	53	33
Viney St. Swithins	34	7	10	17	35	62	31
Whitminster	34	6	8	20	44	91	26

Whitminster left and joined the Stroud & District League and were replaced by Kings Stanley from the GNSL.

2003-04

Almondsbury	34	20	10	4	63	32	70
Tytherington Rocks	34	20	9	5	81	47	69
Patchway Town	34	19	9	6	63	38	63
Taverners	34	17	9	8	53	35	60
Highridge United	34	15	10	9	64	45	55
AXA	34	13	11	10	68	67	50
Thornbury Town	34	13	10	11	51	42	49
Kings Stanley	34	12	13	9	61	53	49
Roman Glass St. George	34	12	12	10	71	63	48
Henbury Old Boys	34	12	7	15	42	52	43
Hardwicke	34	10	11	13	50	64	41
Ellwood	34	10	10	14	54	64	40
Totterdown Port of Bristol	34	10	11	13	58	52	38
Old Georgians	34	8	11	15	64	70	35
Wotton Rovers	34	8	10	16	44	57	34
Pucklechurch Sports	34	8	9	17	44	67	33
D.R.G. Stapleton	34	7	5	22	32	75	23
Viney St. Swithins	34	4	9	21	34	74	21

Patchway Town, Totterdown Port of Bristol and D.R.G. Stapleton all had 3 points deducted.
Almondsbury left and joined the Western League and Tytherington Rocks left and joined the Hellenic League. Longwell Green Sports joined from the Bristol Premier Combination, Sea Mills Park joined from the Bristol Premier Combination and Yate Town Reserves joined from the Bristol & Suburban League. League increased to 19 clubs.

2004-05

Highridge United	36	24	10	2	104	35	82
Longwell Green Sports	36	25	7	4	92	34	82
Ellwood	36	24	5	7	84	36	77
Kings Stanley	36	21	7	8	75	50	70
Roman Glass St. George	36	20	9	7	82	36	69
Patchway Town	36	18	9	9	71	54	63
Thornbury Town	36	17	12	7	64	49	63
Yate Town Reserves	36	17	5	14	84	76	56
Hardwicke	36	17	4	15	70	52	55
Sea Mills Park	36	13	8	15	74	73	47
AXA	36	12	8	16	75	79	44
Totterdown Port of Bristol	36	14	4	18	74	84	46
Wotton Rovers	36	11	9	16	48	65	42
Taverners	36	9	12	15	48	64	39
Henbury Old Boys	36	8	10	18	46	72	34
D.R.G. Stapleton	36	8	4	24	43	96	28
Pucklechurch Sports	36	5	6	25	37	85	21
Old Georgians	36	6	3	27	45	95	21
Viney St. Swithins	36	5	4	27	45	126	19

Longwell Green Sports left and joined the Western League, Old Georgians left and joined the Bristol & Suburban League and Viney St. Swithins left and joined the GNSL. Lydney Town joined from the GNSL. League reduced to 17 clubs.

2005-06

Lydney Town	32	23	7	2	87	28	76
Highridge United	32	20	6	6	73	31	66
Yate Town Reserves	32	17	8	7	61	36	59
Totterdown Port of Bristol	32	16	8	8	70	46	56
Patchway Town	32	17	5	10	55	39	56
Ellwood	32	15	9	8	60	35	54
Taverners	32	15	6	11	56	46	51
Henbury Old Boys	32	17	6	9	56	45	50
Roman Glass St. George	32	15	4	13	49	47	49
Thornbury Town	32	13	5	14	56	56	44
Hardwicke	32	12	6	14	60	61	42
AXA	32	10	8	14	56	59	38
Kings Stanley	32	10	7	15	56	62	37
D.R.G. Stapleton	32	7	6	19	44	79	27
Sea Mills Park	32	6	4	22	36	92	22
Wotton Rovers	32	4	4	24	31	103	16
Pucklechurch Sports	32	3	5	24	31	72	14

Henbury Old Boys had 7 points deducted.